a Silent Voice 2

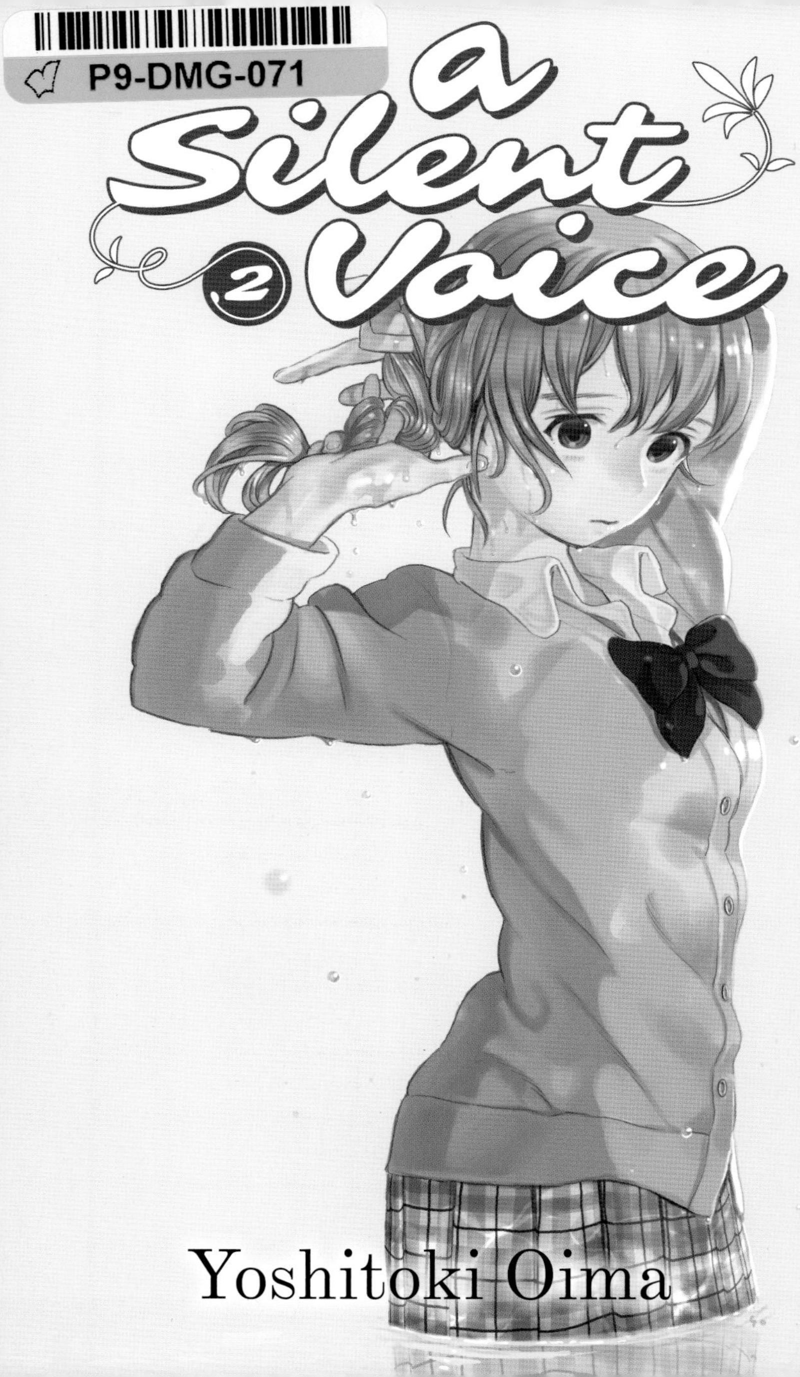

Yoshitoki Oima

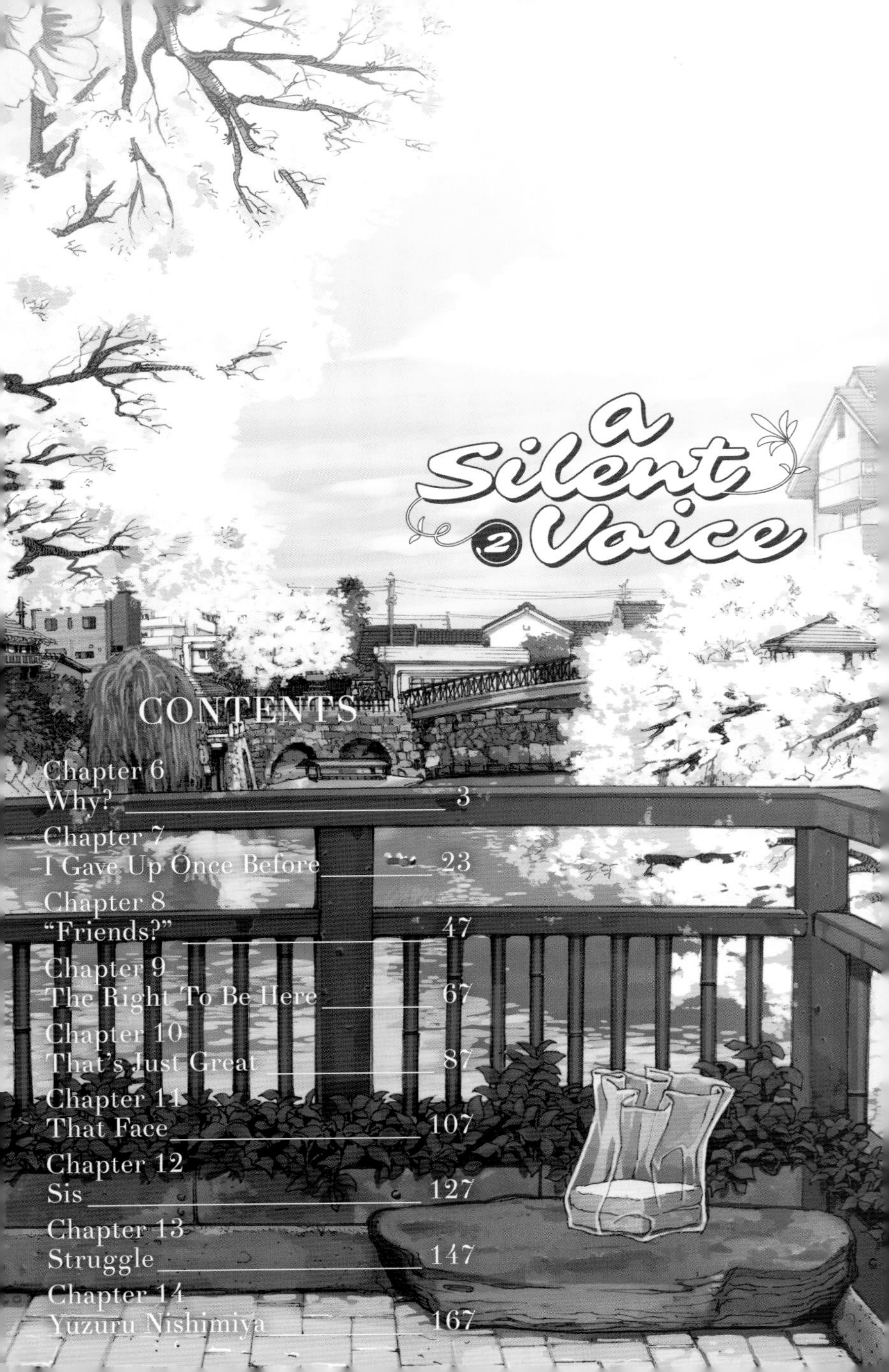

a Silent Voice 2

CONTENTS

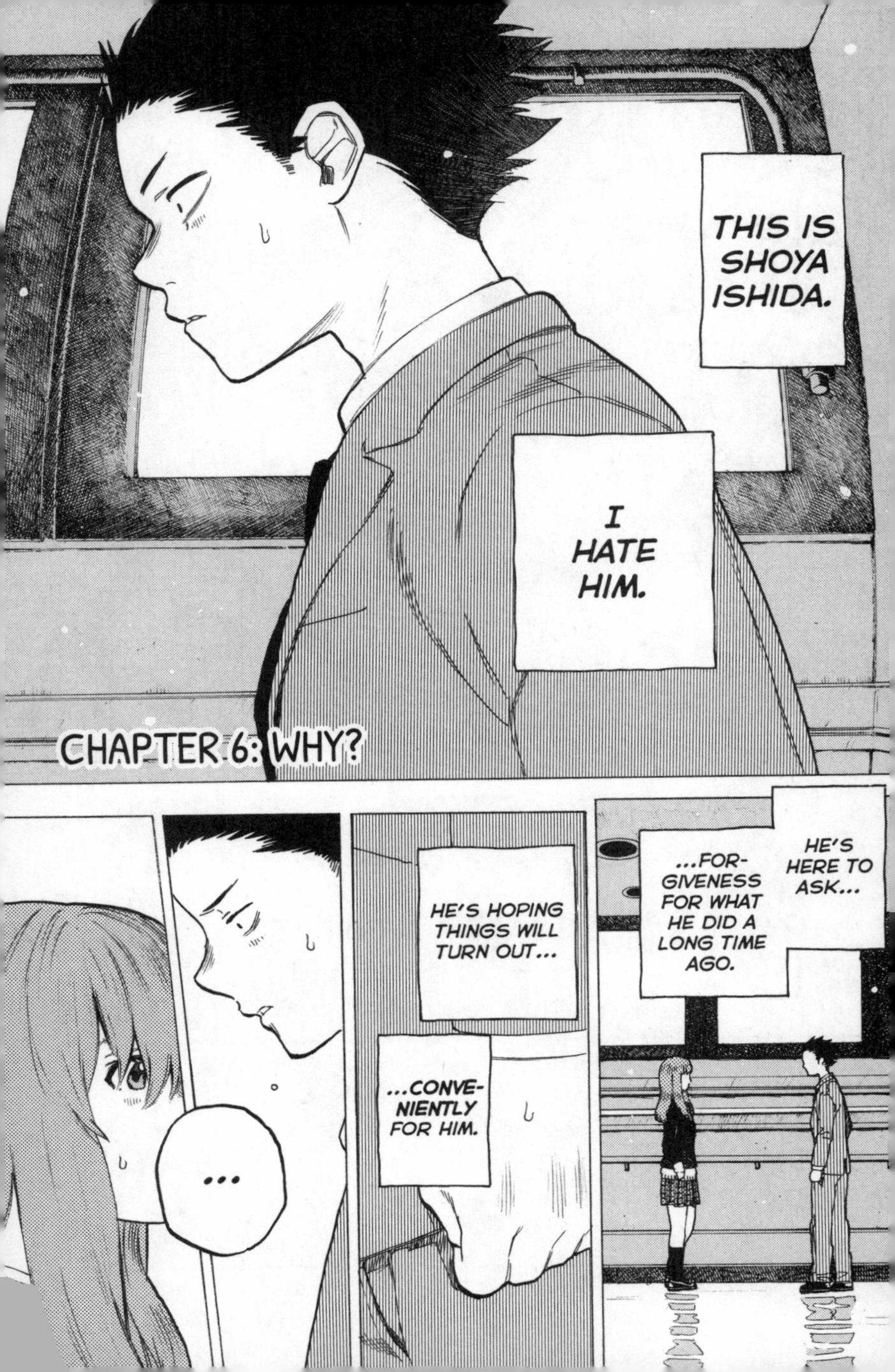
THIS IS SHOYA ISHIDA.
I HATE HIM.
CHAPTER 6: WHY?
HE'S HERE TO ASK...
...FORGIVENESS FOR WHAT HE DID A LONG TIME AGO.
HE'S HOPING THINGS WILL TURN OUT...
...CONVENIENTLY FOR HIM.
...

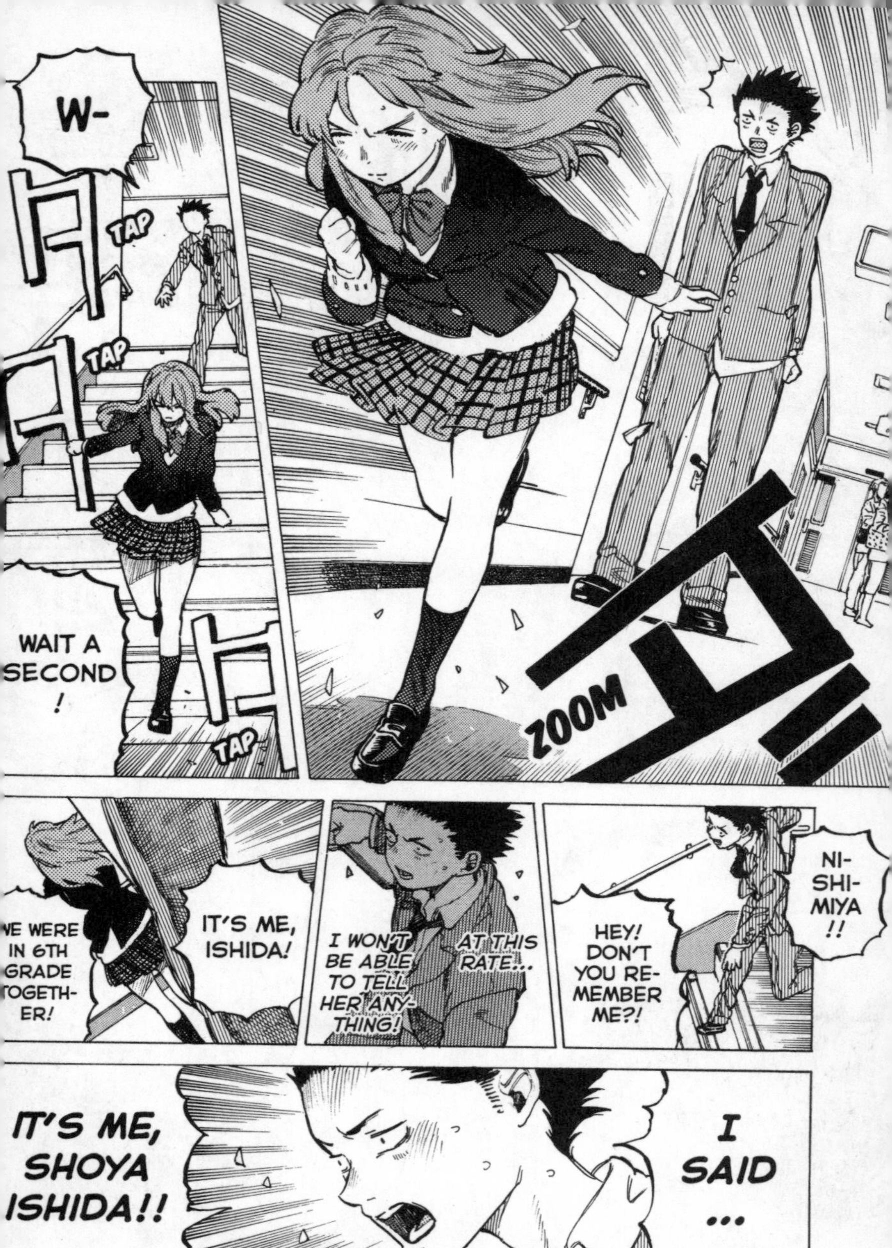
ZOOM
W-
TAP
TAP
WAIT A SECOND!
TAP
NI-SHI-MIYA!!
HEY! DON'T YOU RE-MEMBER ME?!
AT THIS RATE...
I WON'T BE ABLE TO TELL HER ANY-THING!
IT'S ME, ISHIDA!
WE WERE IN 6TH GRADE TOGETH-ER!
I SAID...
IT'S ME, SHOYA ISHIDA!!

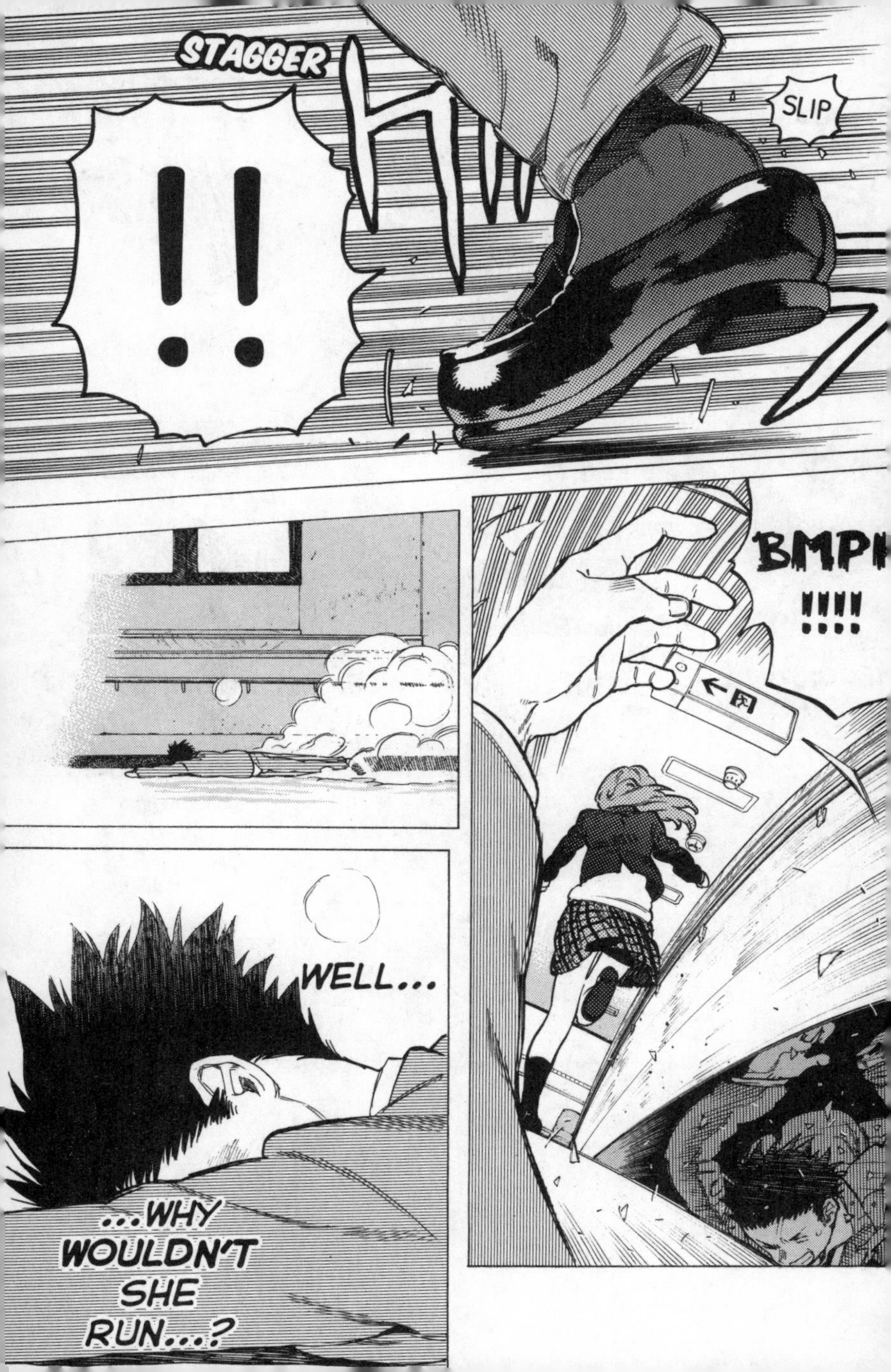
SLIP
STAGGER
!!
BMPH
!!!!!
WELL...
...WHY WOULDN'T SHE RUN...?

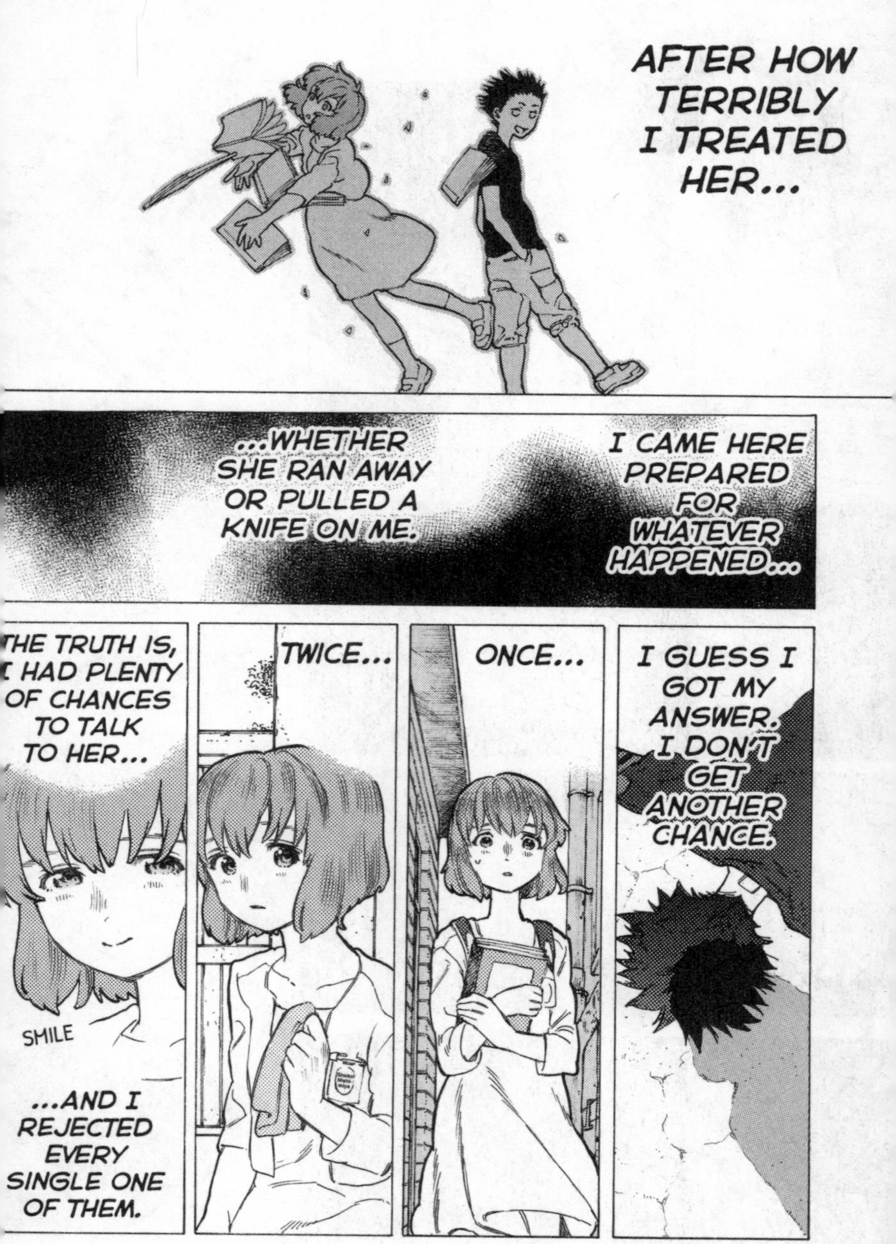
AFTER HOW TERRIBLY I TREATED HER...
I CAME HERE PREPARED FOR WHATEVER HAPPENED...
...WHETHER SHE RAN AWAY OR PULLED A KNIFE ON ME.
I GUESS I GOT MY ANSWER. I DON'T GET ANOTHER CHANCE.
ONCE...
TWICE...
THE TRUTH IS, I HAD PLENTY OF CHANCES TO TALK TO HER...
SMILE
...AND I REJECTED EVERY SINGLE ONE OF THEM.

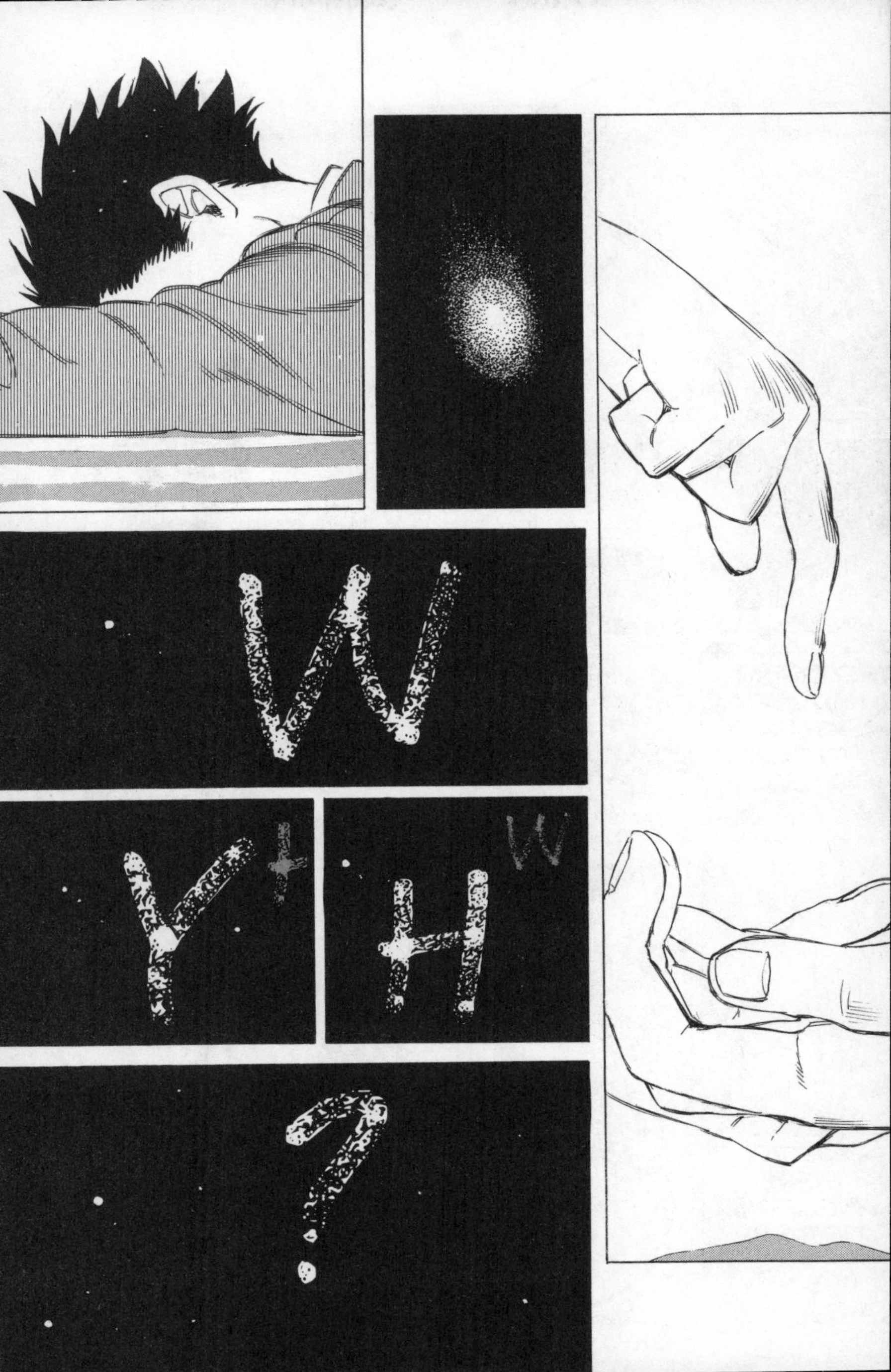
W
H
Y
?

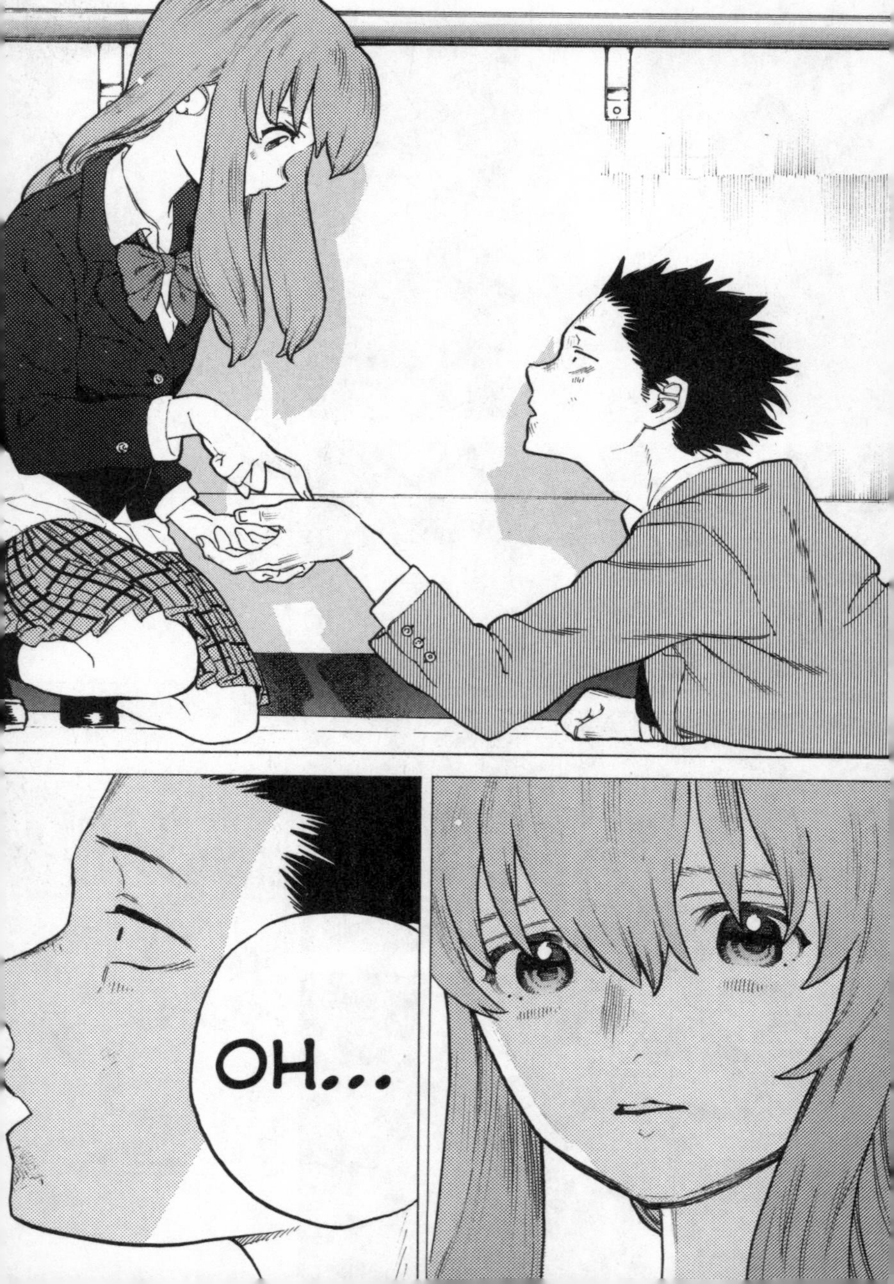
OH...

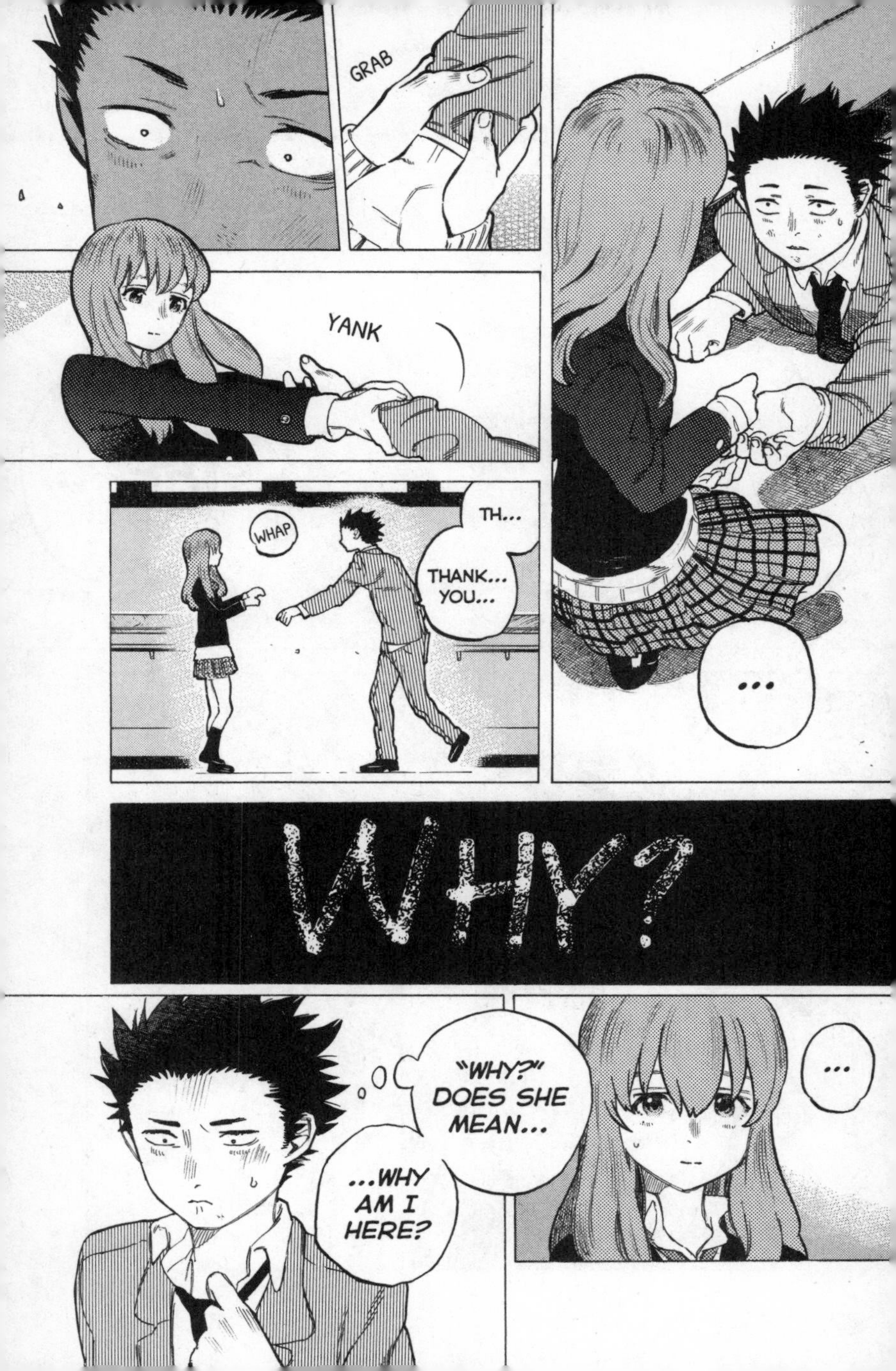
...
GRAB
YANK
TH...
WHAP
THANK... YOU...
WHY?
...
"WHY?" DOES SHE MEAN...
...WHY AM I HERE?

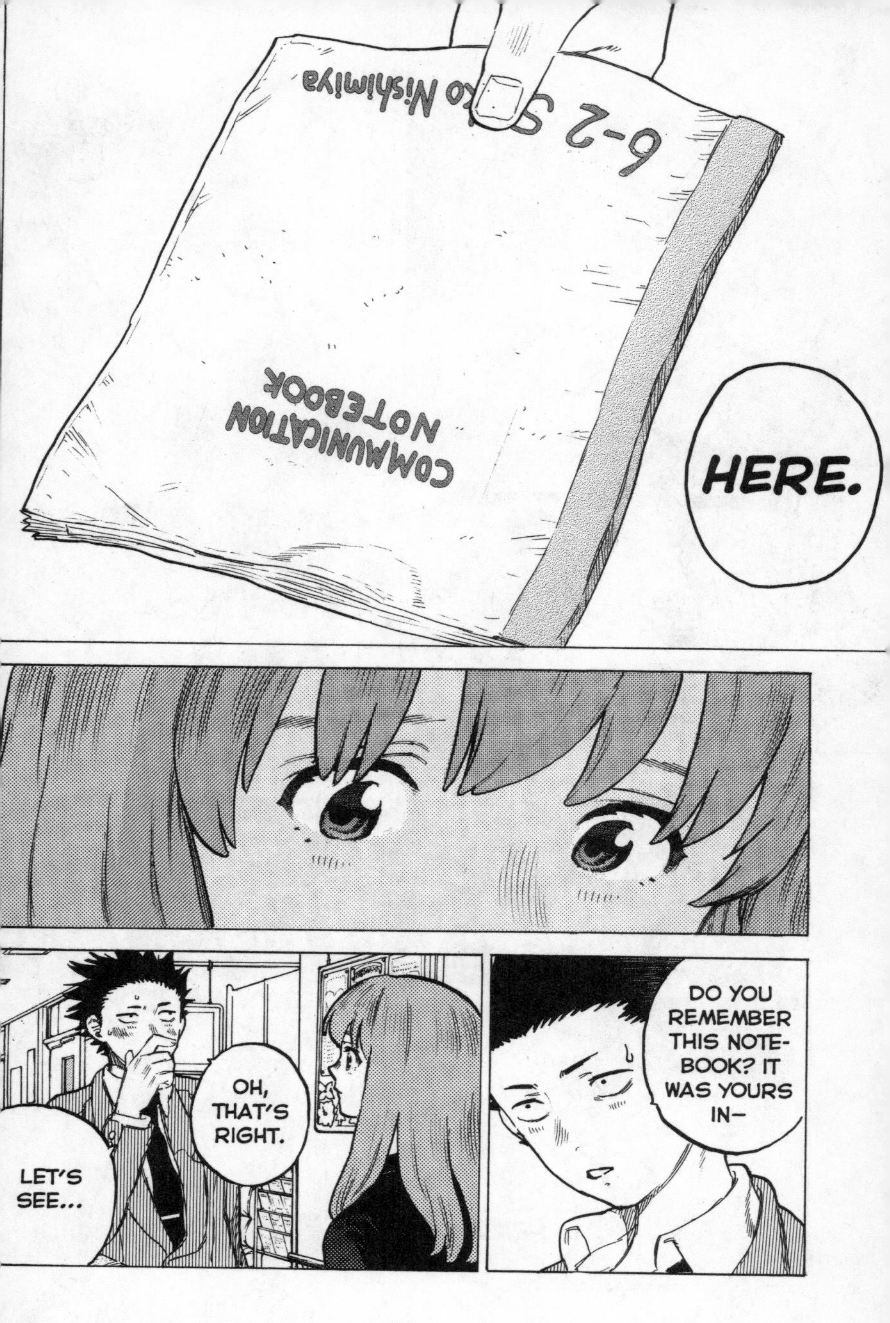
6-2
COMMUNICATION NOTEBOOK
HERE.
DO YOU REMEMBER THIS NOTE-BOOK? IT WAS YOURS IN—
OH, THAT'S RIGHT.
LET'S SEE...

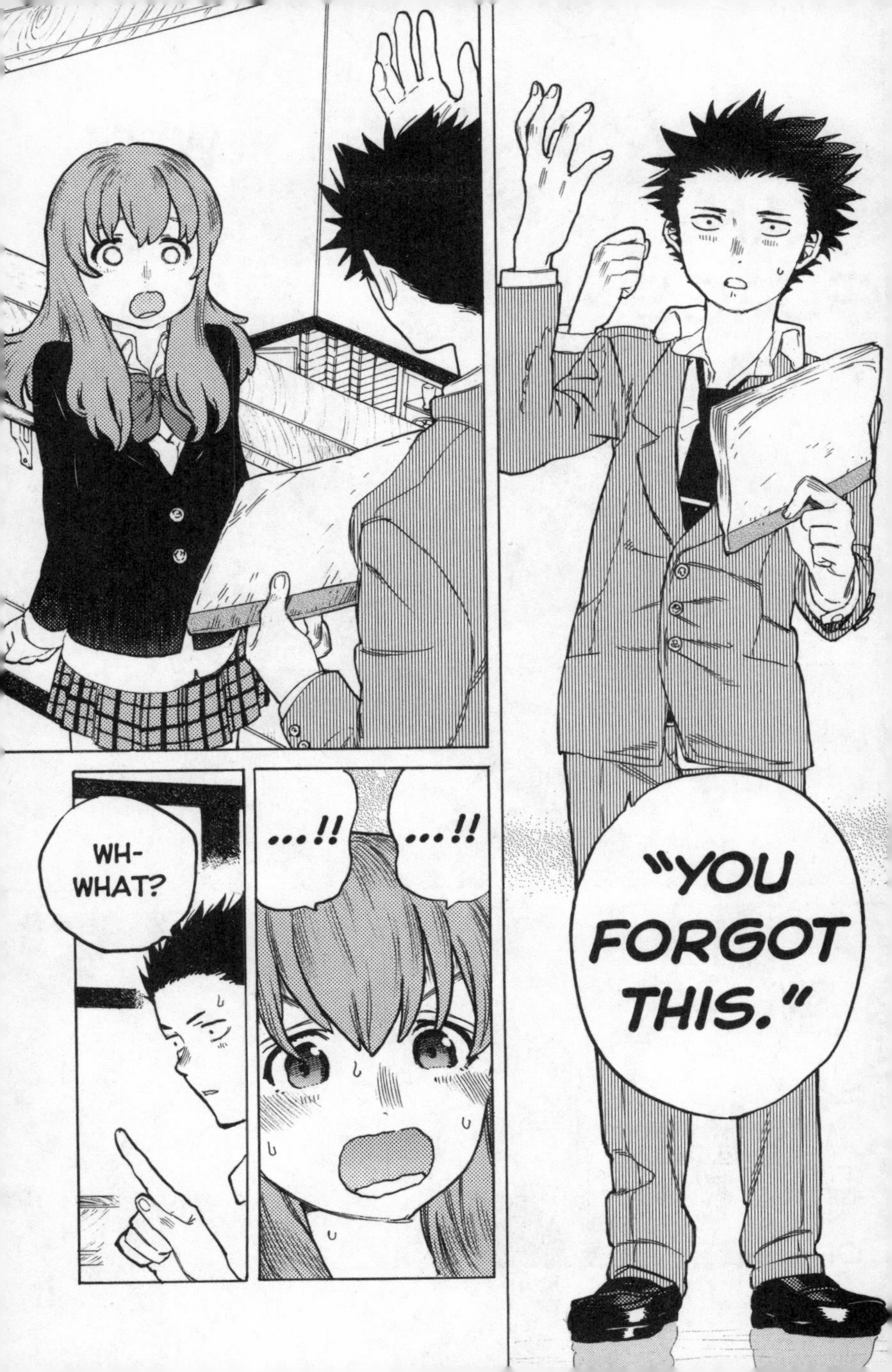
"YOU FORGOT THIS."
...!!
...!!
WH- WHAT?

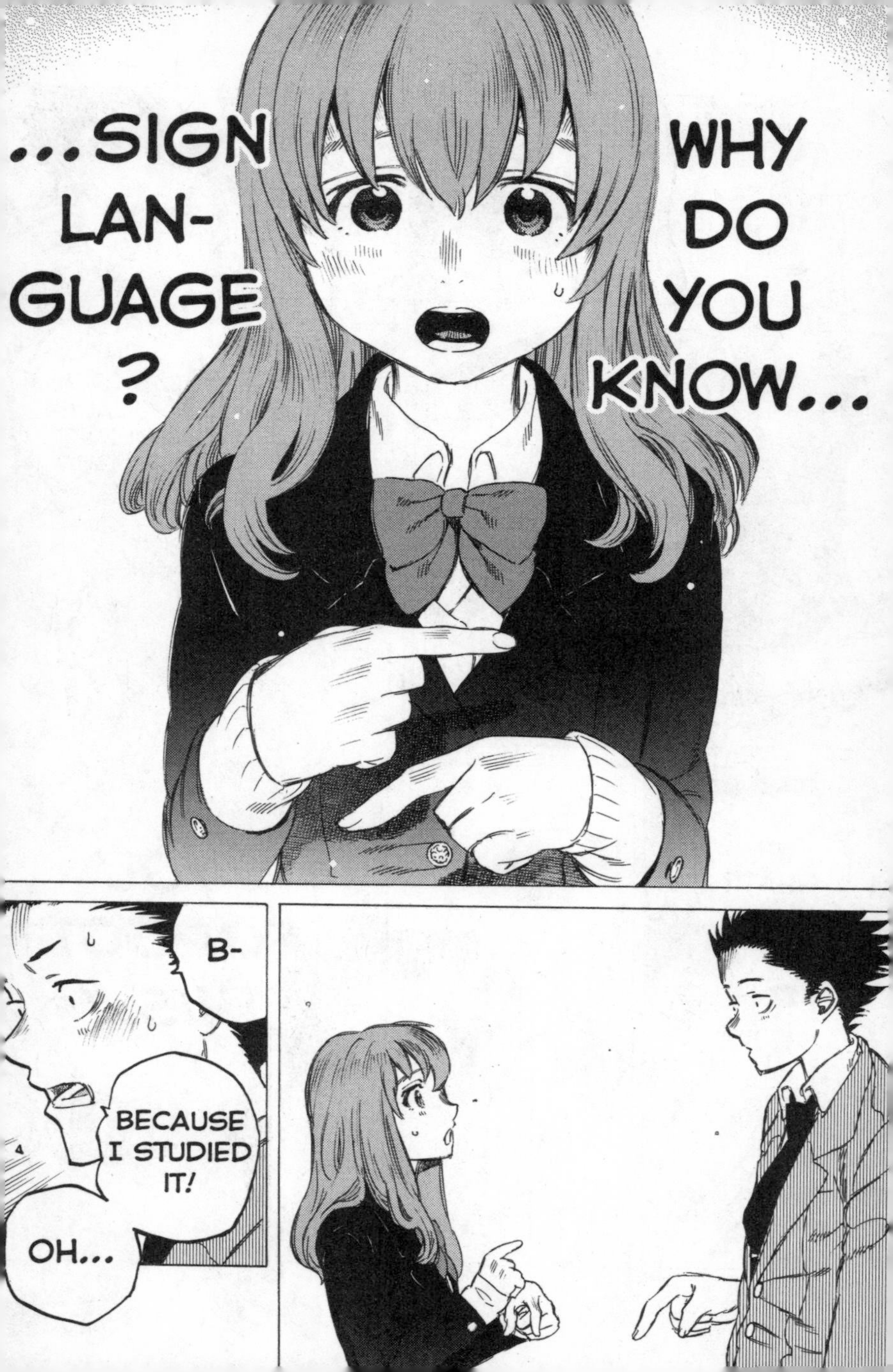
WHY DO YOU KNOW...
...SIGN LAN-GUAGE?
B-
BECAUSE I STUDIED IT!
OH...

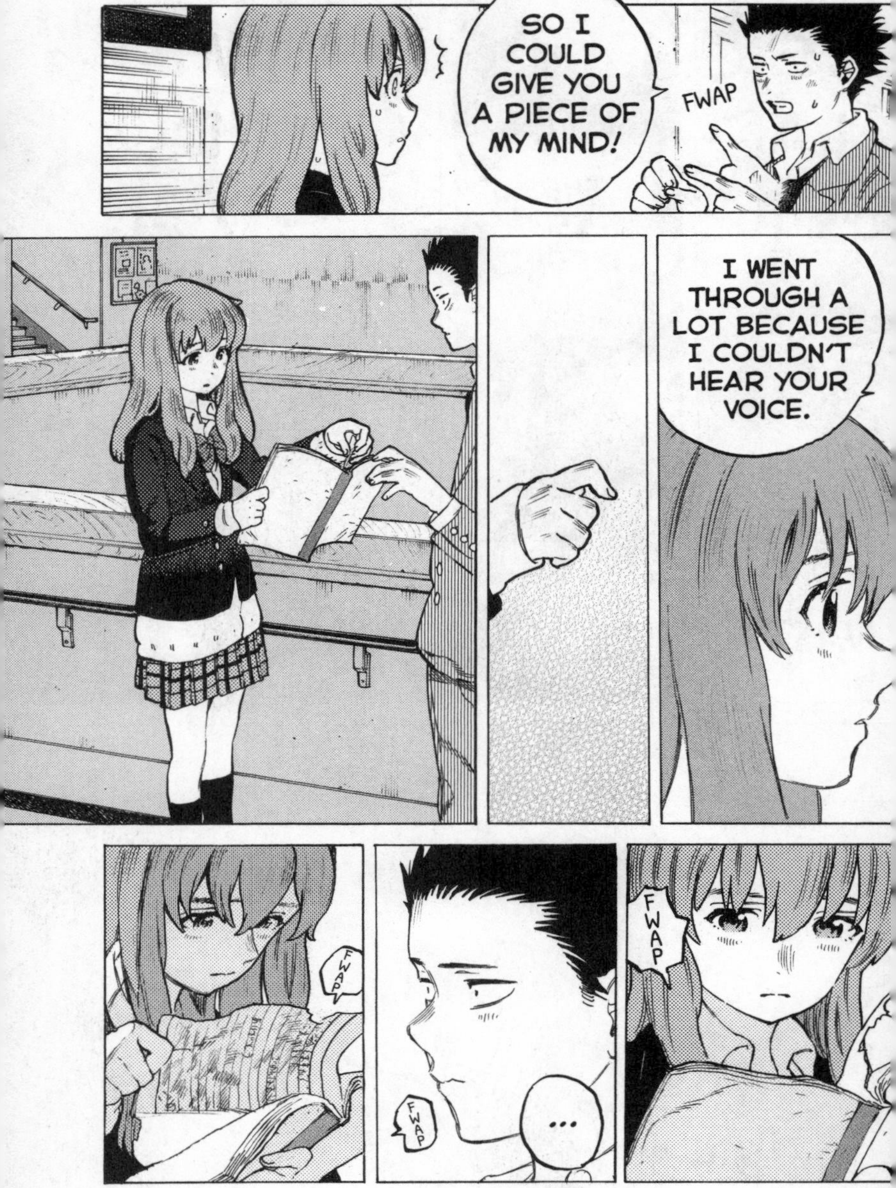
SO I COULD GIVE YOU A PIECE OF MY MIND!
FWAP
I WENT THROUGH A LOT BECAUSE I COULDN'T HEAR YOUR VOICE.
FWAP
...
FWAP
FWAP

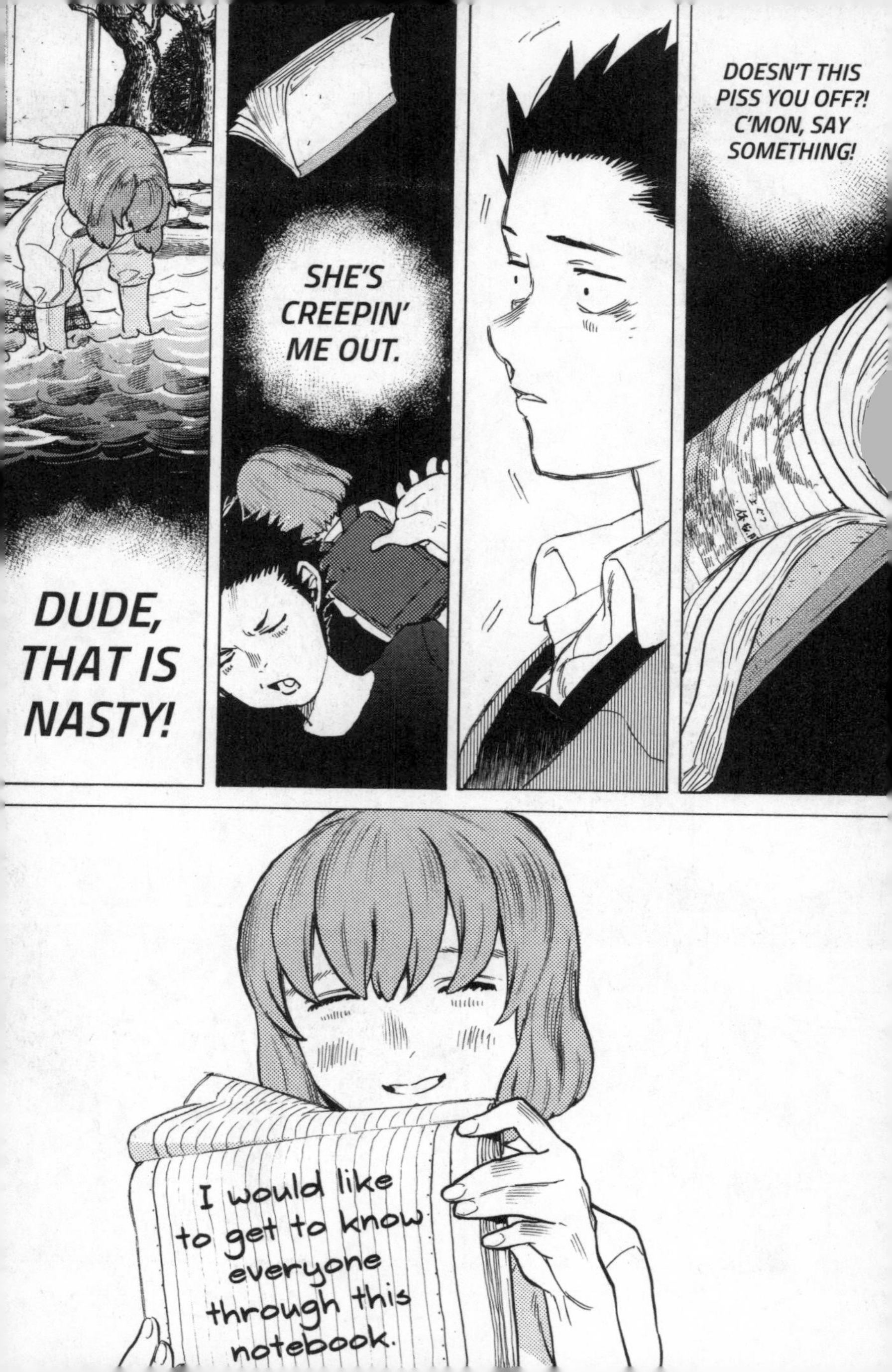
DOESN'T THIS PISS YOU OFF?! C'MON, SAY SOMETHING!
SHE'S CREEPIN' ME OUT.
DUDE, THAT IS NASTY!
I would like to get to know everyone through this notebook.

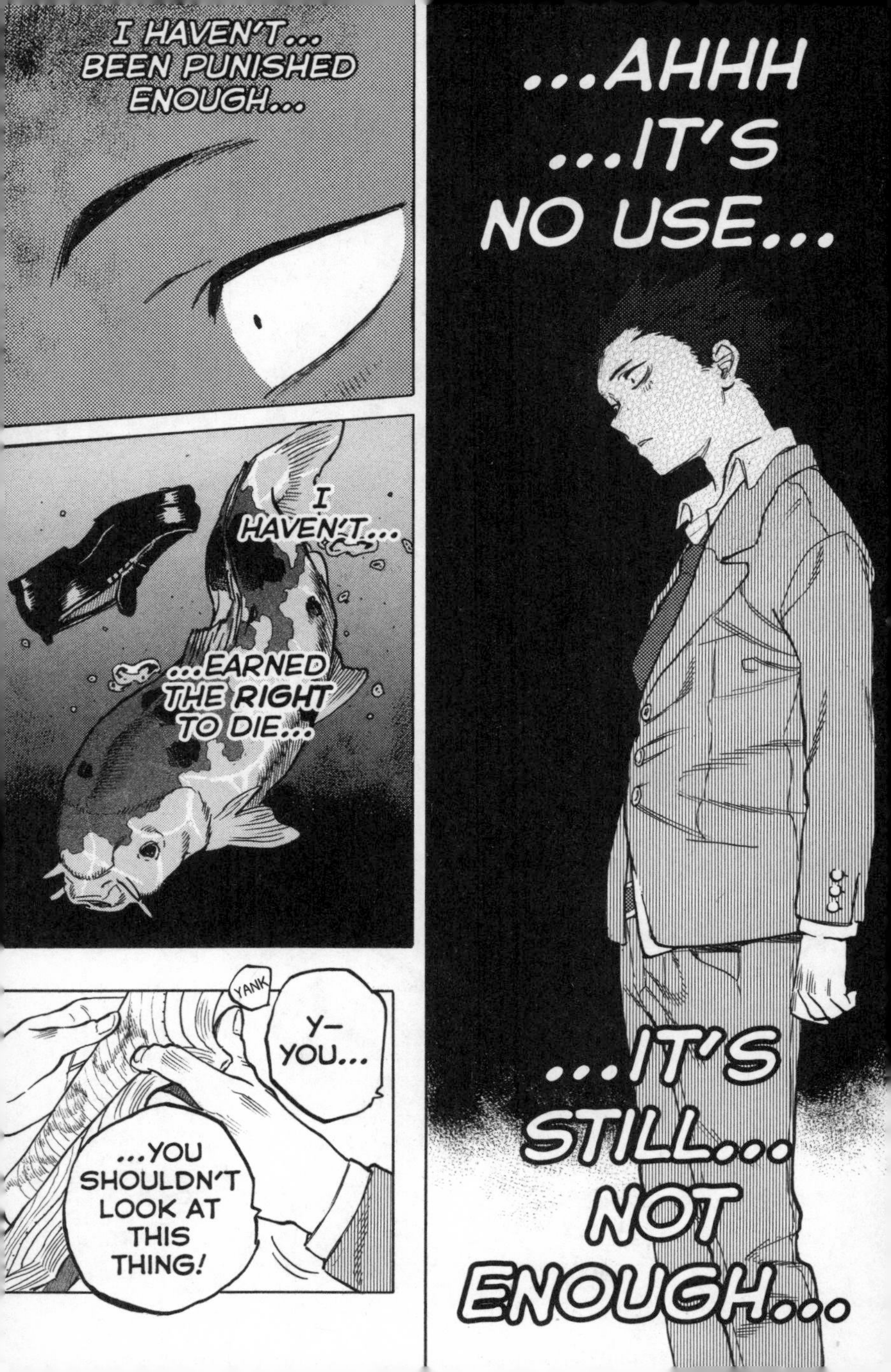

...AHHH ...IT'S NO USE...
...IT'S STILL... NOT ENOUGH...
I HAVEN'T... BEEN PUNISHED ENOUGH...
I HAVEN'T...
...EARNED THE RIGHT TO DIE...
YANK
Y— YOU...
...YOU SHOULDN'T LOOK AT THIS THING!

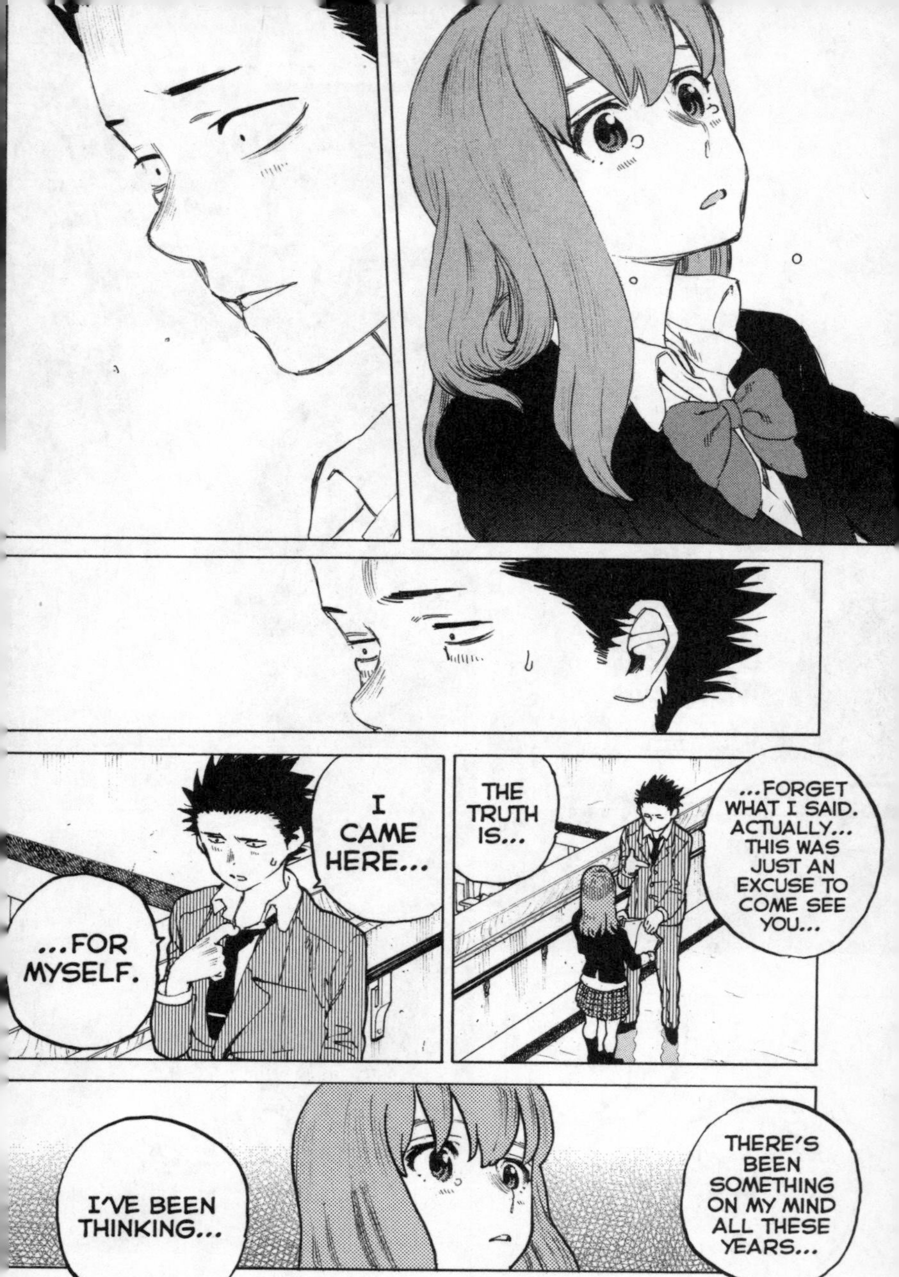
...FORGET WHAT I SAID. ACTUALLY... THIS WAS JUST AN EXCUSE TO COME SEE YOU...
THE TRUTH IS...
I CAME HERE...
...FOR MYSELF.
THERE'S BEEN SOMETHING ON MY MIND ALL THESE YEARS...
I'VE BEEN THINKING...

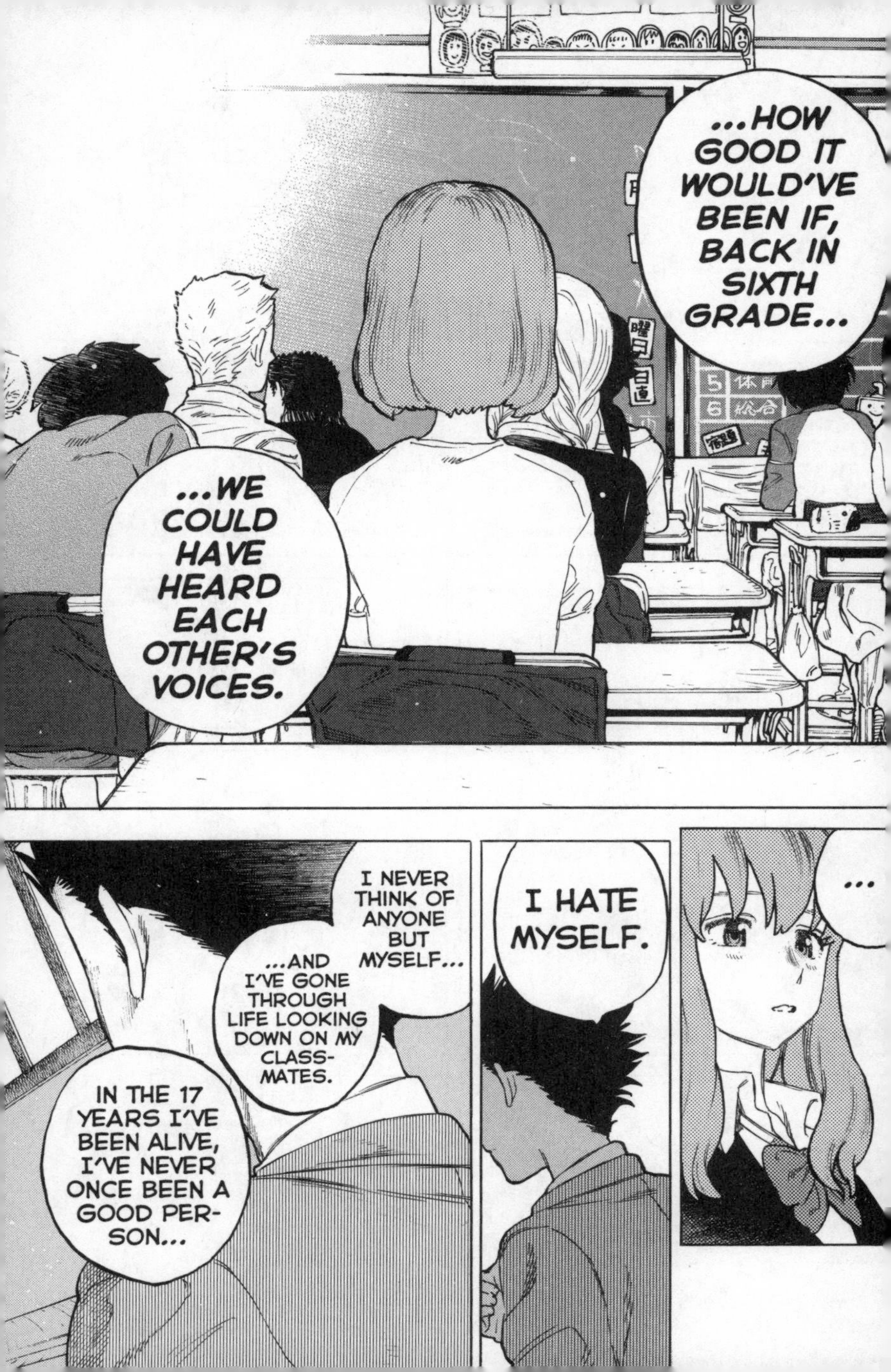
...HOW GOOD IT WOULD'VE BEEN IF, BACK IN SIXTH GRADE...
...WE COULD HAVE HEARD EACH OTHER'S VOICES.
...
I HATE MYSELF.
I NEVER THINK OF ANYONE BUT MYSELF...
...AND I'VE GONE THROUGH LIFE LOOKING DOWN ON MY CLASS-MATES.
IN THE 17 YEARS I'VE BEEN ALIVE, I'VE NEVER ONCE BEEN A GOOD PER-SON...

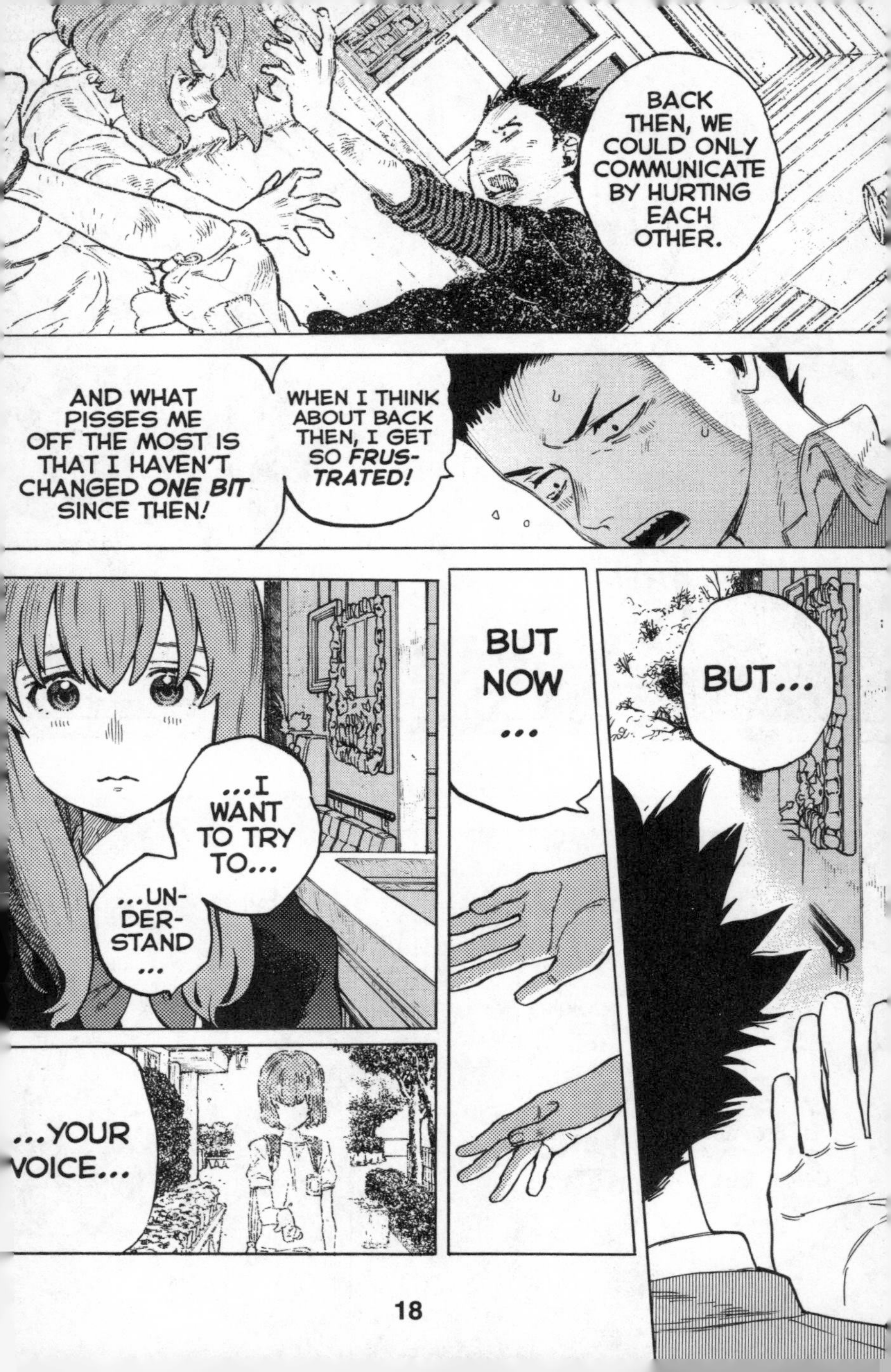
BACK THEN, WE COULD ONLY COMMUNICATE BY HURTING EACH OTHER.
WHEN I THINK ABOUT BACK THEN, I GET SO *FRUSTRATED!*
AND WHAT PISSES ME OFF THE MOST IS THAT I HAVEN'T CHANGED *ONE BIT* SINCE THEN!
BUT...
BUT NOW...
...I WANT TO TRY TO...
...UNDERSTAND...
...YOUR VOICE...

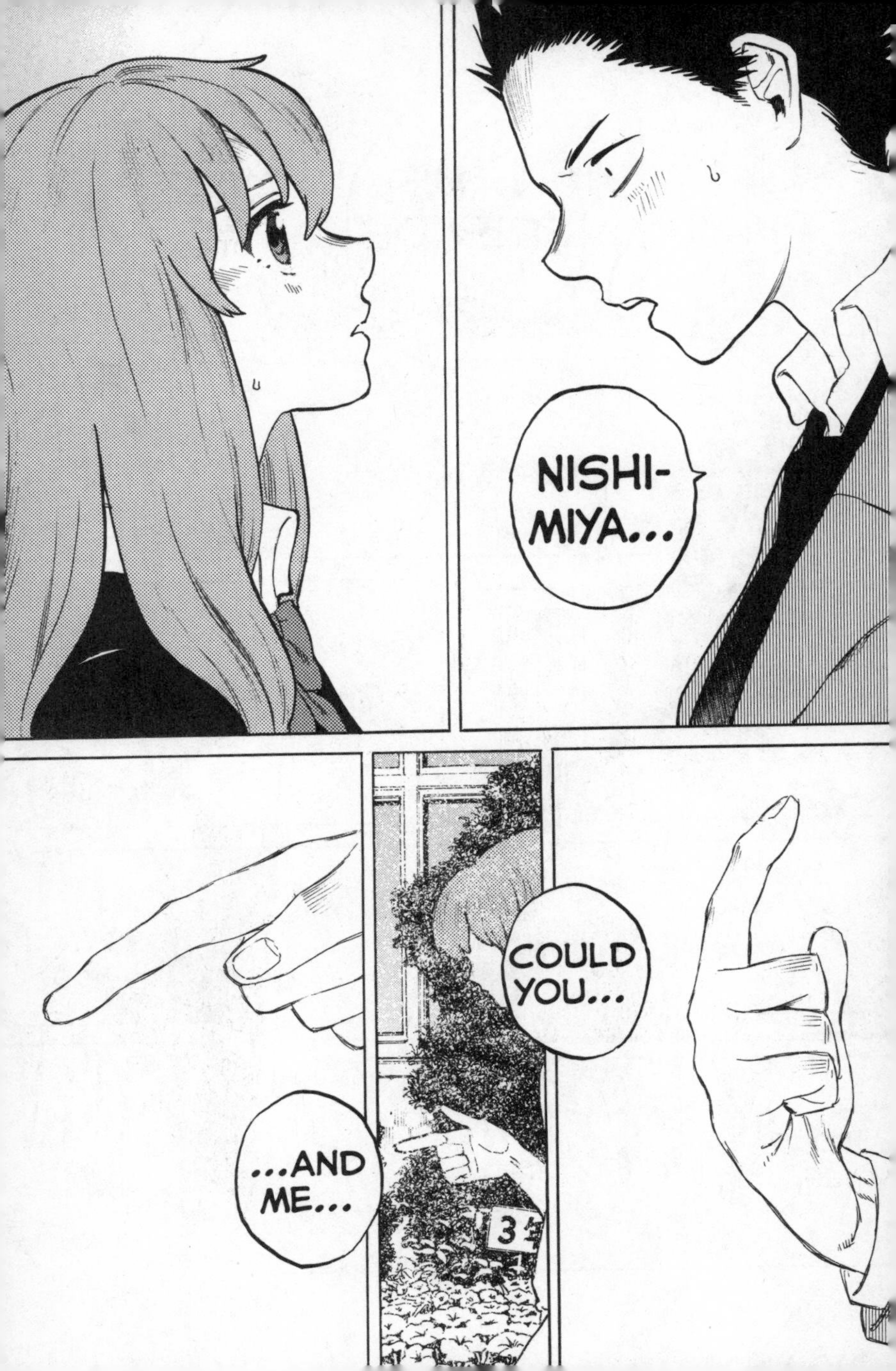
NISHI-MIYA...
COULD YOU...
...AND ME...

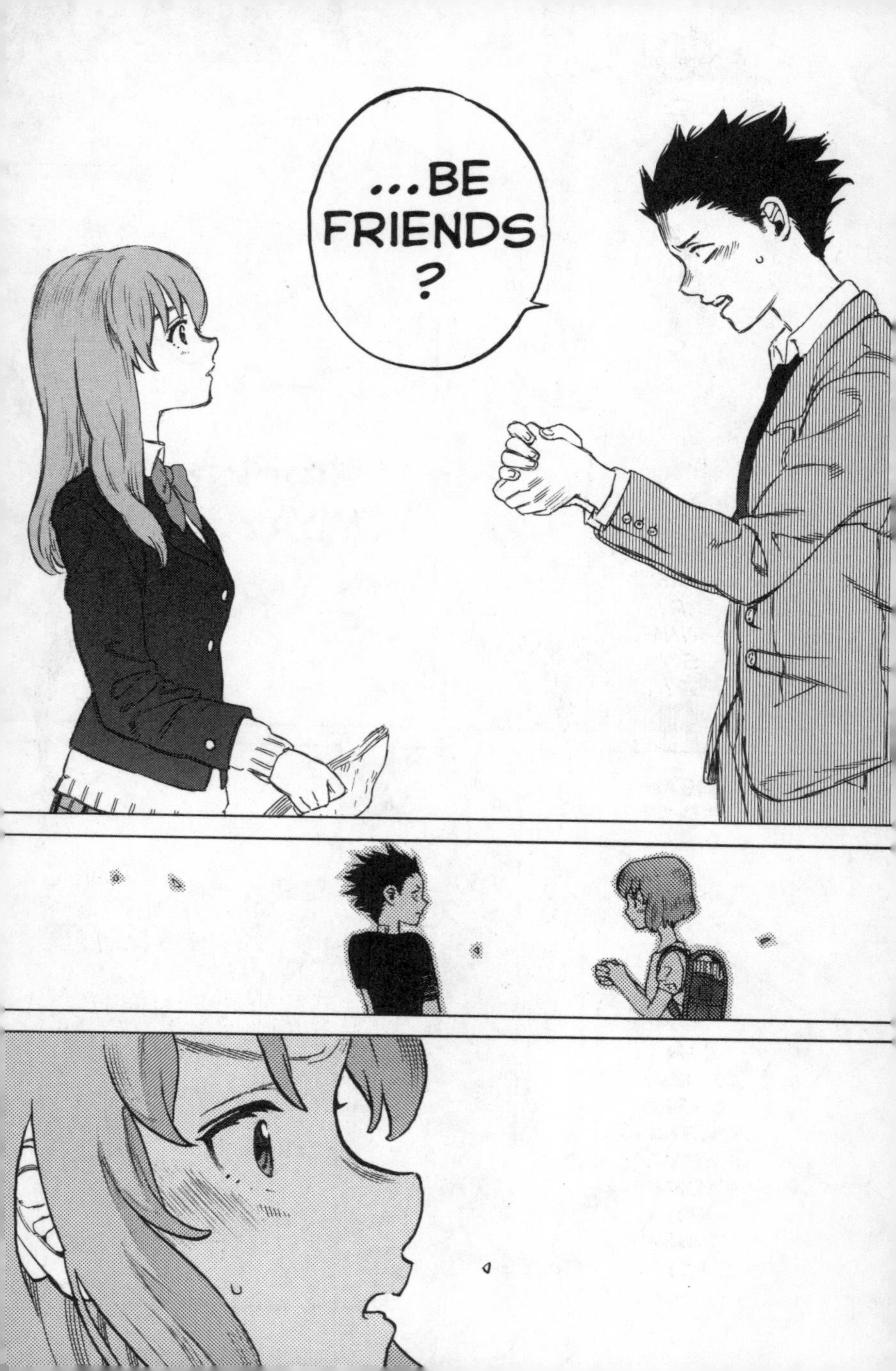
...BE FRIENDS ?

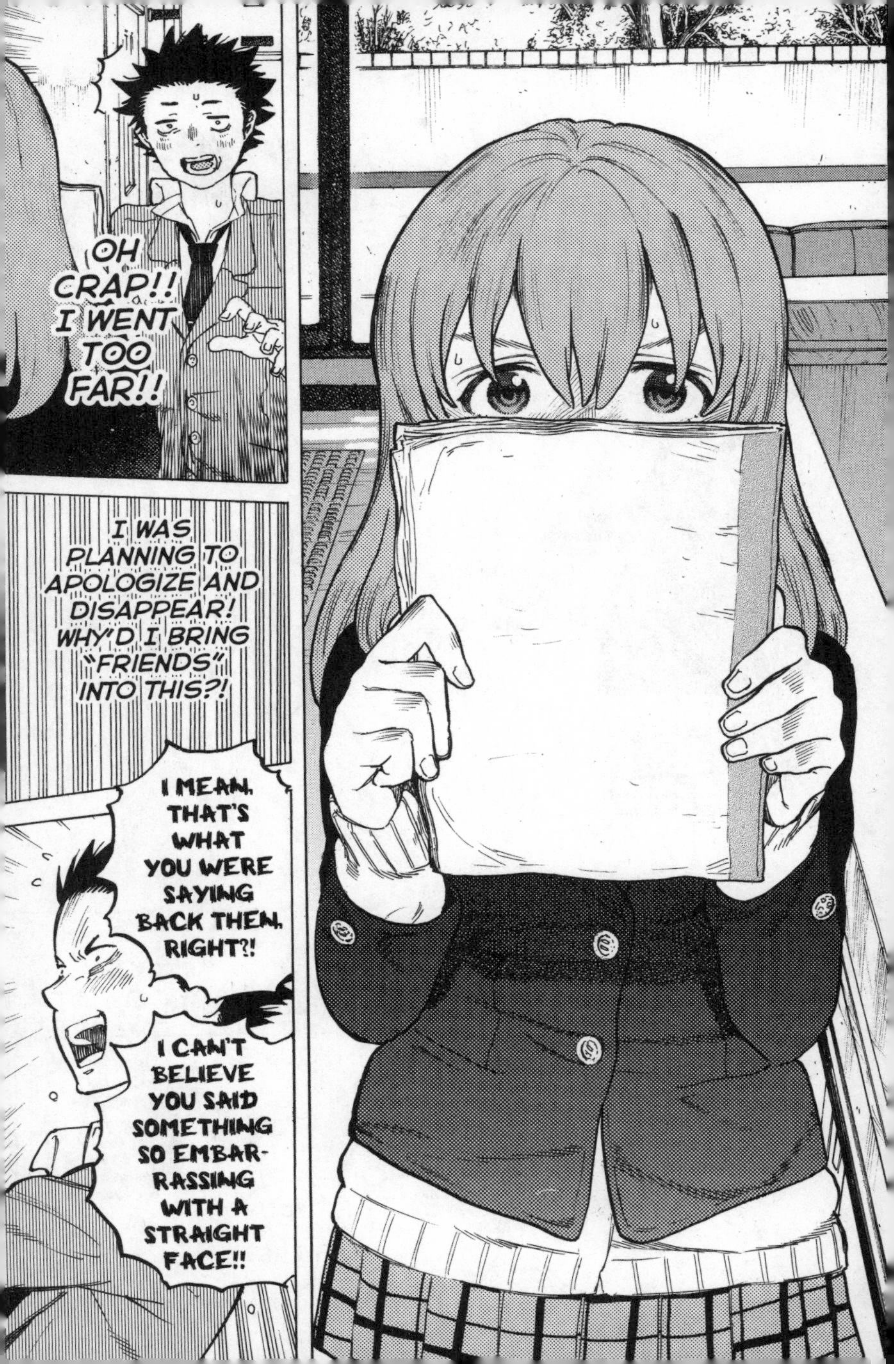
OH CRAP!! I WENT TOO FAR!!
I WAS PLANNING TO APOLOGIZE AND DISAPPEAR! WHY'D I BRING "FRIENDS" INTO THIS?!
I MEAN, THAT'S WHAT YOU WERE SAYING BACK THEN, RIGHT?!
I CAN'T BELIEVE YOU SAID SOMETHING SO EMBAR-RASSING WITH A STRAIGHT FACE!!

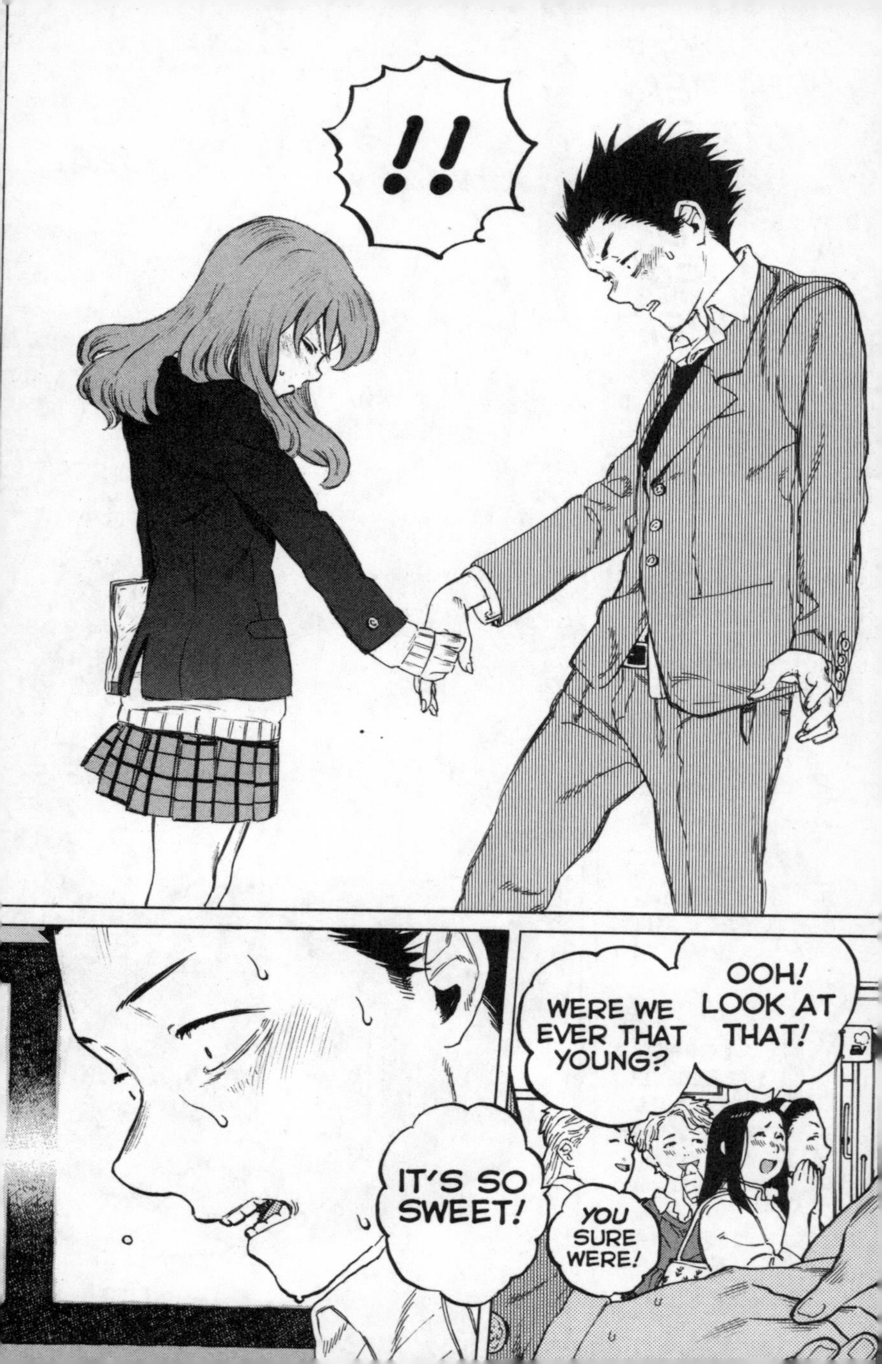
!!
OOH! LOOK AT THAT!
WERE WE EVER THAT YOUNG?
YOU SURE WERE!
IT'S SO SWEET!

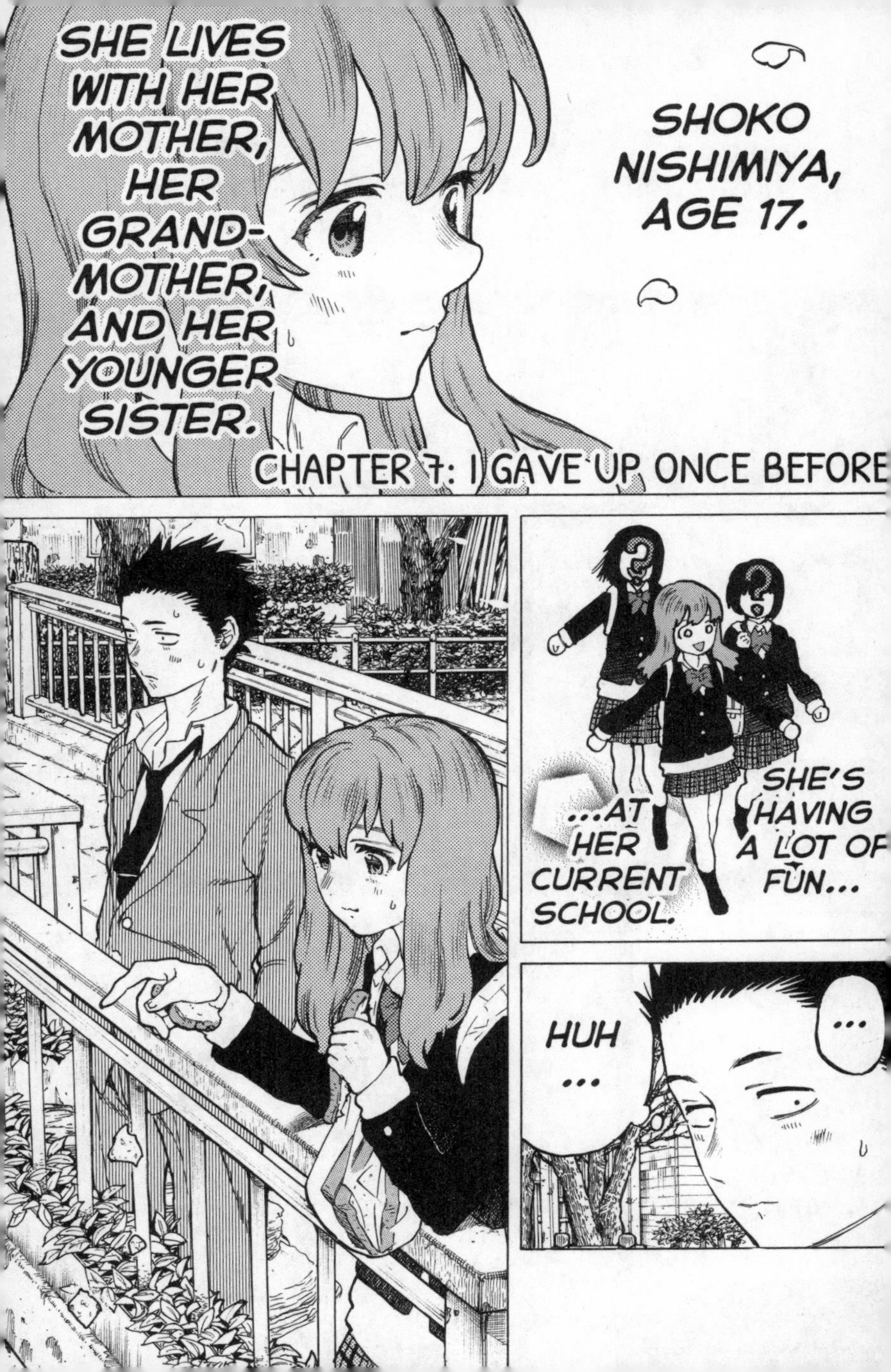
SHOKO NISHIMIYA, AGE 17.
SHE LIVES WITH HER MOTHER, HER GRAND-MOTHER, AND HER YOUNGER SISTER.
CHAPTER 7: I GAVE UP ONCE BEFORE
SHE'S HAVING A LOT OF FUN...
...AT HER CURRENT SCHOOL.
...
HUH ...

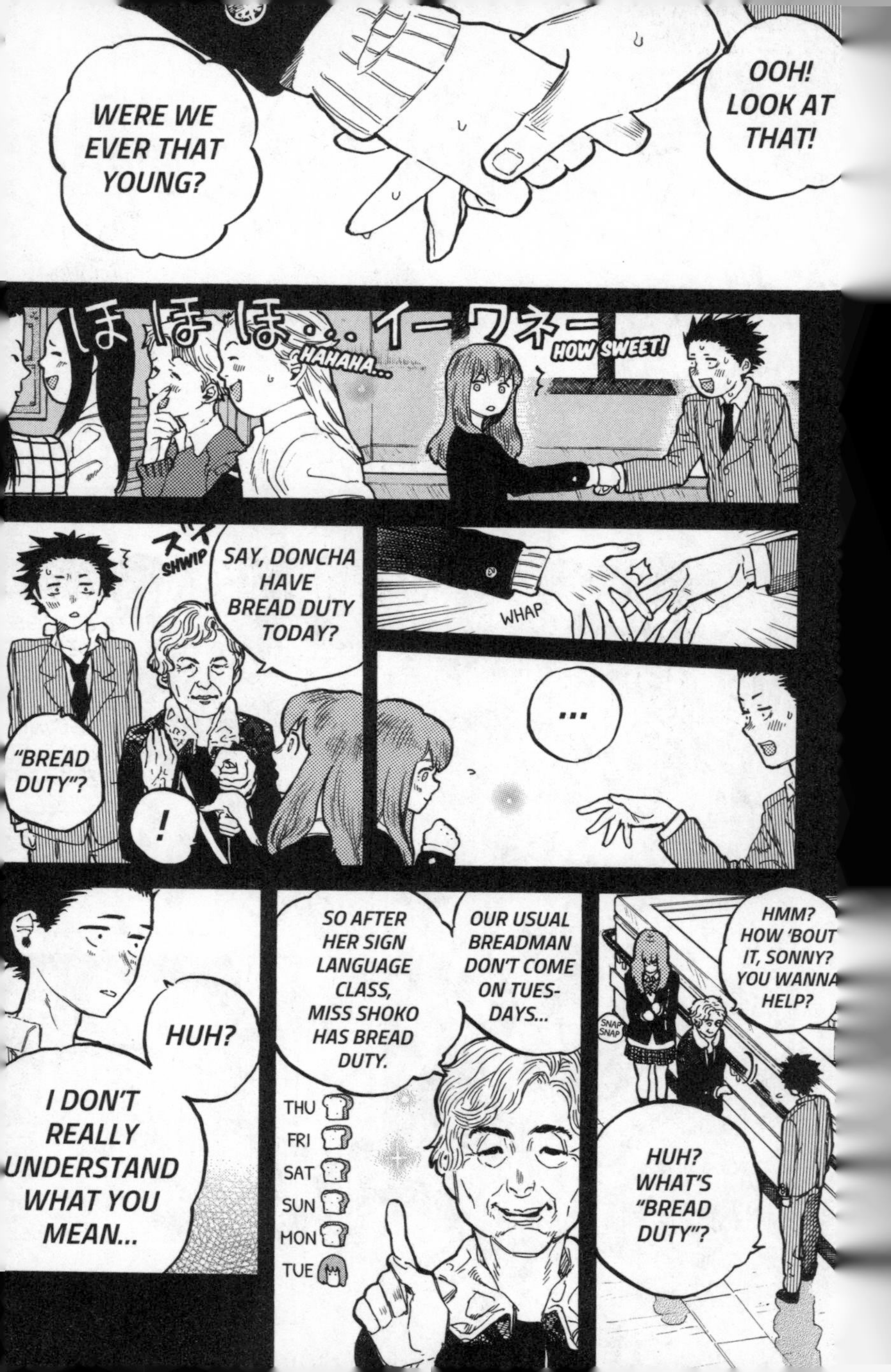
OOH! LOOK AT THAT!
WERE WE EVER THAT YOUNG?
HOW SWEET!
HAHAHA...
WHAP
...
SHWIP
SAY, DONCHA HAVE BREAD DUTY TODAY?
"BREAD DUTY"?
!
HMM? HOW 'BOUT IT, SONNY? YOU WANNA HELP?
SNAP SNAP
HUH? WHAT'S "BREAD DUTY"?
OUR USUAL BREADMAN DON'T COME ON TUES-DAYS...
SO AFTER HER SIGN LANGUAGE CLASS, MISS SHOKO HAS BREAD DUTY.
THU
FRI
SAT
SUN
MON
TUE
HUH?
I DON'T REALLY UNDERSTAND WHAT YOU MEAN...

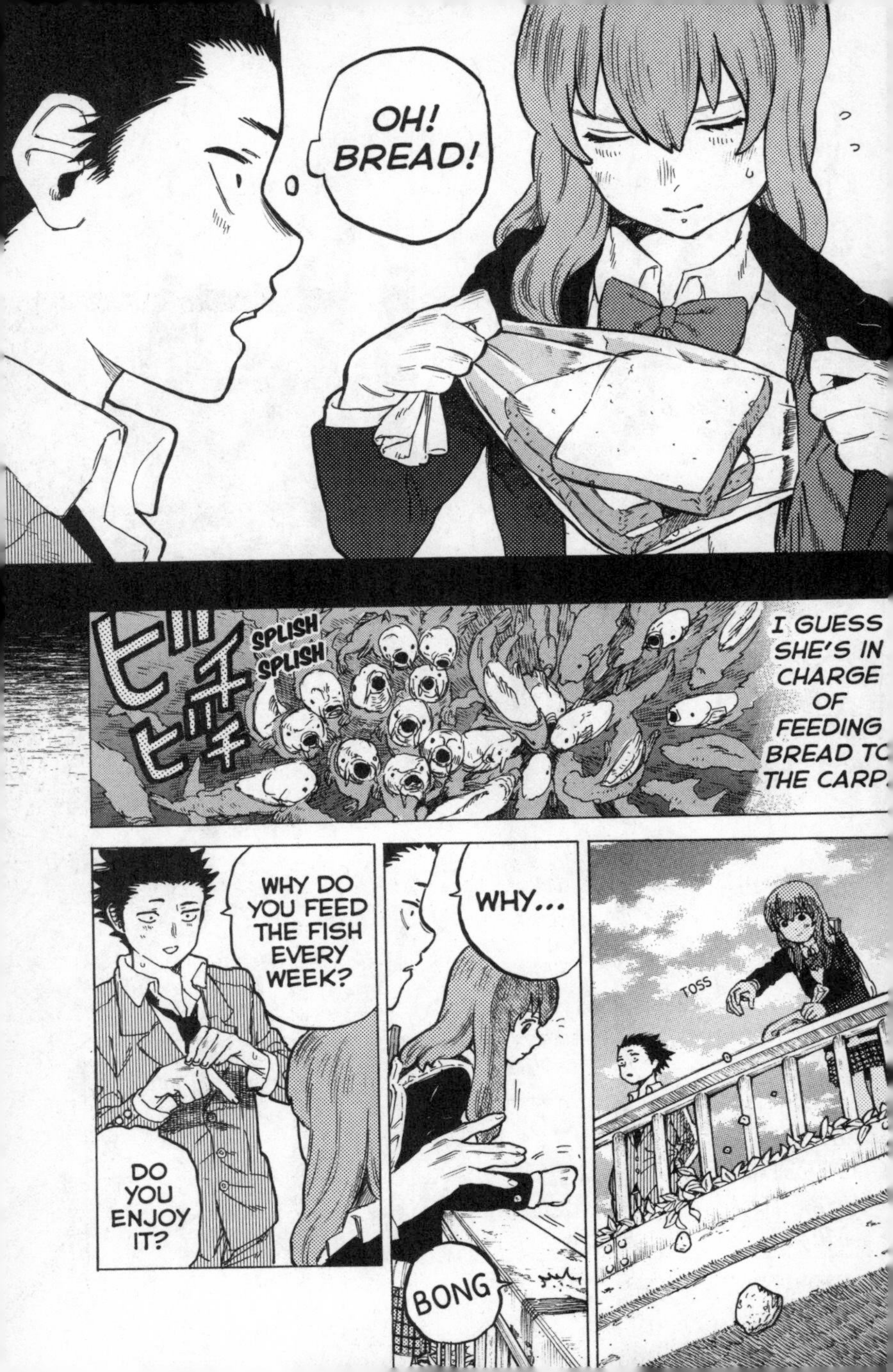
OH! BREAD!
I GUESS SHE'S IN CHARGE OF FEEDING BREAD TO THE CARP.
SPLISH SPLISH
TOSS
WHY...
BONG
WHY DO YOU FEED THE FISH EVERY WEEK?
DO YOU ENJOY IT?

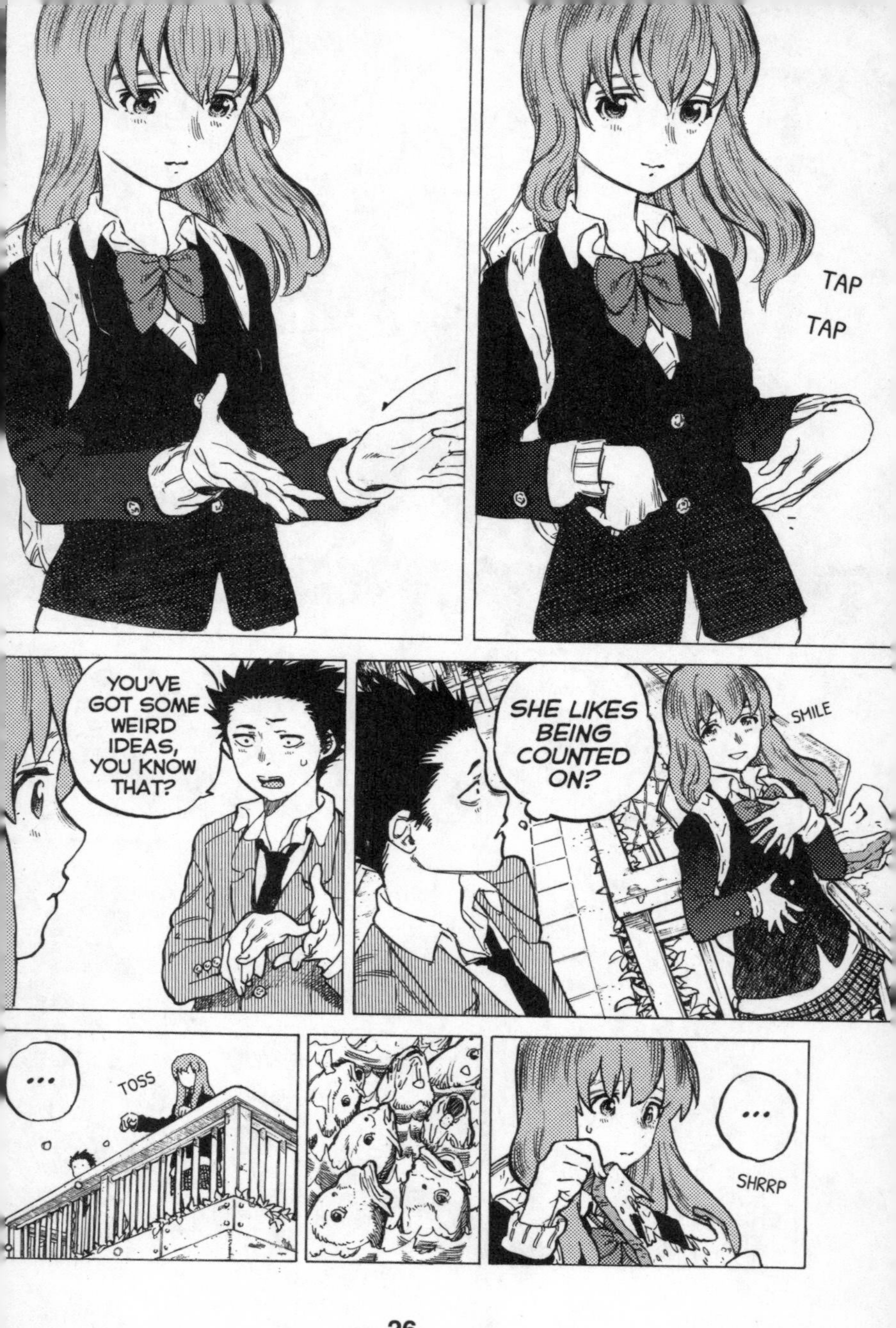
TAP
TAP
SHE LIKES BEING COUNTED ON?
SMILE
YOU'VE GOT SOME WEIRD IDEAS, YOU KNOW THAT?
...
SHRRP
...
TOSS

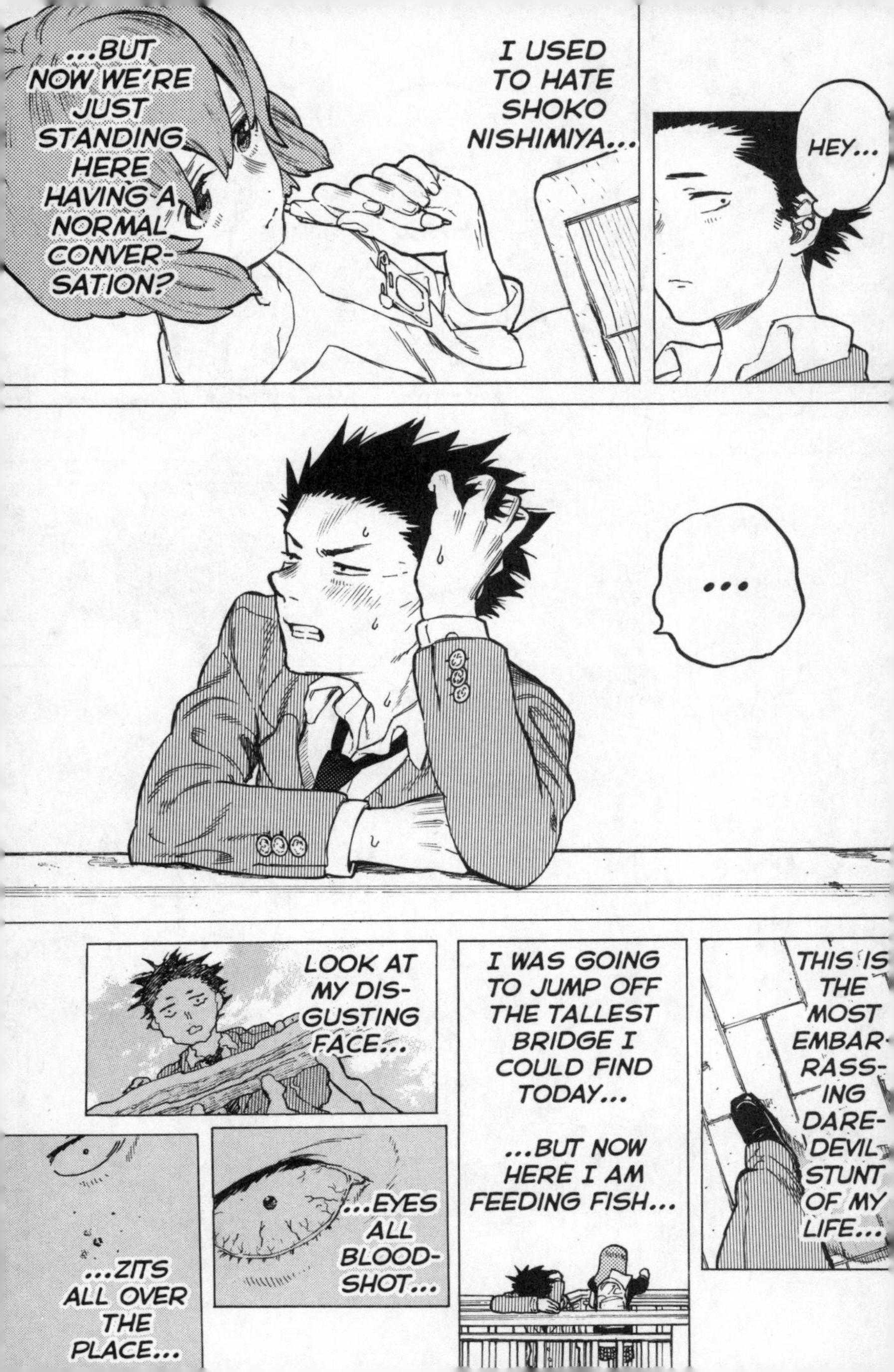
HEY...
I USED TO HATE SHOKO NISHIMIYA...
...BUT NOW WE'RE JUST STANDING HERE HAVING A NORMAL CONVERSATION?
...
THIS IS THE MOST EMBARRASSING DAREDEVIL STUNT OF MY LIFE...
I WAS GOING TO JUMP OFF THE TALLEST BRIDGE I COULD FIND TODAY...
...BUT NOW HERE I AM FEEDING FISH...
LOOK AT MY DISGUSTING FACE...
...EYES ALL BLOODSHOT...
...ZITS ALL OVER THE PLACE...

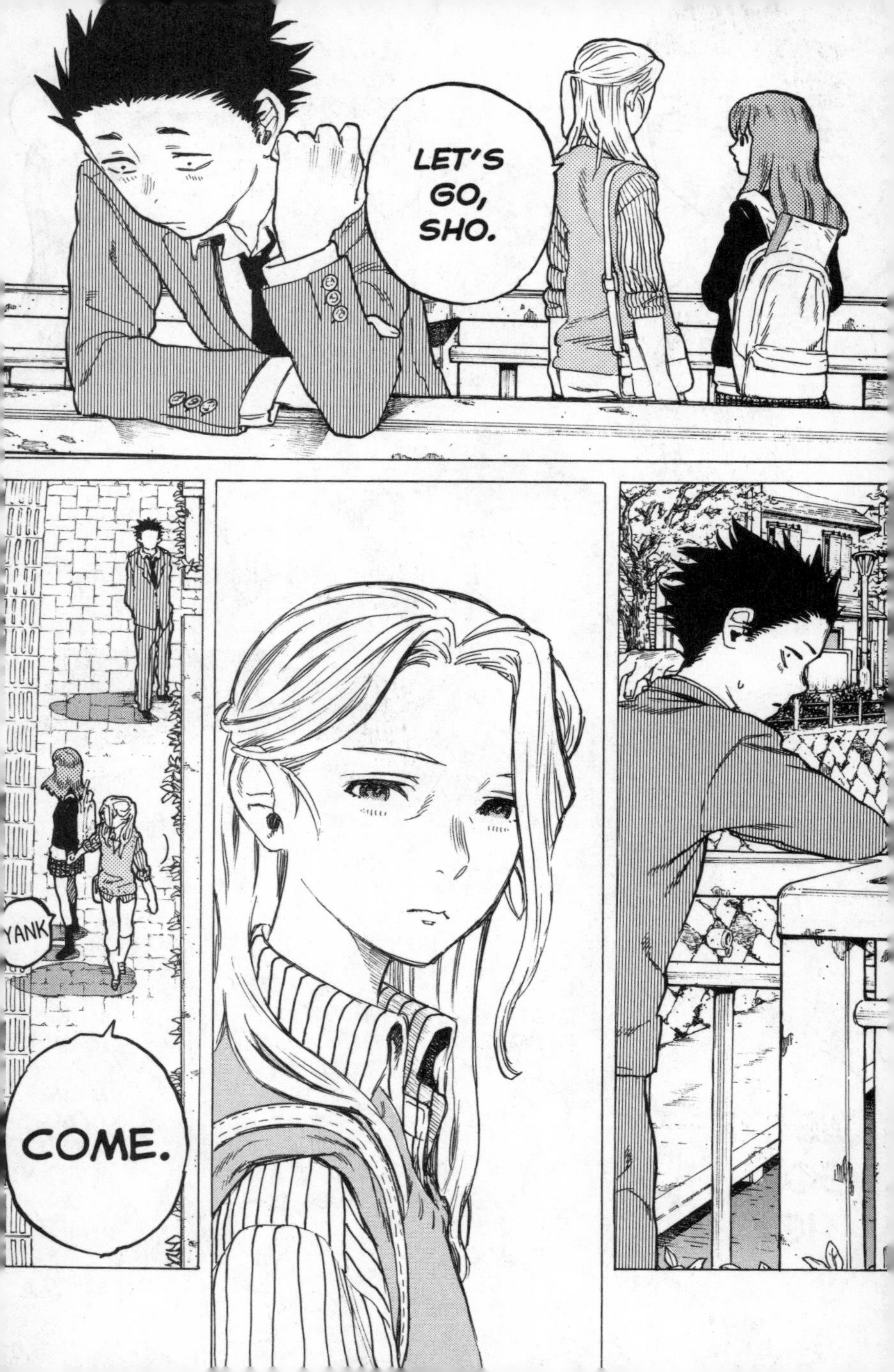
LET'S GO, SHO.
YANK
COME.

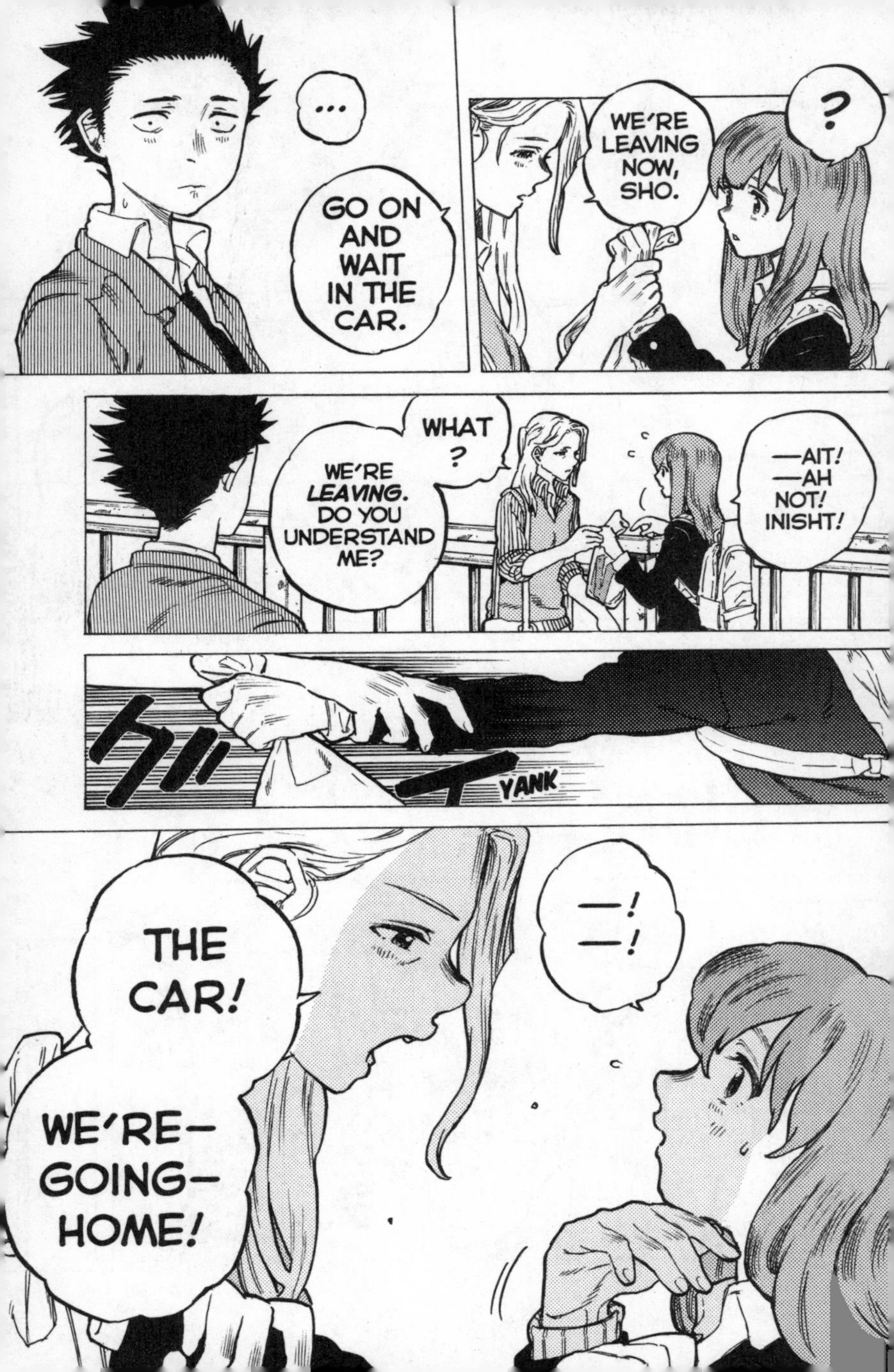
?
WE'RE LEAVING NOW, SHO.
...
GO ON AND WAIT IN THE CAR.
—AIT! —AH NOT! INISHT!
WHAT ?
WE'RE *LEAVING*. DO YOU UNDERSTAND ME?
YANK
—! —!
THE CAR!
WE'RE— GOING— HOME!

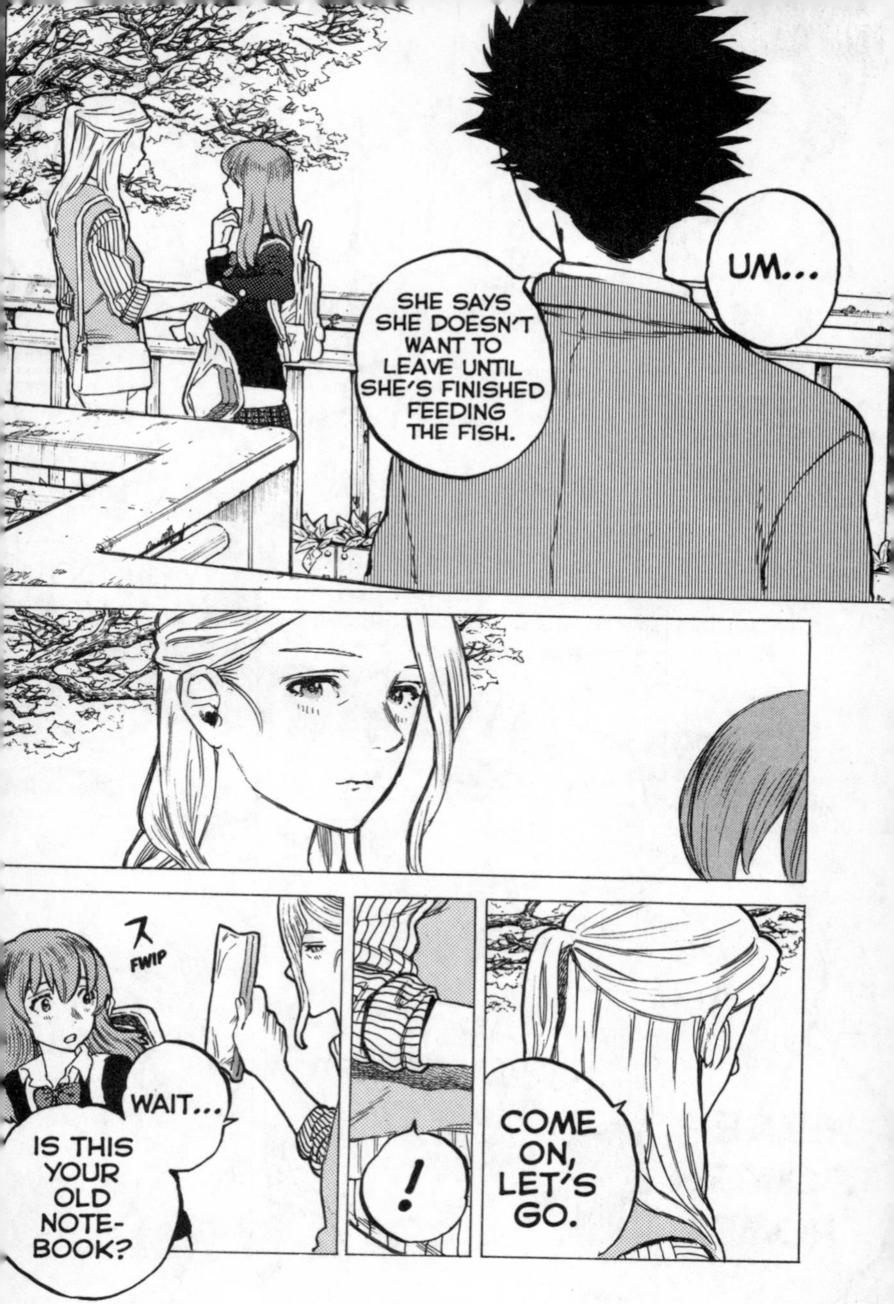
UM...
SHE SAYS SHE DOESN'T WANT TO LEAVE UNTIL SHE'S FINISHED FEEDING THE FISH.
COME ON, LET'S GO.
!
ス
FWIP
WAIT...
IS THIS YOUR OLD NOTE-BOOK?

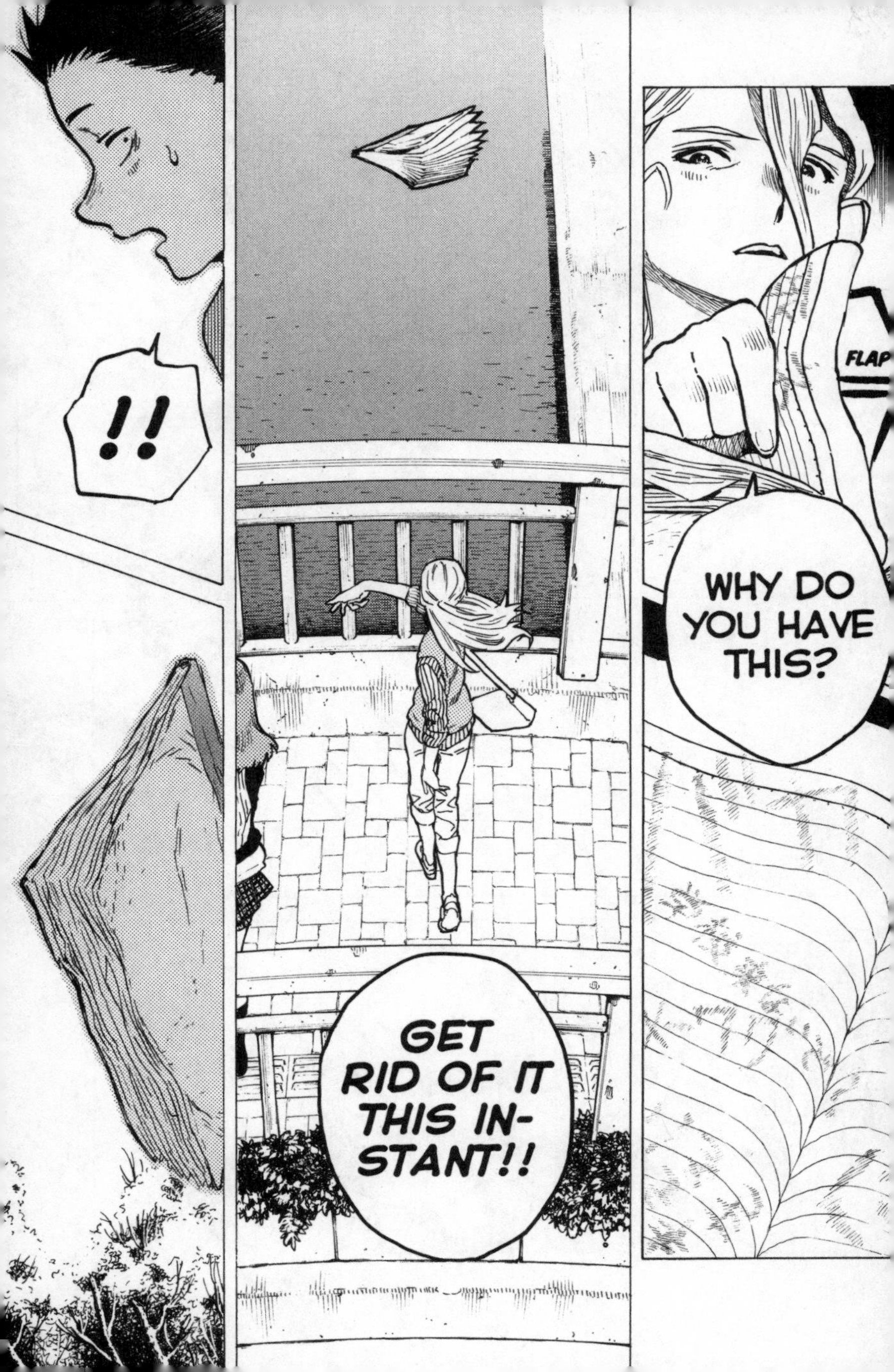
FLAP
WHY DO YOU HAVE THIS?
GET RID OF IT THIS IN-STANT!!
!!

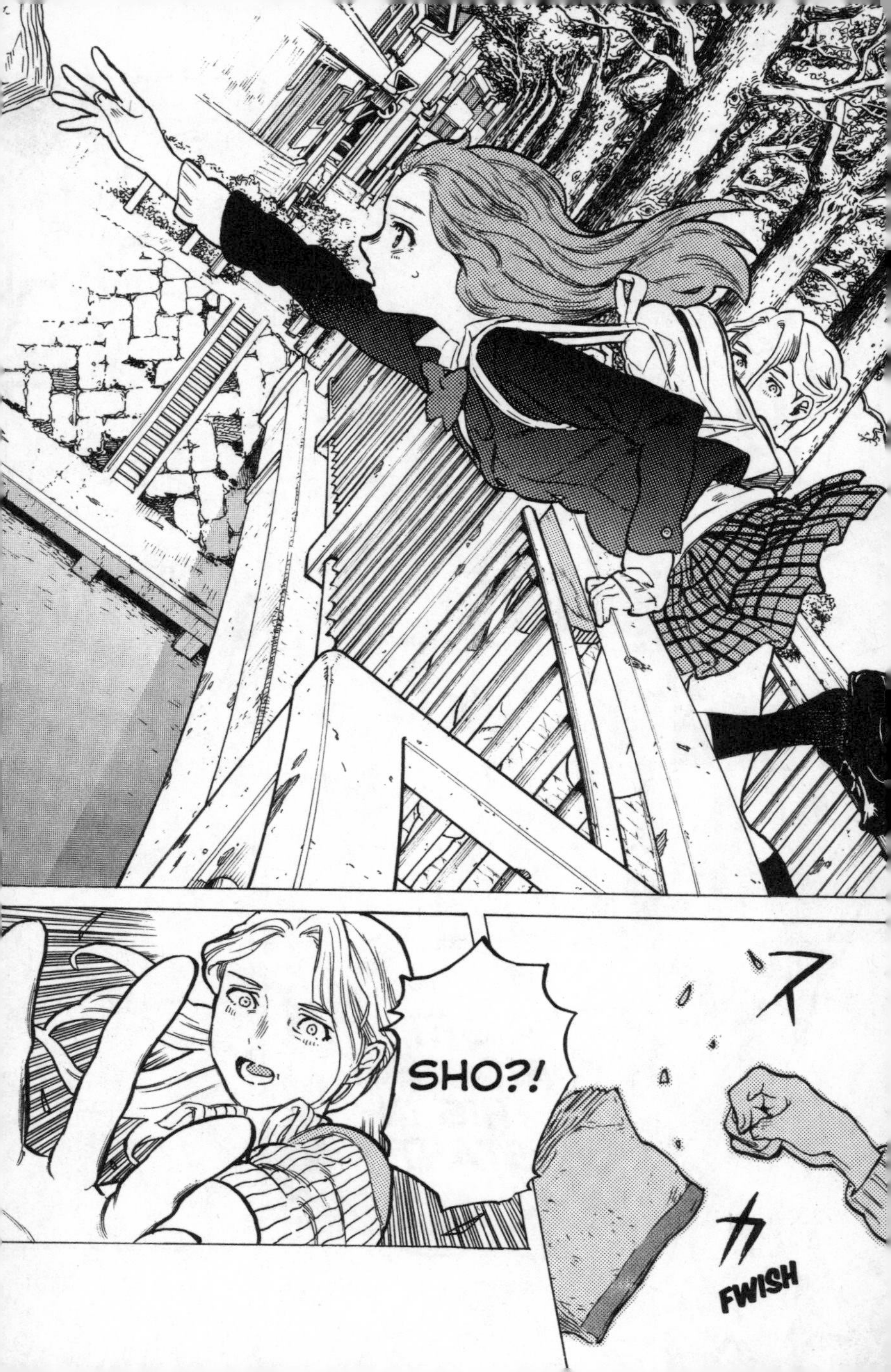
ス
カ
FWISH
SHO?!

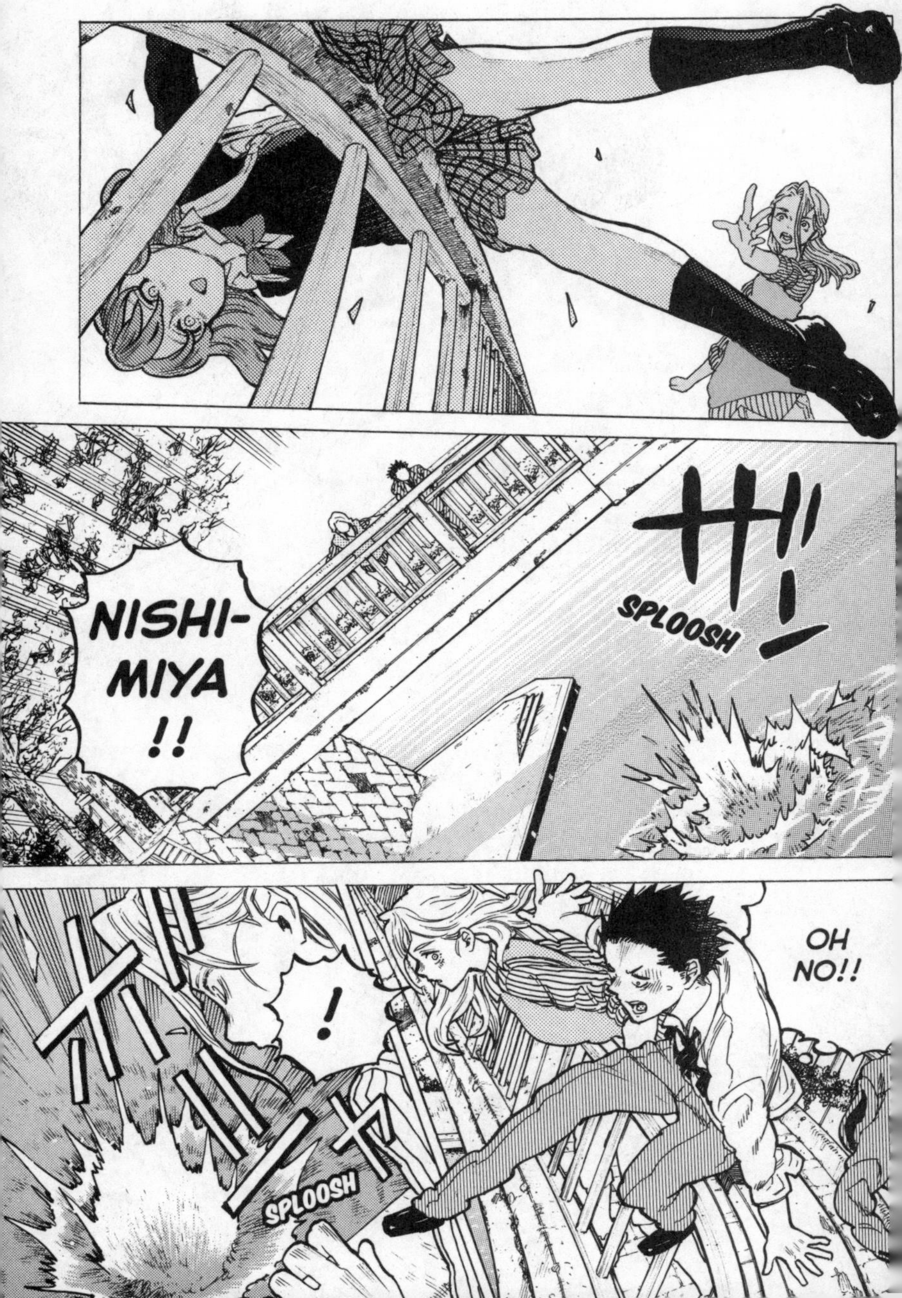
SPLOOSH
NISHI-
MIYA
!!
OH
NO!!
!
SPLOOSH

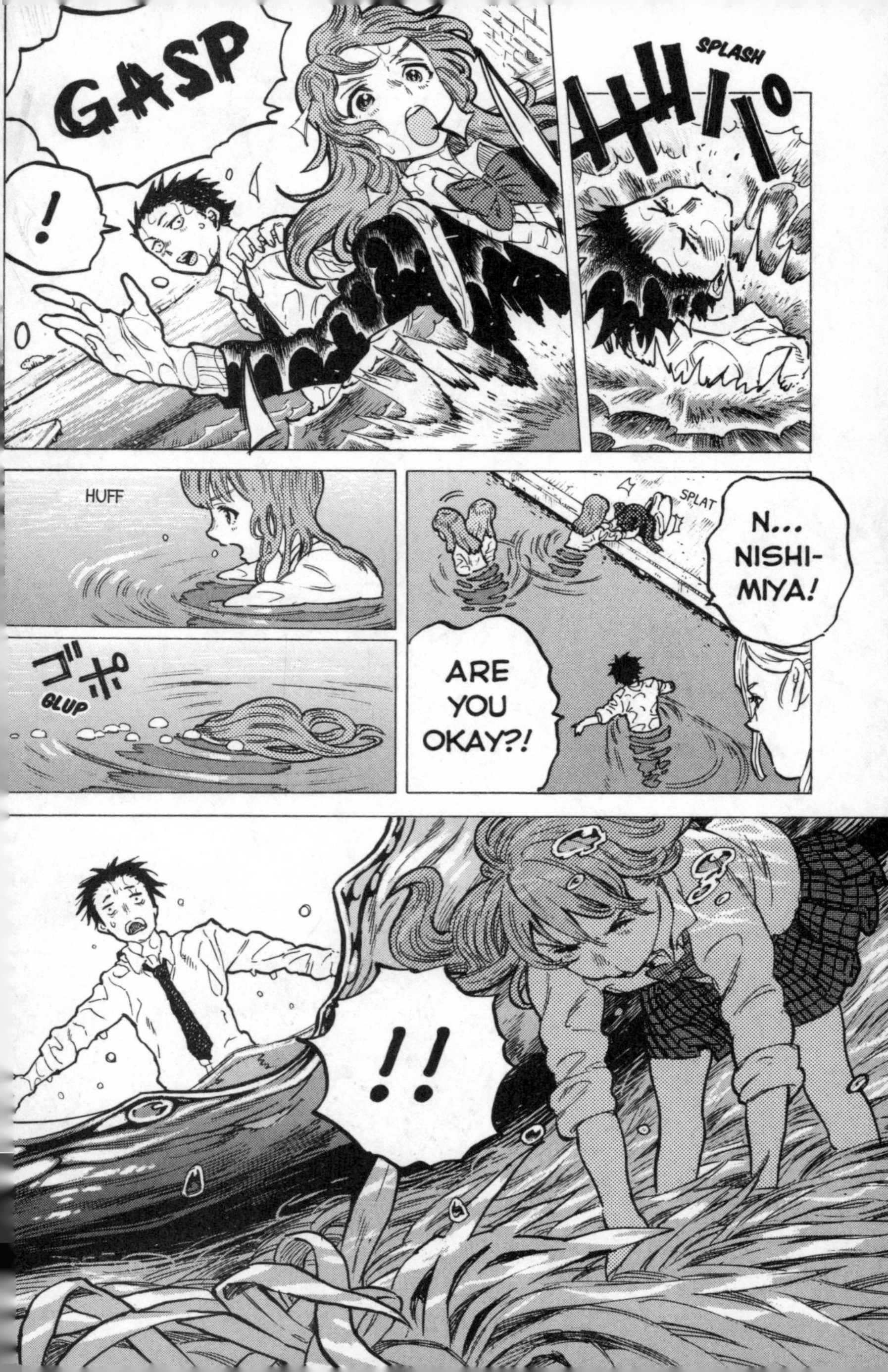
SPLASH
GASP
!
SPLAT
N... NISHI-MIYA!
ARE YOU OKAY?!
HUFF
ゴポ
GLUP
!!

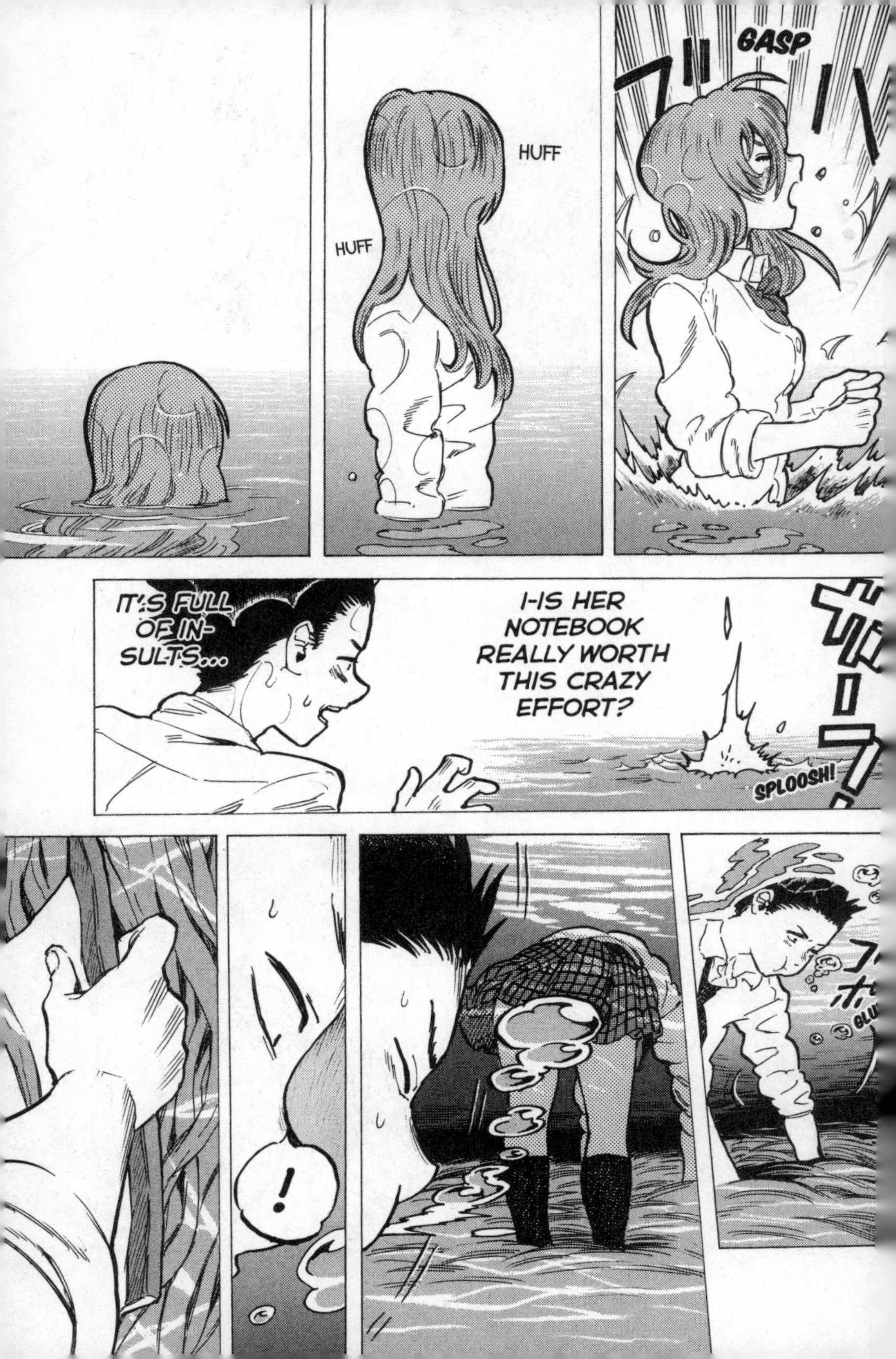
GASP
HUFF
HUFF
I-IS HER NOTEBOOK REALLY WORTH THIS CRAZY EFFORT?
IT'S FULL OF IN-SULTS...
SPLOOSH!
!

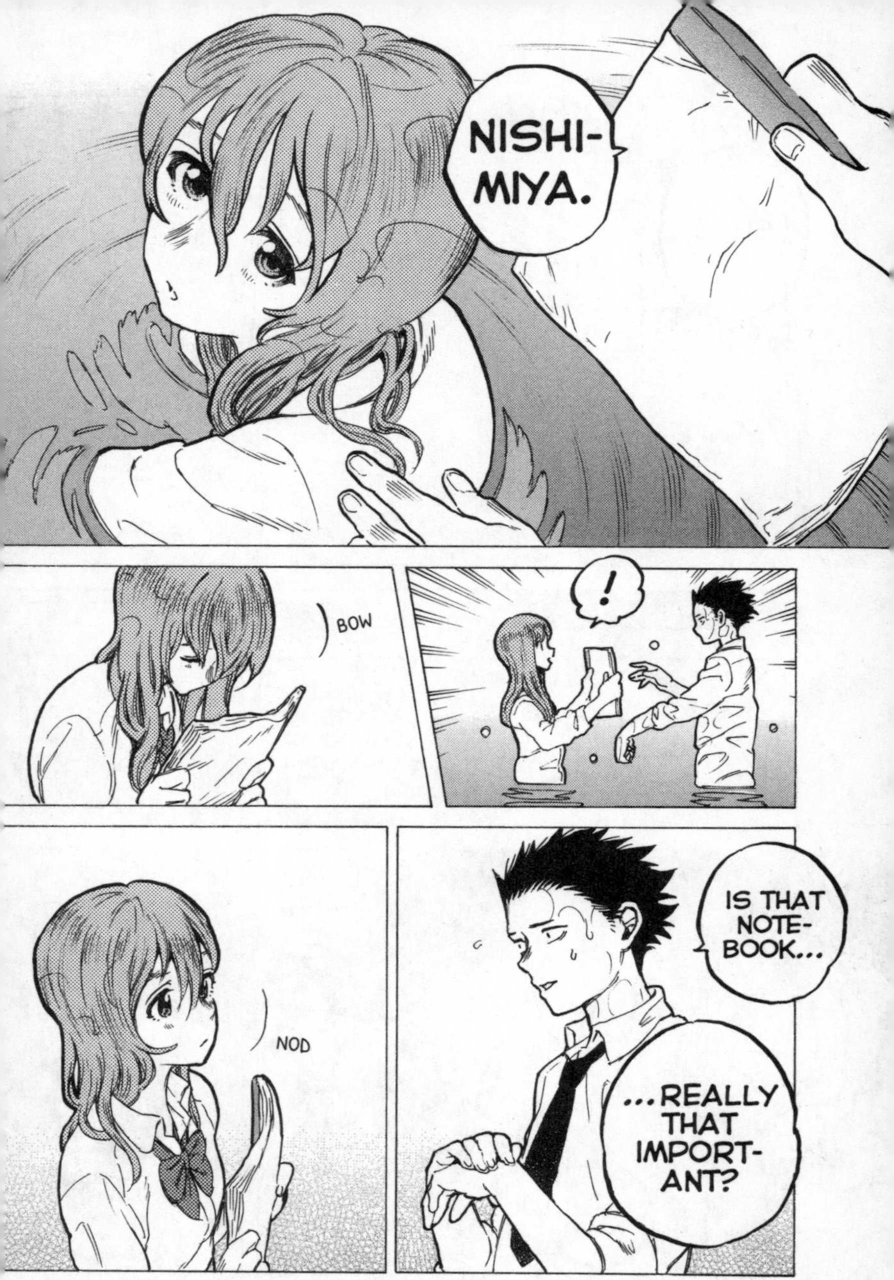
NISHI-MIYA.
!
BOW
IS THAT NOTE-BOOK...
...REALLY THAT IMPORT-ANT?
NOD

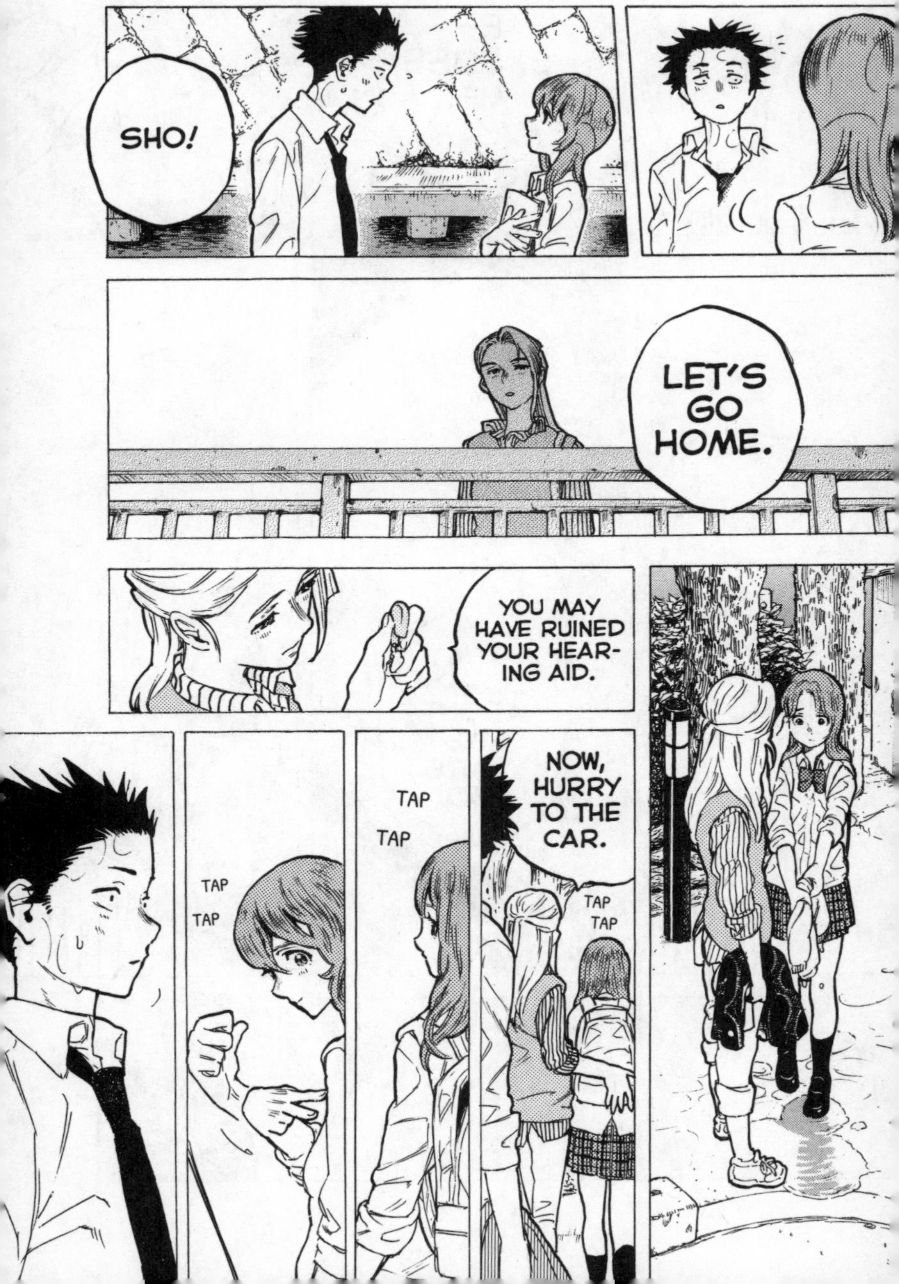
SHO!
LET'S GO HOME.
YOU MAY HAVE RUINED YOUR HEAR-ING AID.
NOW, HURRY TO THE CAR.
TAP TAP
TAP TAP
TAP TAP

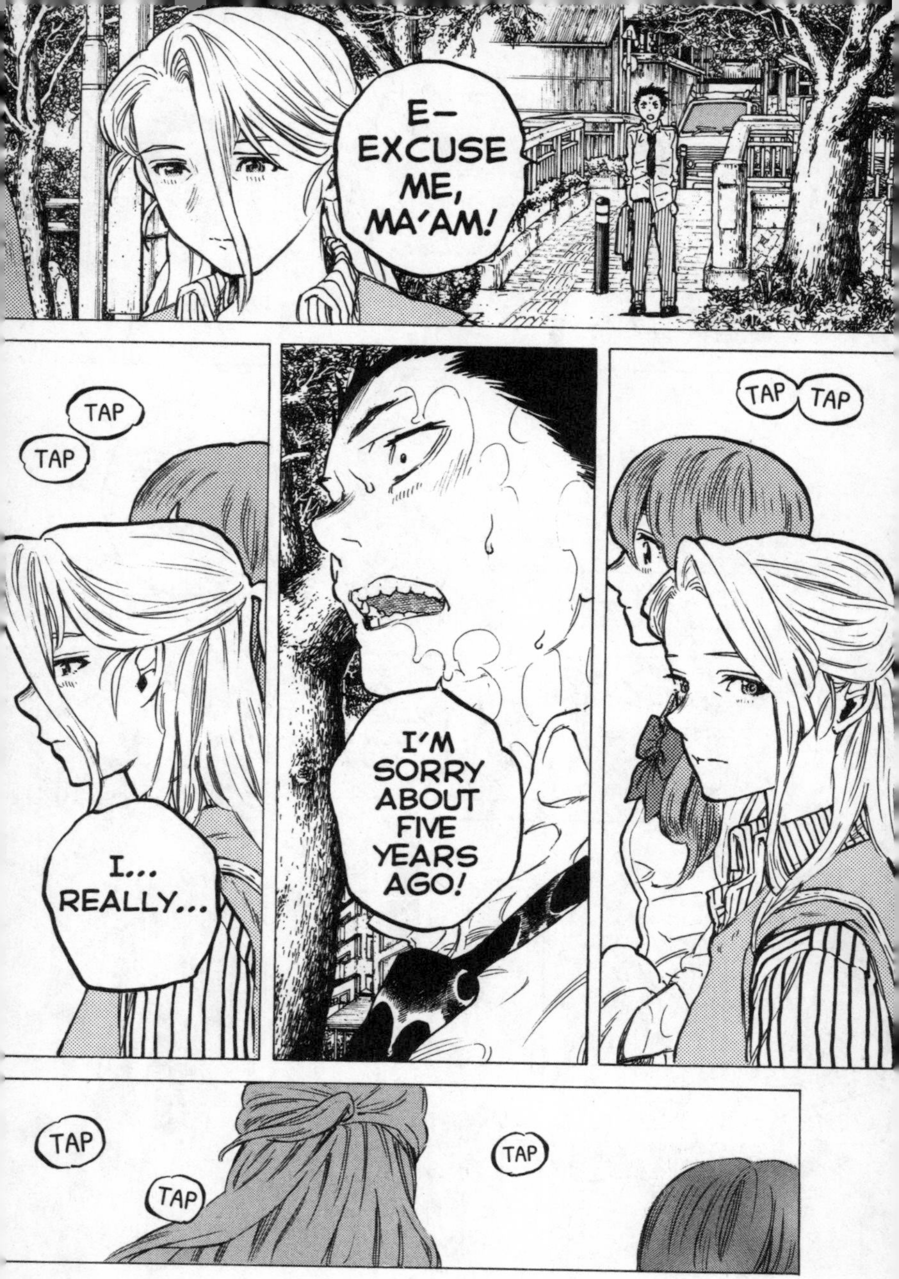
E— EXCUSE ME, MA'AM!
TAP
TAP
I'M SORRY ABOUT FIVE YEARS AGO!
TAP
TAP
I... REALLY...
TAP
TAP
TAP

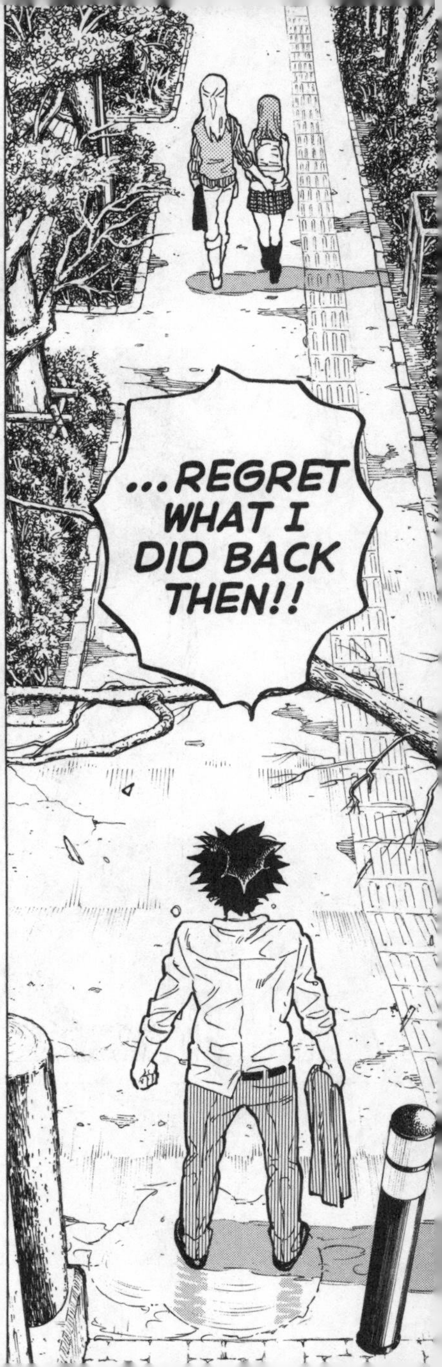
...REGRET WHAT I DID BACK THEN!!
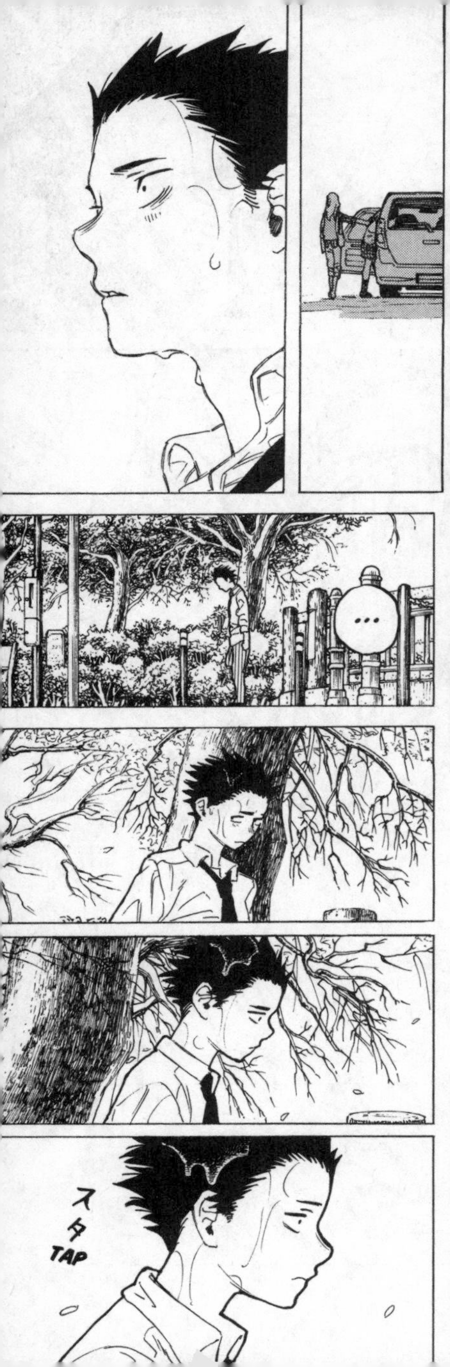
...
スタ
TAP

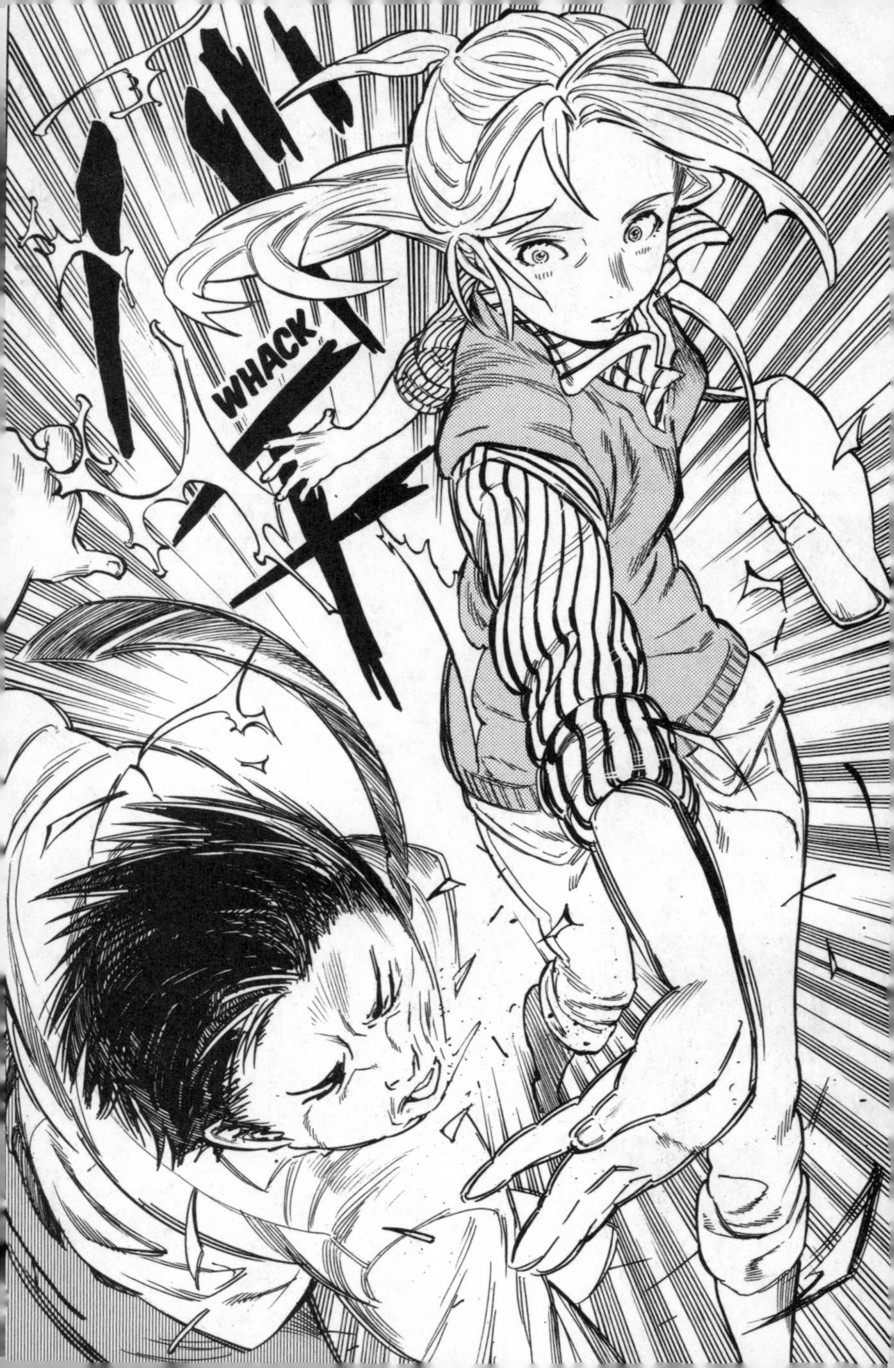
WHACK

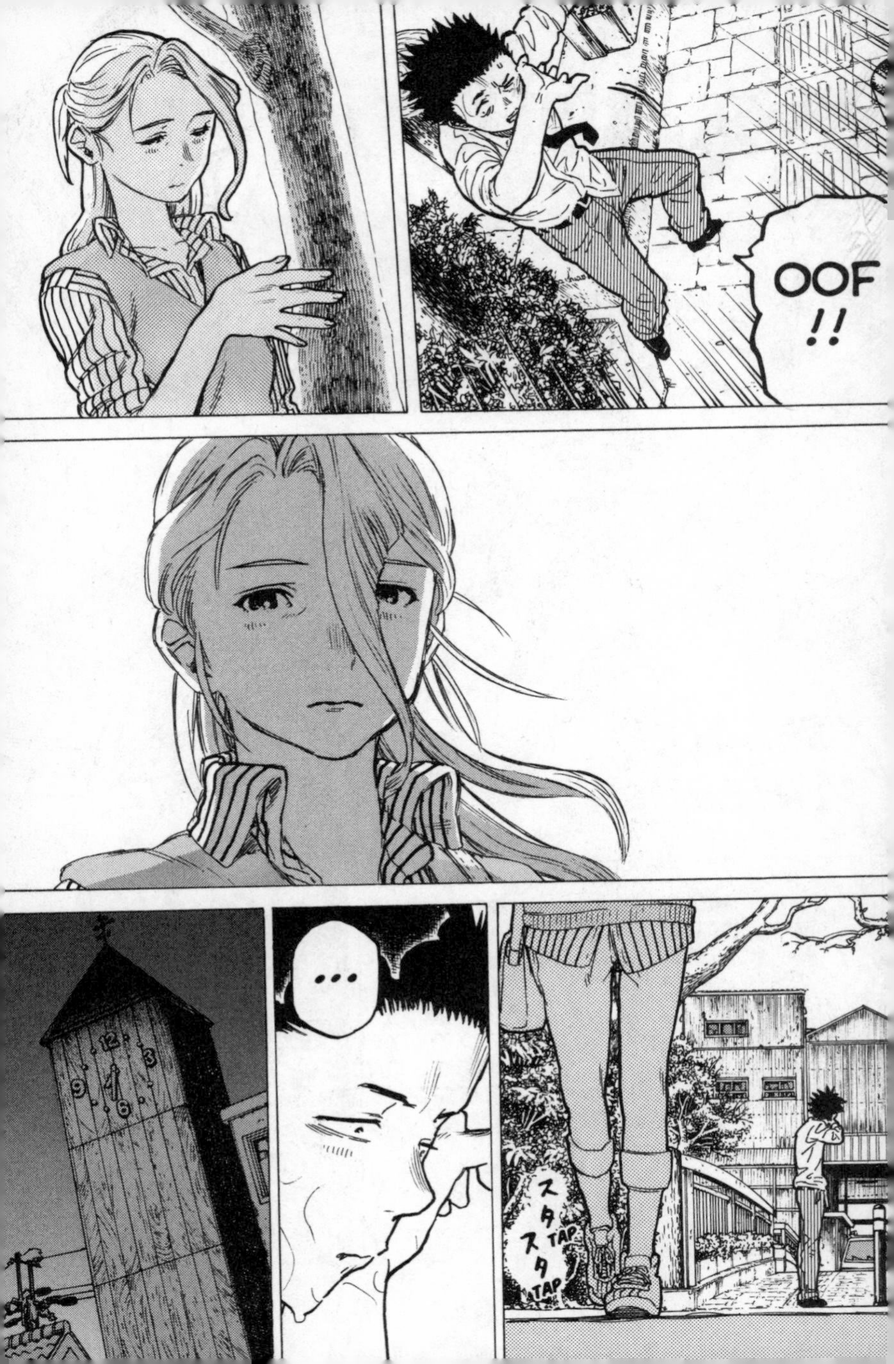
OOF !!
スタスタ
TAP TAP
...

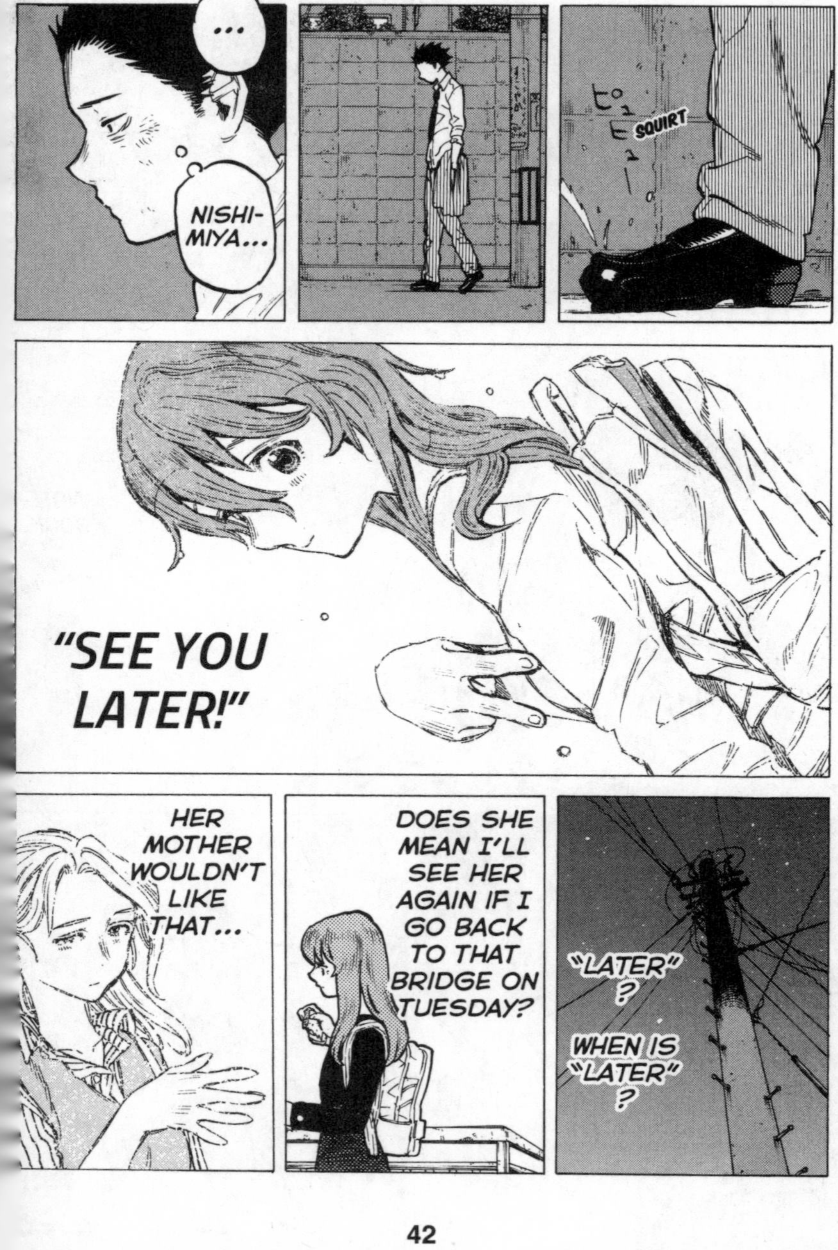
SQUIRT
...
NISHI-MIYA...
"SEE YOU LATER!"
"LATER"?
WHEN IS "LATER"?
DOES SHE MEAN I'LL SEE HER AGAIN IF I GO BACK TO THAT BRIDGE ON TUESDAY?
HER MOTHER WOULDN'T LIKE THAT...

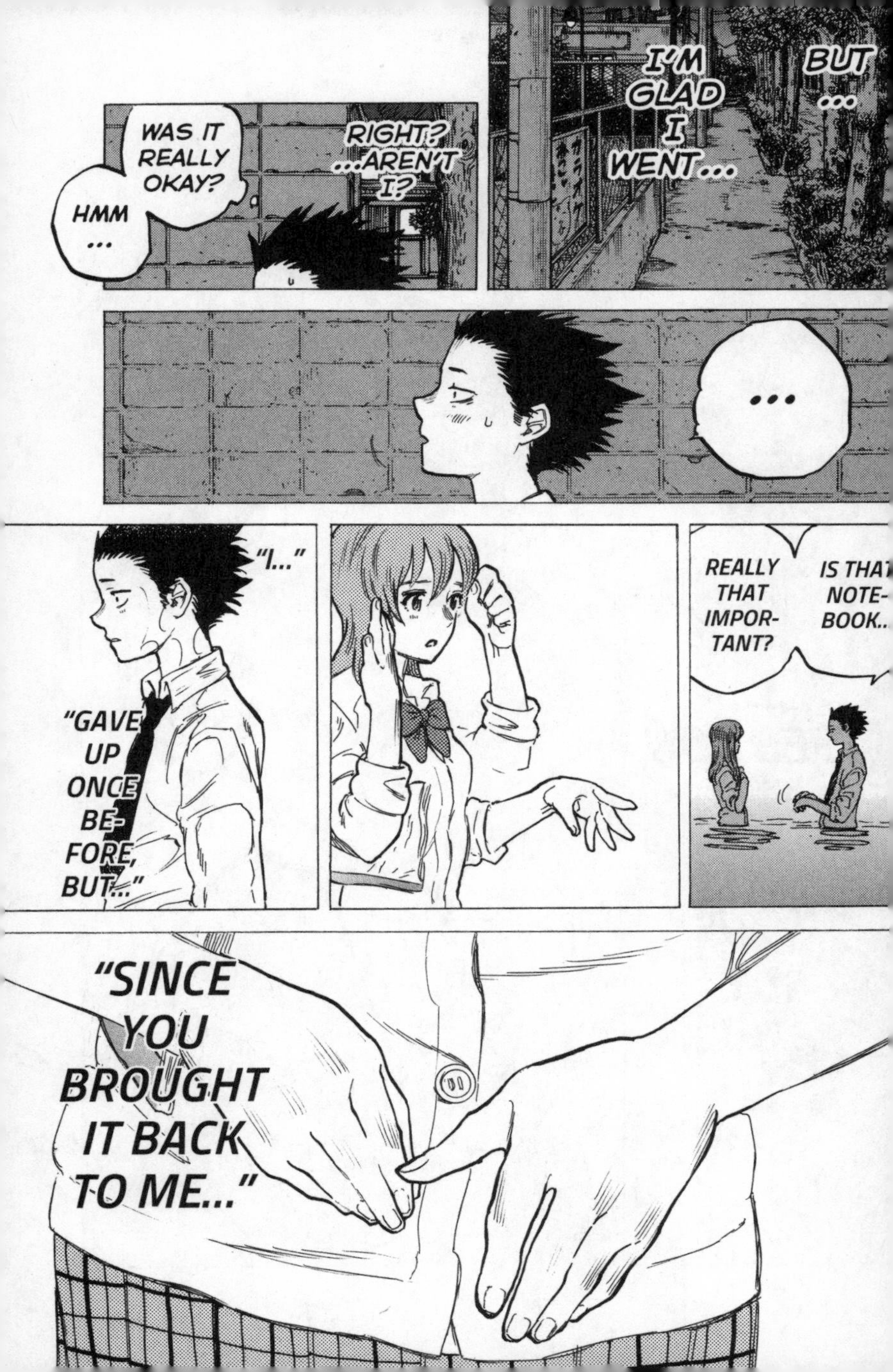
BUT...
I'M GLAD I WENT...
RIGHT? ...AREN'T I?
WAS IT REALLY OKAY?
HMM...
...
IS THAT NOTE-BOOK...
REALLY THAT IMPOR-TANT?
"I..."
"GAVE UP ONCE BE-FORE, BUT..."
"SINCE YOU BROUGHT IT BACK TO ME..."

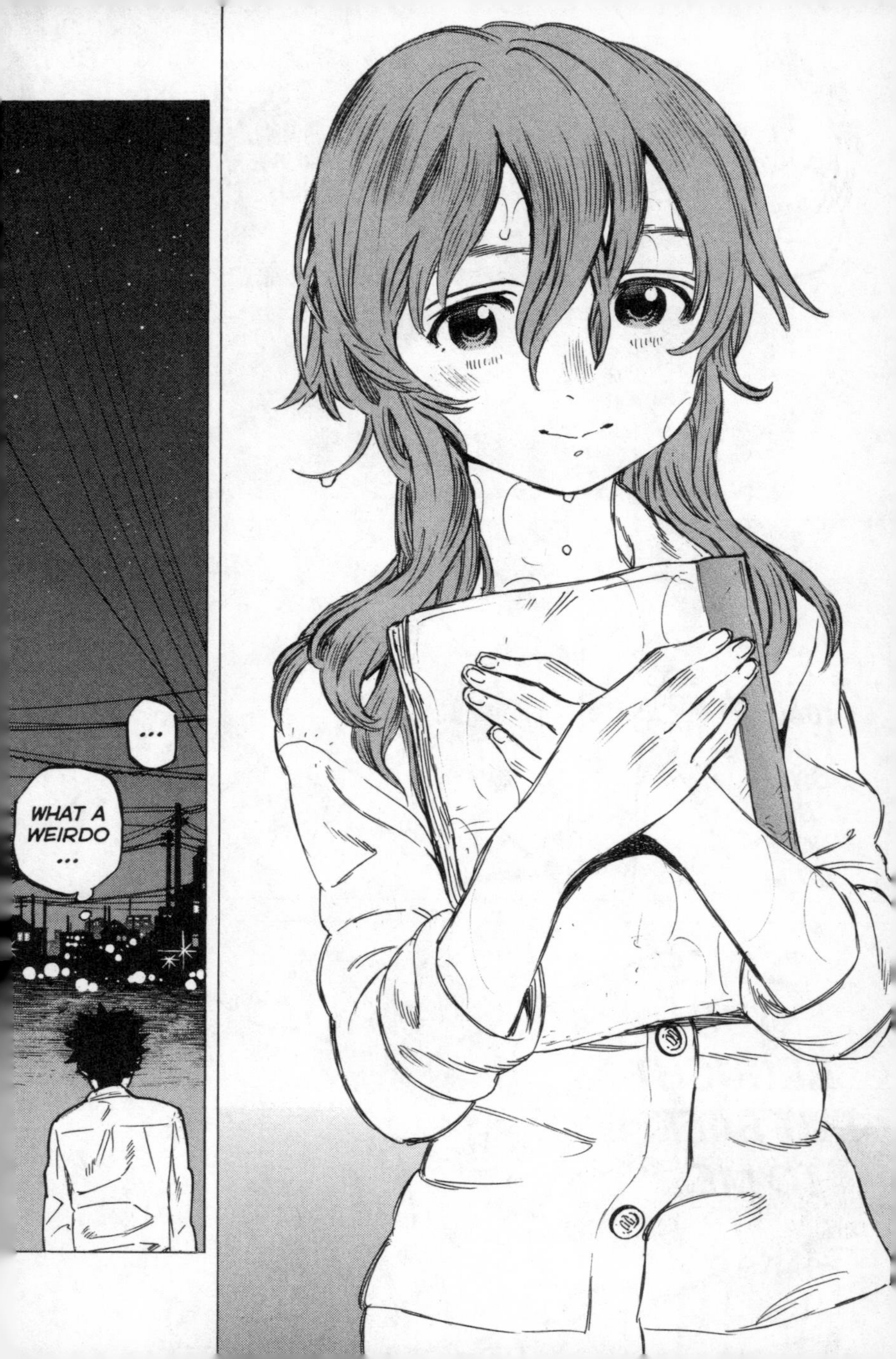
...
WHAT A WEIRDO ...

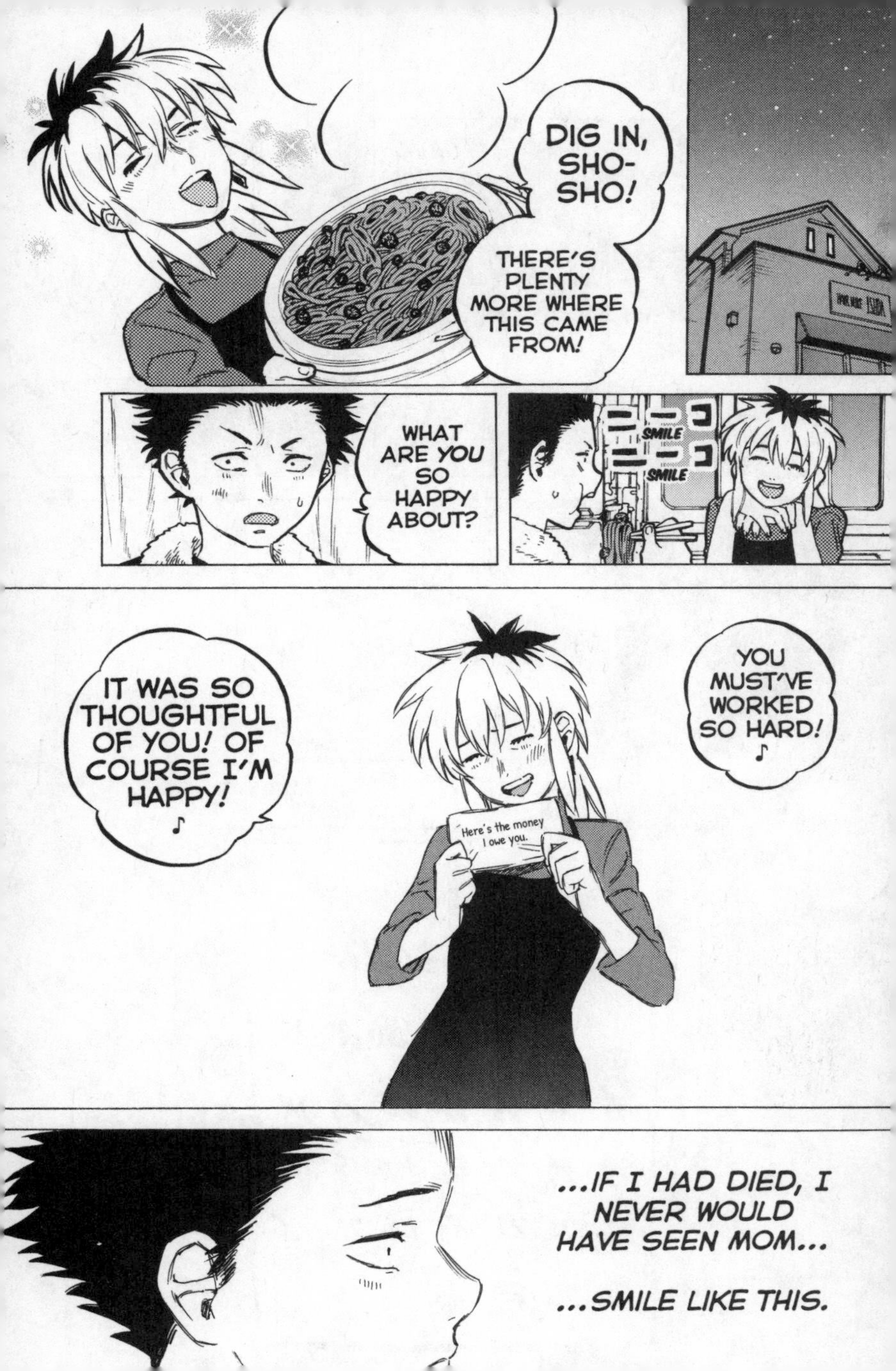

DIG IN, SHO-SHO!
THERE'S PLENTY MORE WHERE THIS CAME FROM!
SMILE
SMILE
WHAT ARE *YOU* SO HAPPY ABOUT?
YOU MUST'VE WORKED SO HARD! ♪
Here's the money I owe you.
IT WAS SO THOUGHTFUL OF YOU! OF COURSE I'M HAPPY! ♪
...IF I HAD DIED, I NEVER WOULD HAVE SEEN MOM...
...SMILE LIKE THIS.

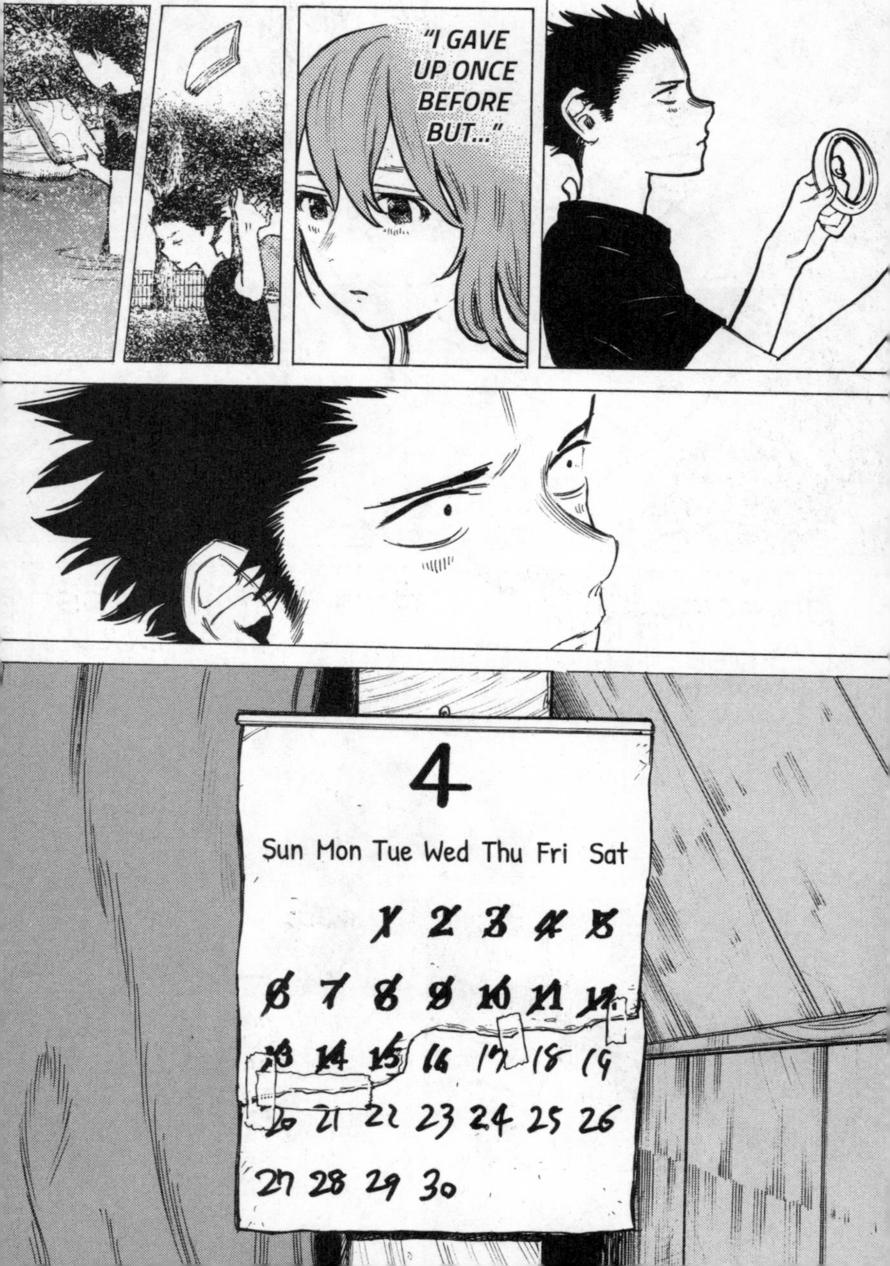
"I GAVE UP ONCE BEFORE BUT..."
4
Sun Mon Tue Wed Thu Fri Sat
1 2 3 4 5
6 7 8 9 10 11 12
13 14 15 16 17 18 19
20 21 22 23 24 25 26
27 28 29 30

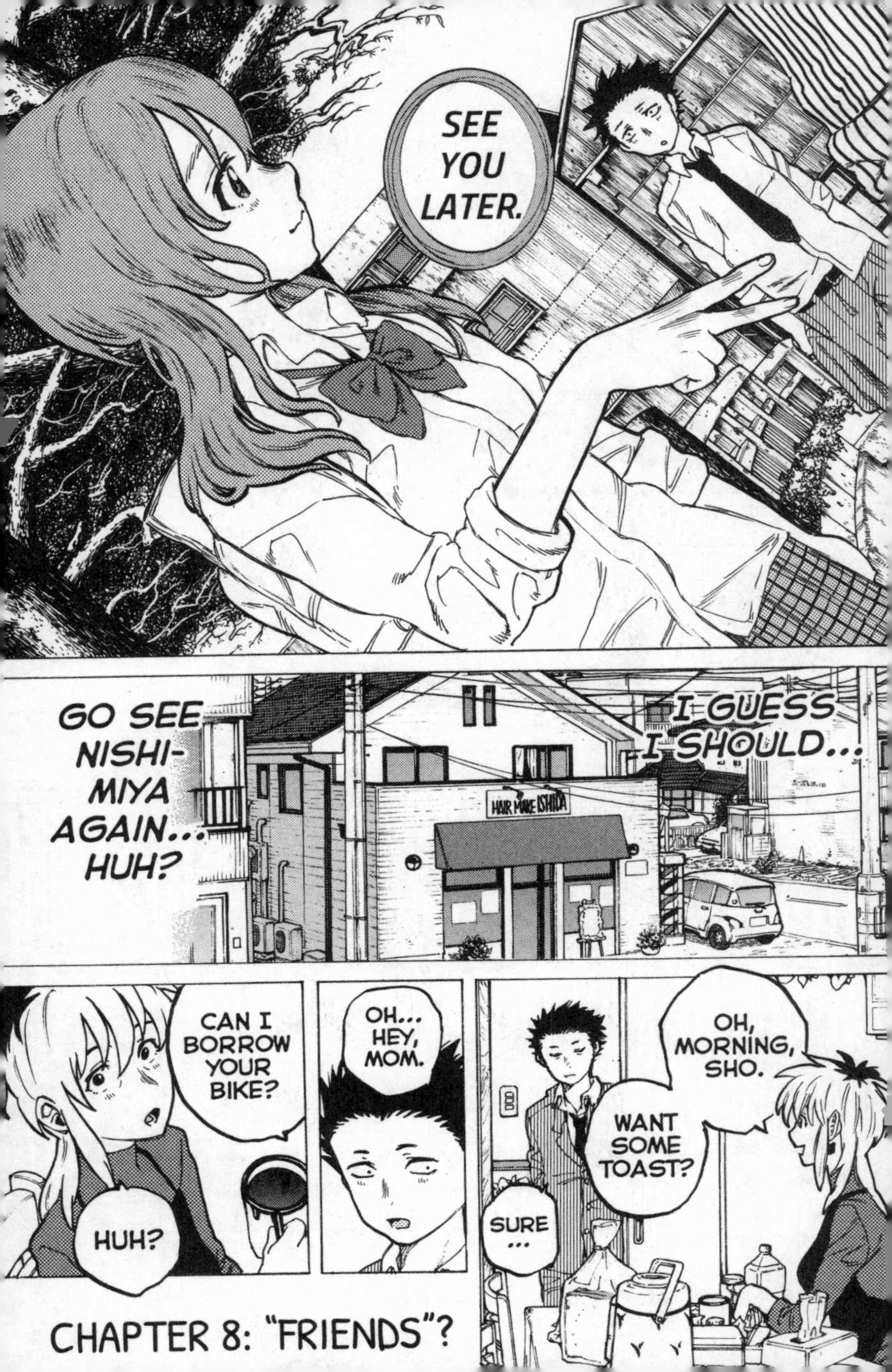
SEE YOU LATER.
I GUESS I SHOULD...
GO SEE NISHIMIYA AGAIN... HUH?
HAIR MAKE ISHIDA
OH, MORNING, SHO.
WANT SOME TOAST?
SURE...
OH... HEY, MOM.
CAN I BORROW YOUR BIKE?
HUH?
CHAPTER 8: "FRIENDS"?

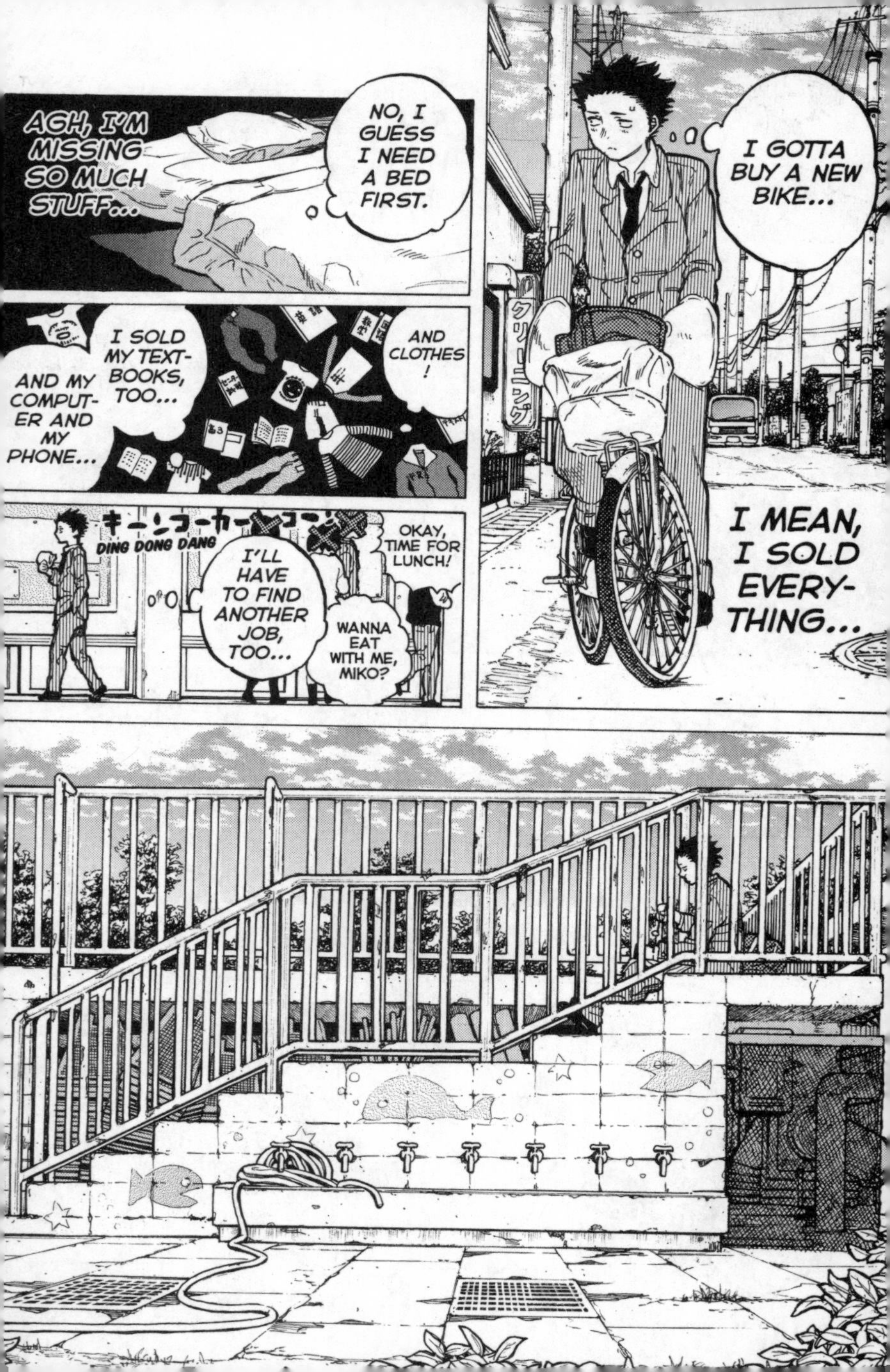
I GOTTA BUY A NEW BIKE...
I MEAN, I SOLD EVERYTHING...
NO, I GUESS I NEED A BED FIRST.
AGH, I'M MISSING SO MUCH STUFF...
AND CLOTHES!
I SOLD MY TEXT-BOOKS, TOO...
AND MY COMPUTER AND MY PHONE...
OKAY, TIME FOR LUNCH!
WANNA EAT WITH ME, MIKO?
I'LL HAVE TO FIND ANOTHER JOB, TOO...
DING DONG DANG

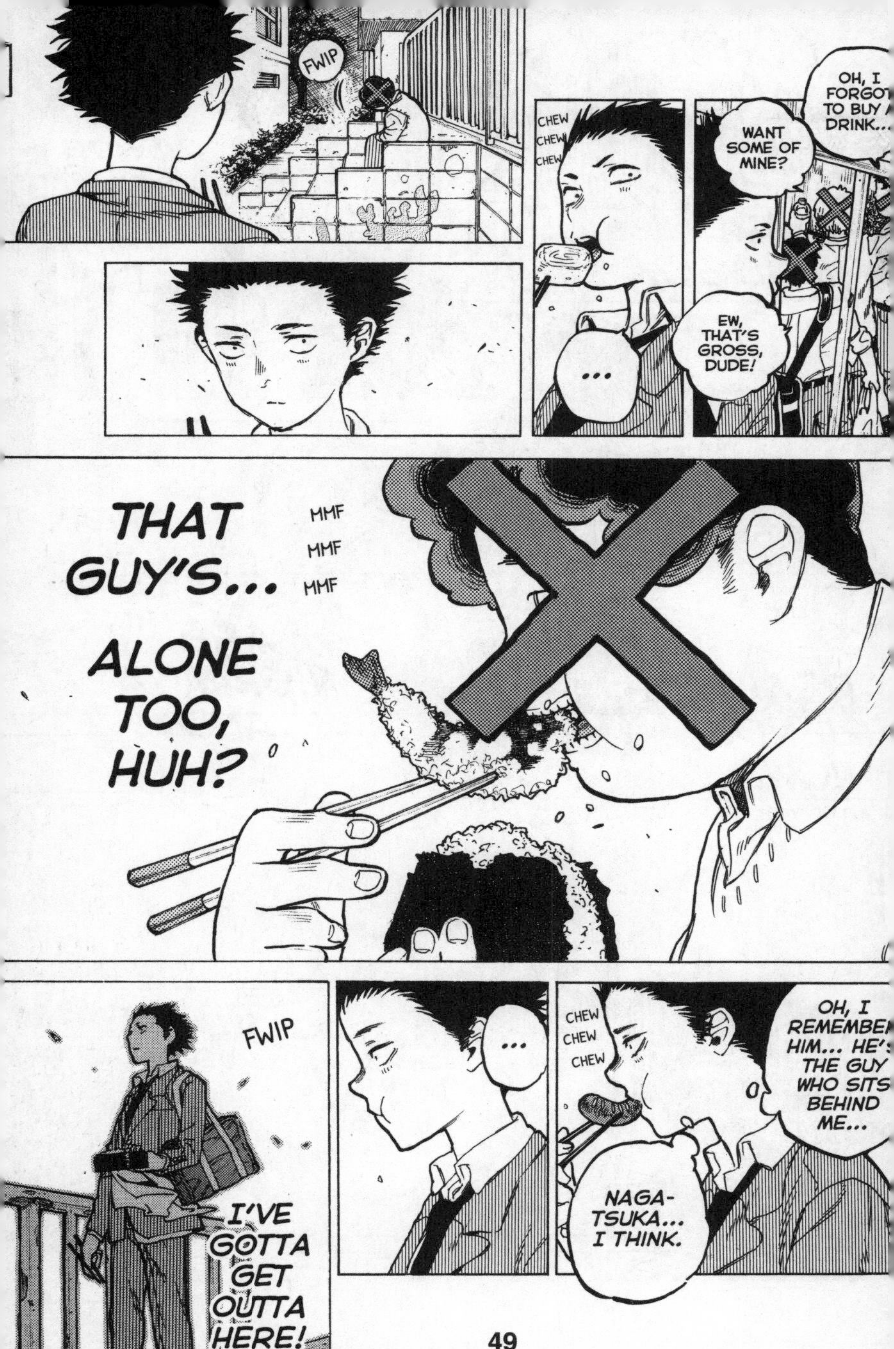
OH, I FORGOT TO BUY A DRINK...
WANT SOME OF MINE?
EW, THAT'S GROSS, DUDE!
CHEW CHEW CHEW
...
FWIP
THAT GUY'S...
MMF MMF MMF
ALONE TOO, HUH?
OH, I REMEMBER HIM... HE'S THE GUY WHO SITS BEHIND ME...
CHEW CHEW CHEW
NAGA-TSUKA... I THINK.
...
FWIP
I'VE GOTTA GET OUTTA HERE!

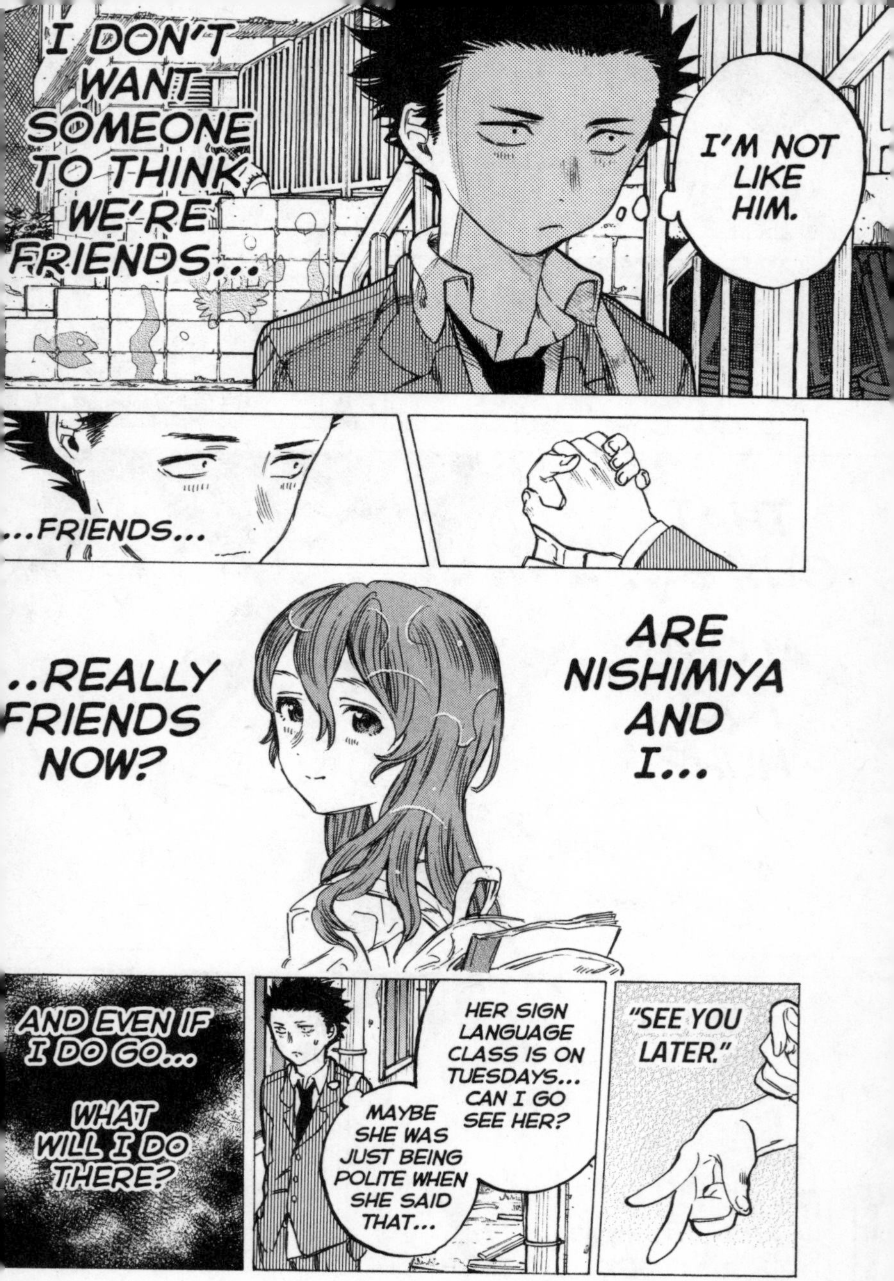
I'M NOT LIKE HIM.
I DON'T WANT SOMEONE TO THINK WE'RE FRIENDS...
...FRIENDS...
ARE NISHIMIYA AND I...
..REALLY FRIENDS NOW?
"SEE YOU LATER."
HER SIGN LANGUAGE CLASS IS ON TUESDAYS... CAN I GO SEE HER?
MAYBE SHE WAS JUST BEING POLITE WHEN SHE SAID THAT...
AND EVEN IF I DO GO...
WHAT WILL I DO THERE?

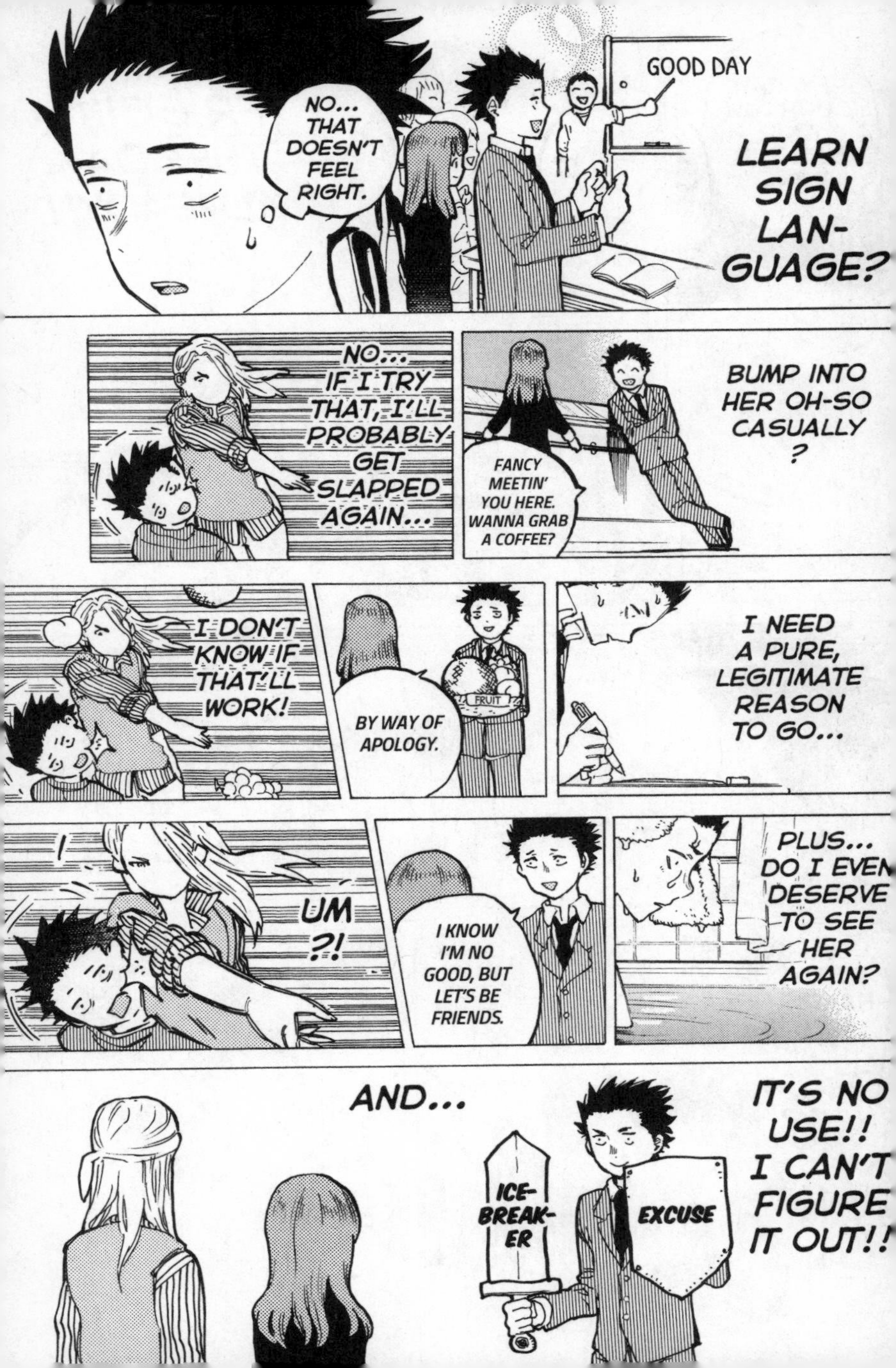
LEARN SIGN LANGUAGE?
GOOD DAY
NO... THAT DOESN'T FEEL RIGHT.
BUMP INTO HER OH-SO CASUALLY?
FANCY MEETIN' YOU HERE. WANNA GRAB A COFFEE?
NO... IF I TRY THAT, I'LL PROBABLY GET SLAPPED AGAIN...
I NEED A PURE, LEGITIMATE REASON TO GO...
FRUIT
BY WAY OF APOLOGY.
I DON'T KNOW IF THAT'LL WORK!
PLUS... DO I EVEN DESERVE TO SEE HER AGAIN?
I KNOW I'M NO GOOD, BUT LET'S BE FRIENDS.
!
UM ?!
IT'S NO USE!! I CAN'T FIGURE IT OUT!!
EXCUSE
ICE-BREAKER
AND...

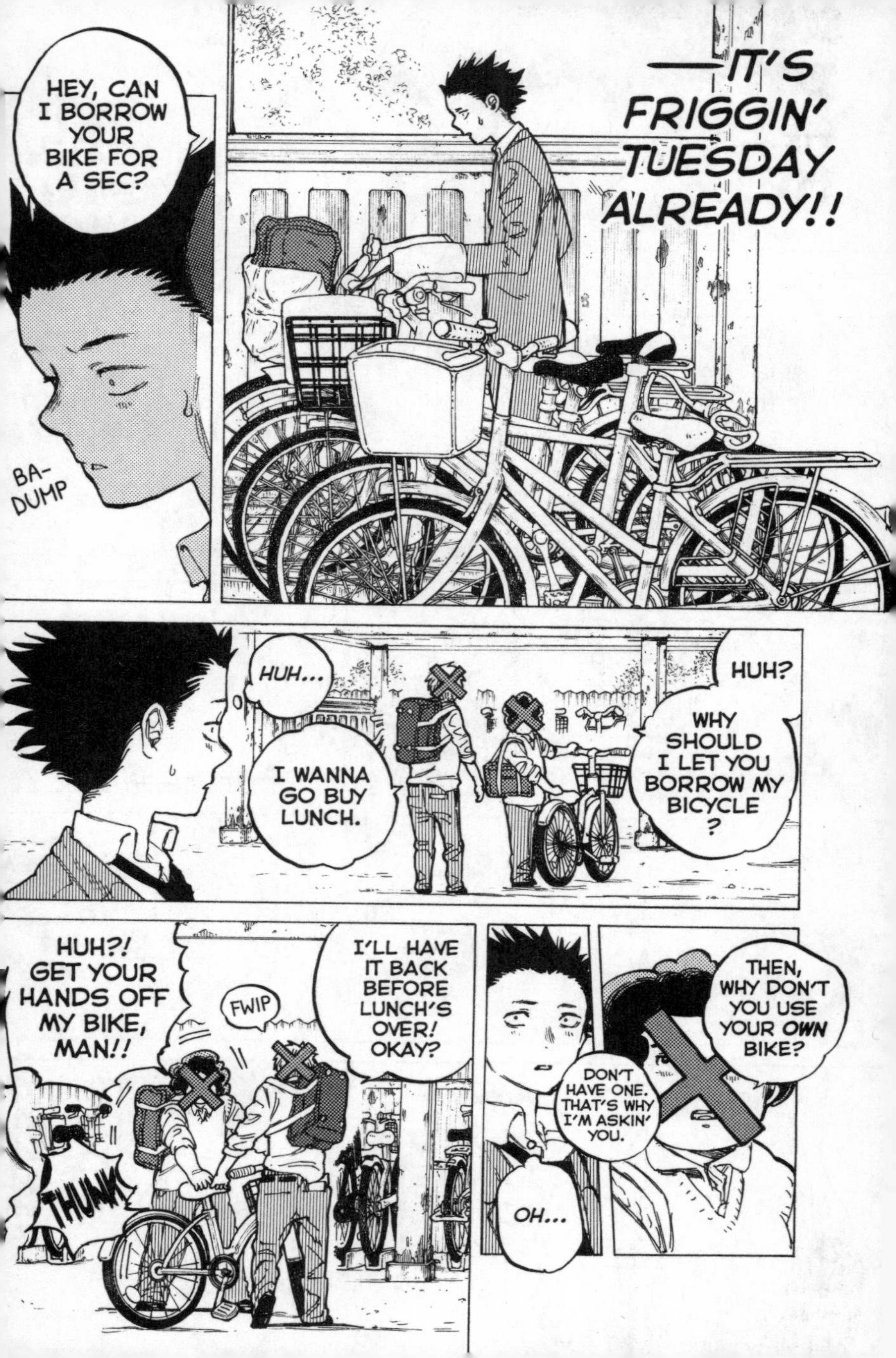
—IT'S FRIGGIN' TUESDAY ALREADY!!
HEY, CAN I BORROW YOUR BIKE FOR A SEC?
BA-DUMP
HUH?
WHY SHOULD I LET YOU BORROW MY BICYCLE?
HUH...
I WANNA GO BUY LUNCH.
THEN, WHY DON'T YOU USE YOUR *OWN* BIKE?
DON'T HAVE ONE. THAT'S WHY I'M ASKIN' YOU.
OH...
I'LL HAVE IT BACK BEFORE LUNCH'S OVER! OKAY?
FWIP
HUH?! GET YOUR HANDS OFF MY BIKE, MAN!!
THUNK

HELP ME!!
RATTLE RATTLE
?
WHY DOESN'T HE JUST LEND THE GUY HIS BIKE?
SOME-BODY HELP ME!!
RATTLE
CRAP!
OUR EYES MET.
AHHHH!!
RATTLE
...
RATTLE
AH!
DON'T I NEED TO CHANGE SOME-THING?

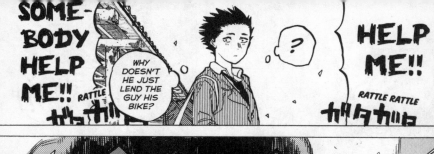

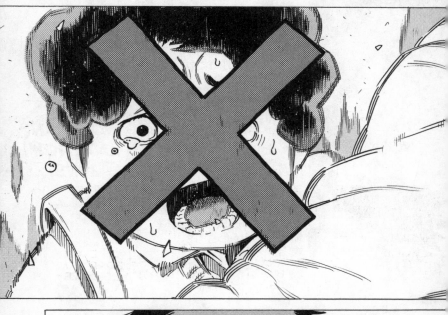

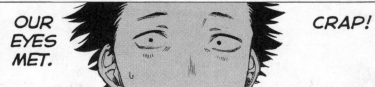

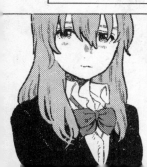

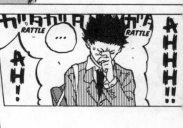

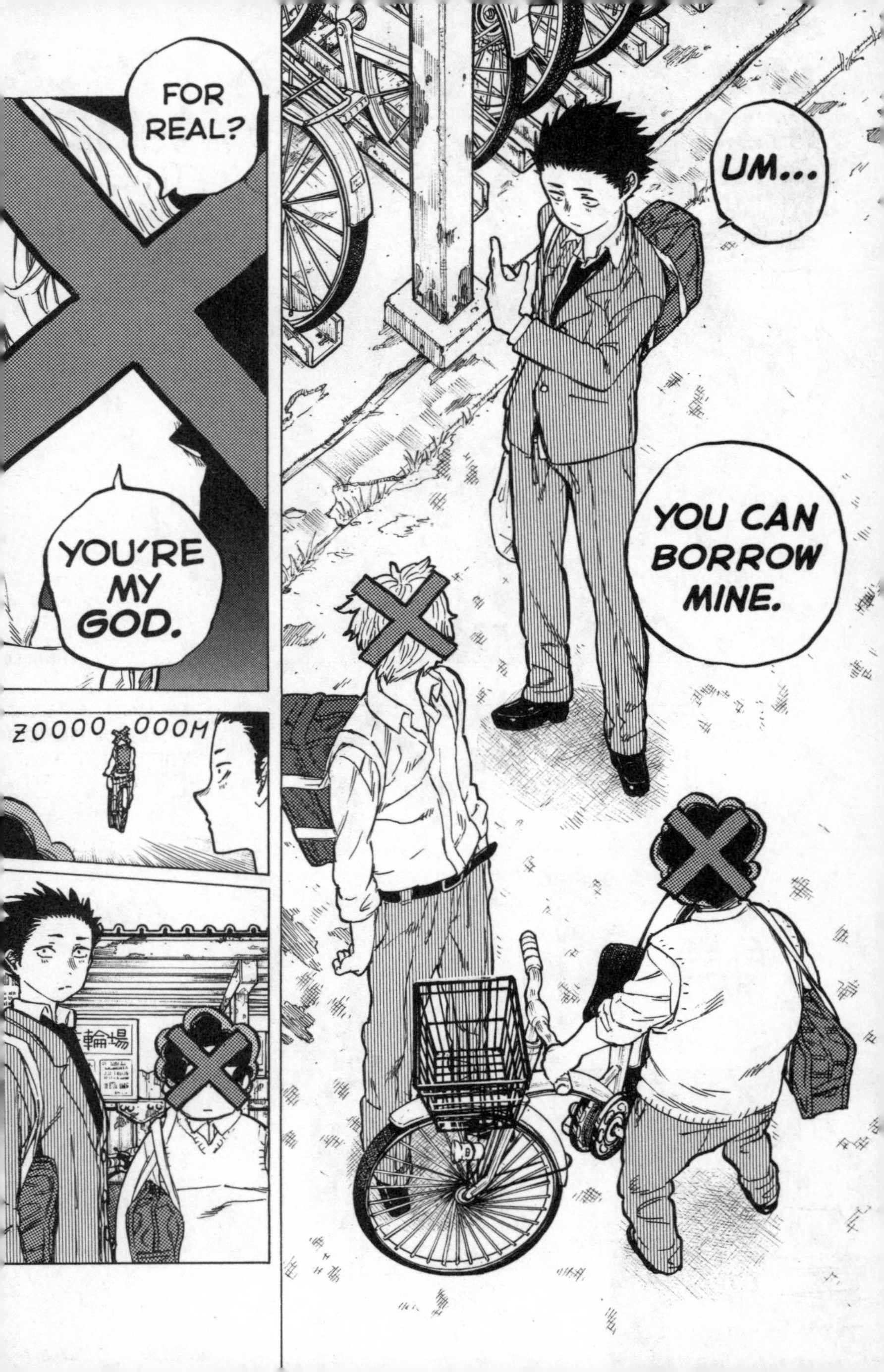
UM...
YOU CAN BORROW MINE.
FOR REAL?
YOU'RE MY GOD.
ZOOOO OOOM

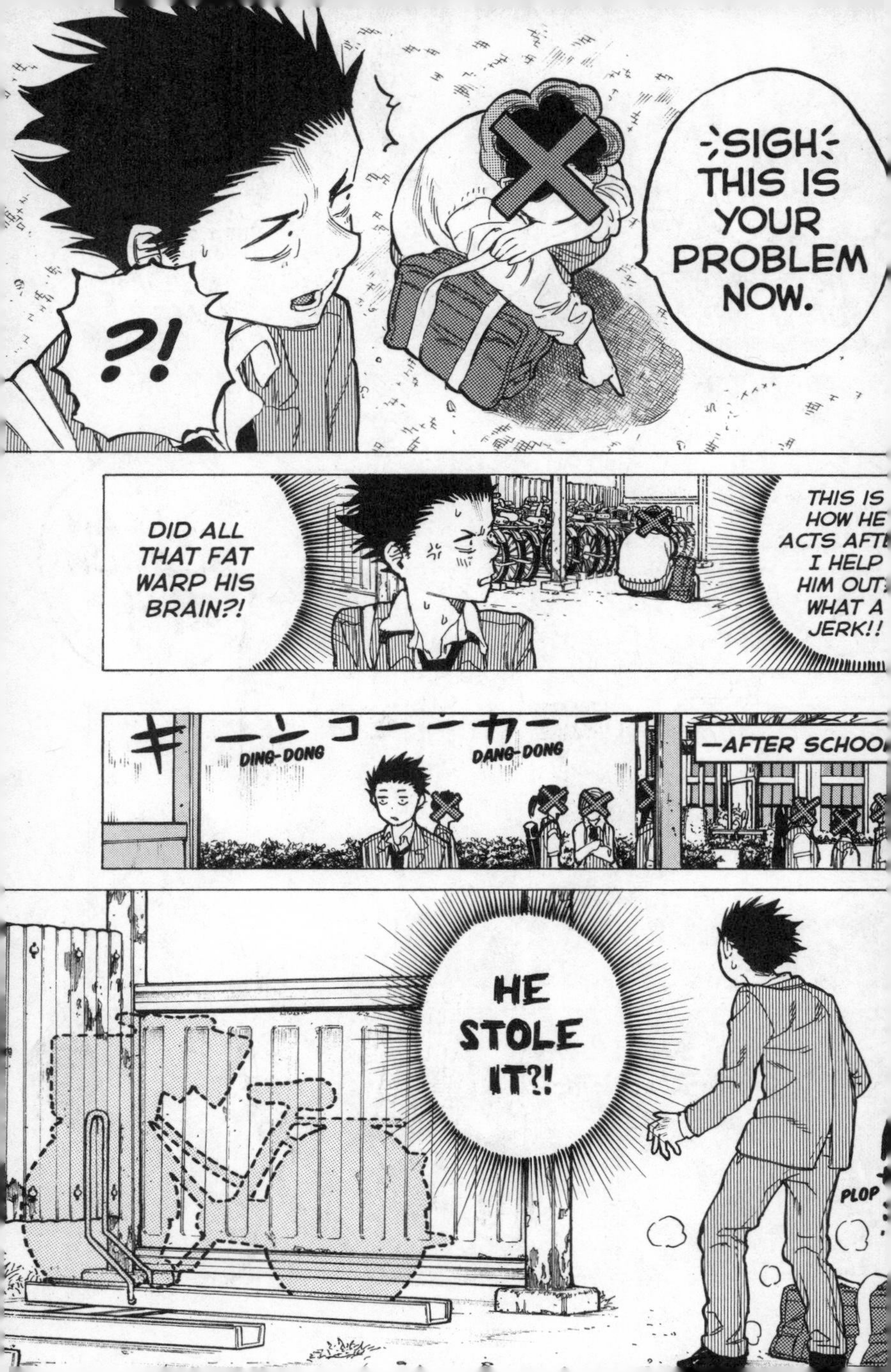
-;SIGH;- THIS IS YOUR PROBLEM NOW.
?!
THIS IS HOW HE ACTS AFT I HELP HIM OUT WHAT A JERK!!
DID ALL THAT FAT WARP HIS BRAIN?!
—AFTER SCHOO
キーーンコーーンカーーー
DING-DONG
DANG-DONG
PLOP
HE STOLE IT?!

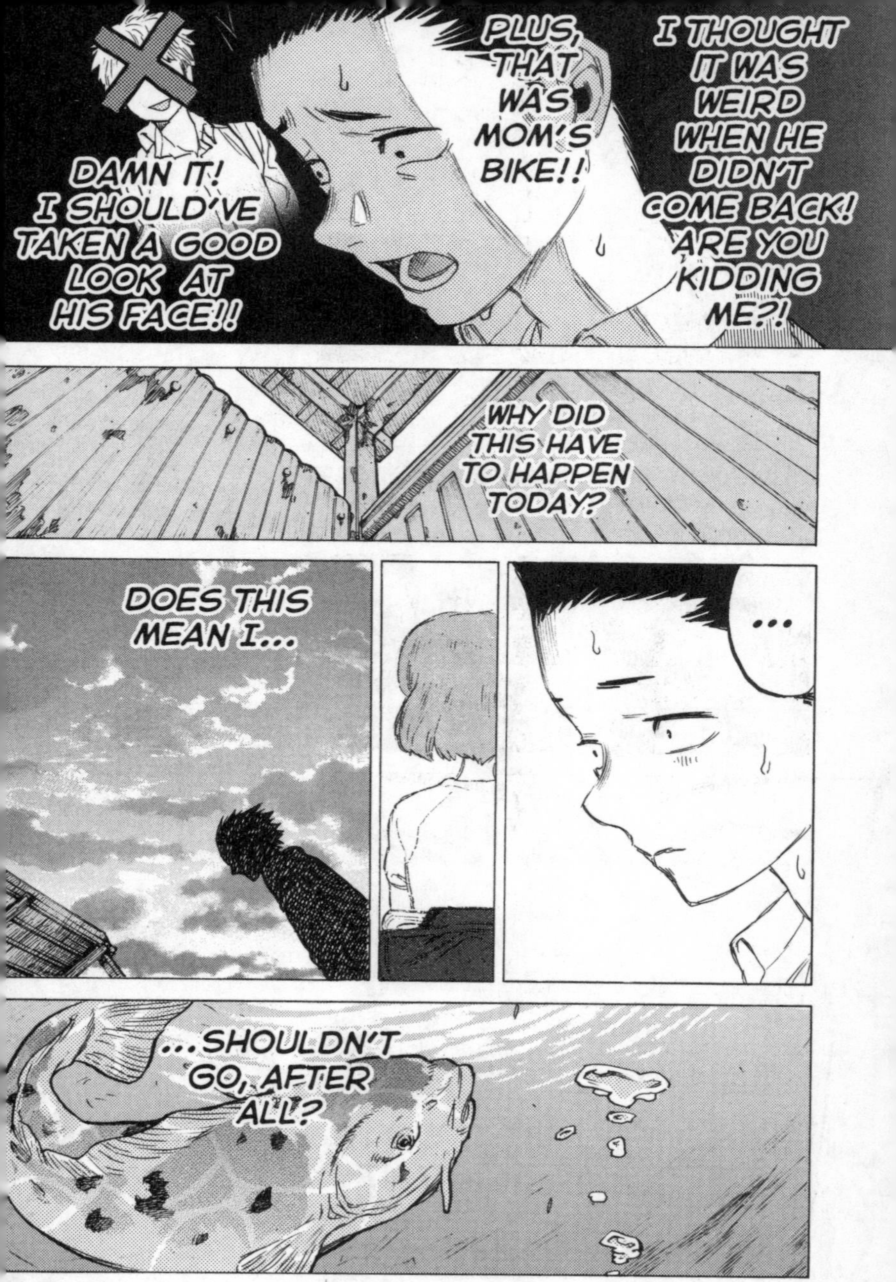
I THOUGHT IT WAS WEIRD WHEN HE DIDN'T COME BACK! ARE YOU KIDDING ME?!
PLUS, THAT WAS MOM'S BIKE!!
DAMN IT! I SHOULD'VE TAKEN A GOOD LOOK AT HIS FACE!!
WHY DID THIS HAVE TO HAPPEN TODAY?
...
DOES THIS MEAN I...
...SHOULDN'T GO, AFTER ALL?

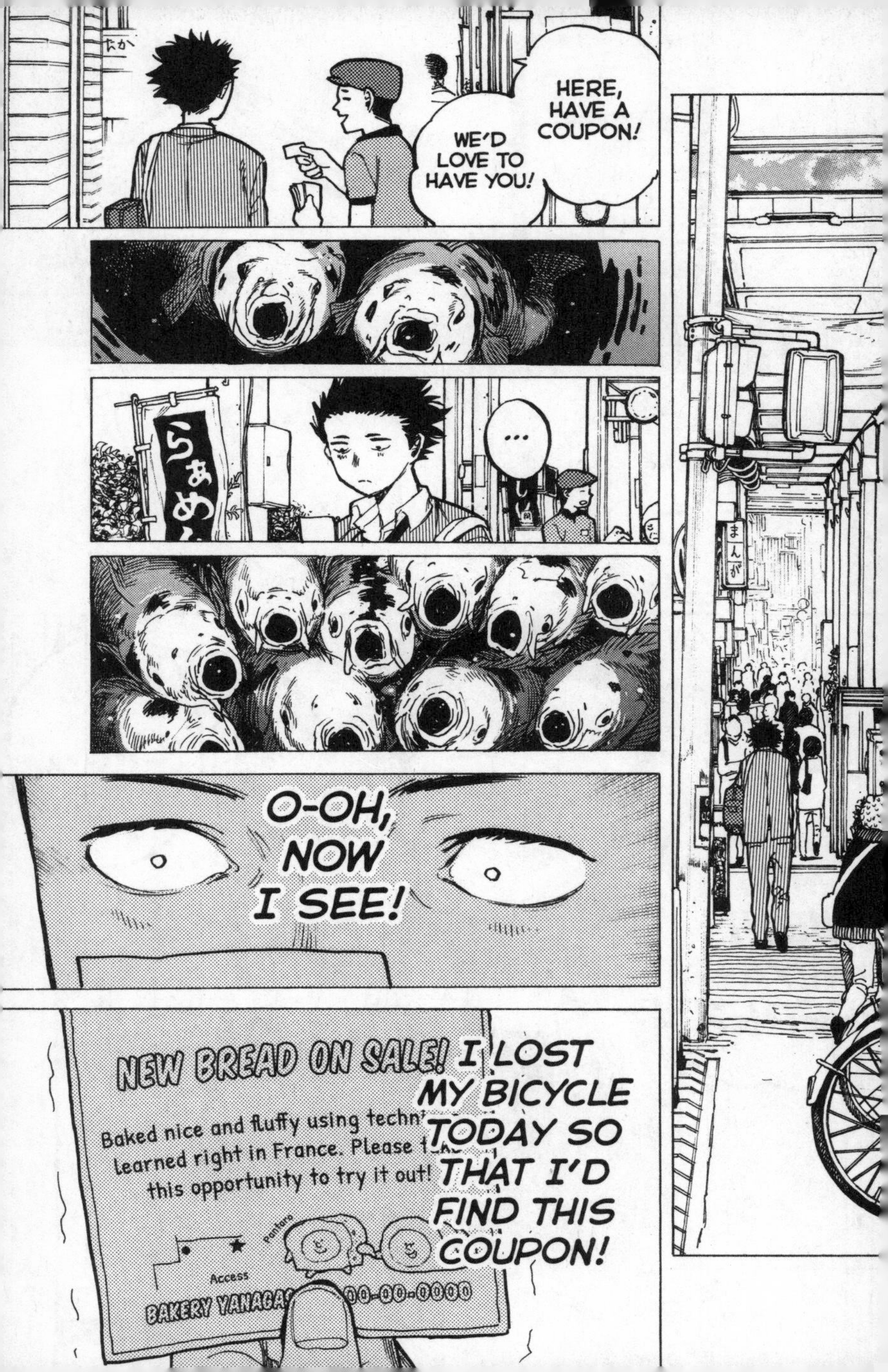
まんが
HERE, HAVE A COUPON!
WE'D LOVE TO HAVE YOU!
...
O-OH, NOW I SEE!
NEW BREAD ON SALE!
Baked nice and fluffy using techn
learned right in France. Please t
this opportunity to try it out!
Pantaro
Access
BAKERY YANAGA
00-00-0000
I LOST MY BICYCLE TODAY SO THAT I'D FIND THIS COUPON!

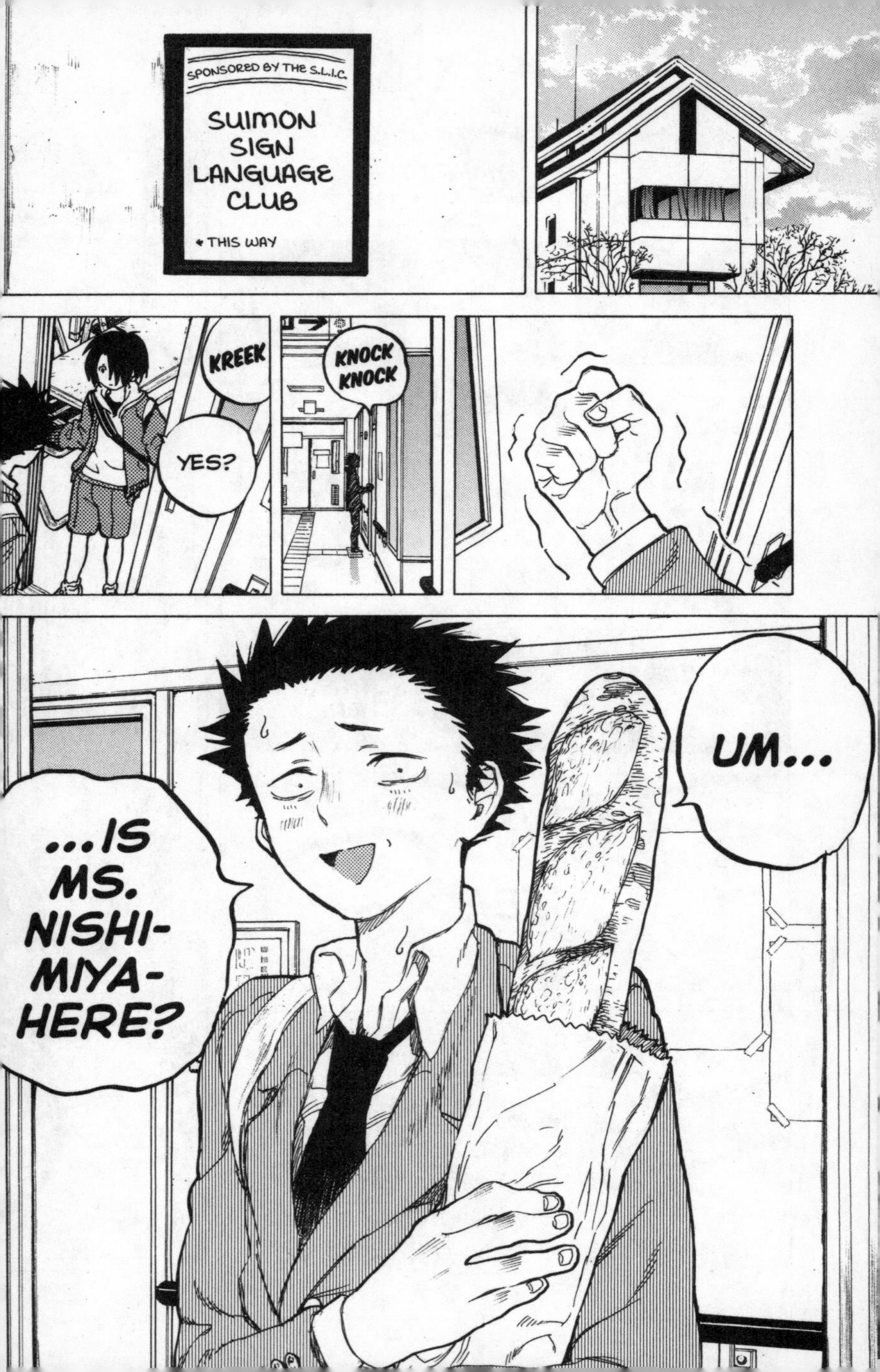
SPONSORED BY THE S.L.I.C.
SUIMON SIGN LANGUAGE CLUB
THIS WAY
KNOCK KNOCK
KREEK
YES?
UM...
...IS MS. NISHI-MIYA-HERE?

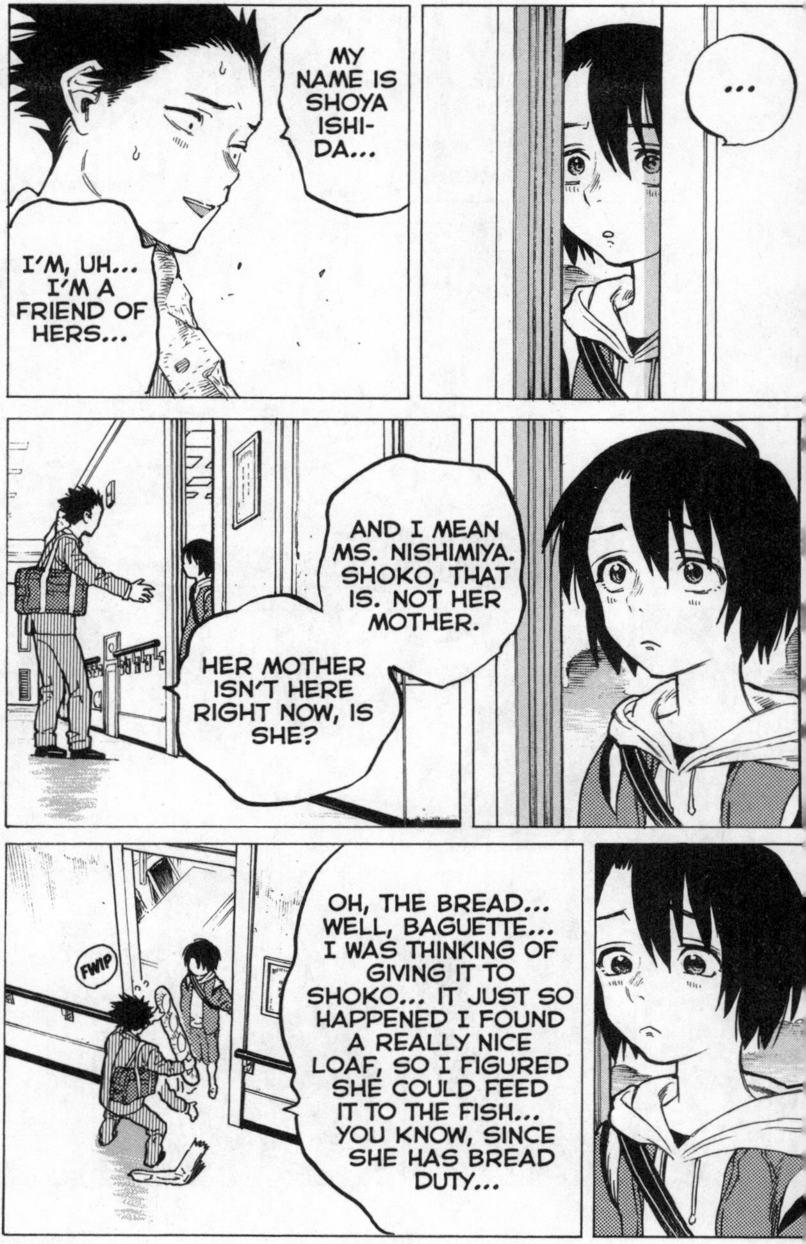
...
MY NAME IS SHOYA ISHIDA...
I'M, UH... I'M A FRIEND OF HERS...
AND I MEAN MS. NISHIMIYA. SHOKO, THAT IS. NOT HER MOTHER.
HER MOTHER ISN'T HERE RIGHT NOW, IS SHE?
OH, THE BREAD... WELL, BAGUETTE... I WAS THINKING OF GIVING IT TO SHOKO... IT JUST SO HAPPENED I FOUND A REALLY NICE LOAF, SO I FIGURED SHE COULD FEED IT TO THE FISH... YOU KNOW, SINCE SHE HAS BREAD DUTY...
FWIP

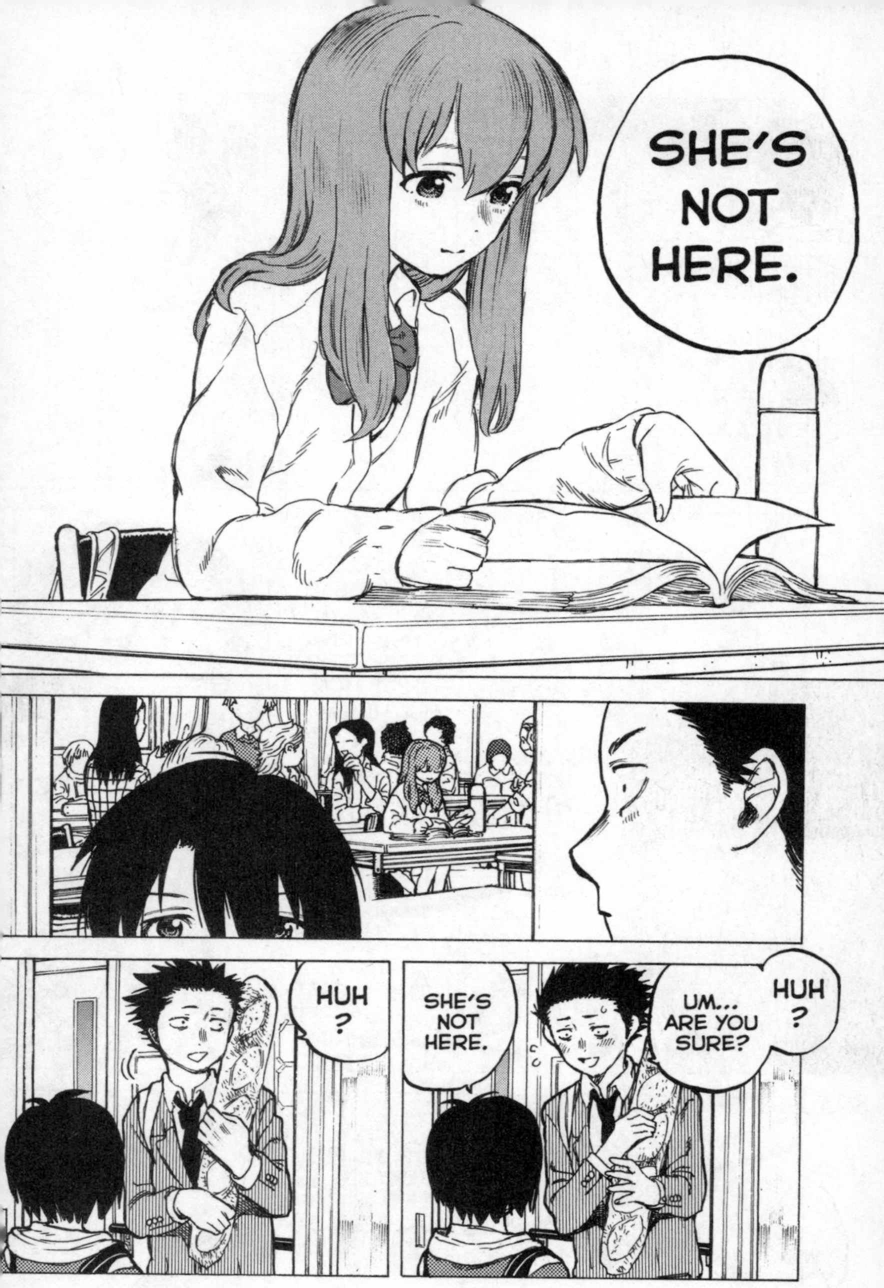
SHE'S NOT HERE.
HUH ?
UM... ARE YOU SURE?
SHE'S NOT HERE.
HUH ?

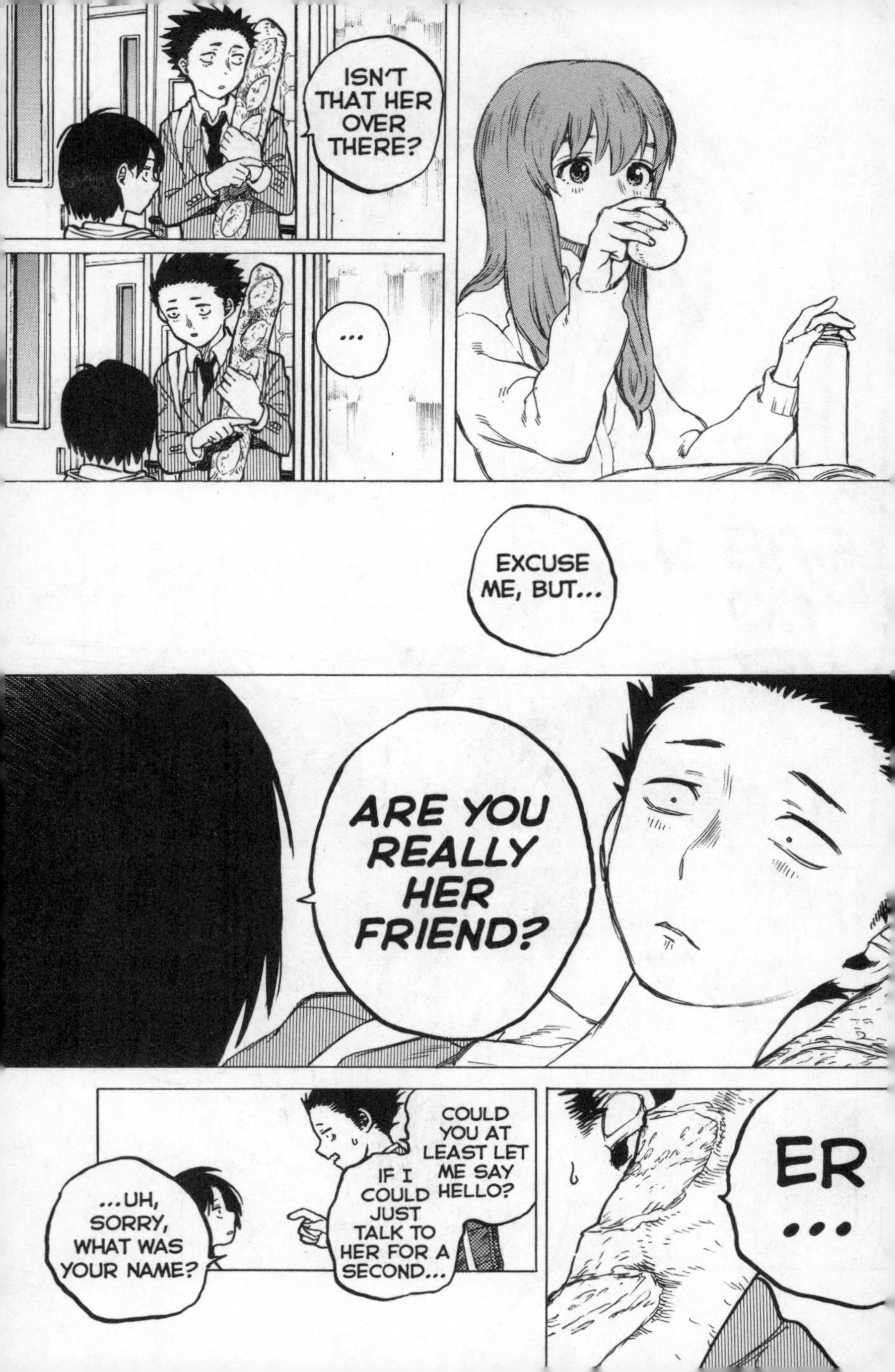
ISN'T THAT HER OVER THERE?
...
EXCUSE ME, BUT...
ARE YOU REALLY HER FRIEND?
ER ...
COULD YOU AT LEAST LET ME SAY HELLO?
IF I COULD JUST TALK TO HER FOR A SECOND...
...UH, SORRY, WHAT WAS YOUR NAME?

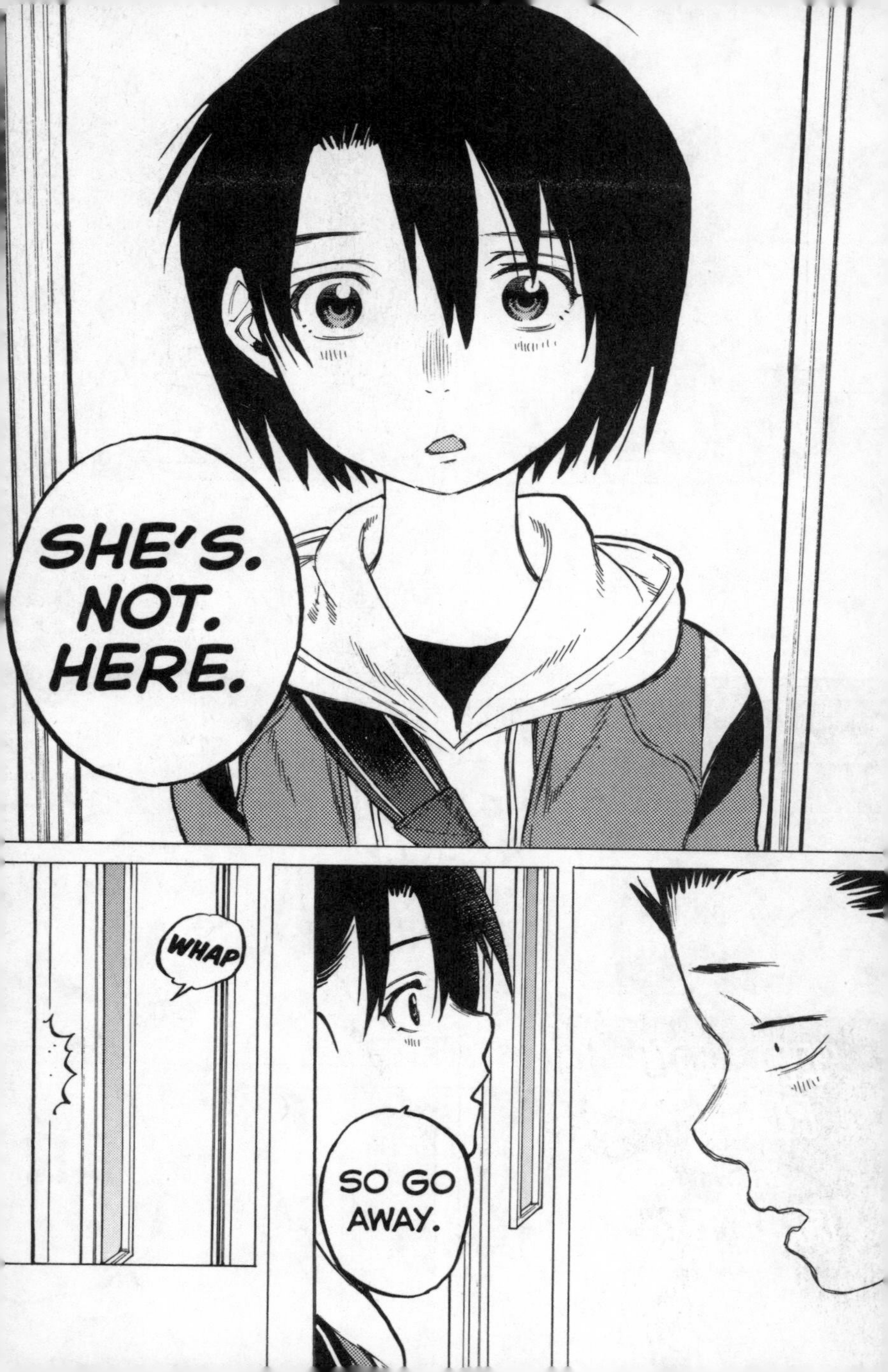
SHE'S. NOT. HERE.
SO GO AWAY.
WHAP

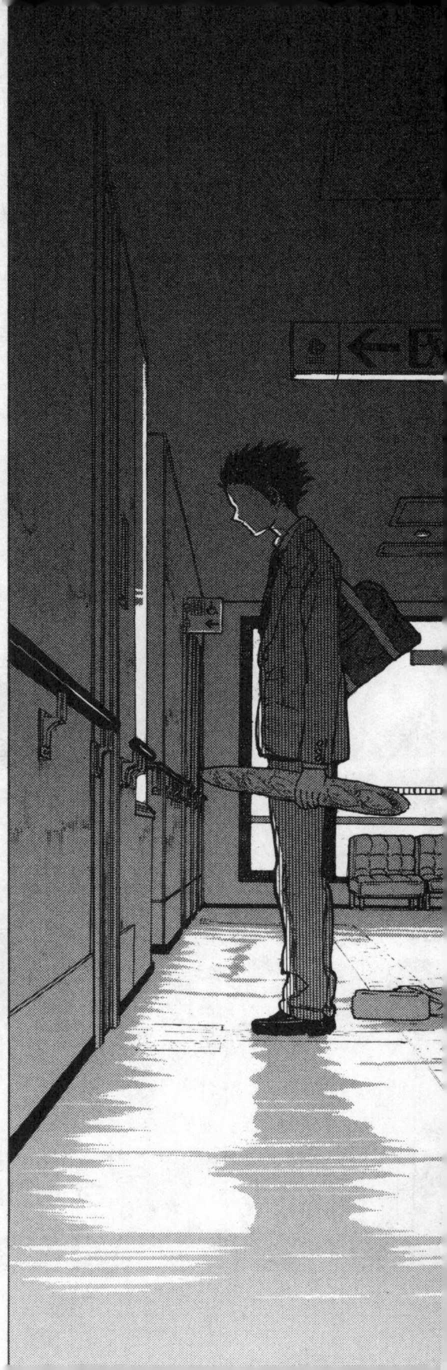

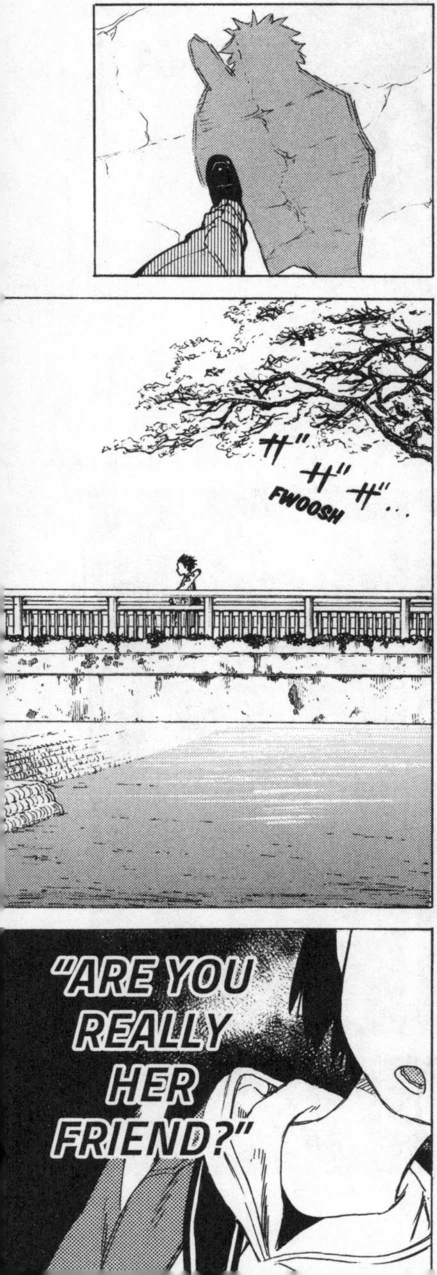
ザ ザ ザ…
FWOOSH
"ARE YOU REALLY HER FRIEND?"

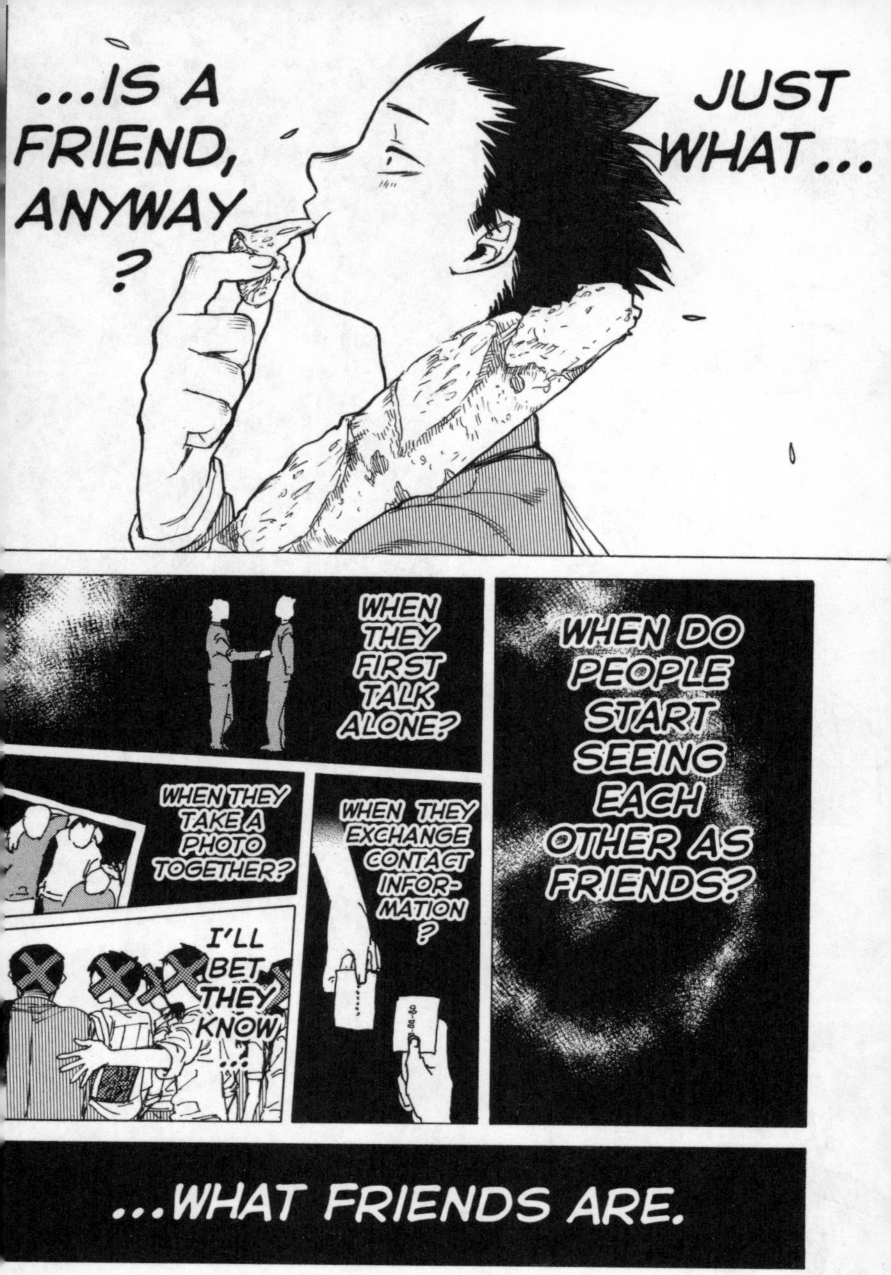
JUST WHAT...
...IS A FRIEND, ANYWAY?
WHEN DO PEOPLE START SEEING EACH OTHER AS FRIENDS?
WHEN THEY FIRST TALK ALONE?
WHEN THEY EXCHANGE CONTACT INFORMATION?
WHEN THEY TAKE A PHOTO TOGETHER?
I'LL BET THEY KNOW...
...WHAT FRIENDS ARE.

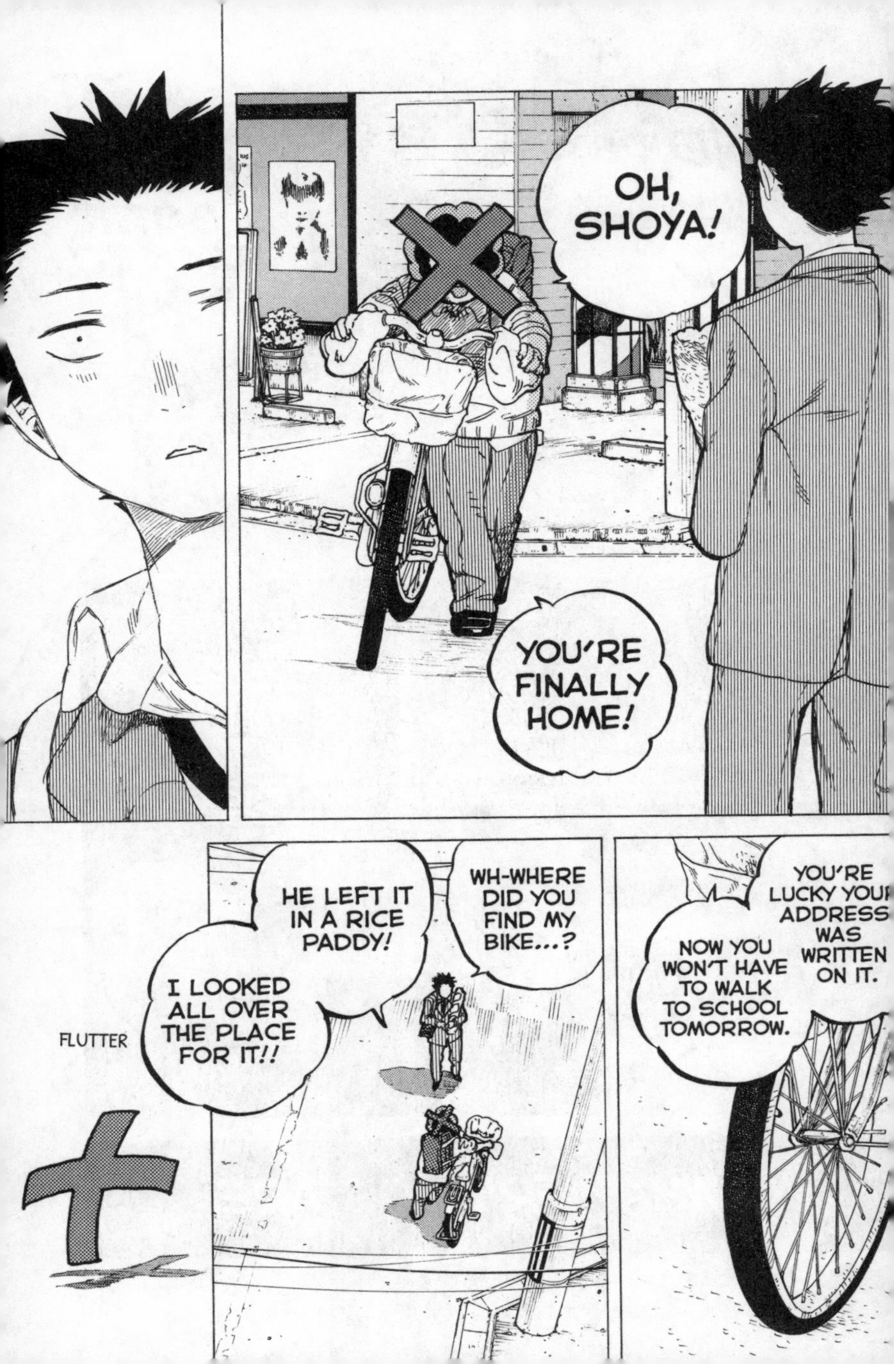
OH, SHOYA!
YOU'RE FINALLY HOME!
YOU'RE LUCKY YOUR ADDRESS WAS WRITTEN ON IT.
NOW YOU WON'T HAVE TO WALK TO SCHOOL TOMORROW.
WH-WHERE DID YOU FIND MY BIKE...?
HE LEFT IT IN A RICE PADDY!
I LOOKED ALL OVER THE PLACE FOR IT!!
FLUTTER

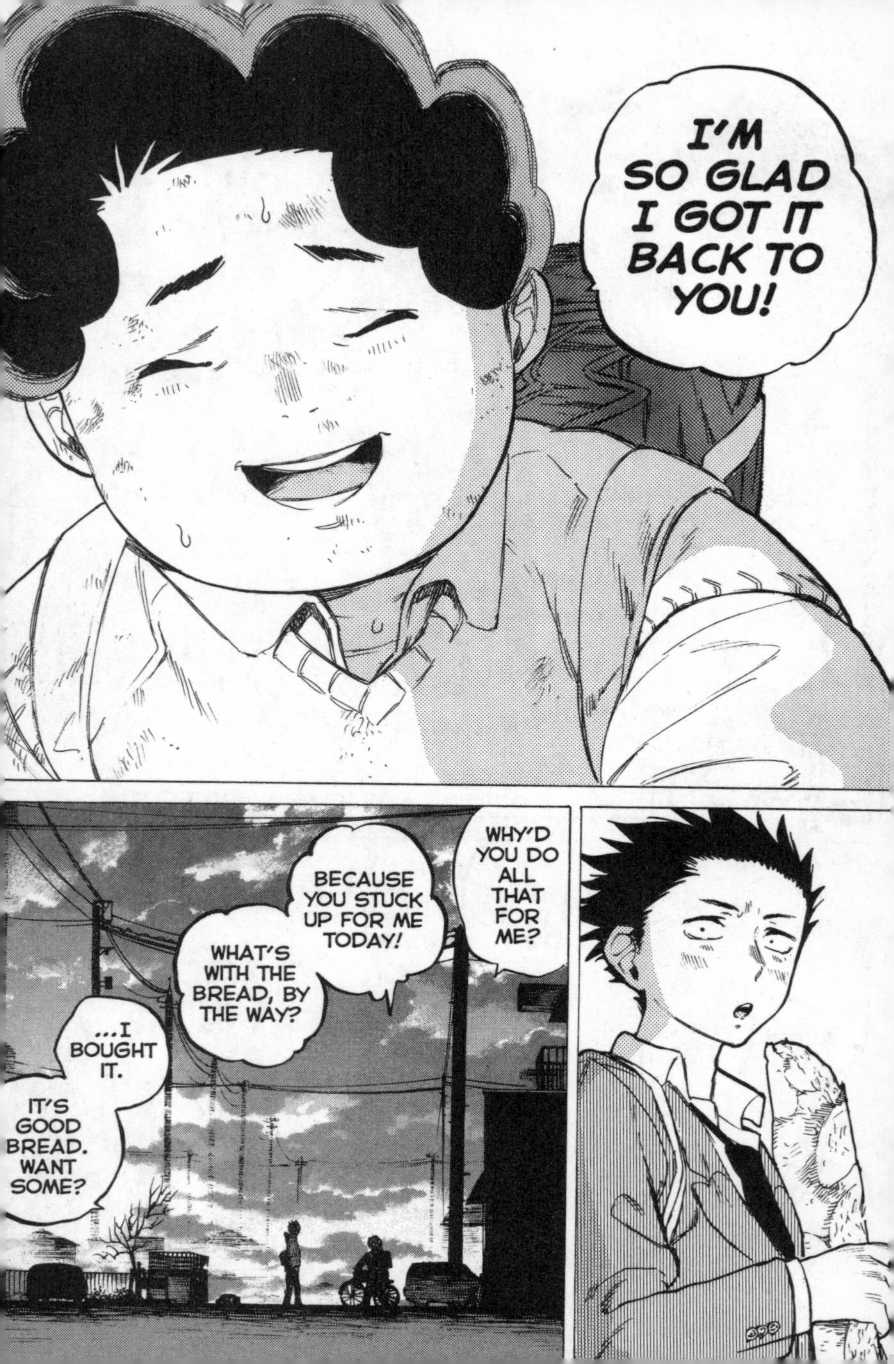
I'M SO GLAD I GOT IT BACK TO YOU!
WHY'D YOU DO ALL THAT FOR ME?
BECAUSE YOU STUCK UP FOR ME TODAY!
WHAT'S WITH THE BREAD, BY THE WAY?
...I BOUGHT IT.
IT'S GOOD BREAD. WANT SOME?

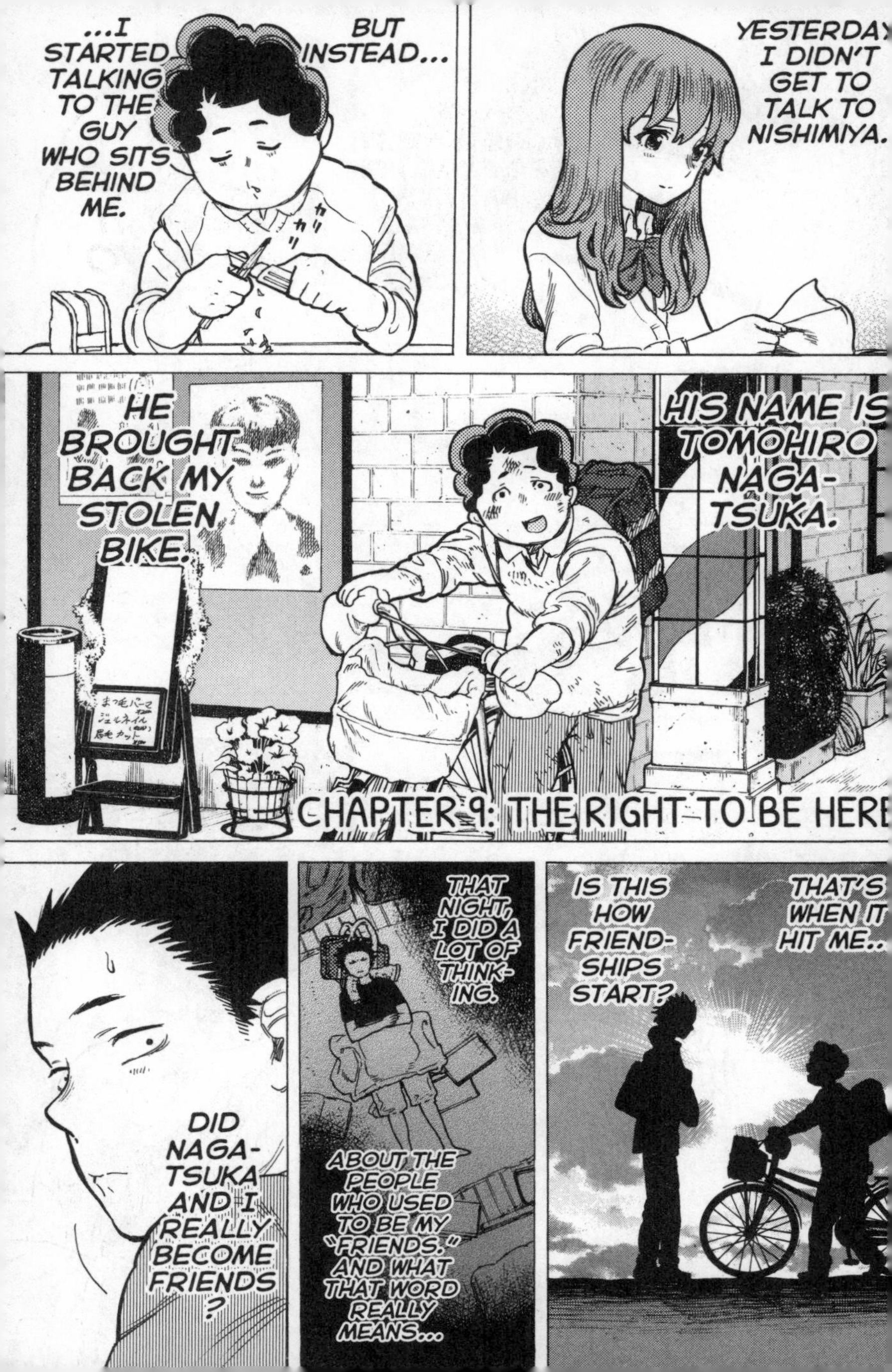
YESTERDAY I DIDN'T GET TO TALK TO NISHIMIYA.
BUT INSTEAD...
...I STARTED TALKING TO THE GUY WHO SITS BEHIND ME.
カリ カリ
HIS NAME IS TOMOHIRO NAGATSUKA.
HE BROUGHT BACK MY STOLEN BIKE.
CHAPTER 9: THE RIGHT TO BE HERE
THAT'S WHEN IT HIT ME...
IS THIS HOW FRIENDSHIPS START?
THAT NIGHT, I DID A LOT OF THINKING.
ABOUT THE PEOPLE WHO USED TO BE MY "FRIENDS," AND WHAT THAT WORD REALLY MEANS...
DID NAGATSUKA AND I REALLY BECOME FRIENDS?

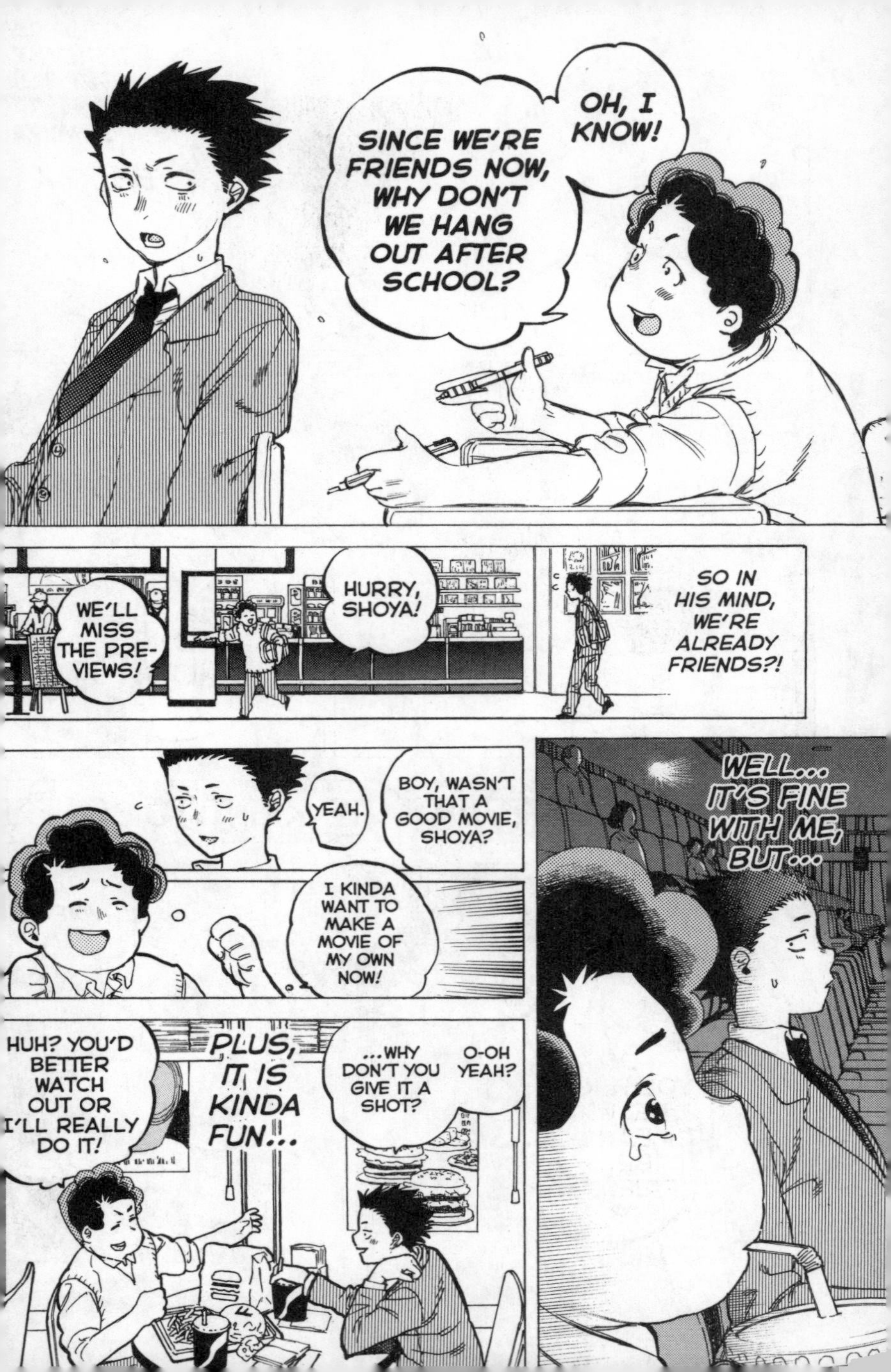
OH, I KNOW!
SINCE WE'RE FRIENDS NOW, WHY DON'T WE HANG OUT AFTER SCHOOL?
SO IN HIS MIND, WE'RE ALREADY FRIENDS?!
HURRY, SHOYA!
WE'LL MISS THE PRE-VIEWS!
WELL... IT'S FINE WITH ME, BUT...
BOY, WASN'T THAT A GOOD MOVIE, SHOYA?
YEAH.
I KINDA WANT TO MAKE A MOVIE OF MY OWN NOW!
O-OH YEAH?
...WHY DON'T YOU GIVE IT A SHOT?
PLUS, IT IS KINDA FUN...
HUH? YOU'D BETTER WATCH OUT OR I'LL REALLY DO IT!

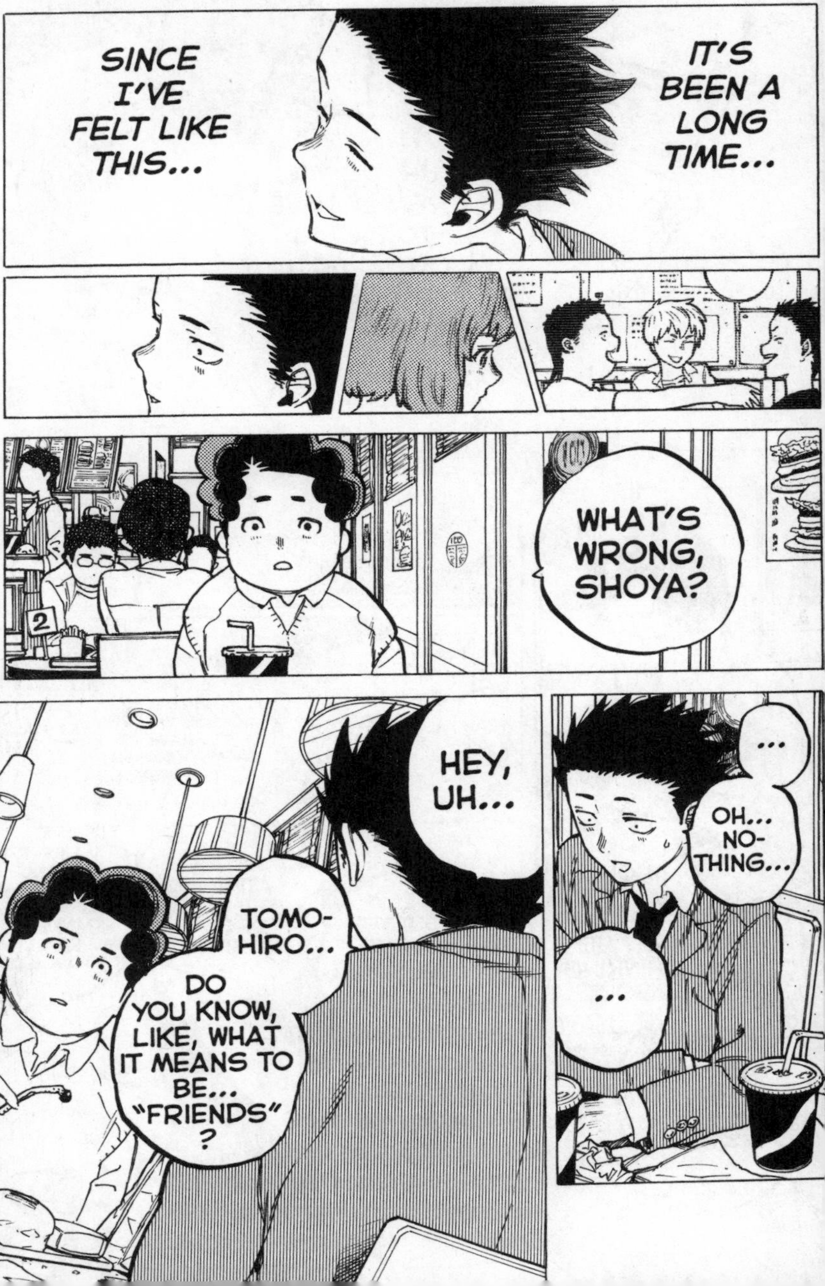
IT'S BEEN A LONG TIME...
SINCE I'VE FELT LIKE THIS...
WHAT'S WRONG, SHOYA?
...
OH... NO-THING...
...
HEY, UH...
TOMO-HIRO...
DO YOU KNOW, LIKE, WHAT IT MEANS TO BE... "FRIENDS"?

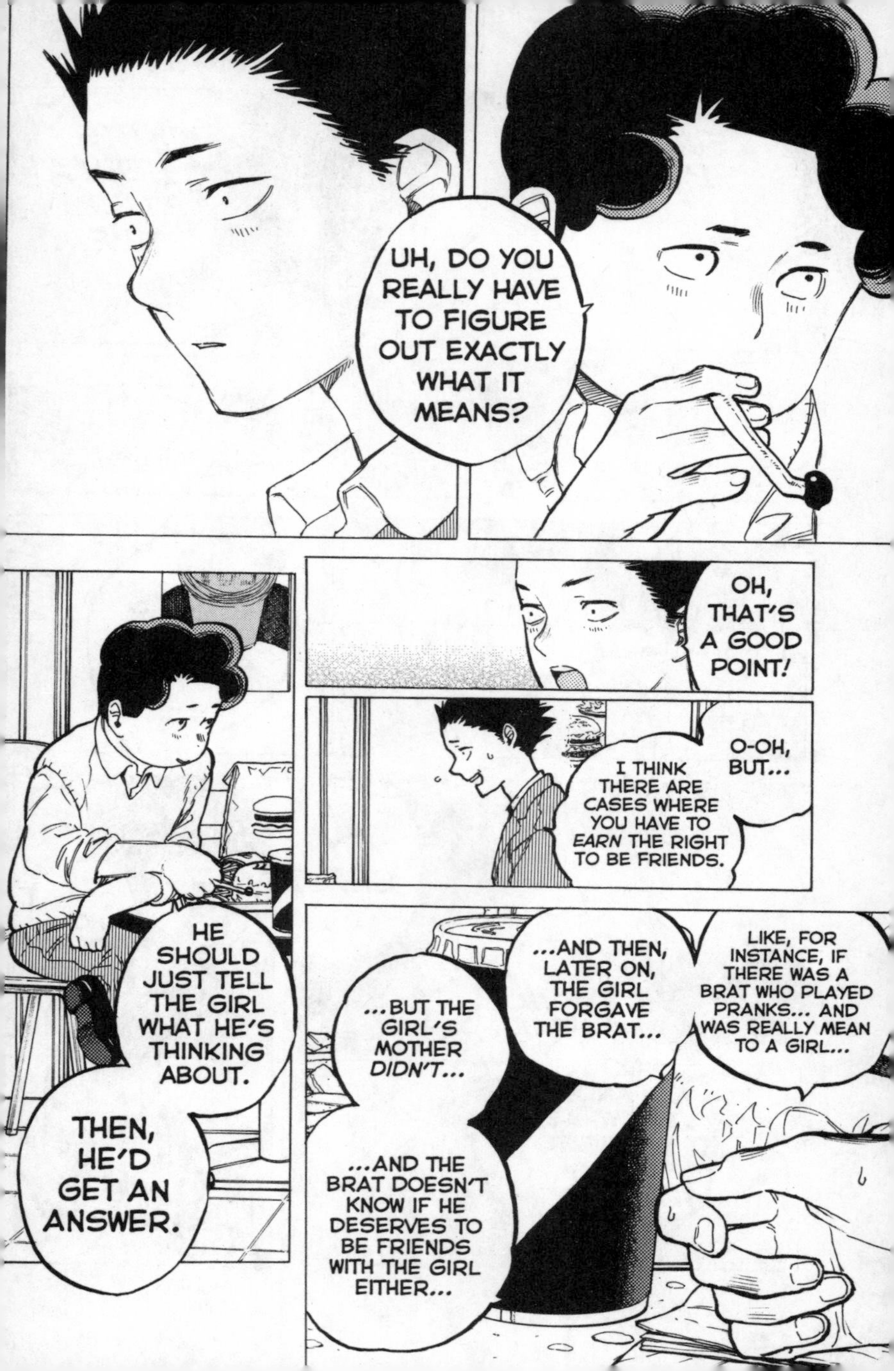
UH, DO YOU REALLY HAVE TO FIGURE OUT EXACTLY WHAT IT MEANS?
OH, THAT'S A GOOD POINT!
O-OH, BUT...
I THINK THERE ARE CASES WHERE YOU HAVE TO *EARN* THE RIGHT TO BE FRIENDS.
LIKE, FOR INSTANCE, IF THERE WAS A BRAT WHO PLAYED PRANKS... AND WAS REALLY MEAN TO A GIRL...
...AND THEN, LATER ON, THE GIRL FORGAVE THE BRAT...
...BUT THE GIRL'S MOTHER *DIDN'T*...
...AND THE BRAT DOESN'T KNOW IF HE DESERVES TO BE FRIENDS WITH THE GIRL EITHER...
HE SHOULD JUST TELL THE GIRL WHAT HE'S THINKING ABOUT.
THEN, HE'D GET AN ANSWER.

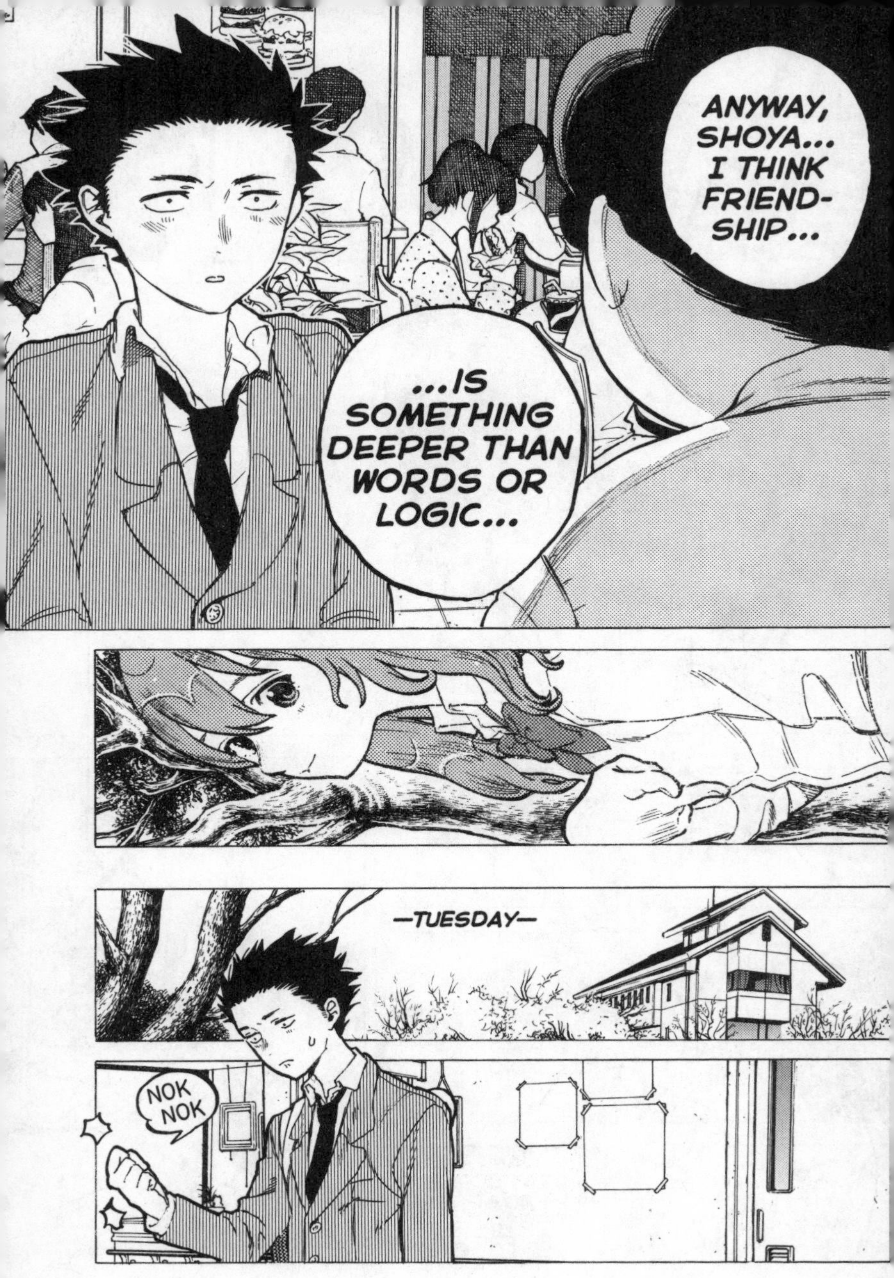
ANYWAY, SHOYA... I THINK FRIEND-SHIP...
...IS SOMETHING DEEPER THAN WORDS OR LOGIC...
—TUESDAY—
NOK NOK

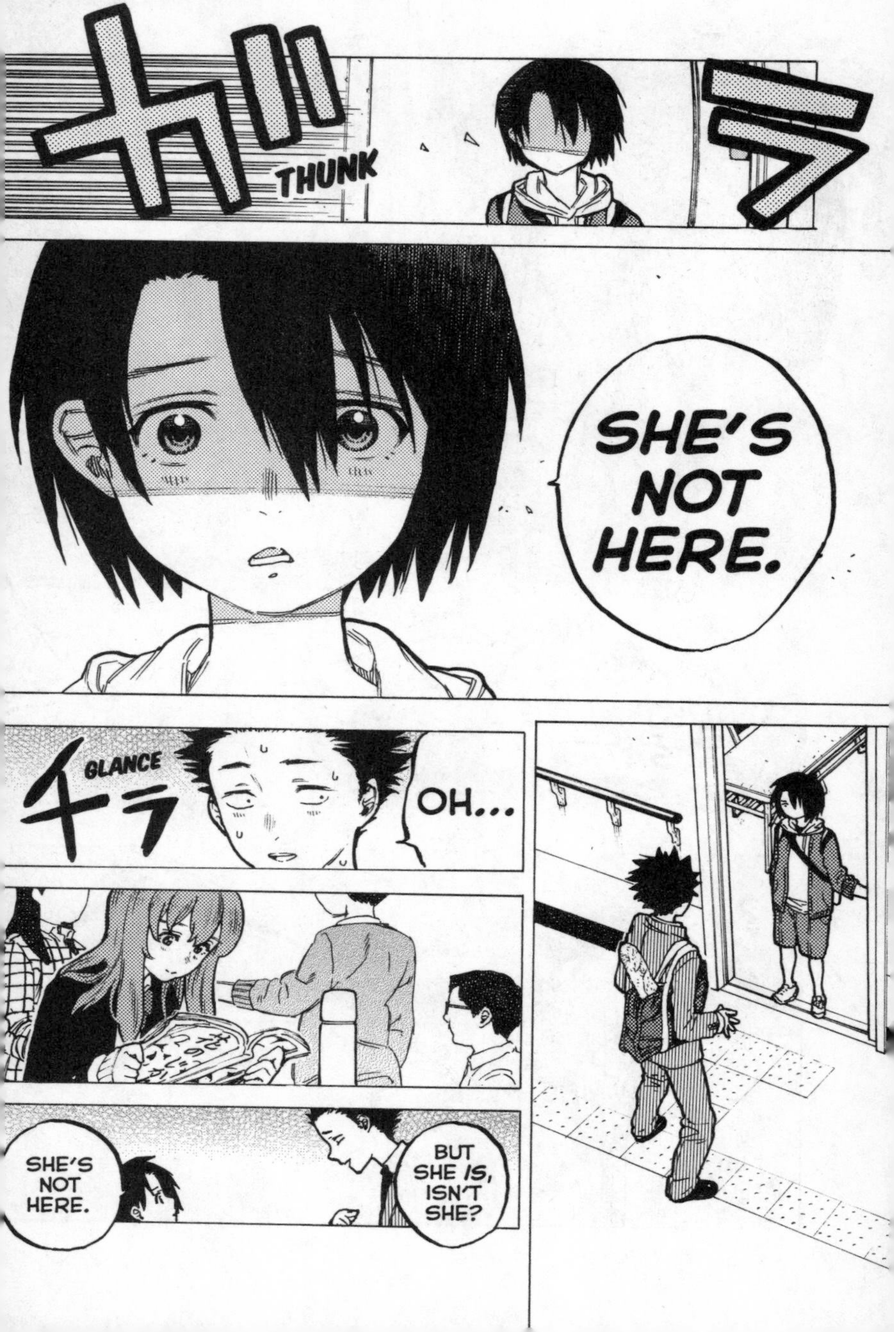
ガラ
THUNK
SHE'S NOT HERE.
OH...
チラ
GLANCE
BUT SHE IS, ISN'T SHE?
SHE'S NOT HERE.

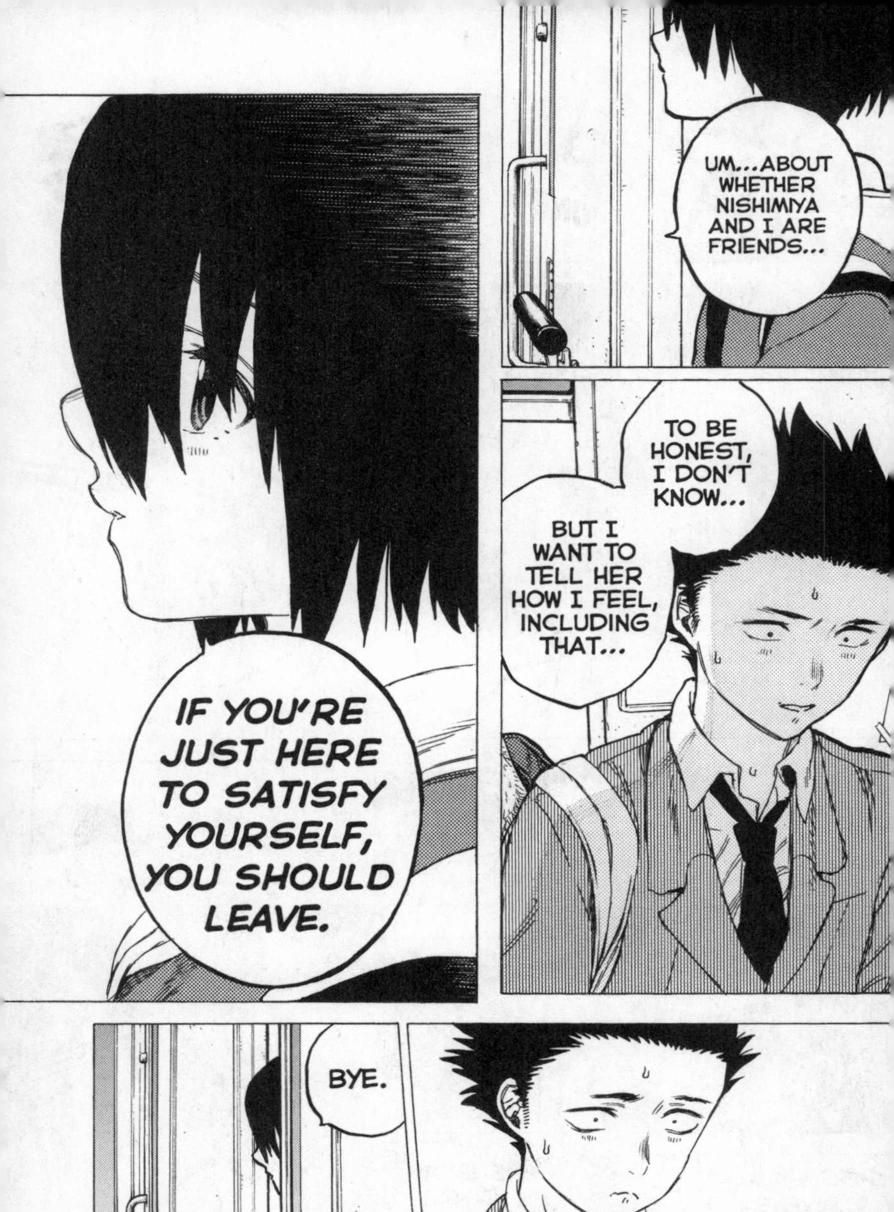
UM...ABOUT WHETHER NISHIMIYA AND I ARE FRIENDS...
TO BE HONEST, I DON'T KNOW...
BUT I WANT TO TELL HER HOW I FEEL, INCLUDING THAT...
IF YOU'RE JUST HERE TO SATISFY YOURSELF, YOU SHOULD LEAVE.
BYE.

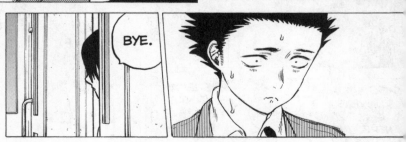

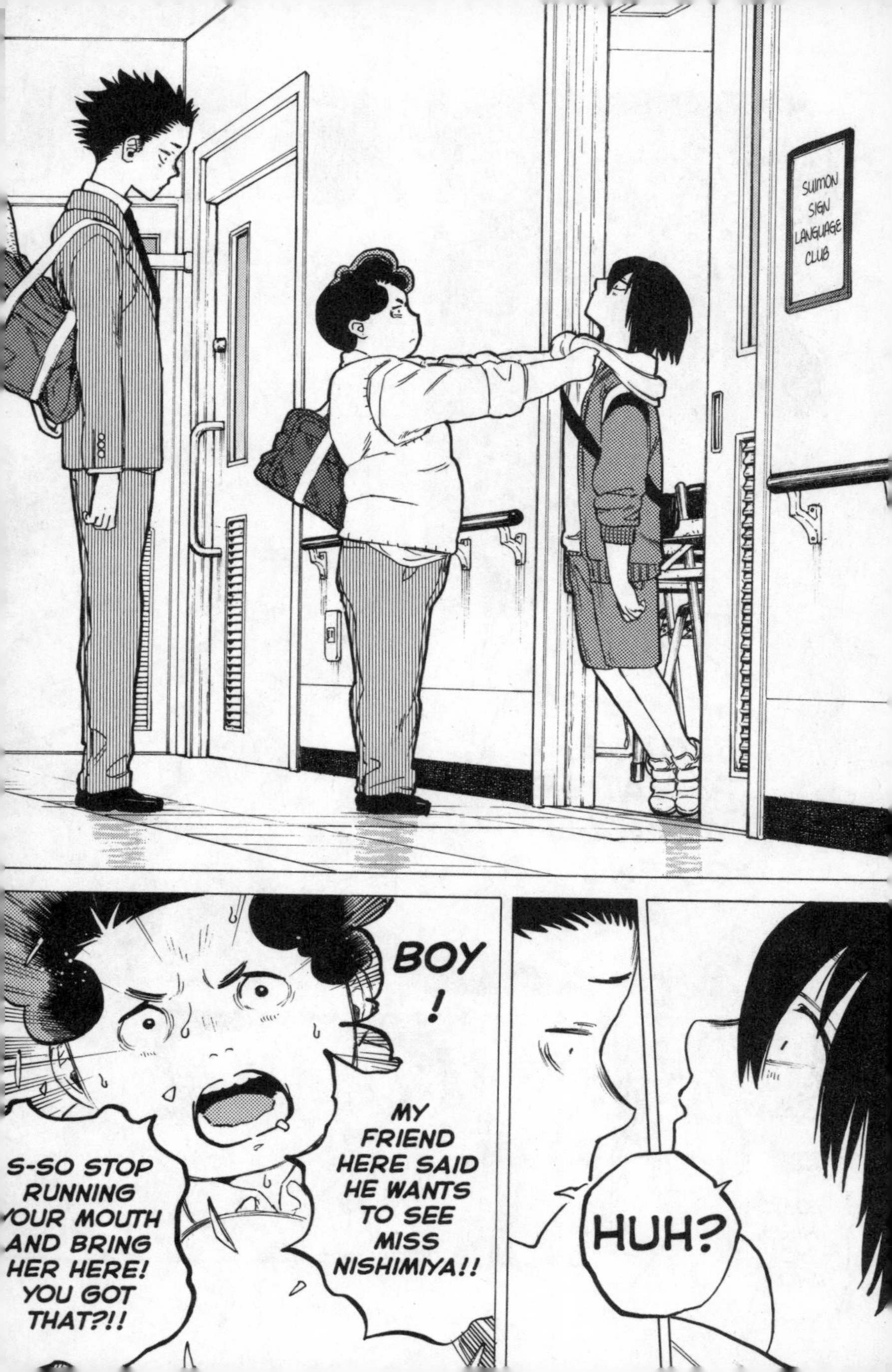
SUIMON SIGN LANGUAGE CLUB
HUH?
BOY!
MY FRIEND HERE SAID HE WANTS TO SEE MISS NISHIMIYA!!
S-SO STOP RUNNING YOUR MOUTH AND BRING HER HERE! YOU GOT THAT?!!

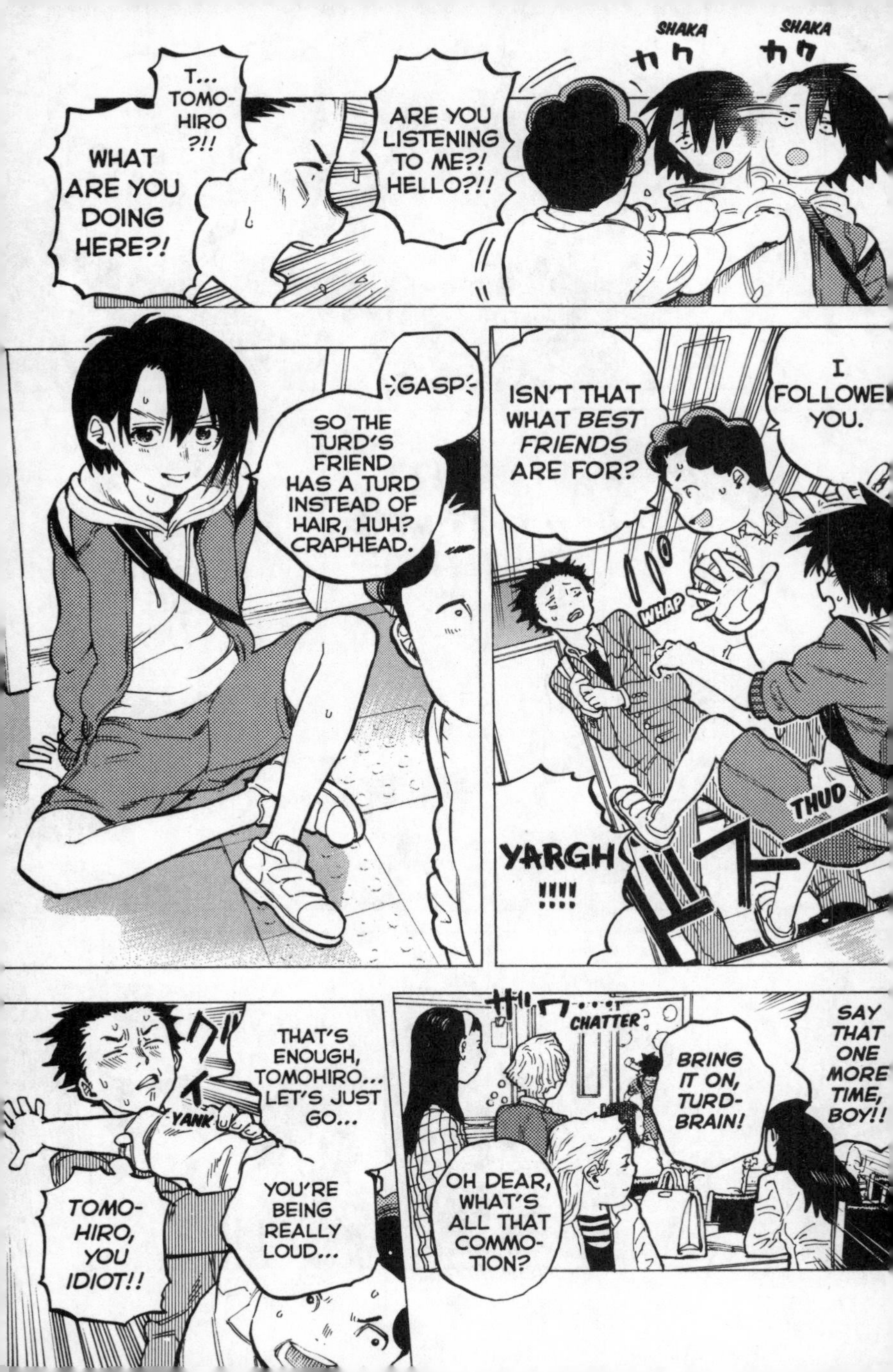
SHAKA
SHAKA
ARE YOU LISTENING TO ME?! HELLO?!!
T... TOMOHIRO ?!!
WHAT ARE YOU DOING HERE?!
I FOLLOWE YOU.
ISN'T THAT WHAT *BEST FRIENDS* ARE FOR?
WHAP
THUD
YARGH !!!!!
GASP
SO THE TURD'S FRIEND HAS A TURD INSTEAD OF HAIR, HUH? CRAPHEAD.
SAY THAT ONE MORE TIME, BOY!!
BRING IT ON, TURD-BRAIN!
CHATTER
OH DEAR, WHAT'S ALL THAT COMMOTION?
THAT'S ENOUGH, TOMOHIRO... LET'S JUST GO...
YANK
YOU'RE BEING REALLY LOUD...
TOMOHIRO, YOU *IDIOT!!*

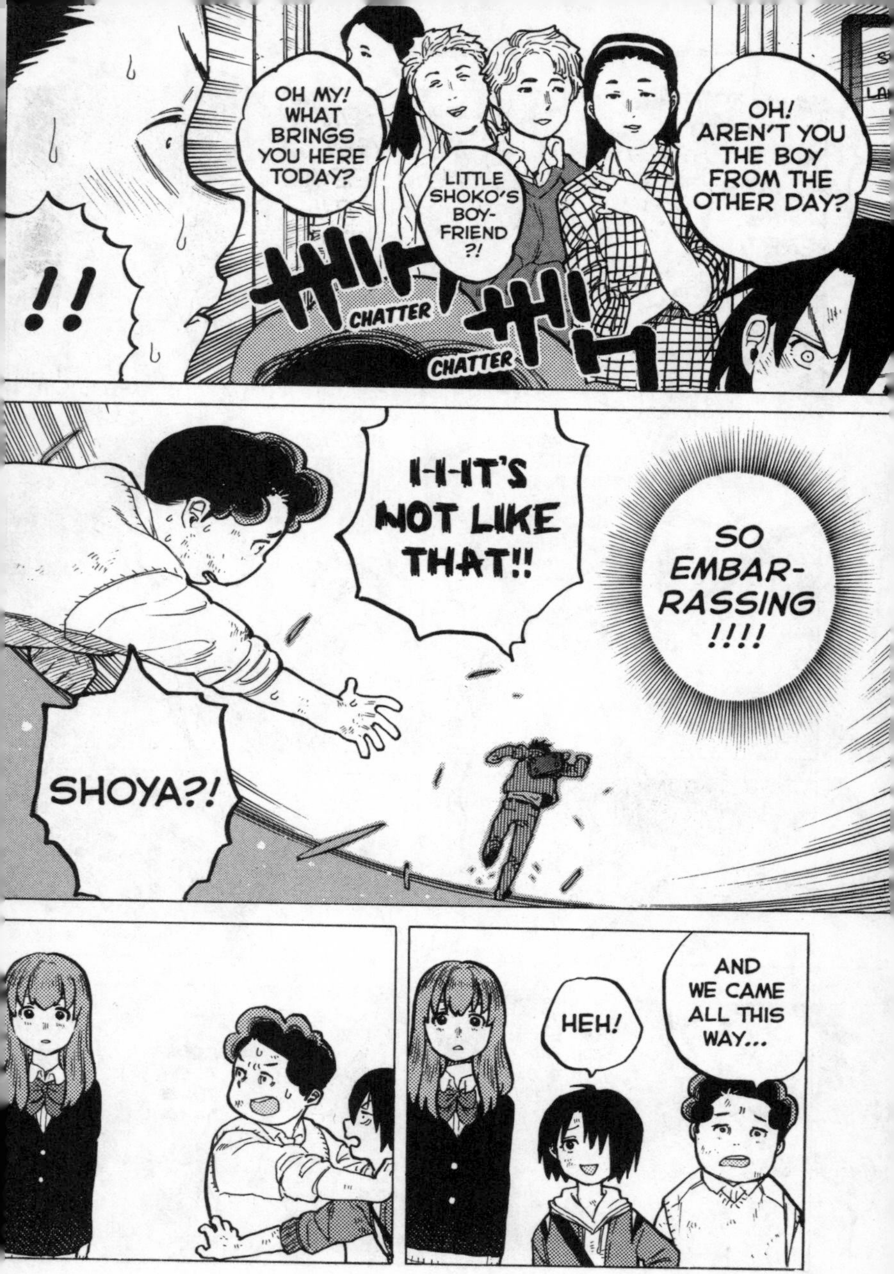
OH! AREN'T YOU THE BOY FROM THE OTHER DAY?
LITTLE SHOKO'S BOY-FRIEND?!
OH MY! WHAT BRINGS YOU HERE TODAY?
CHATTER
CHATTER
!!
SO EMBARRASSING!!!!
I-I-IT'S NOT LIKE THAT!!
SHOYA?!
AND WE CAME ALL THIS WAY...
HEH!

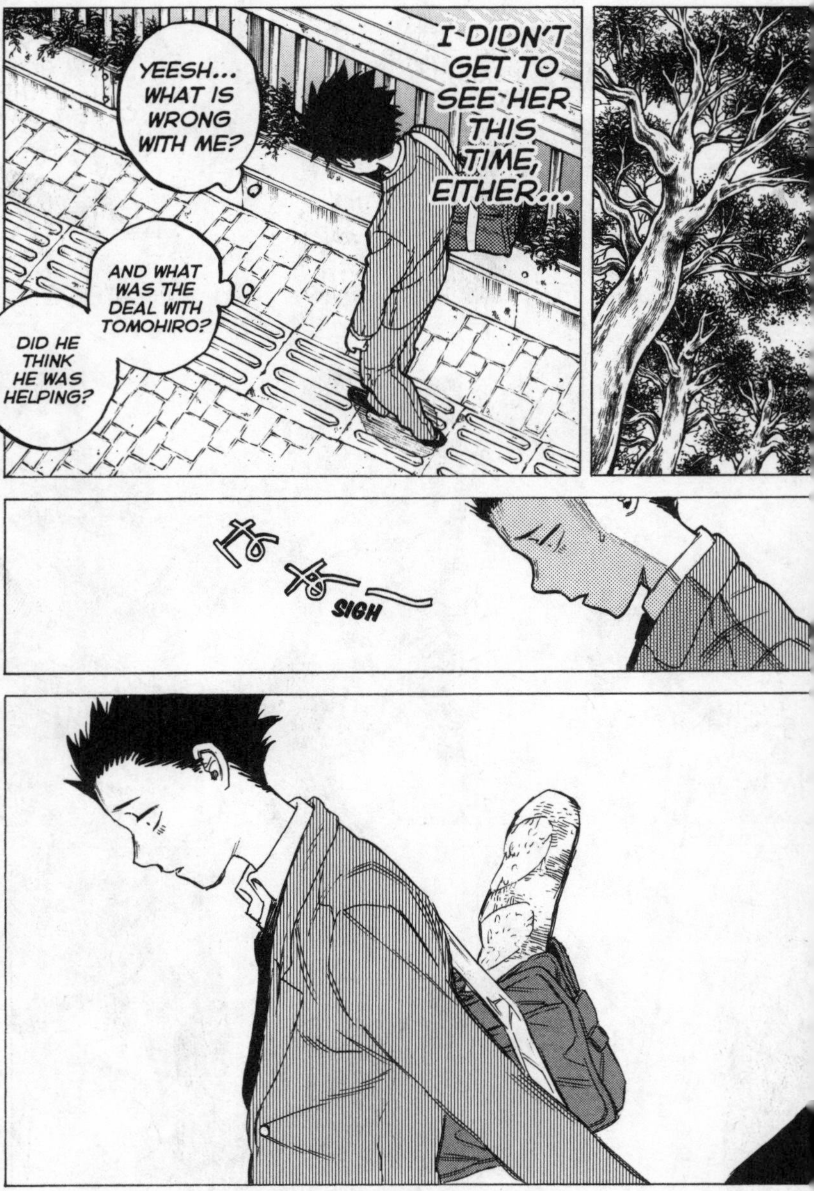

I DIDN'T GET TO SEE HER THIS TIME, EITHER...
YEESH... WHAT IS WRONG WITH ME?
AND WHAT WAS THE DEAL WITH TOMOHIRO?
DID HE THINK HE WAS HELPING?
SIGH

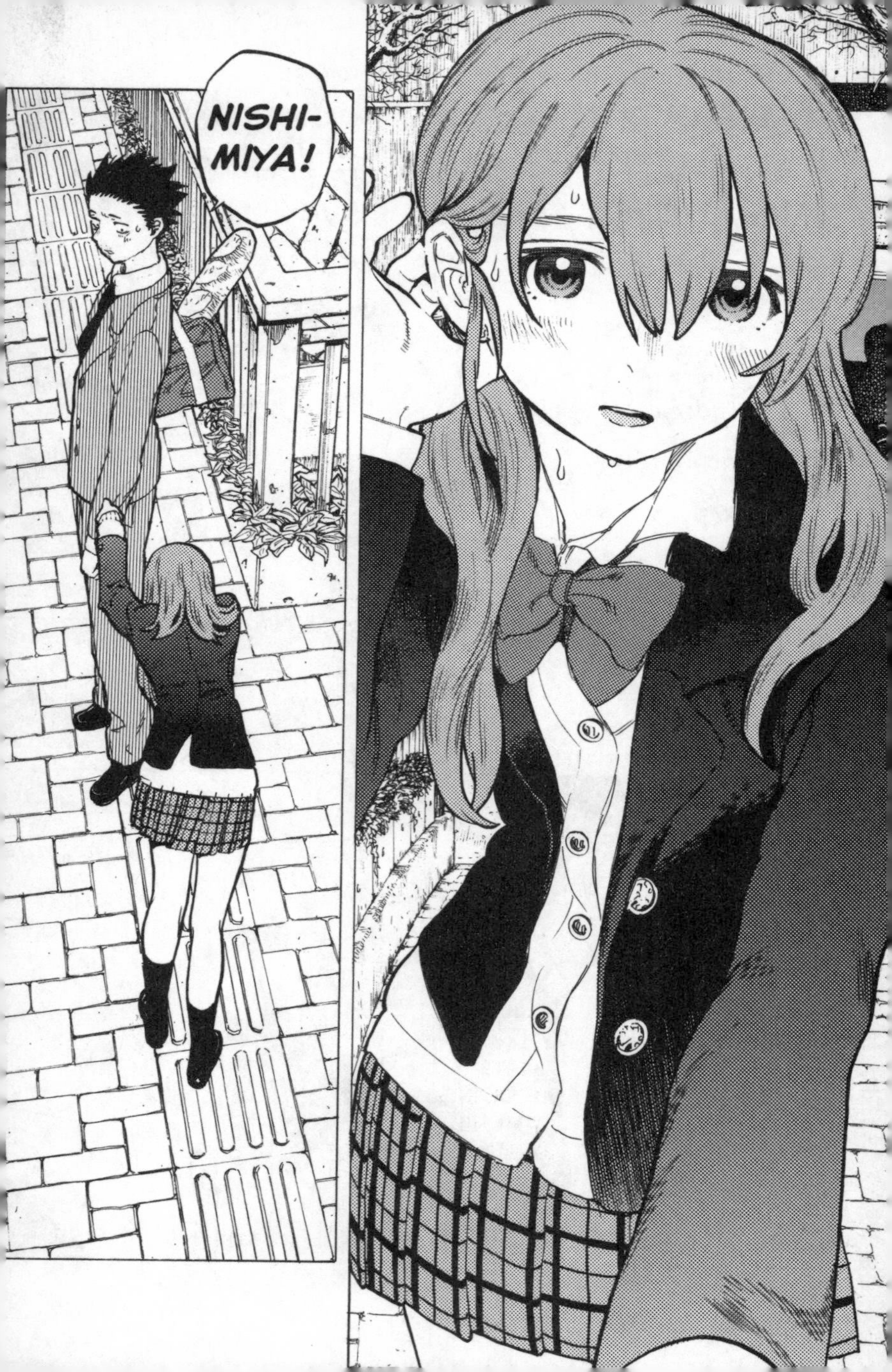
NISHI-MIYA!

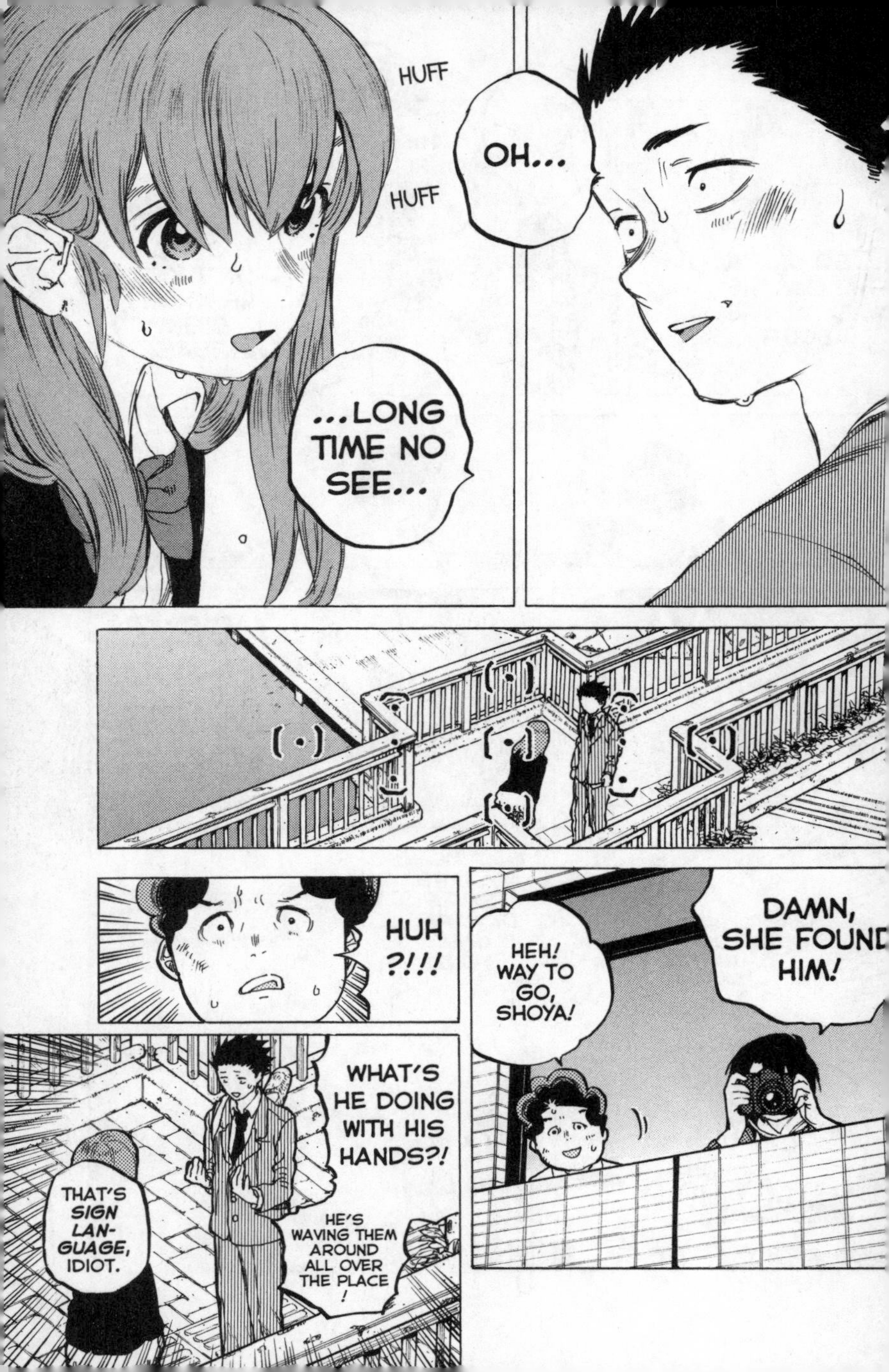
OH...
HUFF
HUFF
...LONG TIME NO SEE...
DAMN, SHE FOUND HIM!
HEH! WAY TO GO, SHOYA!
HUH ?!!!
WHAT'S HE DOING WITH HIS HANDS?!
HE'S WAVING THEM AROUND ALL OVER THE PLACE !
THAT'S *SIGN LANGUAGE*, IDIOT.

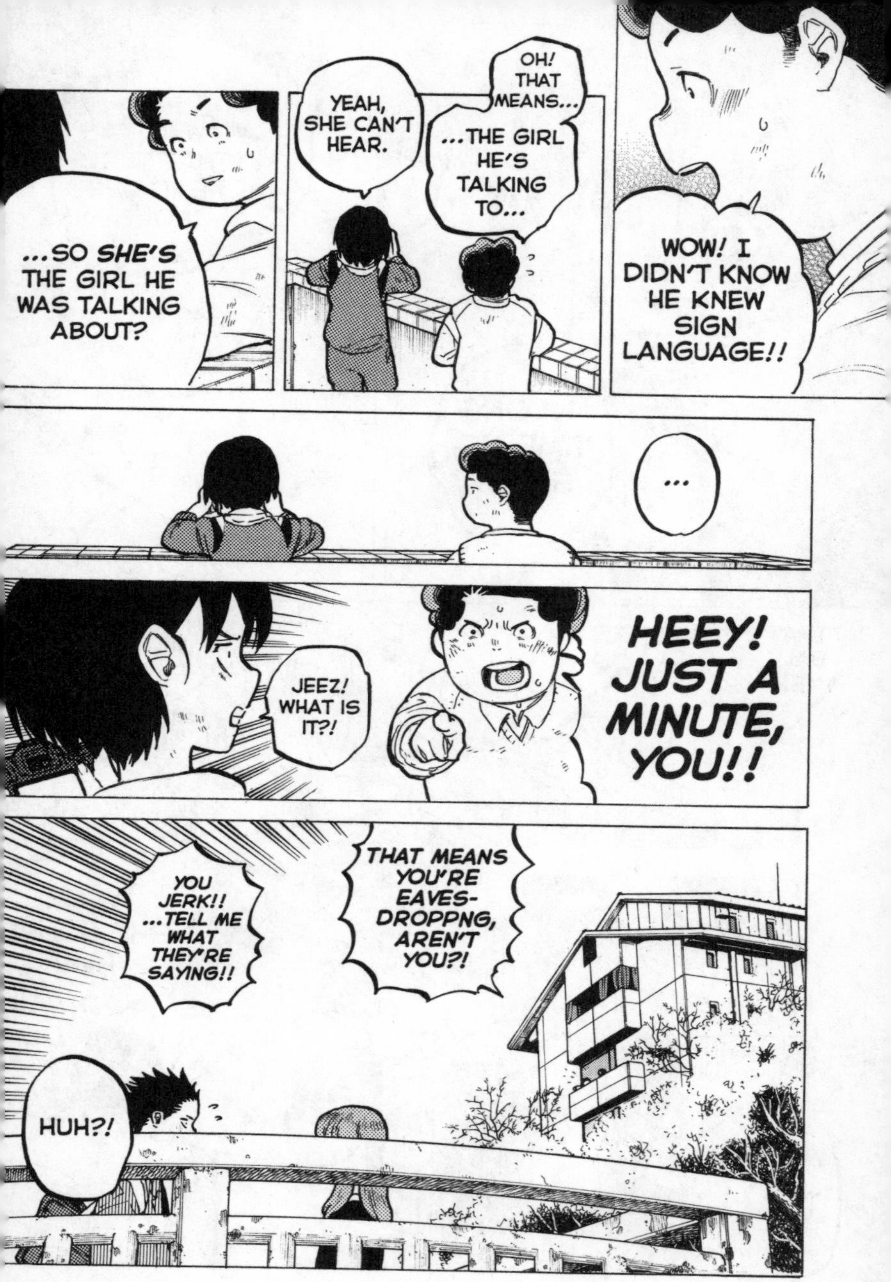
WOW! I DIDN'T KNOW HE KNEW SIGN LANGUAGE!!
OH! THAT MEANS...
...THE GIRL HE'S TALKING TO...
YEAH, SHE CAN'T HEAR.
...SO SHE'S THE GIRL HE WAS TALKING ABOUT?
...
HEEY! JUST A MINUTE, YOU!!
JEEZ! WHAT IS IT?!
THAT MEANS YOU'RE EAVES-DROPPNG, AREN'T YOU?!
YOU JERK!! ...TELL ME WHAT THEY'RE SAYING!!
HUH?!

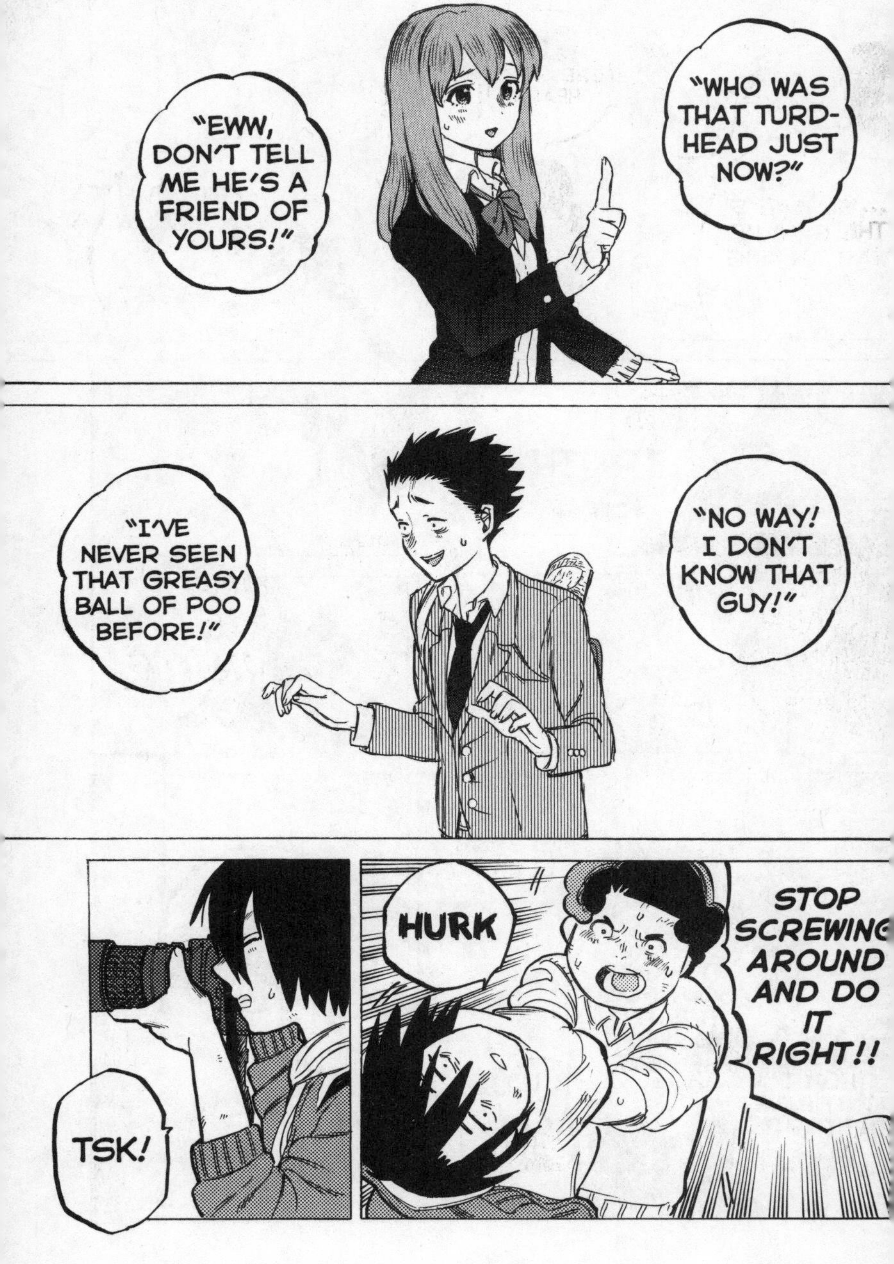
"WHO WAS THAT TURD-HEAD JUST NOW?"
"EWW, DON'T TELL ME HE'S A FRIEND OF YOURS!"
"NO WAY! I DON'T KNOW THAT GUY!"
"I'VE NEVER SEEN THAT GREASY BALL OF POO BEFORE!"
STOP SCREWING AROUND AND DO IT RIGHT!!
HURK
TSK!

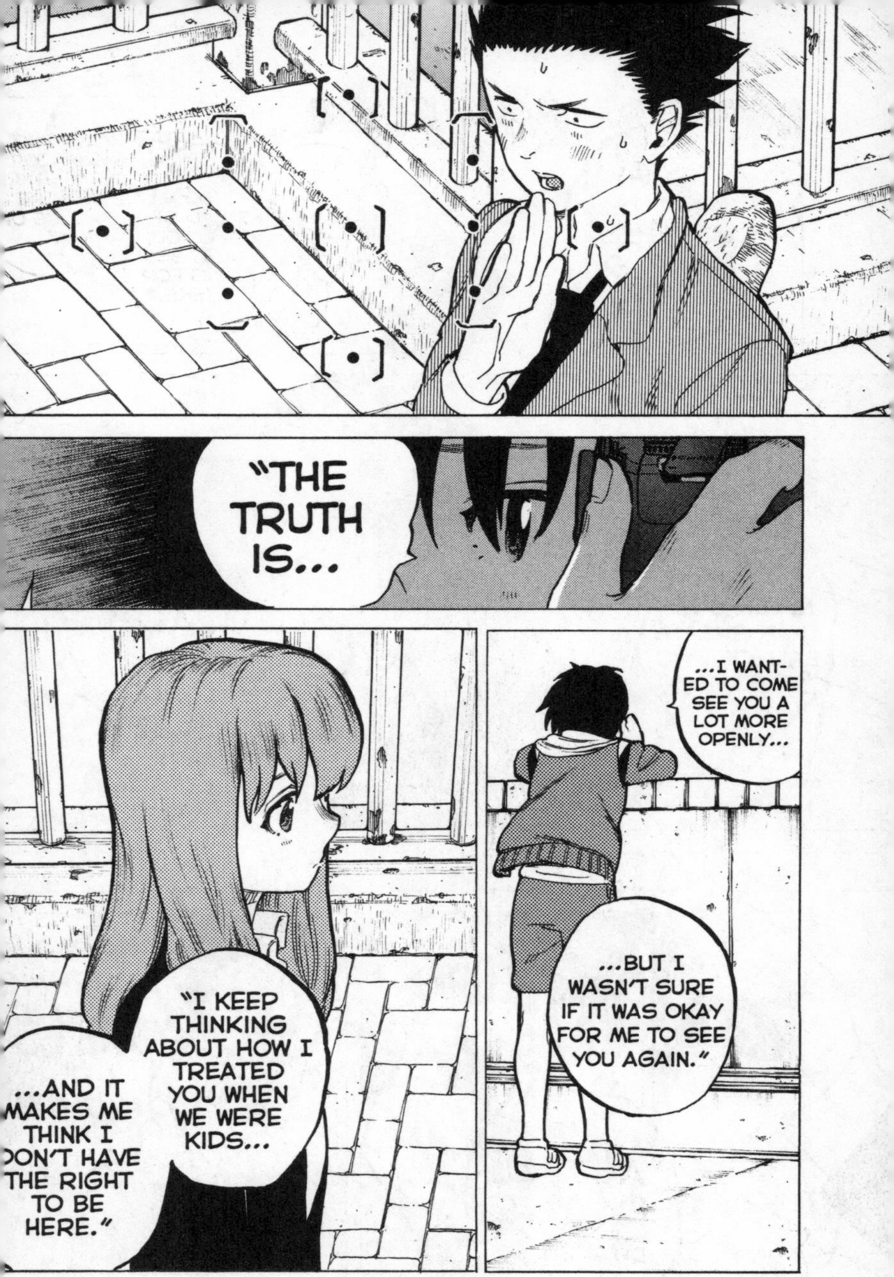
"THE TRUTH IS...
...I WANTED TO COME SEE YOU A LOT MORE OPENLY...
...BUT I WASN'T SURE IF IT WAS OKAY FOR ME TO SEE YOU AGAIN."
"I KEEP THINKING ABOUT HOW I TREATED YOU WHEN WE WERE KIDS...
...AND IT MAKES ME THINK I DON'T HAVE THE RIGHT TO BE HERE."

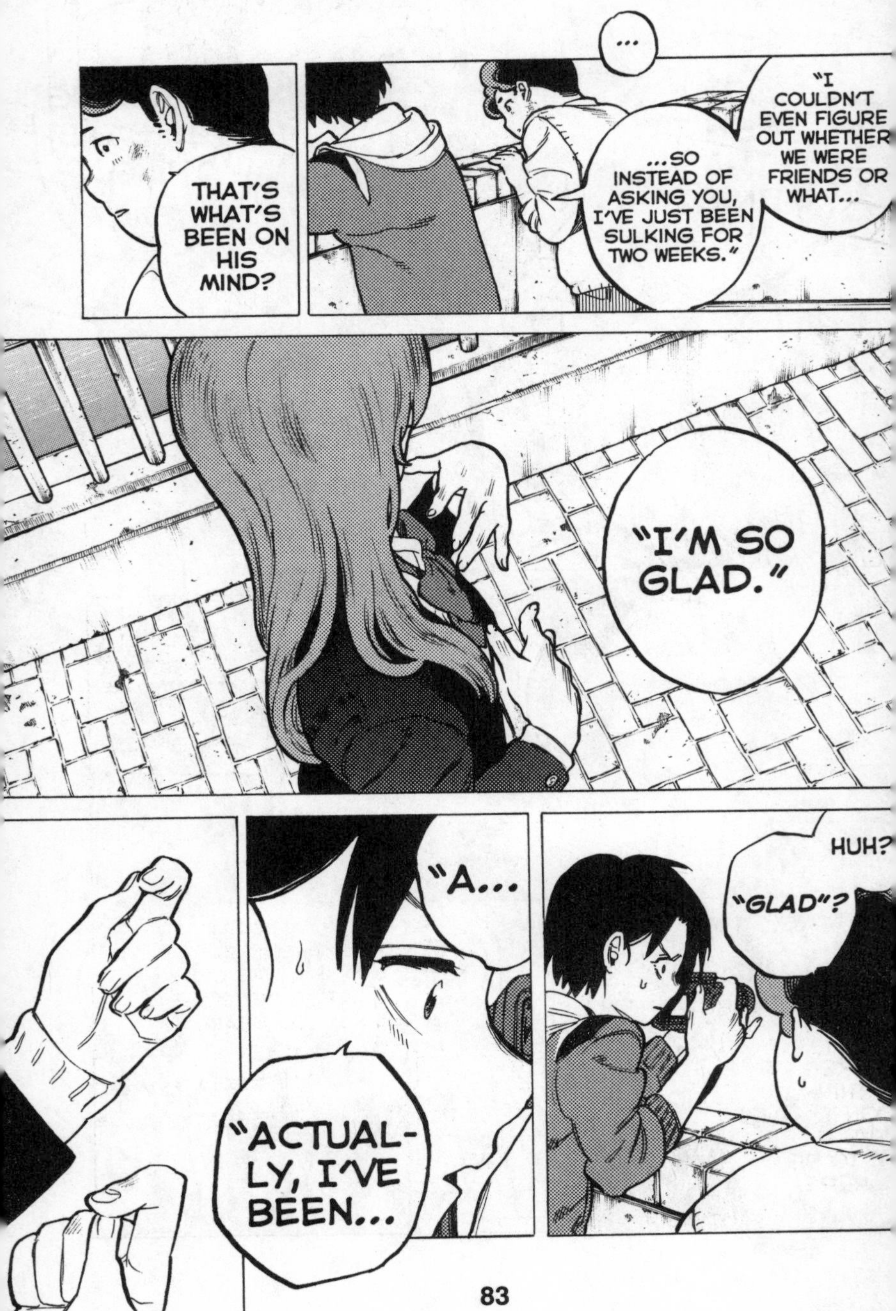
...
"I COULDN'T EVEN FIGURE OUT WHETHER WE WERE FRIENDS OR WHAT...
...SO INSTEAD OF ASKING YOU, I'VE JUST BEEN SULKING FOR TWO WEEKS."
THAT'S WHAT'S BEEN ON HIS MIND?
"I'M SO GLAD."
HUH?
"GLAD"?
"A...
"ACTUAL-LY, I'VE BEEN...

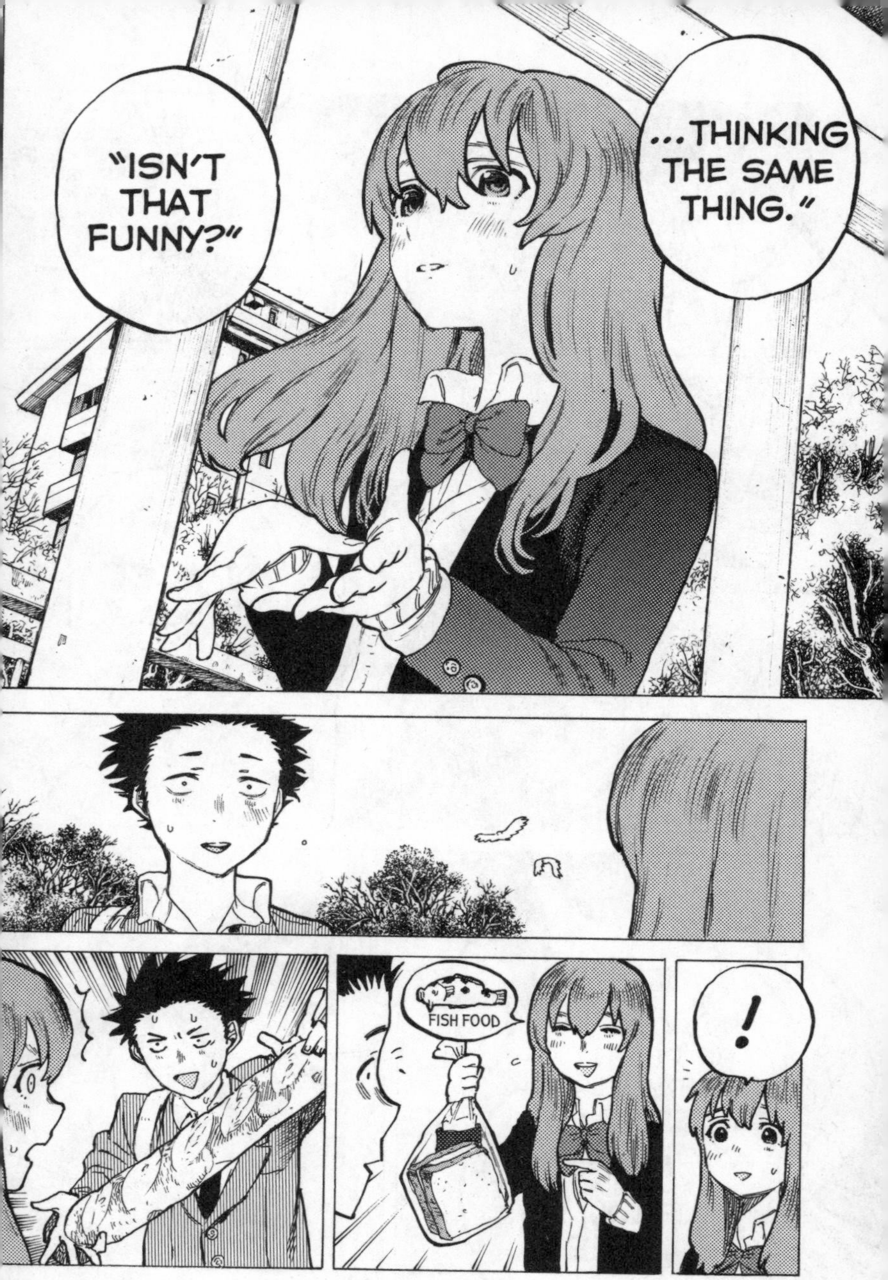
...THINKING THE SAME THING."
"ISN'T THAT FUNNY?"
!
FISH FOOD

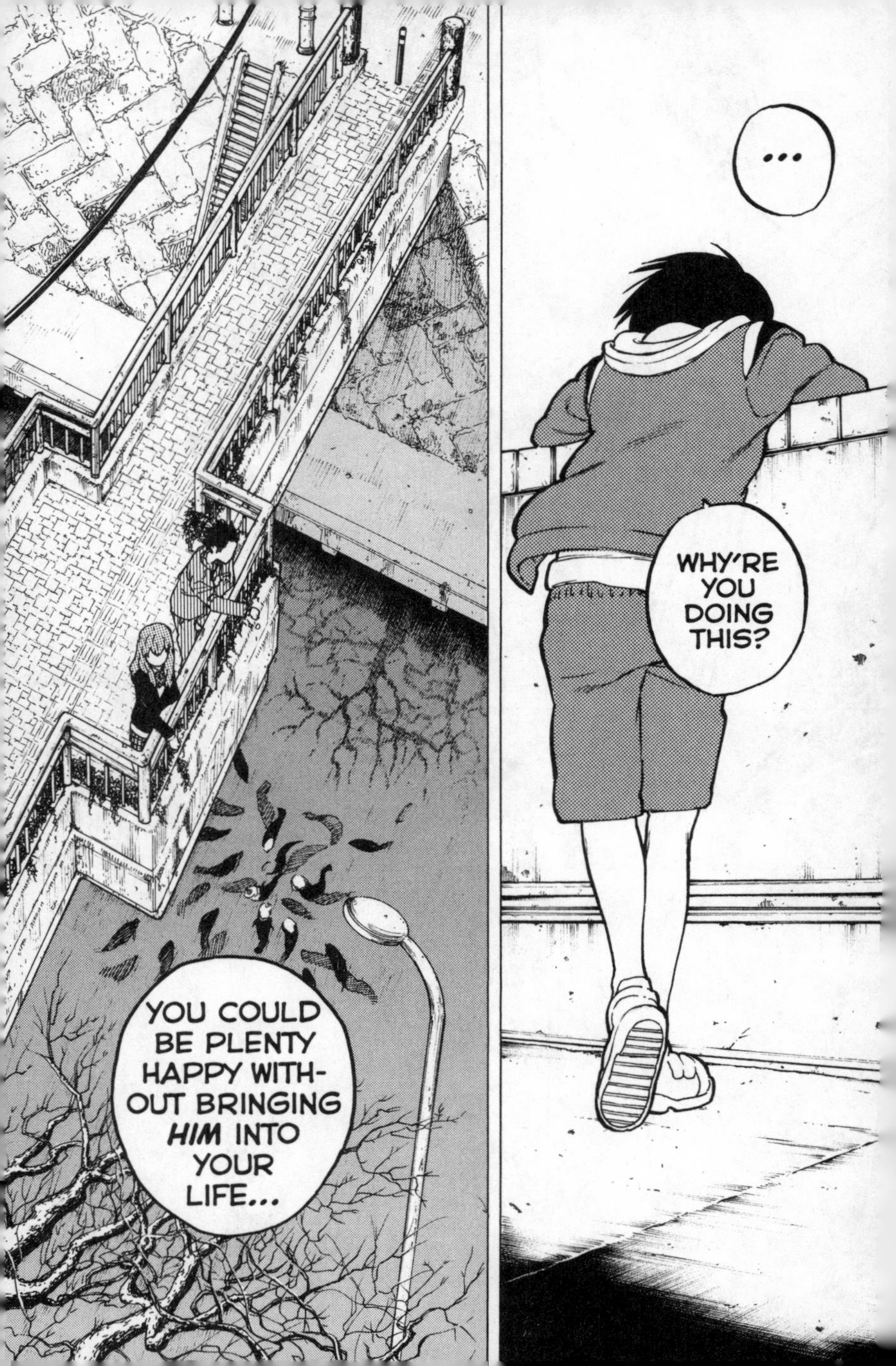
...
WHY'RE YOU DOING THIS?
YOU COULD BE PLENTY HAPPY WITH-OUT BRINGING *HIM* INTO YOUR LIFE...

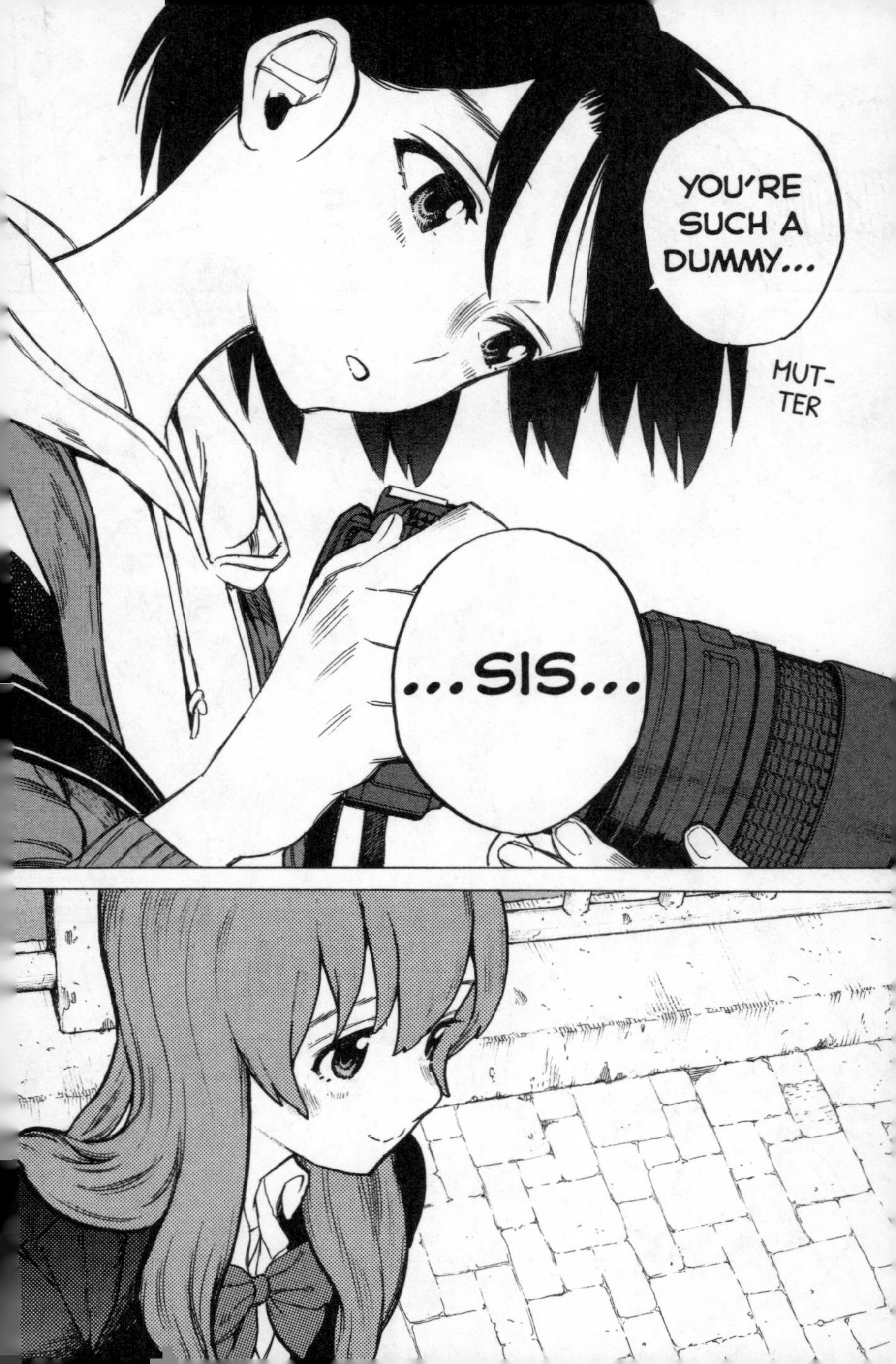
YOU'RE SUCH A DUMMY...
MUT-TER
...SIS...

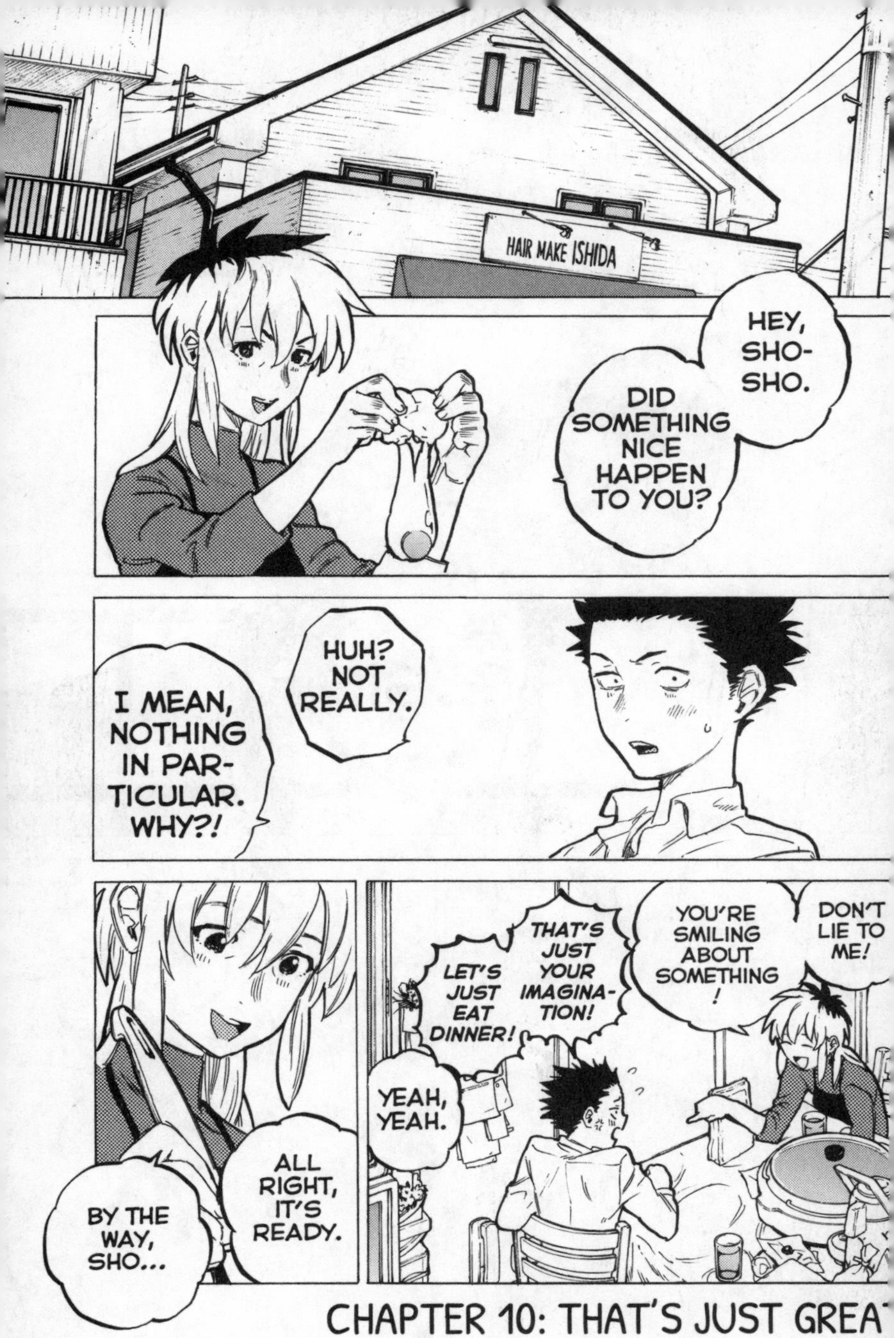
HAIR MAKE ISHIDA
HEY, SHO-SHO.
DID SOMETHING NICE HAPPEN TO YOU?
HUH? NOT REALLY.
I MEAN, NOTHING IN PARTICULAR. WHY?!
DON'T LIE TO ME!
YOU'RE SMILING ABOUT SOMETHING!
THAT'S JUST YOUR IMAGINATION!
LET'S JUST EAT DINNER!
YEAH, YEAH.
ALL RIGHT, IT'S READY.
BY THE WAY, SHO...

CHAPTER 10: THAT'S JUST GREAT

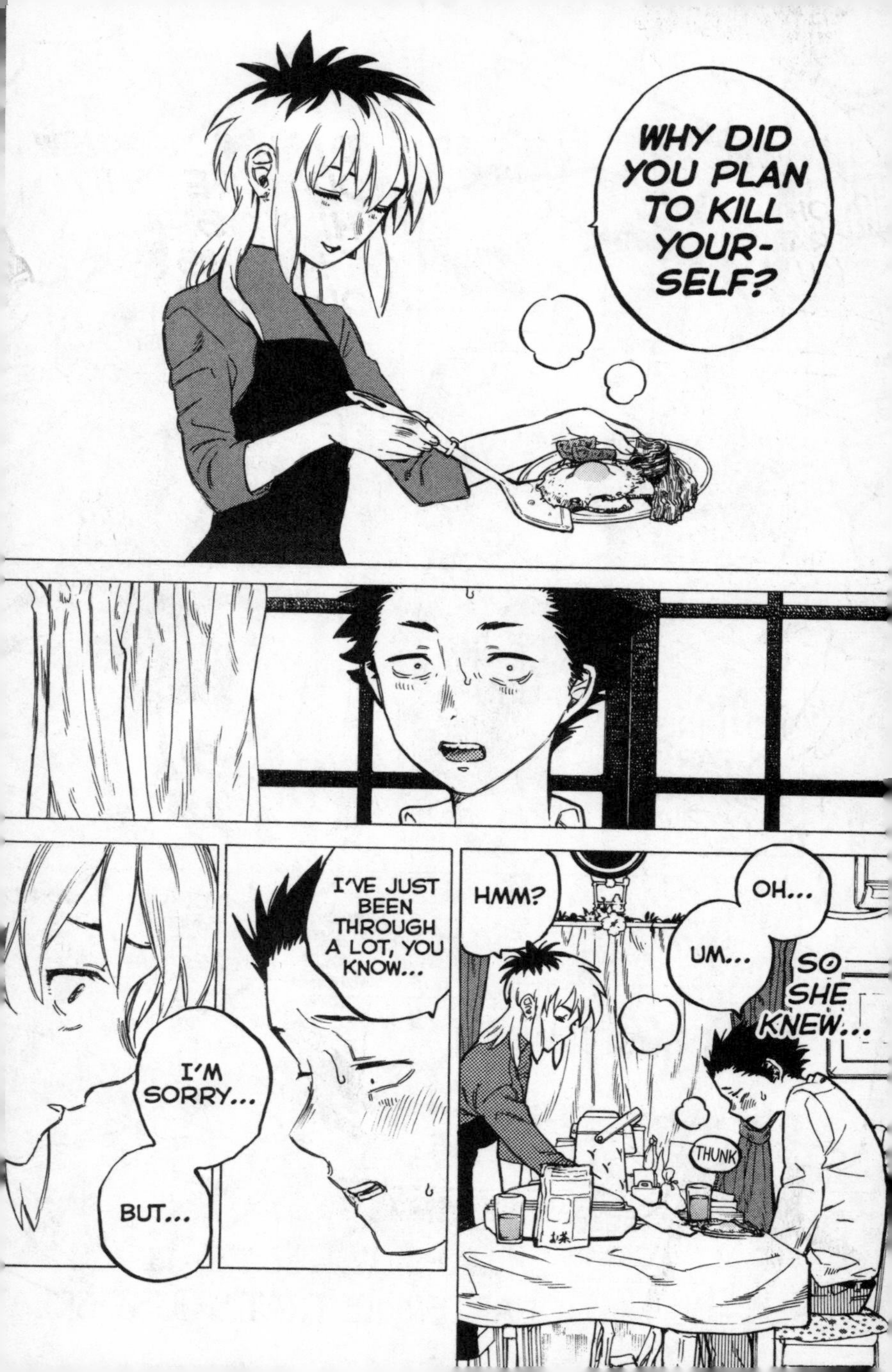
WHY DID YOU PLAN TO KILL YOUR-SELF?
OH...
UM...
SO SHE KNEW...
HMM?
THUNK
I'VE JUST BEEN THROUGH A LOT, YOU KNOW...
I'M SORRY...
BUT...

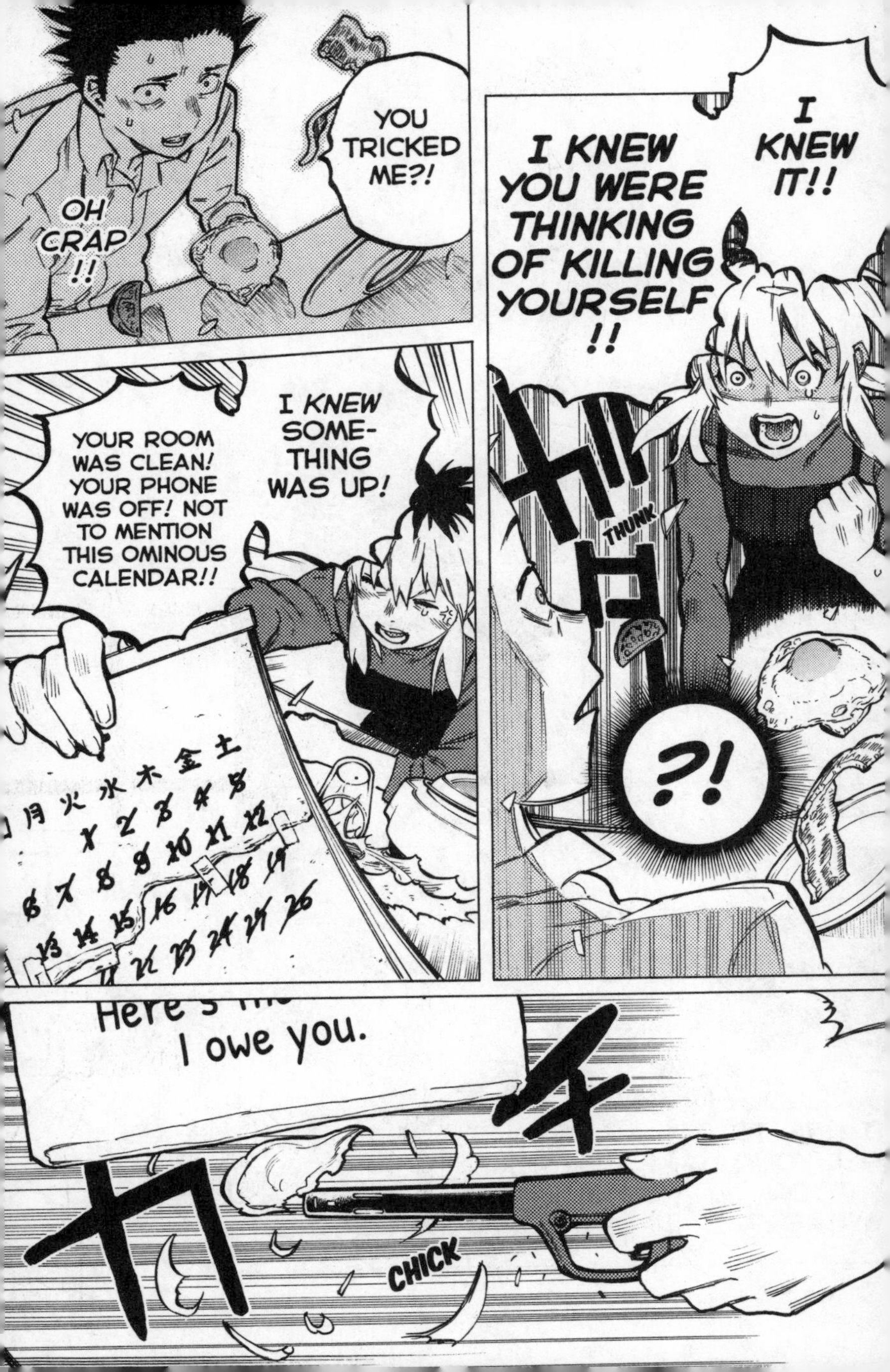
I KNEW IT!!
I KNEW YOU WERE THINKING OF KILLING YOURSELF!!
THUNK
?!
YOU TRICKED ME?!
OH CRAP!!
I KNEW SOME-THING WAS UP!
YOUR ROOM WAS CLEAN! YOUR PHONE WAS OFF! NOT TO MENTION THIS OMINOUS CALENDAR!!
月 火 水 木 金 土
Here's
I owe you.
CHICK

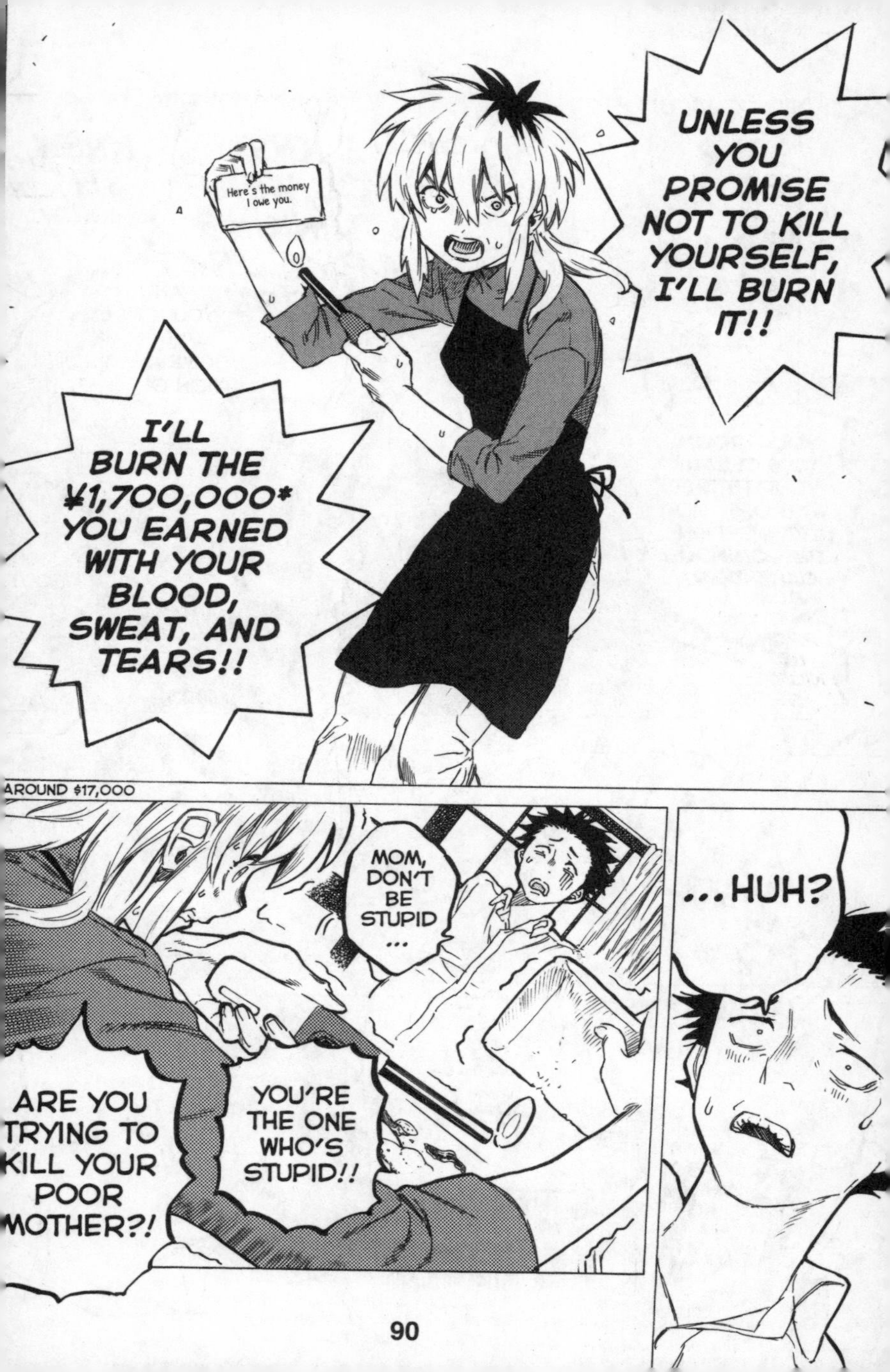
Here's the money I owe you.
UNLESS YOU PROMISE NOT TO KILL YOURSELF, I'LL BURN IT!!
I'LL BURN THE ¥1,700,000* YOU EARNED WITH YOUR BLOOD, SWEAT, AND TEARS!!
AROUND $17,000
...HUH?
MOM, DON'T BE STUPID...
YOU'RE THE ONE WHO'S STUPID!!
ARE YOU TRYING TO KILL YOUR POOR MOTHER?!

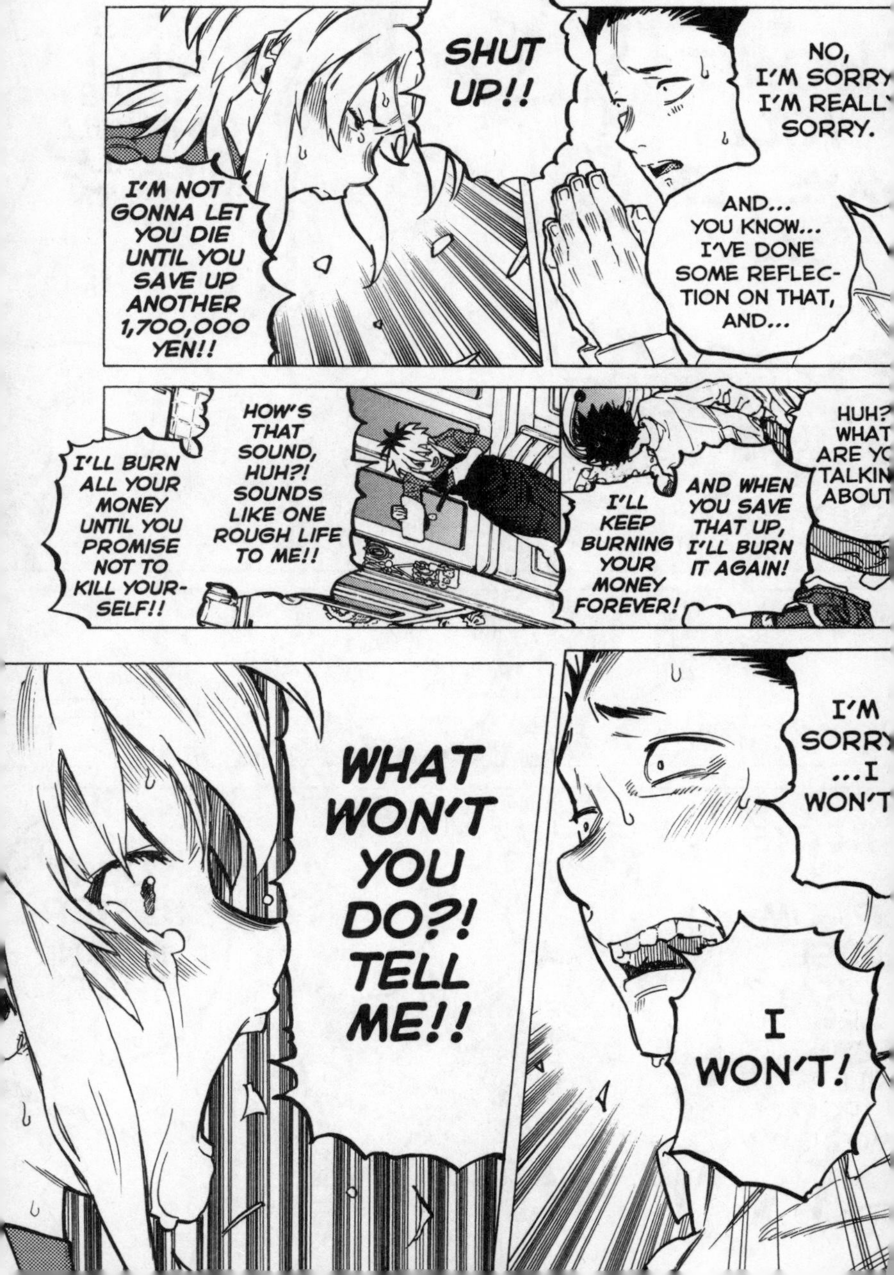

NO, I'M SORRY I'M REALLY SORRY.
AND... YOU KNOW... I'VE DONE SOME REFLECTION ON THAT, AND...
SHUT UP!!
I'M NOT GONNA LET YOU DIE UNTIL YOU SAVE UP ANOTHER 1,700,000 YEN!!
HUH? WHAT ARE YO TALKIN ABOUT
AND WHEN YOU SAVE THAT UP, I'LL BURN IT AGAIN!
I'LL KEEP BURNING YOUR MONEY FOREVER!
HOW'S THAT SOUND, HUH?! SOUNDS LIKE ONE ROUGH LIFE TO ME!!
I'LL BURN ALL YOUR MONEY UNTIL YOU PROMISE NOT TO KILL YOURSELF!!
I'M SORRY ...I WON'T
I WON'T!
WHAT WON'T YOU DO?! TELL ME!!

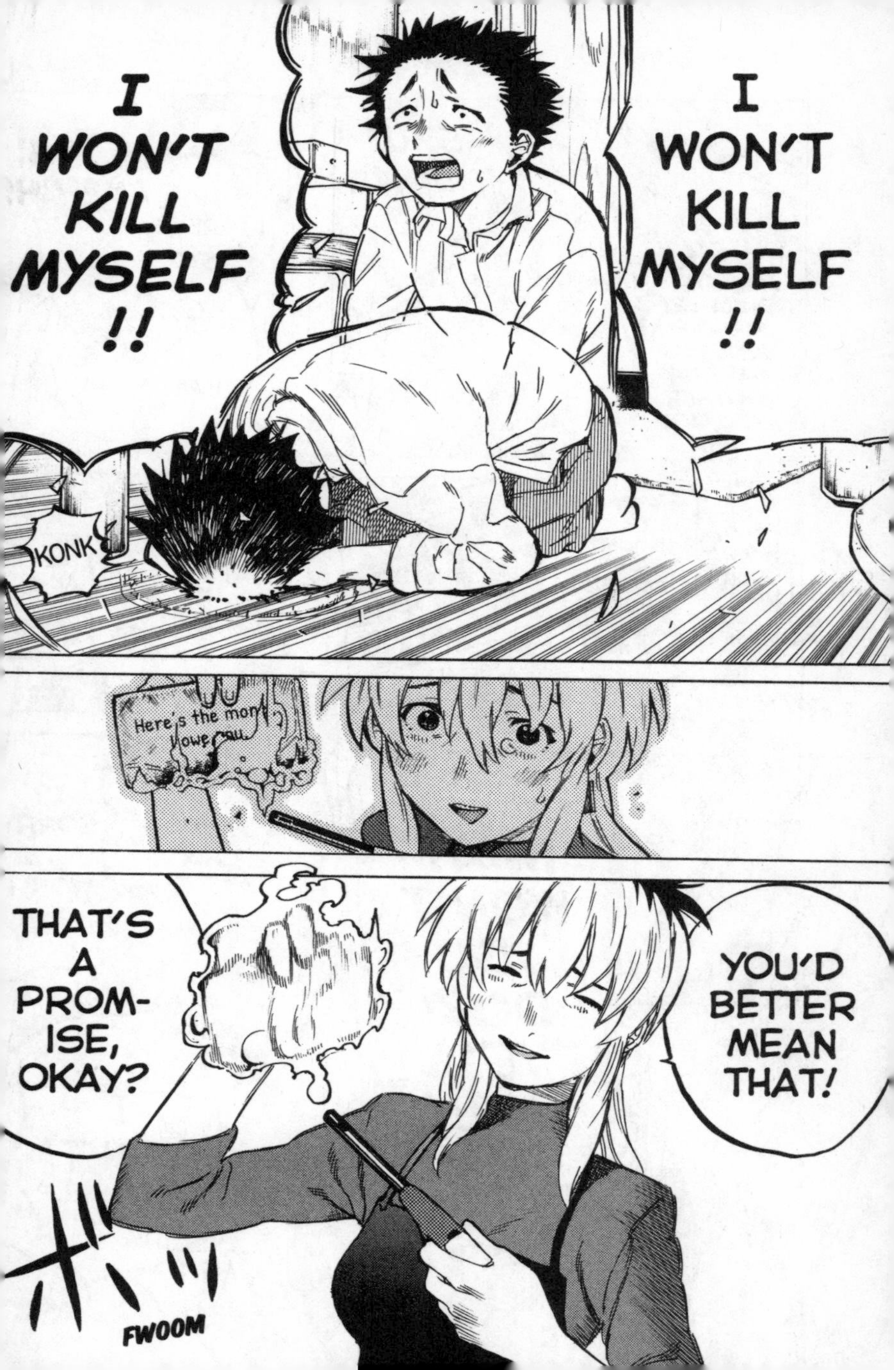

I WON'T KILL MYSELF!!
I WON'T KILL MYSELF!!
KONK
Here's the mon I owe you.
YOU'D BETTER MEAN THAT!
THAT'S A PROM-ISE, OKAY?
FWOOM

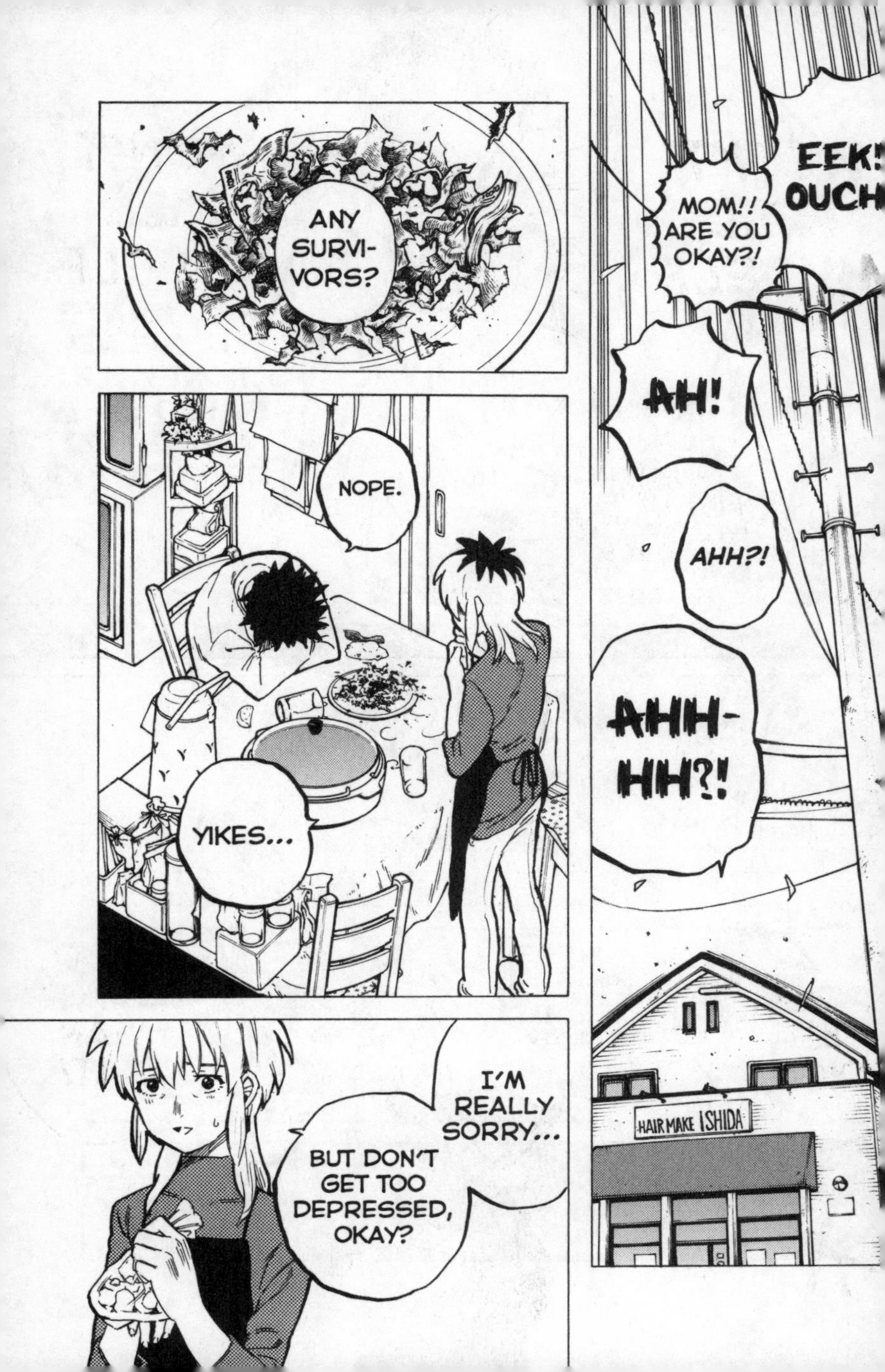
EEK!
OUCH
MOM!! ARE YOU OKAY?!
AH!
AHH?!
AHH-HH?!
HAIR MAKE ISHIDA
ANY SURVI-VORS?
NOPE.
YIKES...
I'M REALLY SORRY...
BUT DON'T GET TOO DEPRESSED, OKAY?

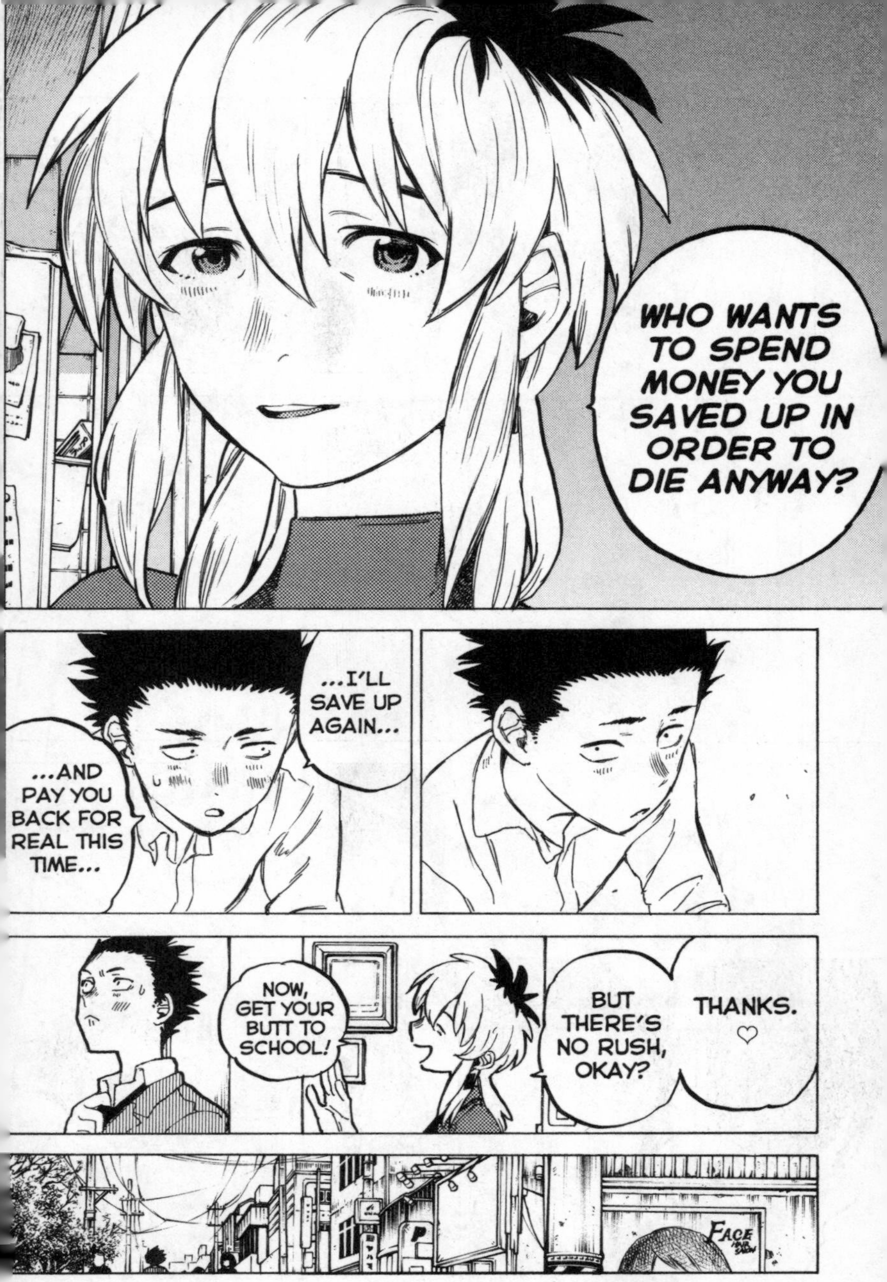
WHO WANTS TO SPEND MONEY YOU SAVED UP IN ORDER TO DIE ANYWAY?
...I'LL SAVE UP AGAIN...
...AND PAY YOU BACK FOR REAL THIS TIME...
THANKS. ♡
BUT THERE'S NO RUSH, OKAY?
NOW, GET YOUR BUTT TO SCHOOL!
FACE

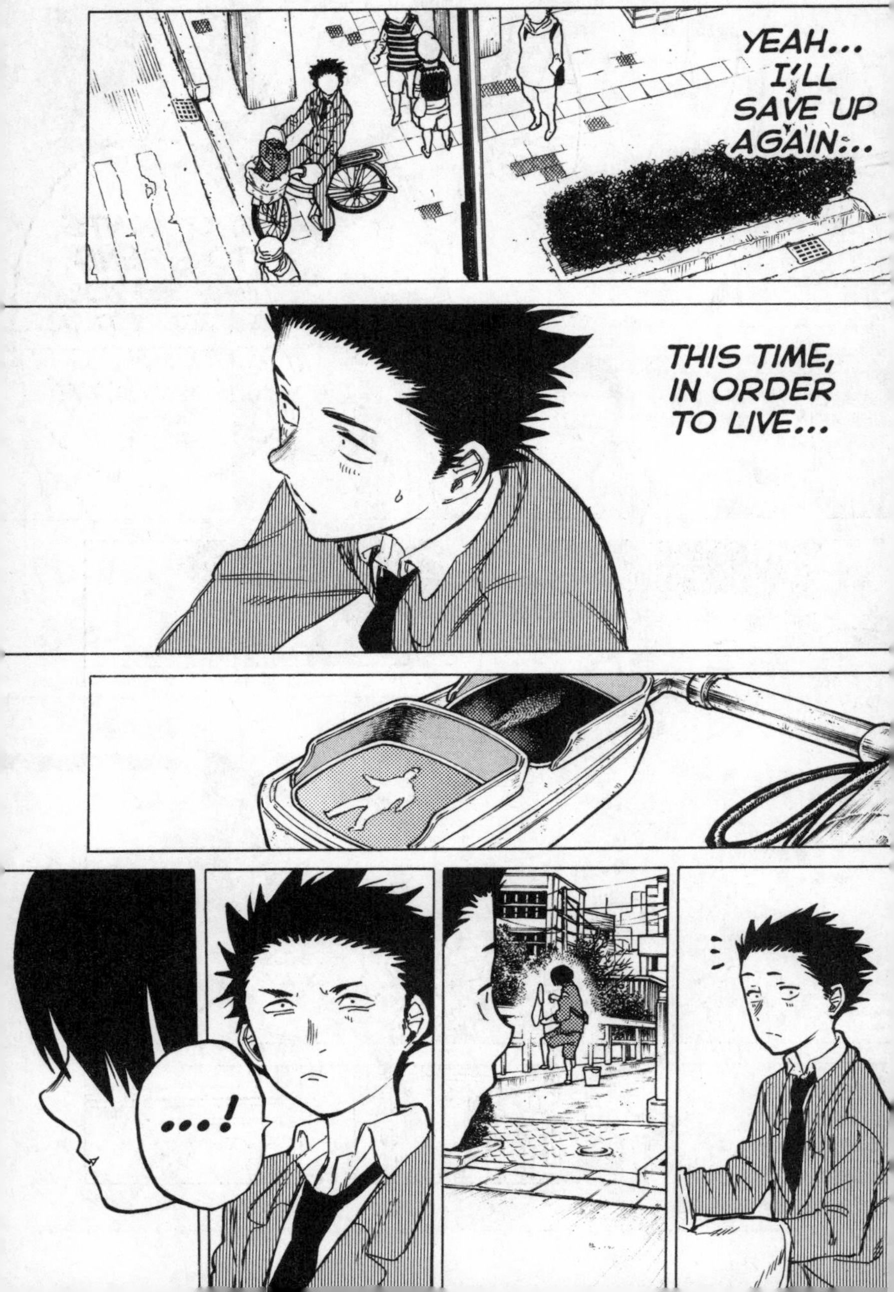
YEAH... I'LL SAVE UP AGAIN...
THIS TIME, IN ORDER TO LIVE...
...!

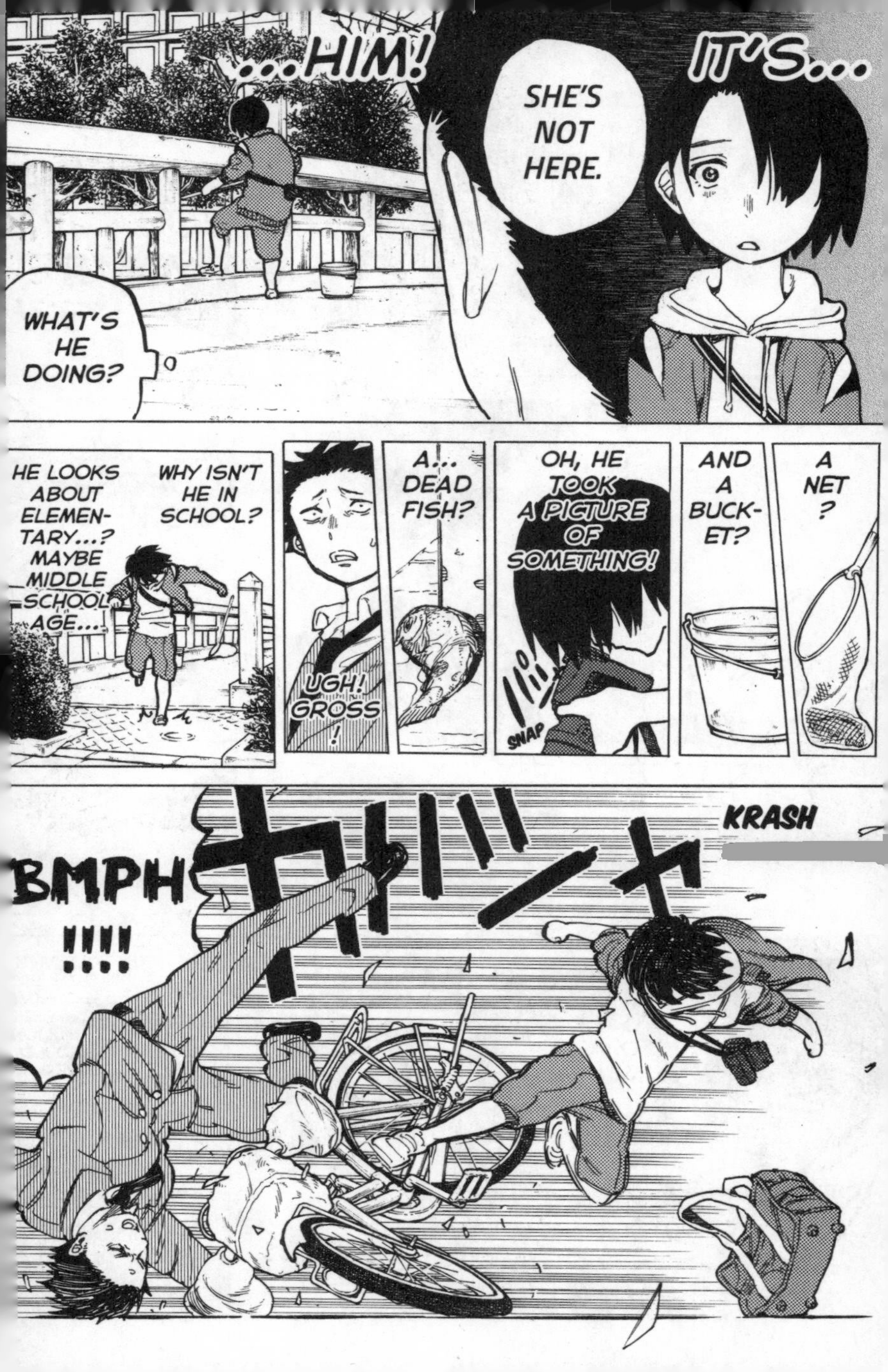
IT'S...
...HIM!
SHE'S NOT HERE.
WHAT'S HE DOING?
A NET ?
AND A BUCK-ET?
OH, HE TOOK A PICTURE OF SOMETHING!
SNAP
A... DEAD FISH?
UGH! GROSS !
WHY ISN'T HE IN SCHOOL?
HE LOOKS ABOUT ELEMEN-TARY...? MAYBE MIDDLE SCHOOL AGE...
KRASH
BMPH !!!!!

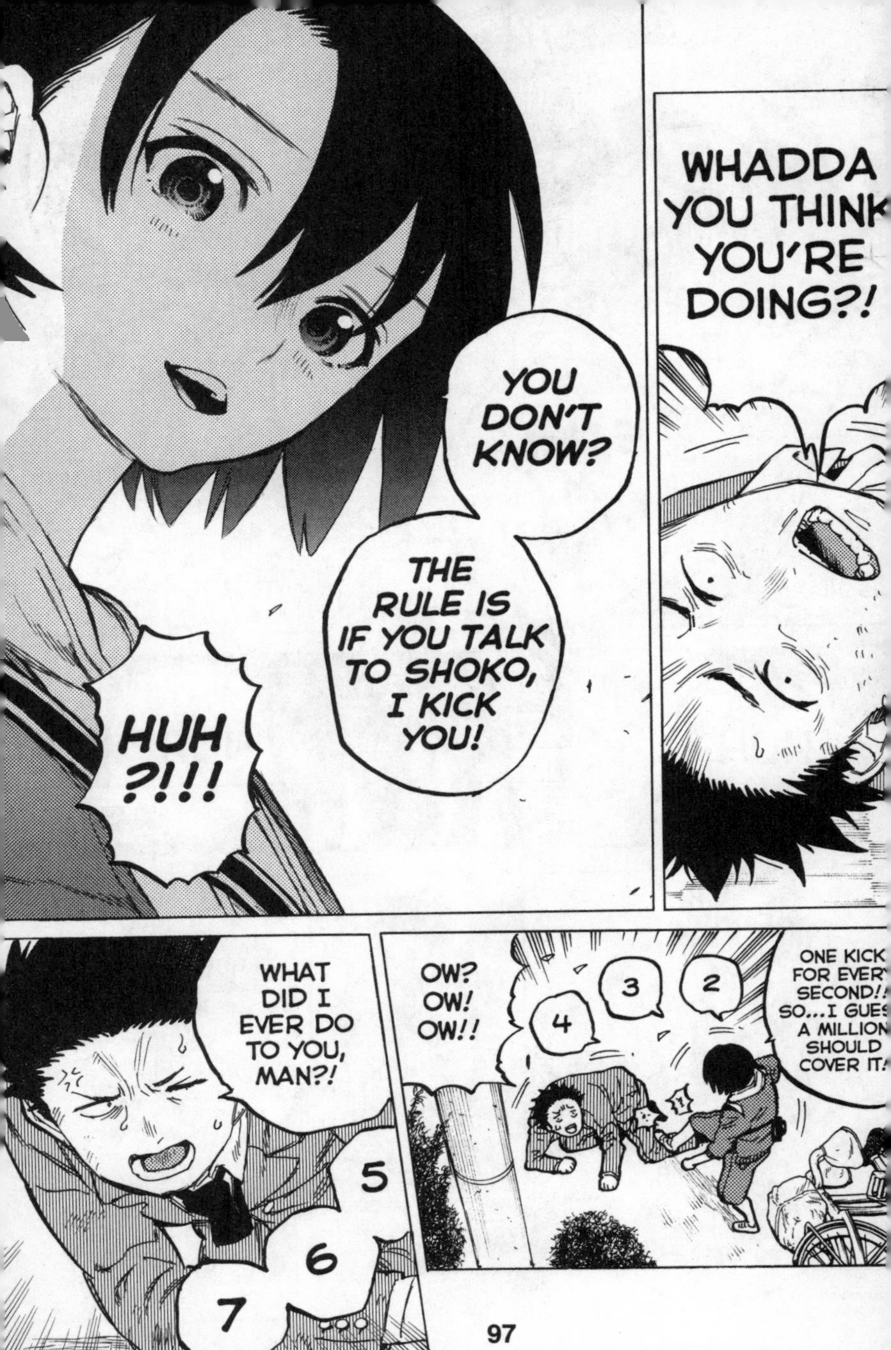
WHADDA YOU THINK YOU'RE DOING?!
YOU DON'T KNOW?
THE RULE IS IF YOU TALK TO SHOKO, I KICK YOU!
HUH ?!!!
ONE KICK FOR EVER SECOND!! SO...I GUES A MILLION SHOULD COVER IT!
2
3
4
OW? OW! OW!!
WHAT DID I EVER DO TO YOU, MAN?!
5
6
7

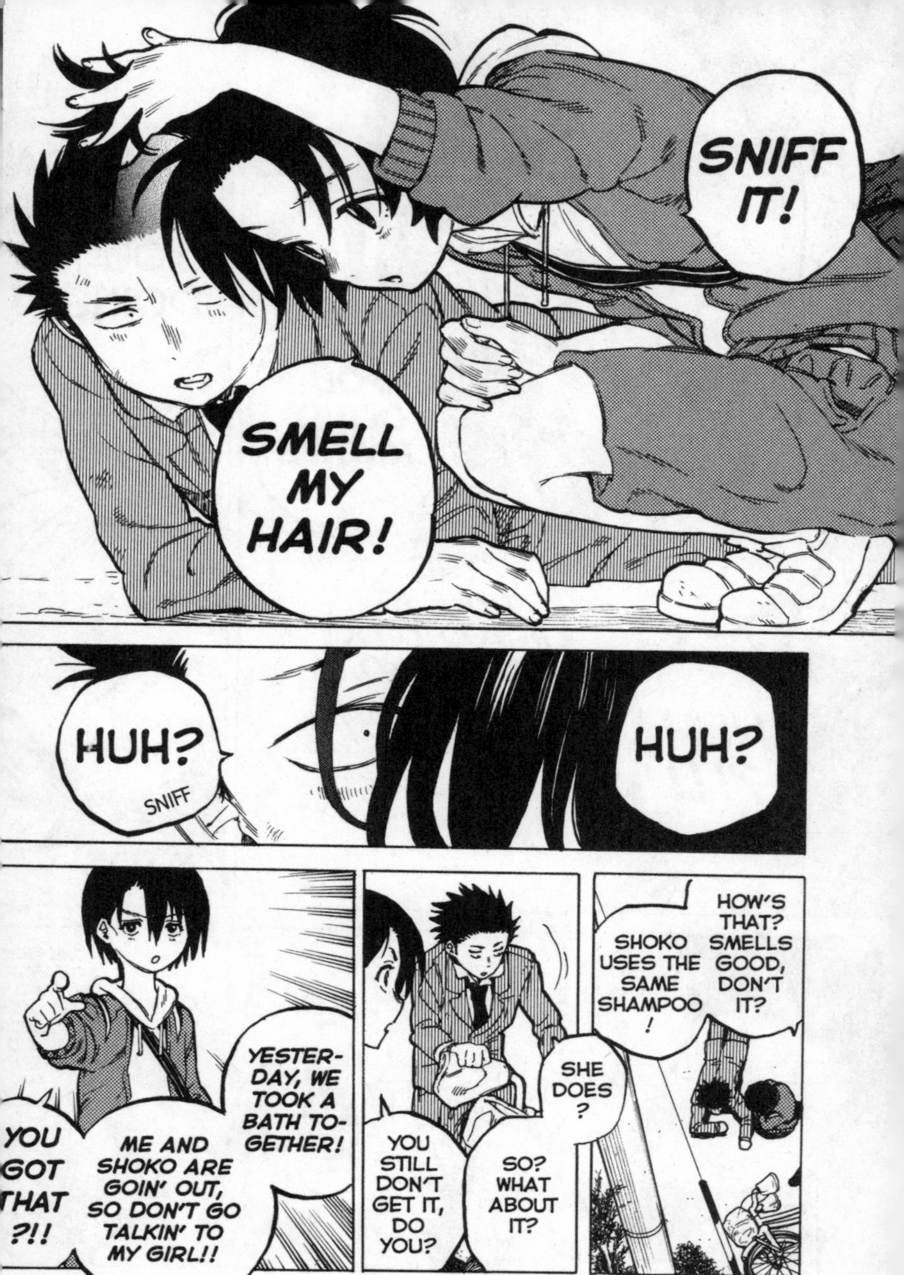
SNIFF IT!
SMELL MY HAIR!
HUH?
HUH?
SNIFF
HOW'S THAT? SMELLS GOOD, DON'T IT?
SHOKO USES THE SAME SHAMPOO!
SHE DOES?
SO? WHAT ABOUT IT?
YOU STILL DON'T GET IT, DO YOU?
YESTER-DAY, WE TOOK A BATH TO-GETHER!
ME AND SHOKO ARE GOIN' OUT, SO DON'T GO TALKIN' TO MY GIRL!!
YOU GOT THAT?!!

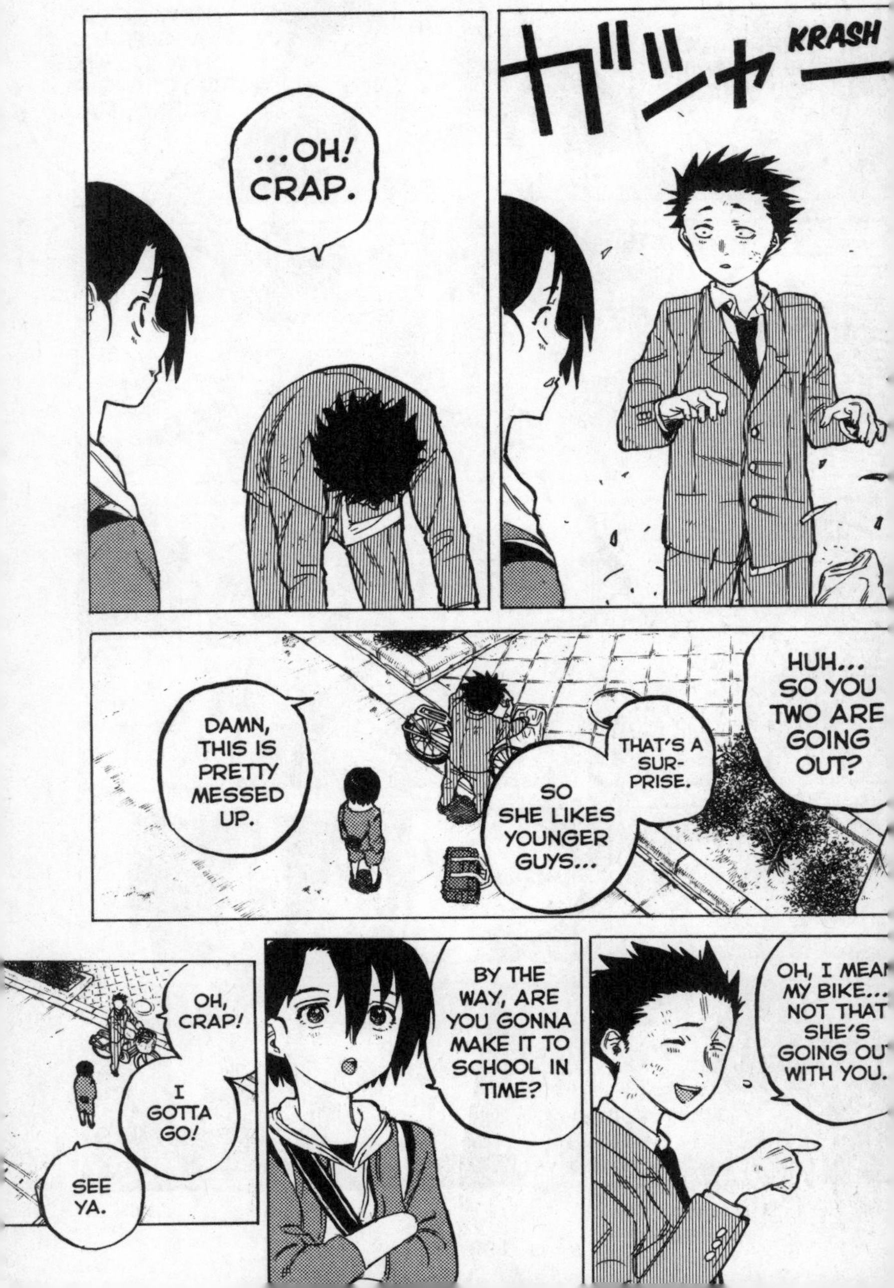
ガシャー
KRASH
...OH! CRAP.
HUH... SO YOU TWO ARE GOING OUT?
THAT'S A SUR-PRISE.
SO SHE LIKES YOUNGER GUYS...
DAMN, THIS IS PRETTY MESSED UP.
OH, I MEAN MY BIKE... NOT THAT SHE'S GOING OUT WITH YOU.
BY THE WAY, ARE YOU GONNA MAKE IT TO SCHOOL IN TIME?
OH, CRAP!
I GOTTA GO!
SEE YA.

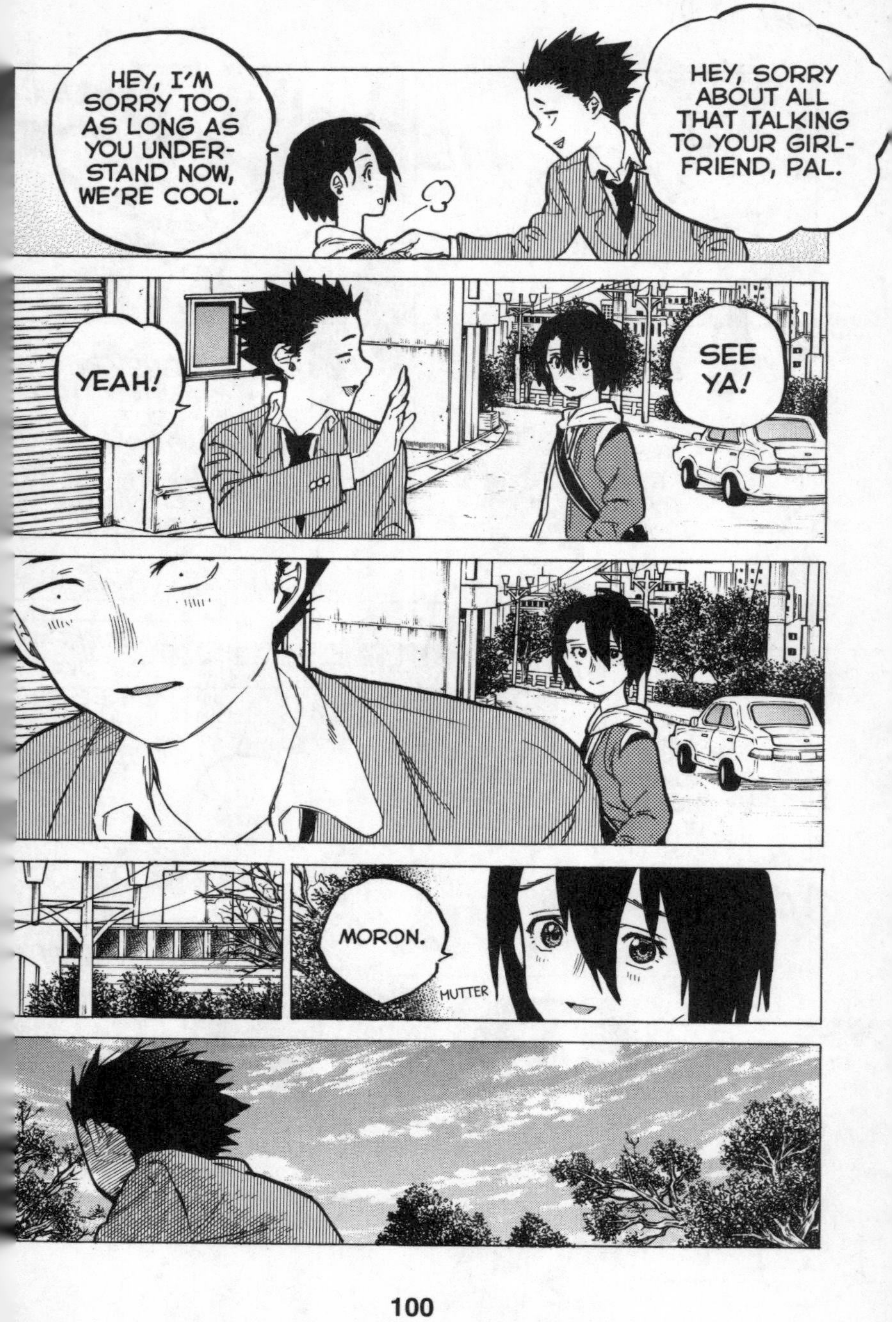
HEY, SORRY ABOUT ALL THAT TALKING TO YOUR GIRL-FRIEND, PAL.
HEY, I'M SORRY TOO. AS LONG AS YOU UNDER-STAND NOW, WE'RE COOL.
SEE YA!
YEAH!
MORON.
MUTTER

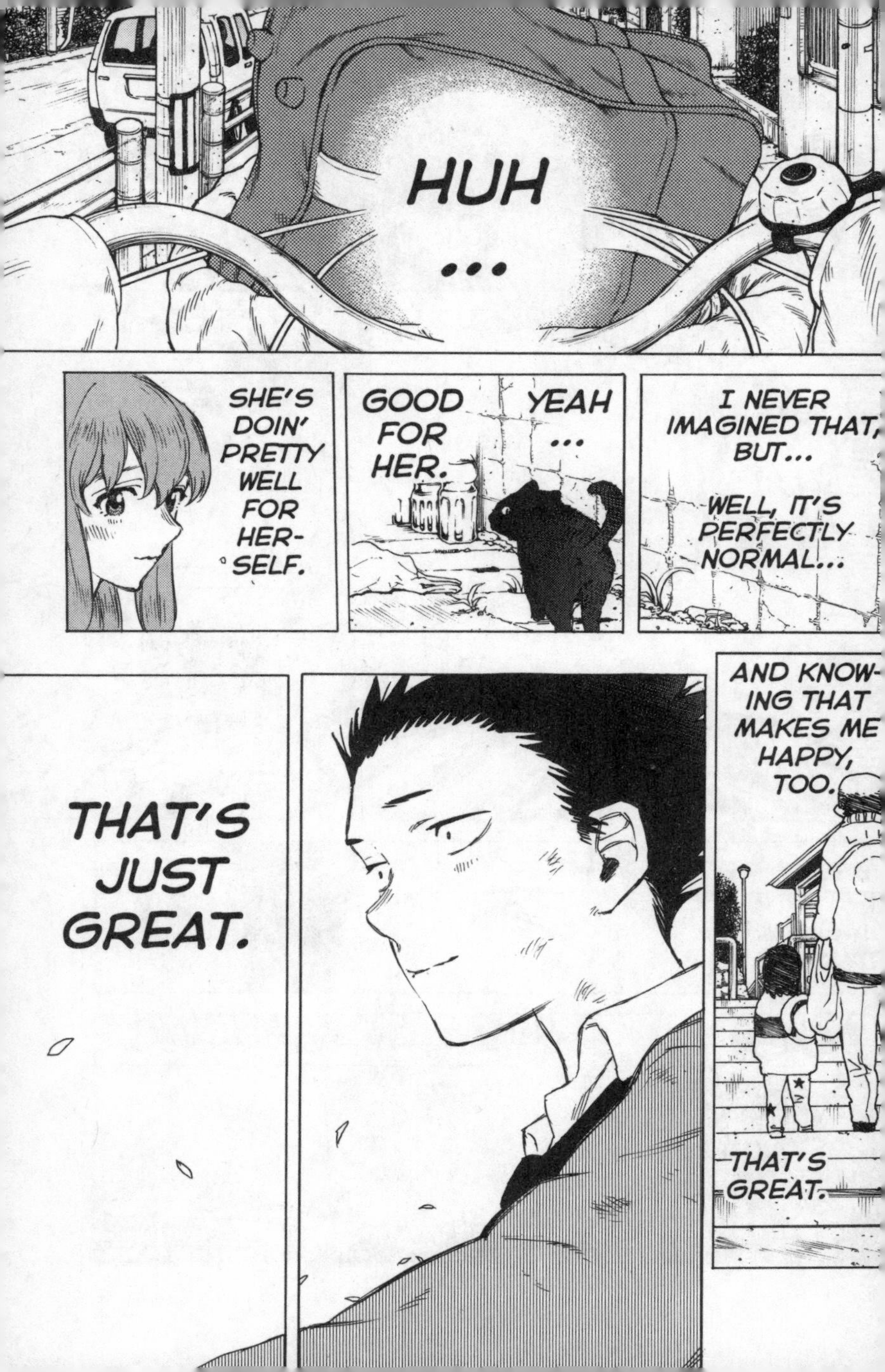
HUH
...
I NEVER IMAGINED THAT, BUT...
WELL, IT'S PERFECTLY NORMAL...
YEAH...
GOOD FOR HER.
SHE'S DOIN' PRETTY WELL FOR HER-SELF.
AND KNOW-ING THAT MAKES ME HAPPY, TOO.
THAT'S GREAT.
THAT'S JUST GREAT.

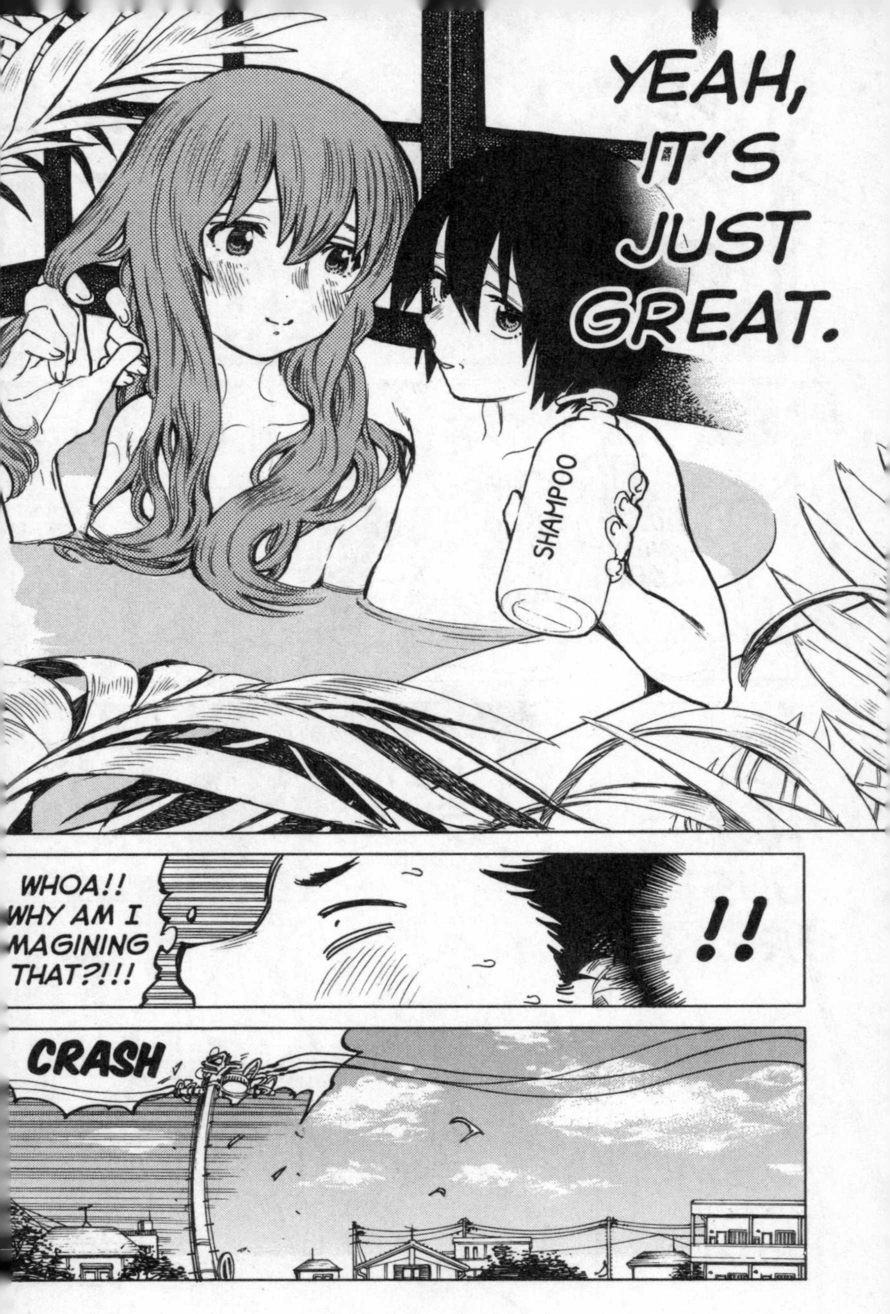
YEAH, IT'S JUST GREAT.
SHAMPOO
!!
WHOA!! WHY AM I MAGINING THAT?!!!
CRASH

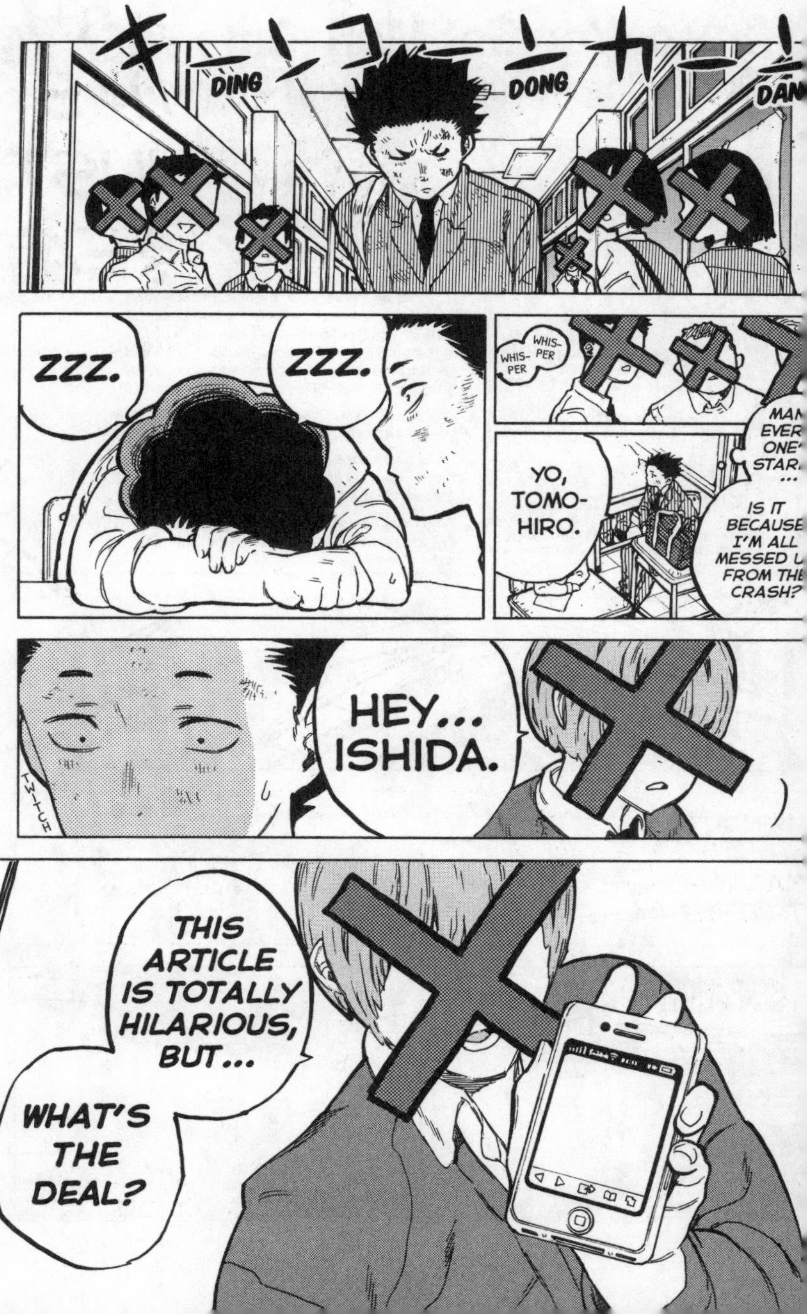

キーンコーンカーン
DING
DONG
DAN
WHIS-PER WHIS-PER
MAN EVER ONE' STAR ...
IS IT BECAUSE I'M ALL MESSED U FROM THE CRASH?
YO, TOMO-HIRO.
ZZZ.
ZZZ.
HEY... ISHIDA.
TWITCH
THIS ARTICLE IS TOTALLY HILARIOUS, BUT...
WHAT'S THE DEAL?

Breaking News/Residents/Current Ranking #8

"Any of You Got More Guts Than Me?"

-Bragging About His Acts of Public Nuisance-

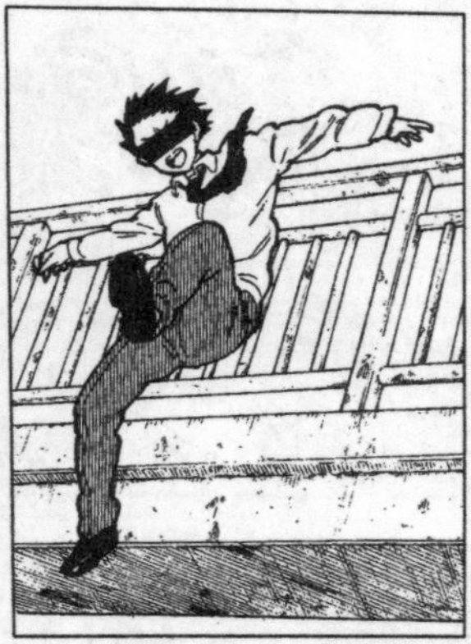

According to the school this male student attends, the incident is still under investigation.

Blog it 0 Tweet! 2 Share 9 Print this Page

■ Now, when community sites are all the rage, they are used in many ways...

Criticism floods his blog. A boy jumping into a river. At a glance, it might seem like a common occurance. But shouldn't responsible adults viewing such tomfoolery knit their brows?
"Any of You Got More Guts Than Me?"
In the public venue at which he took this photo, there is a small bridge used by the residents of the town. And under said bridge, the town raises koi carp.

According to Mr. Takasu, who feeds the carp here six days a week, "lately, the carp seem a little under the weather."

Looking over the boy's post history, this is not his first offense. He has jumped off bridges many times in the past, calling these jumps "daredevil stunts!"

Why does he do it? Bragging rights? War stories? Fun? Bets? Creating material? Whatever his motivation, his acts have now been seen worldwide...

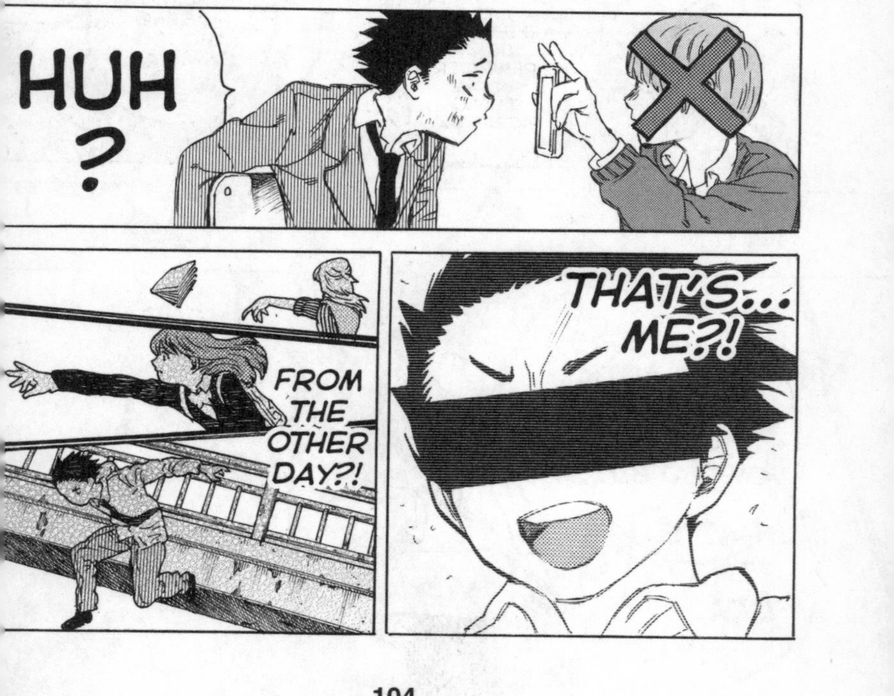
HUH?
THAT'S... ME?!
FROM THE OTHER DAY?!

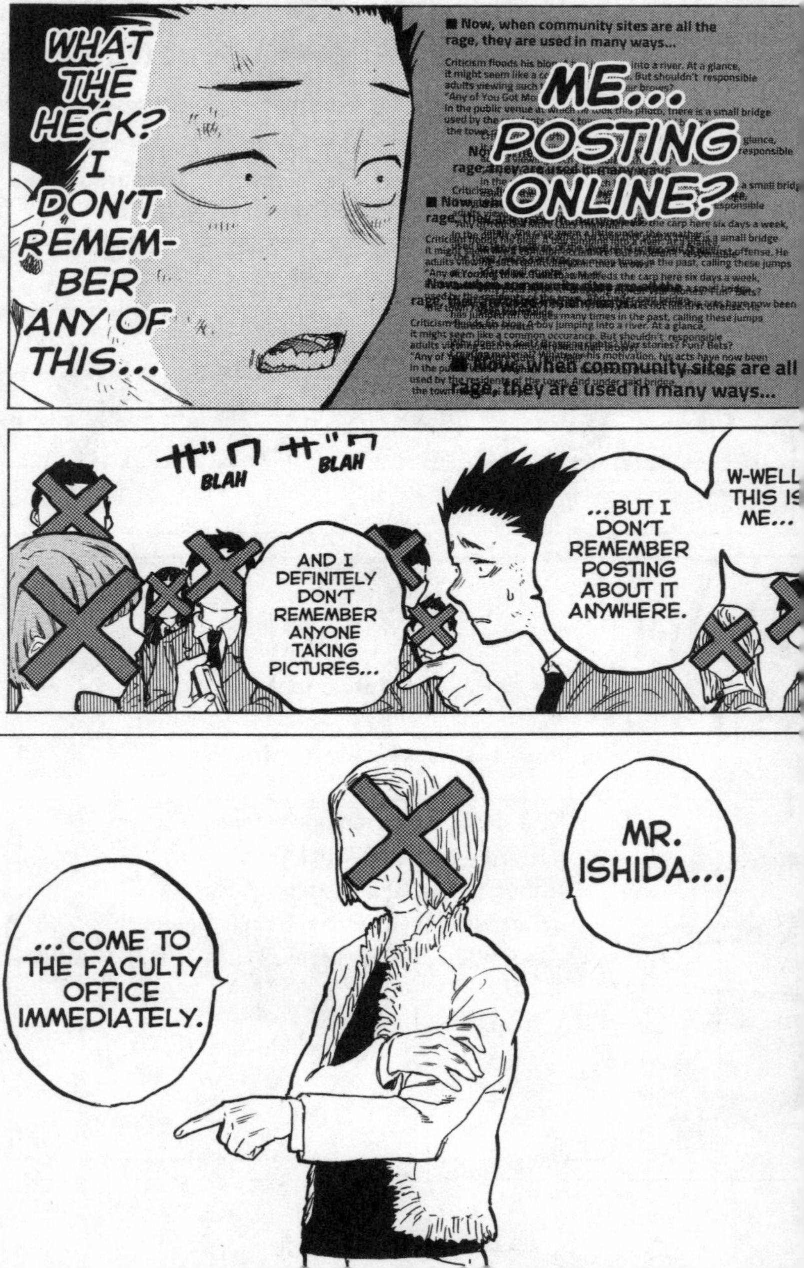
■ Now, when community sites are all the rage, they are used in many ways...
ME... POSTING ONLINE?
WHAT THE HECK? I DON'T REMEMBER ANY OF THIS...
W-WELL THIS IS ME...
...BUT I DON'T REMEMBER POSTING ABOUT IT ANYWHERE.
AND I DEFINITELY DON'T REMEMBER ANYONE TAKING PICTURES...
ザワ BLAH
ザワ BLAH
MR. ISHIDA...
...COME TO THE FACULTY OFFICE IMMEDIATELY.

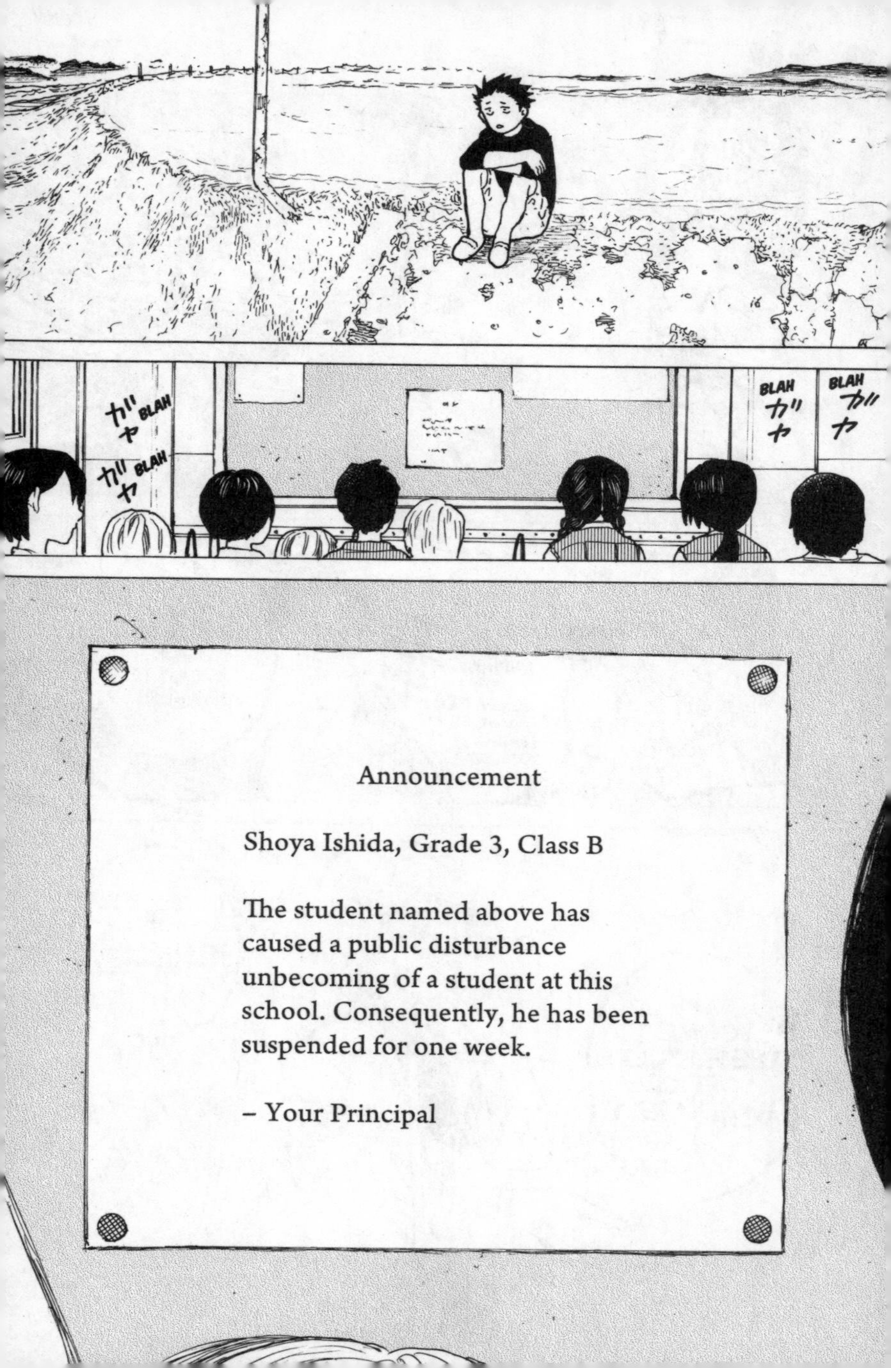
BLAH ガヤ
BLAH ガヤ
ガヤ BLAH
ガヤ BLAH
Announcement
Shoya Ishida, Grade 3, Class B
The student named above has caused a public disturbance unbecoming of a student at this school. Consequently, he has been suspended for one week.
– Your Principal

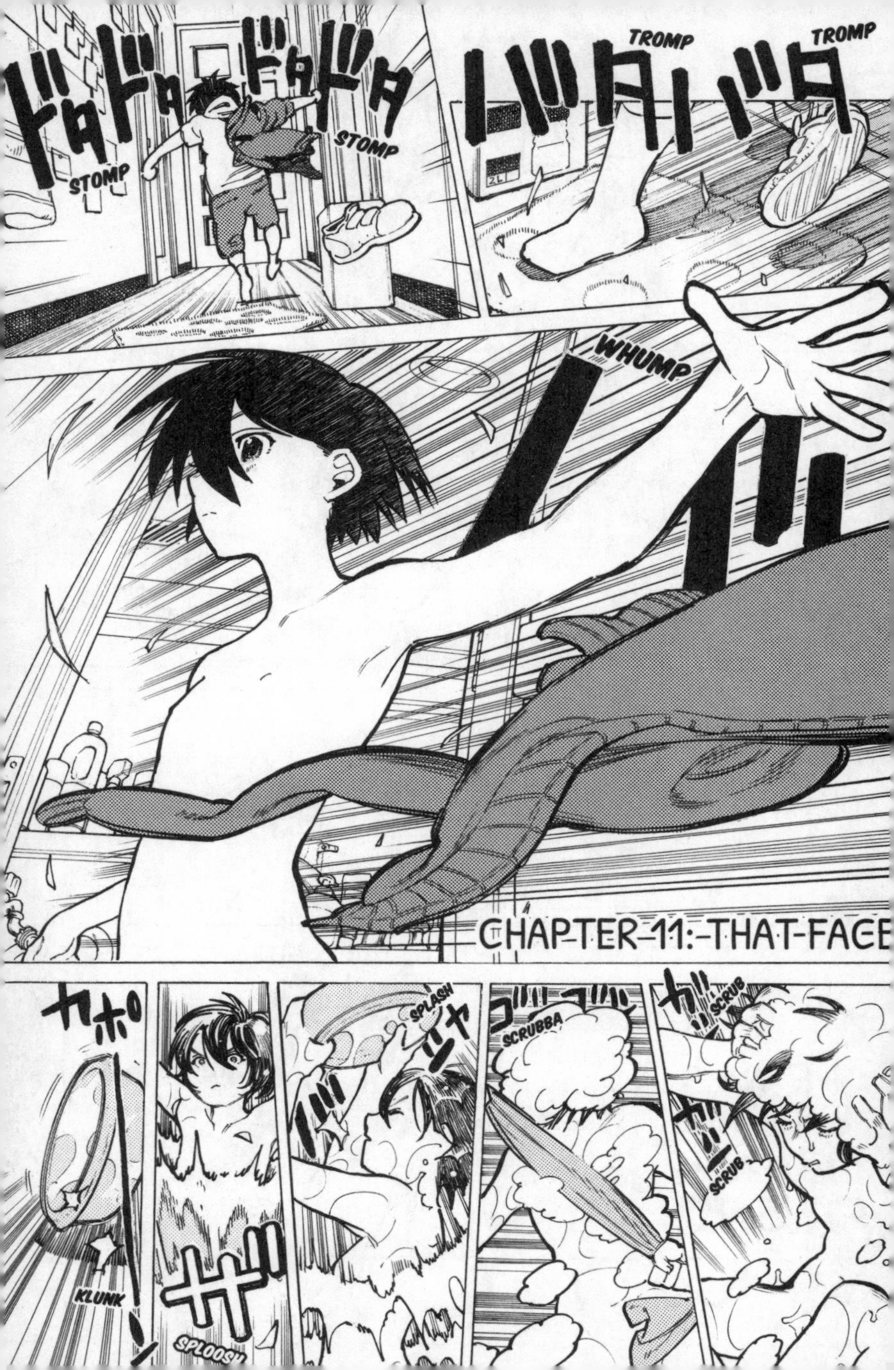
TROMP
TROMP
STOMP
STOMP
WHUMP
CHAPTER 11: THAT FACE
SCRUB
SCRUB
SCRUBBA
SPLASH
SPLOOSH
KLUNK

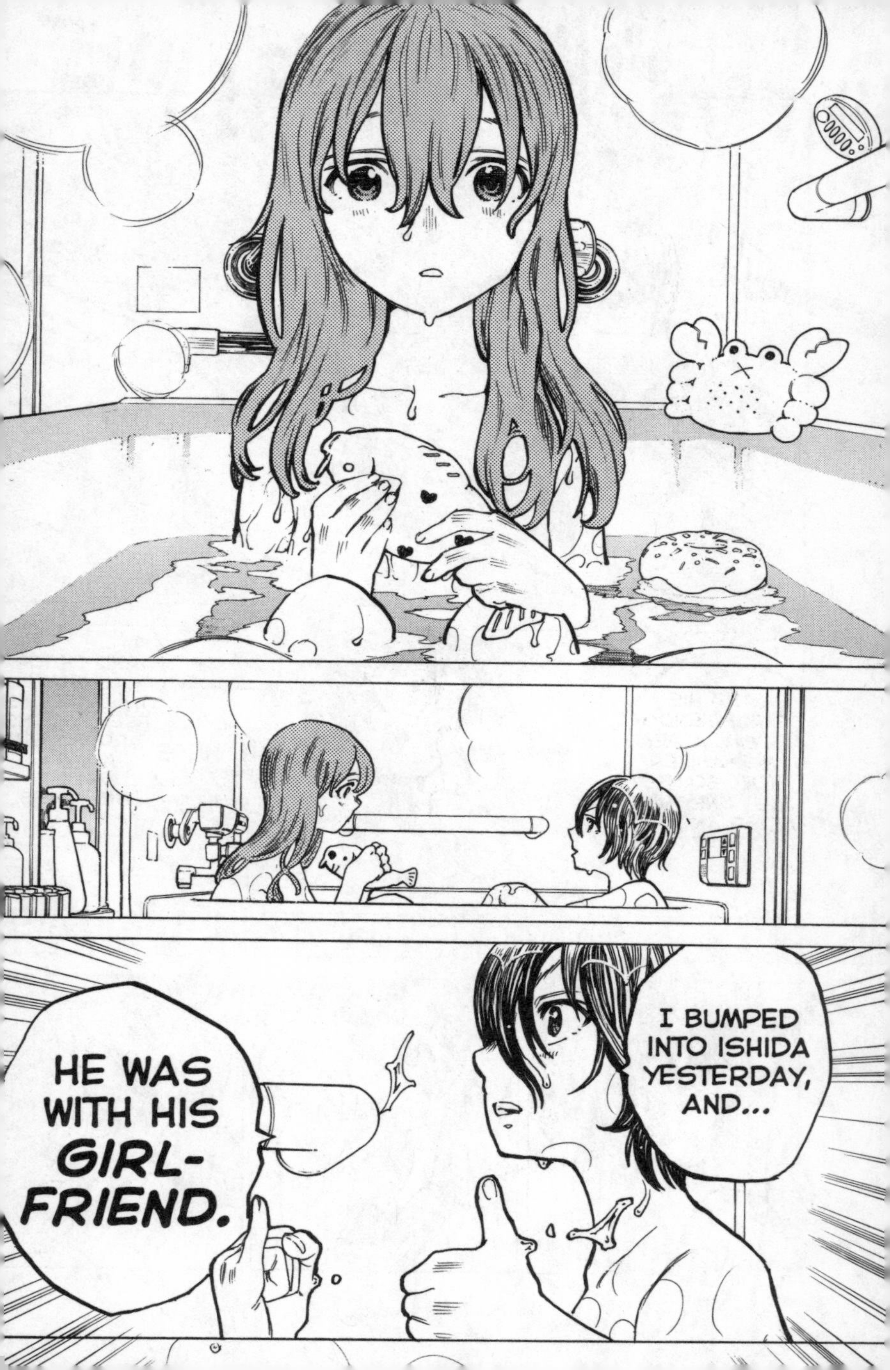
I BUMPED INTO ISHIDA YESTERDAY, AND...
HE WAS WITH HIS GIRL-FRIEND.

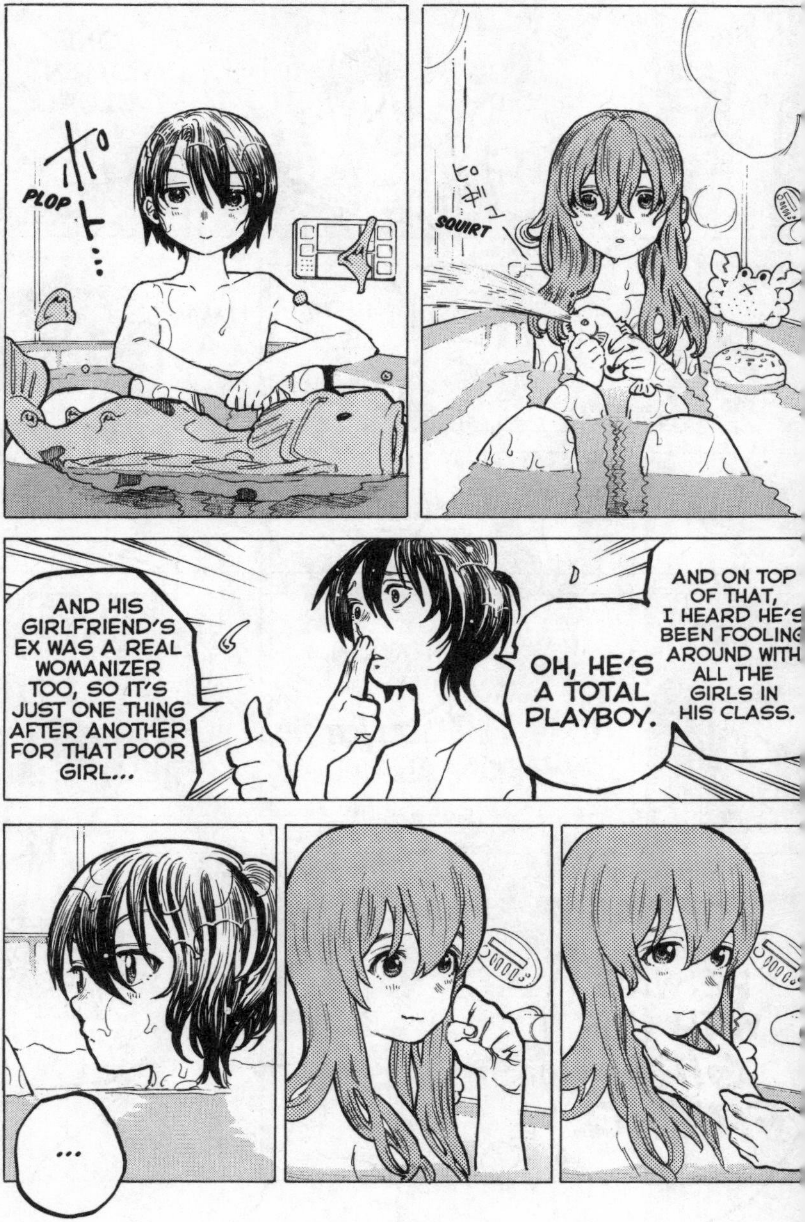
ピギュ
SQUIRT
ポト…
PLOP
OH, HE'S A TOTAL PLAYBOY.
AND ON TOP OF THAT, I HEARD HE'S BEEN FOOLING AROUND WITH ALL THE GIRLS IN HIS CLASS.
AND HIS GIRLFRIEND'S EX WAS A REAL WOMANIZER TOO, SO IT'S JUST ONE THING AFTER ANOTHER FOR THAT POOR GIRL...
...

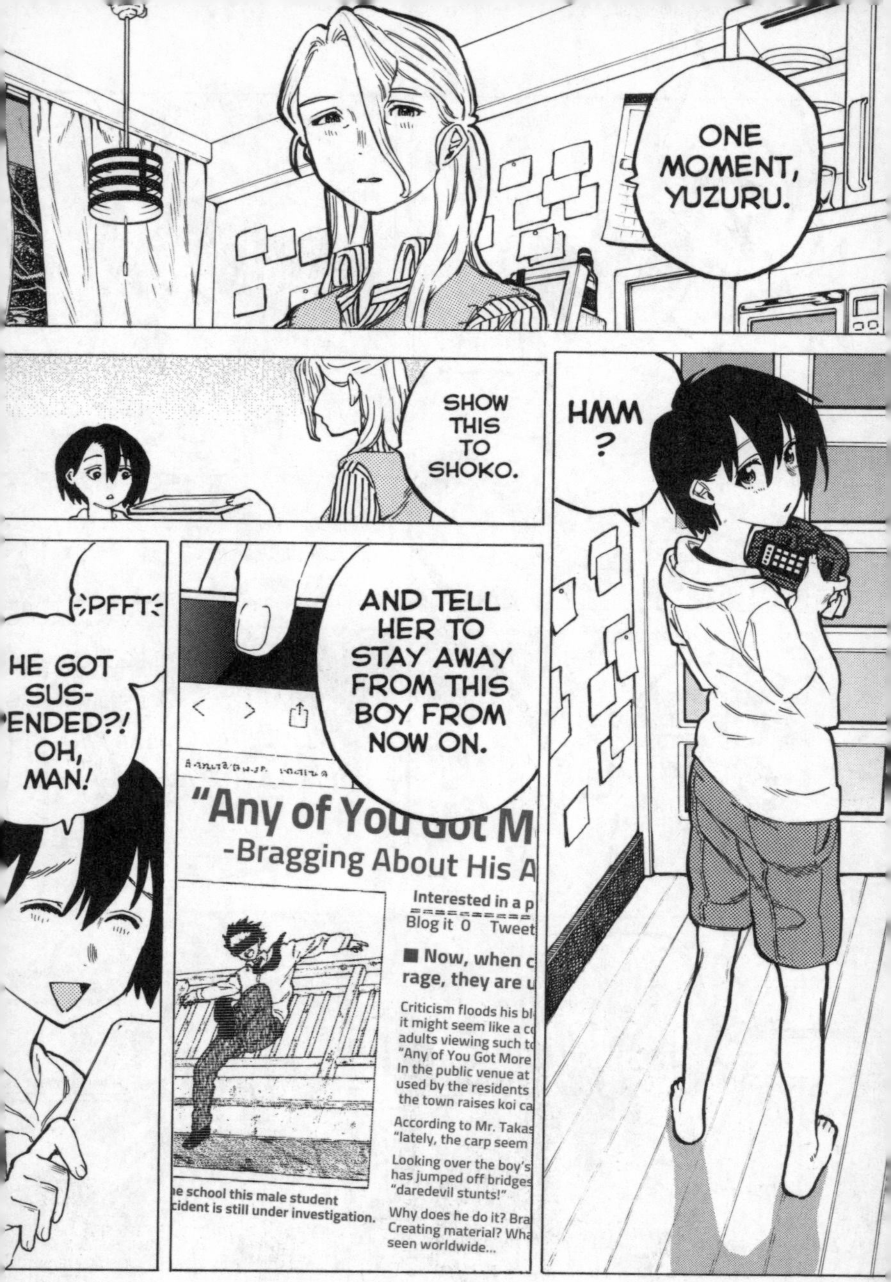
ONE MOMENT, YUZURU.
HMM ?
SHOW THIS TO SHOKO.
AND TELL HER TO STAY AWAY FROM THIS BOY FROM NOW ON.
"Any of You Got M
-Bragging About His A
Interested in a p
Blog it 0 Tweet
■ Now, when c
rage, they are u
Criticism floods his bl
it might seem like a c
adults viewing such t
"Any of You Got More
In the public venue at
used by the residents
the town raises koi ca
According to Mr. Takas
"lately, the carp seem
Looking over the boy's
has jumped off bridges
"daredevil stunts!"
Why does he do it? Bra
Creating material? Wha
seen worldwide...
e school this male student
cident is still under investigation.
PFFT
HE GOT SUS-ENDED?! OH, MAN!

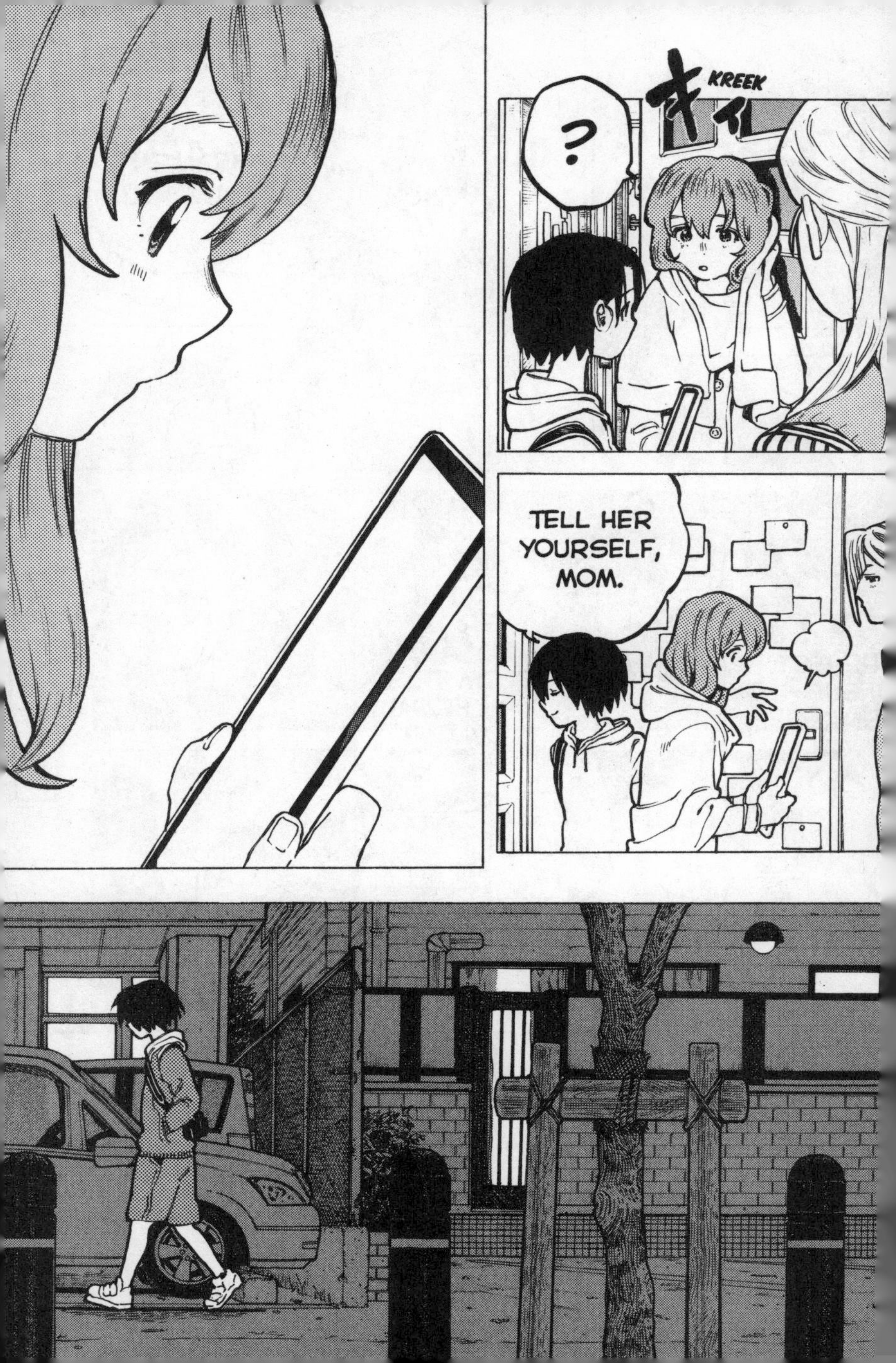
KREEK
キイ
?
TELL HER YOURSELF, MOM.

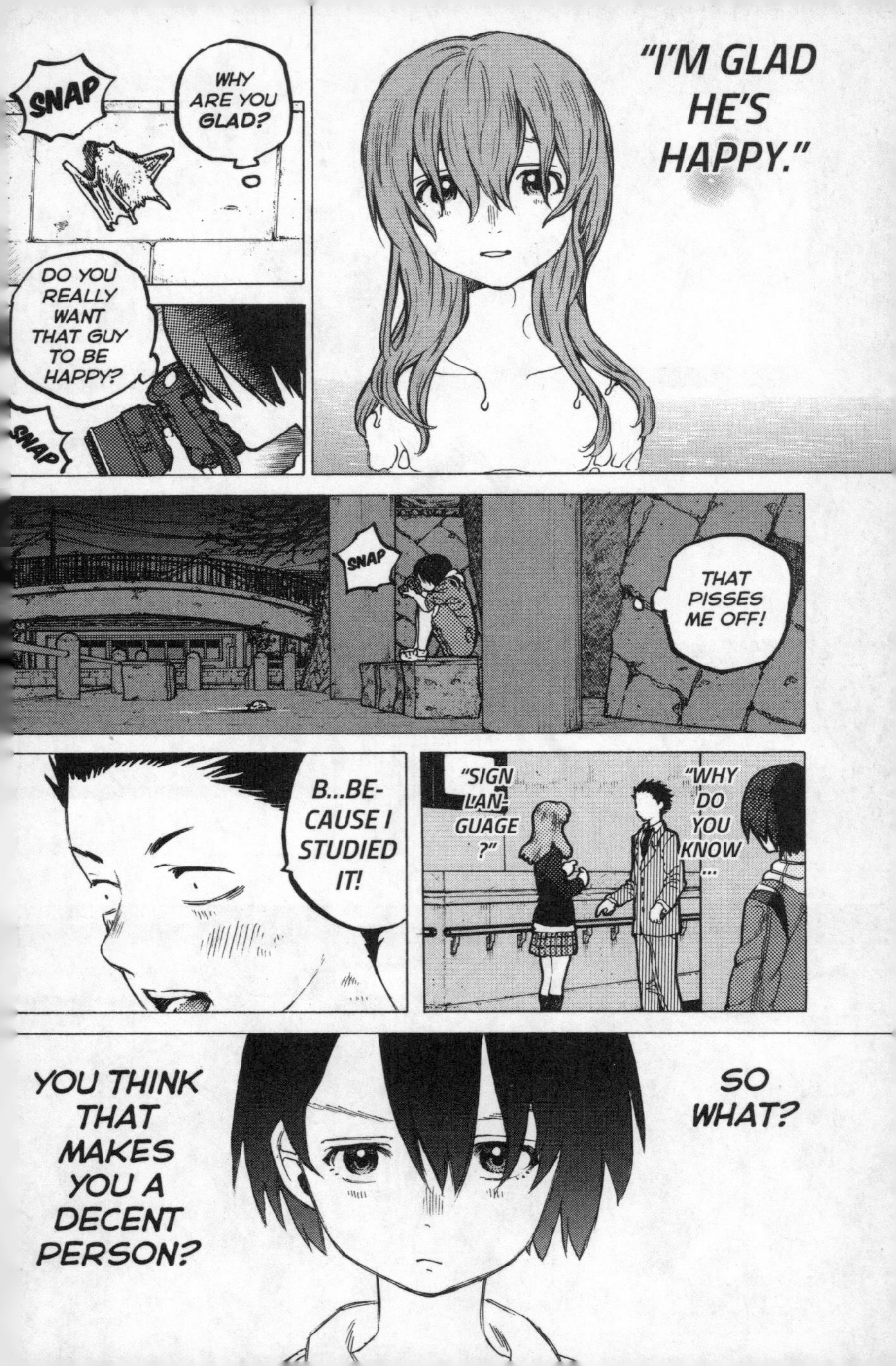
"I'M GLAD HE'S HAPPY."
SNAP
WHY ARE YOU GLAD?
DO YOU REALLY WANT THAT GUY TO BE HAPPY?
SNAP
THAT PISSES ME OFF!
SNAP
"WHY DO YOU KNOW...
"SIGN LANGUAGE?"
B...BECAUSE I STUDIED IT!
SO WHAT?
YOU THINK THAT MAKES YOU A DECENT PERSON?

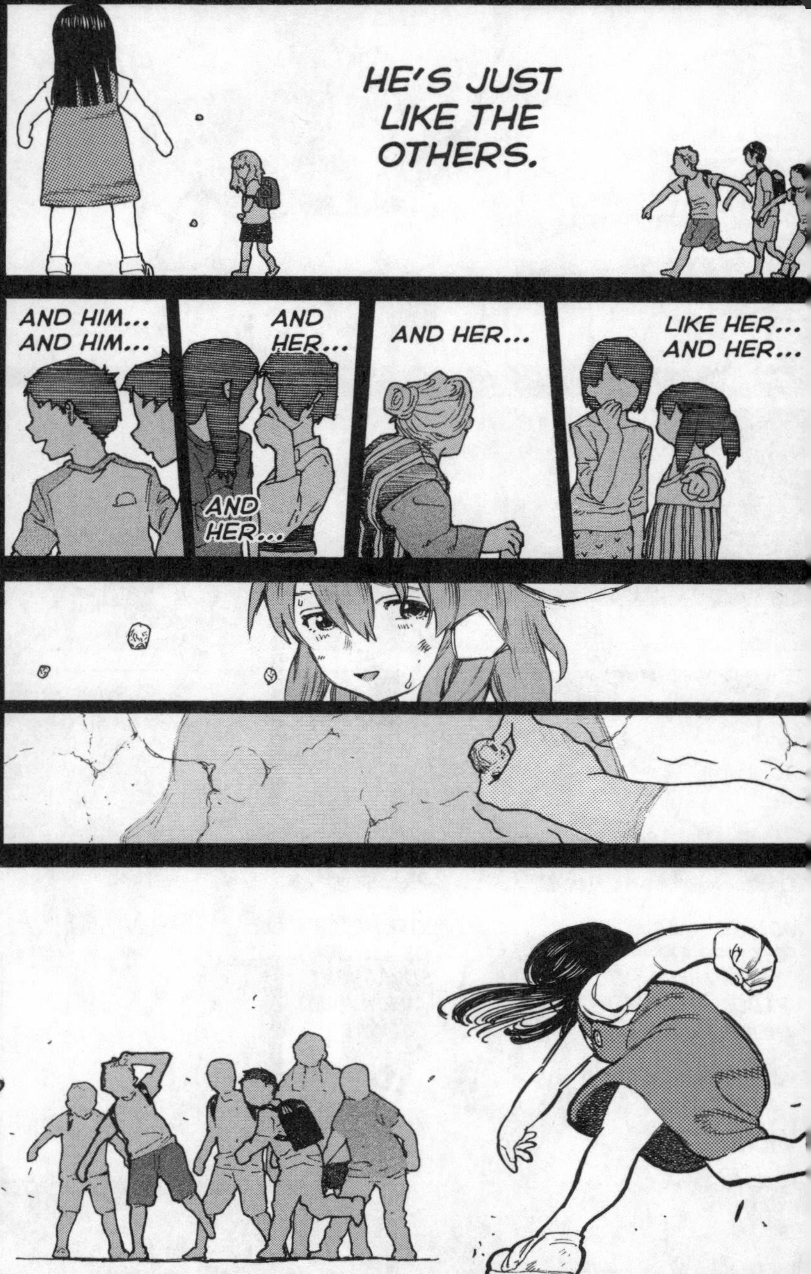
HE'S JUST LIKE THE OTHERS.
LIKE HER... AND HER...
AND HER...
AND HER...
AND HER...
AND HIM... AND HIM...

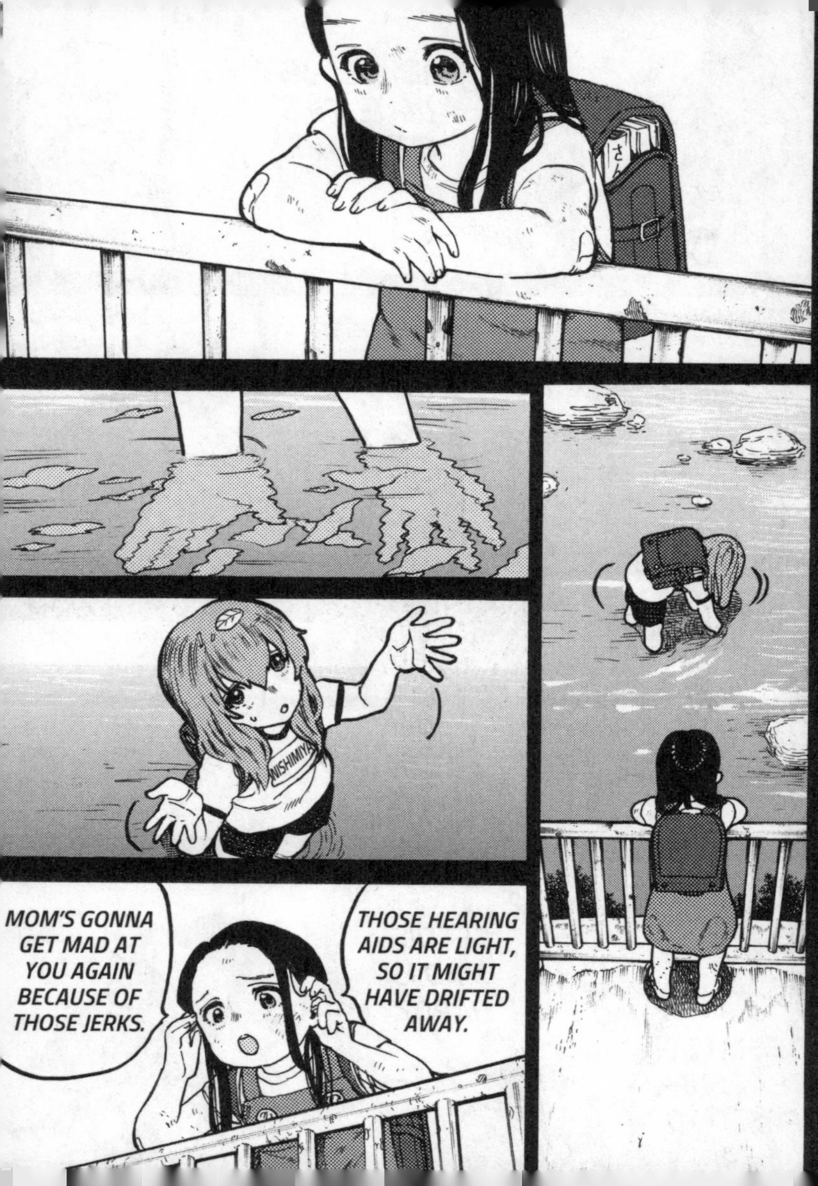
NISHIMIYA
THOSE HEARING AIDS ARE LIGHT, SO IT MIGHT HAVE DRIFTED AWAY.
MOM'S GONNA GET MAD AT YOU AGAIN BECAUSE OF THOSE JERKS.

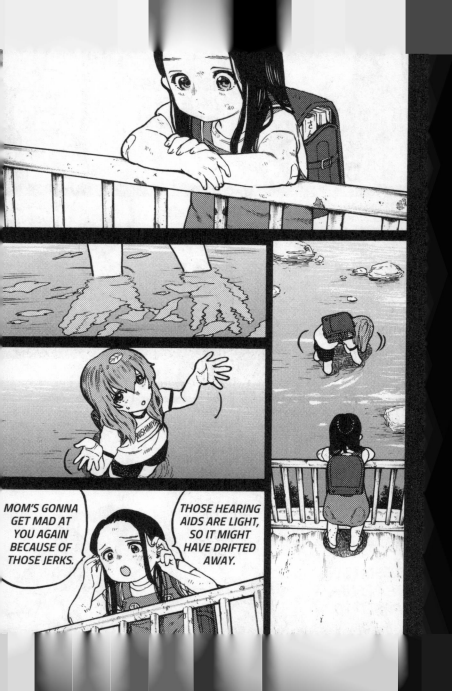

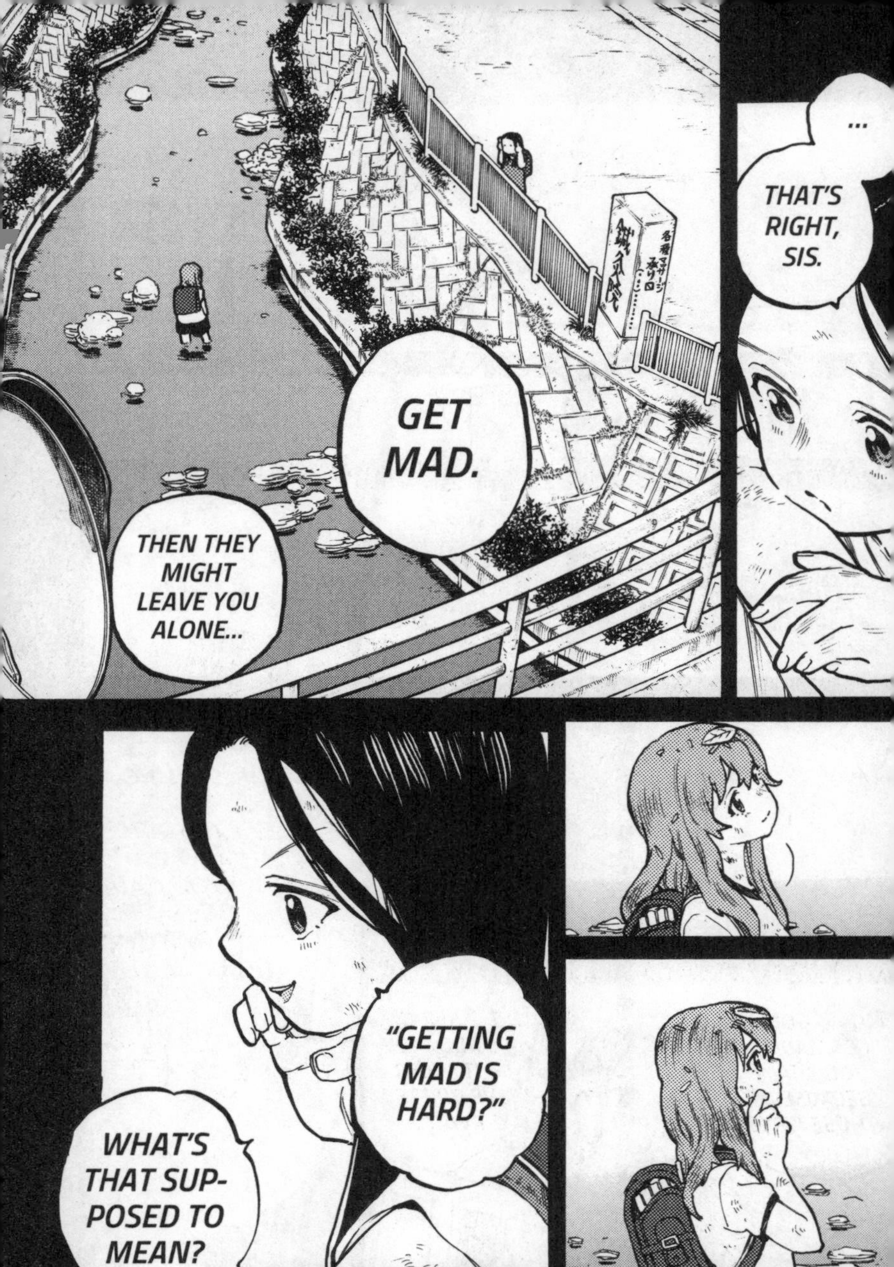
...
THAT'S RIGHT, SIS.
GET MAD.
THEN THEY MIGHT LEAVE YOU ALONE...
"GETTING MAD IS HARD?"
WHAT'S THAT SUP-POSED TO MEAN?

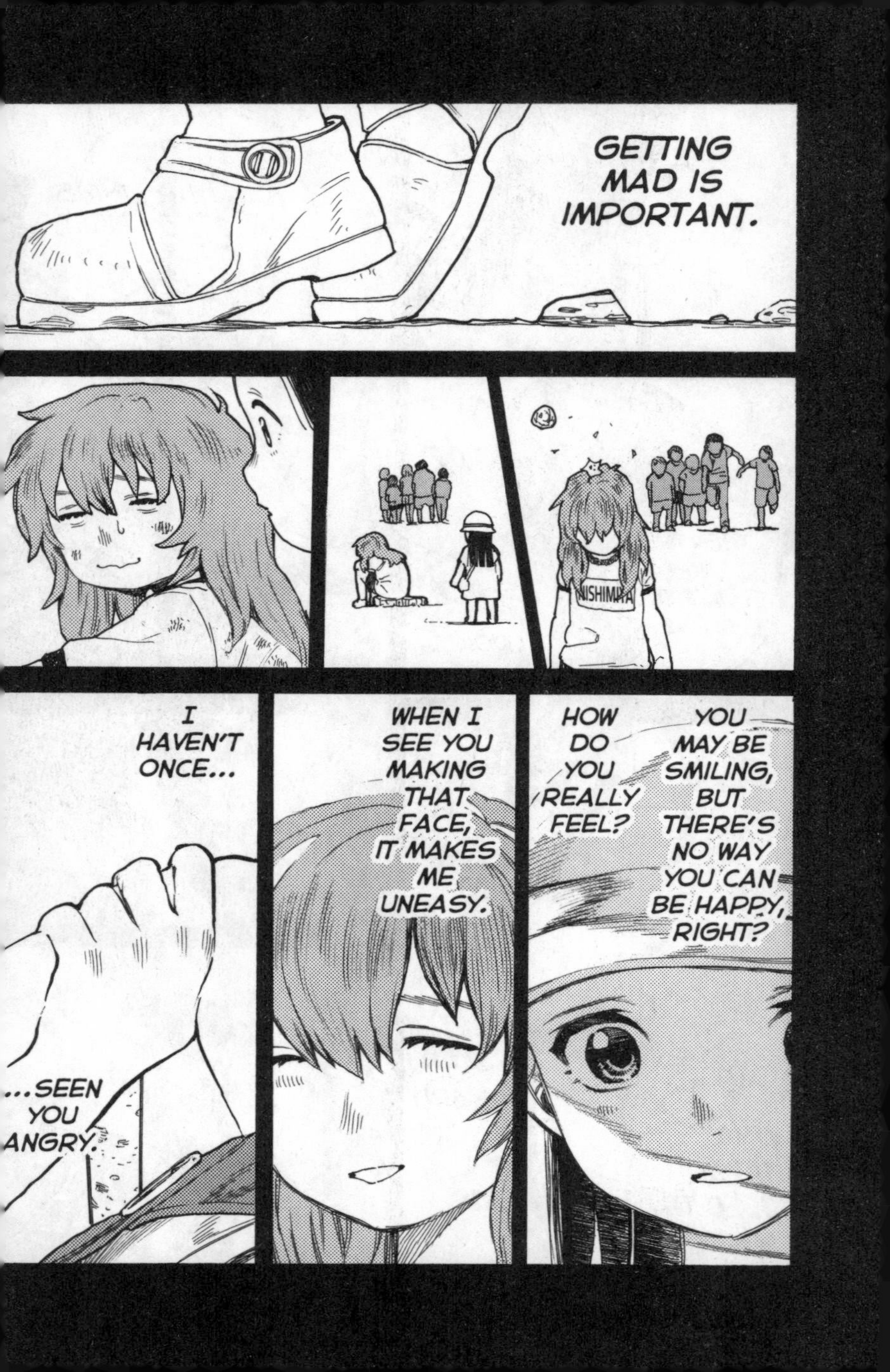
GETTING MAD IS IMPORTANT.
YOU MAY BE SMILING, BUT THERE'S NO WAY YOU CAN BE HAPPY, RIGHT?
HOW DO YOU REALLY FEEL?
WHEN I SEE YOU MAKING THAT FACE, IT MAKES ME UNEASY.
I HAVEN'T ONCE...
...SEEN YOU ANGRY.

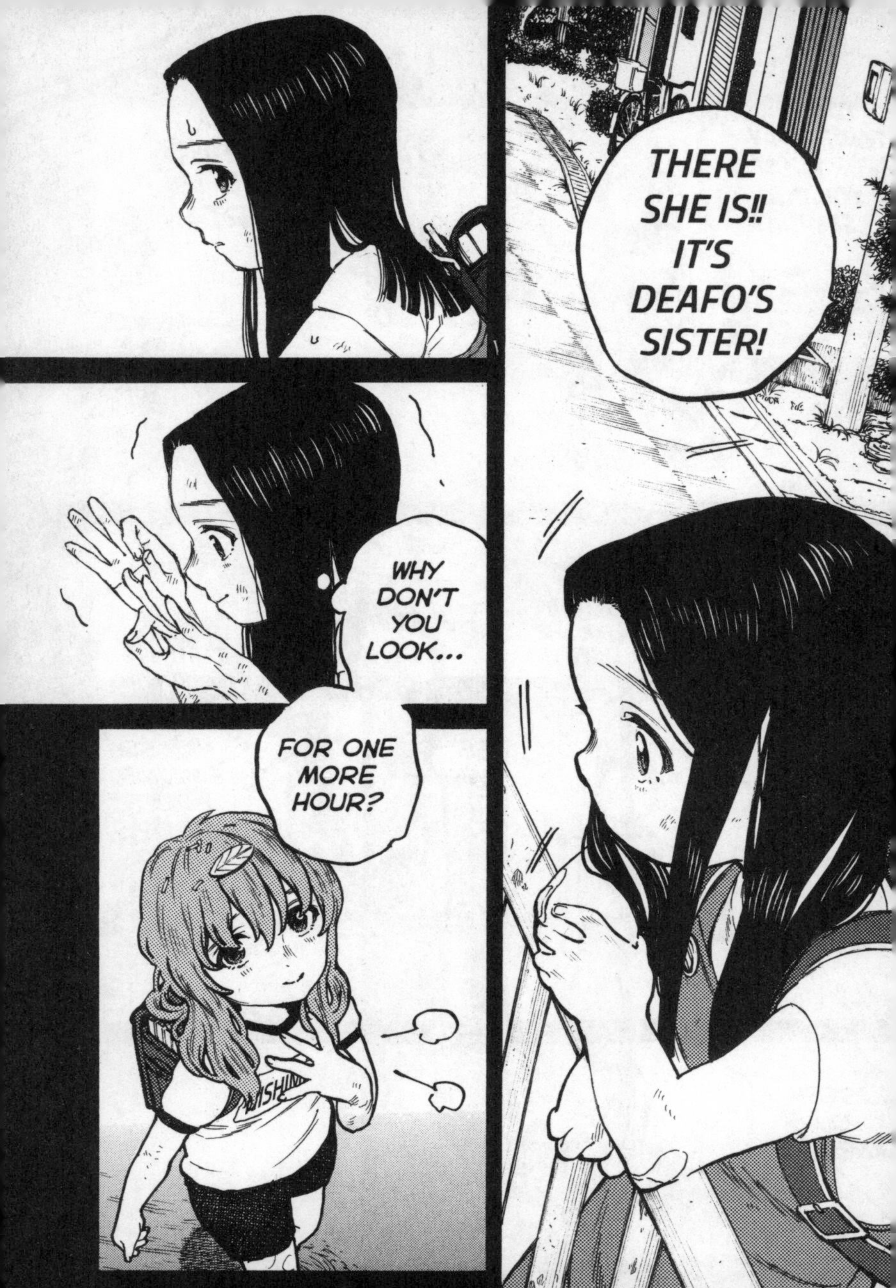
THERE SHE IS!! IT'S DEAFO'S SISTER!
WHY DON'T YOU LOOK...
FOR ONE MORE HOUR?

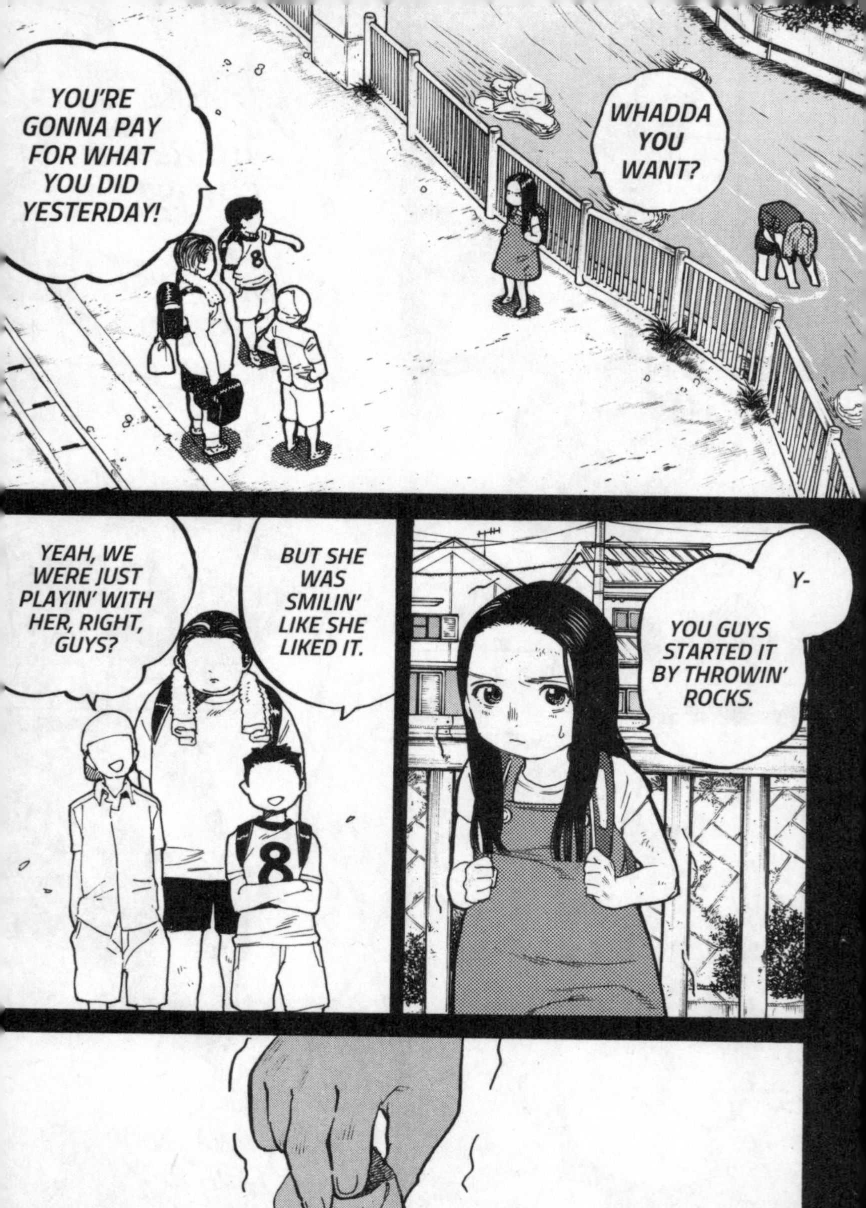
WHADDA YOU WANT?
YOU'RE GONNA PAY FOR WHAT YOU DID YESTERDAY!
Y-
YOU GUYS STARTED IT BY THROWIN' ROCKS.
BUT SHE WAS SMILIN' LIKE SHE LIKED IT.
YEAH, WE WERE JUST PLAYIN' WITH HER, RIGHT, GUYS?

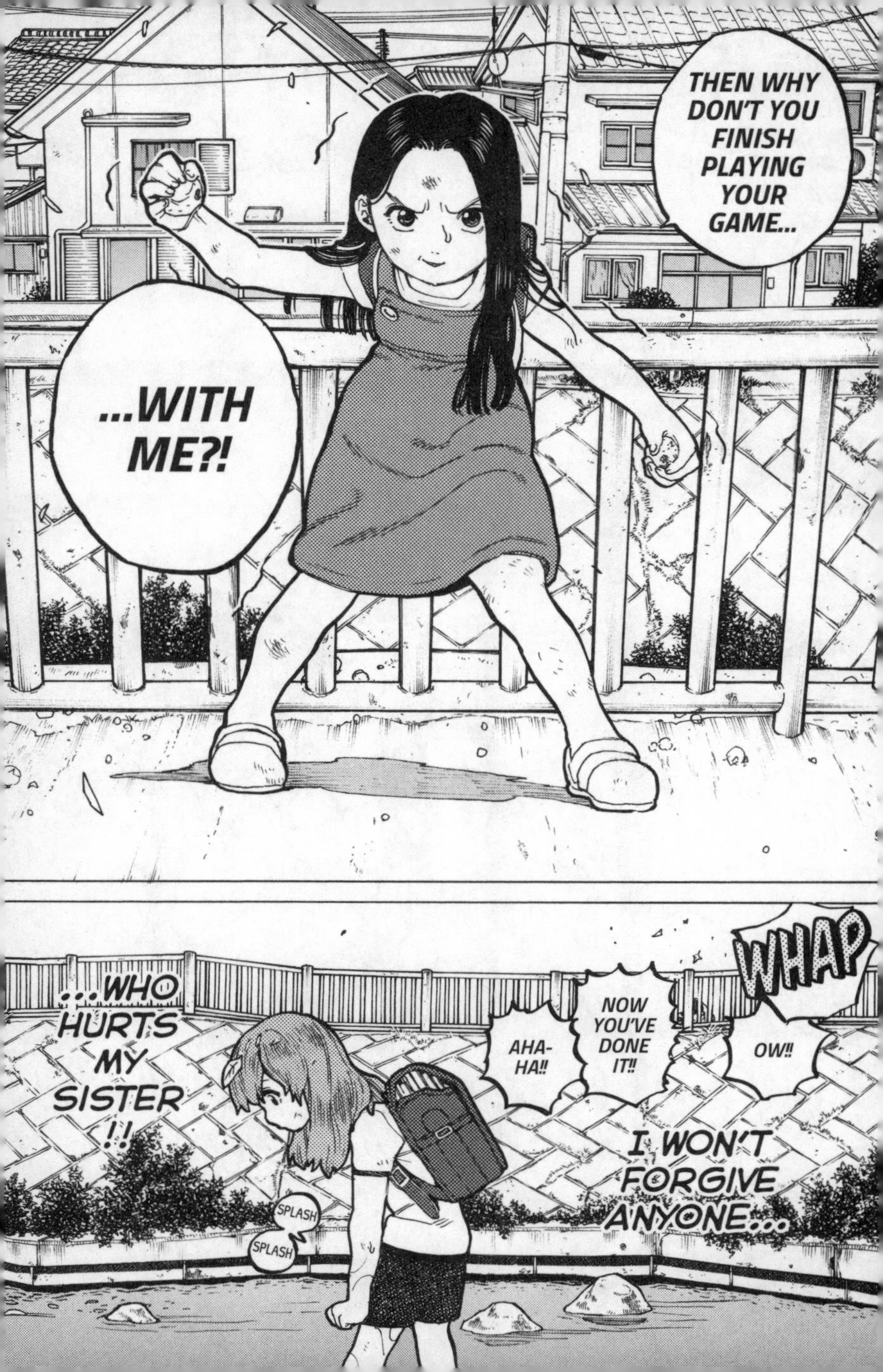
THEN WHY DON'T YOU FINISH PLAYING YOUR GAME...
...WITH ME?!
WHAP
OW!!
NOW YOU'VE DONE IT!!
AHA-HA!!
I WON'T FORGIVE ANYONE...
...WHO HURTS MY SISTER!!
SPLASH
SPLASH

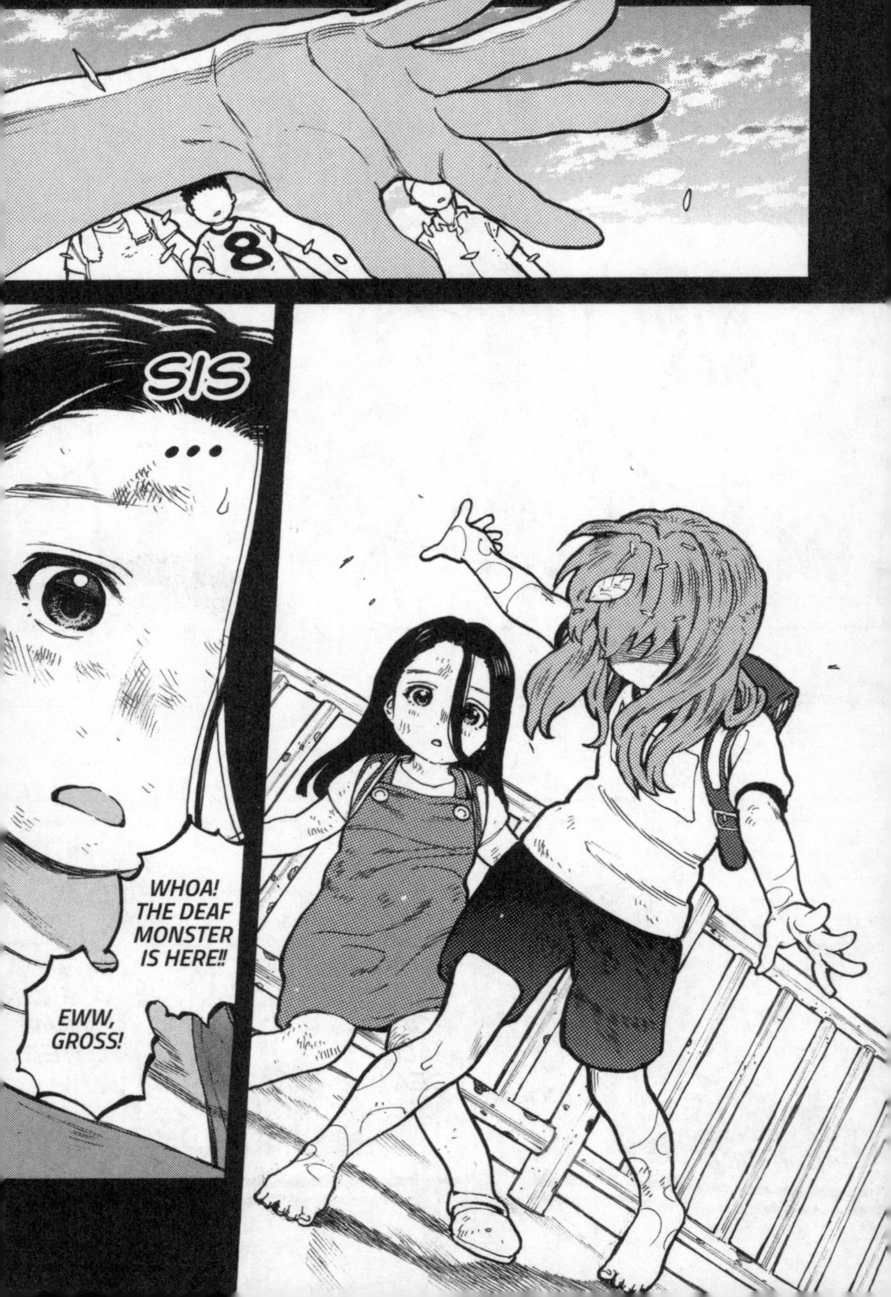
SIS
...
WHOA! THE DEAF MONSTER IS HERE!!
EWW, GROSS!

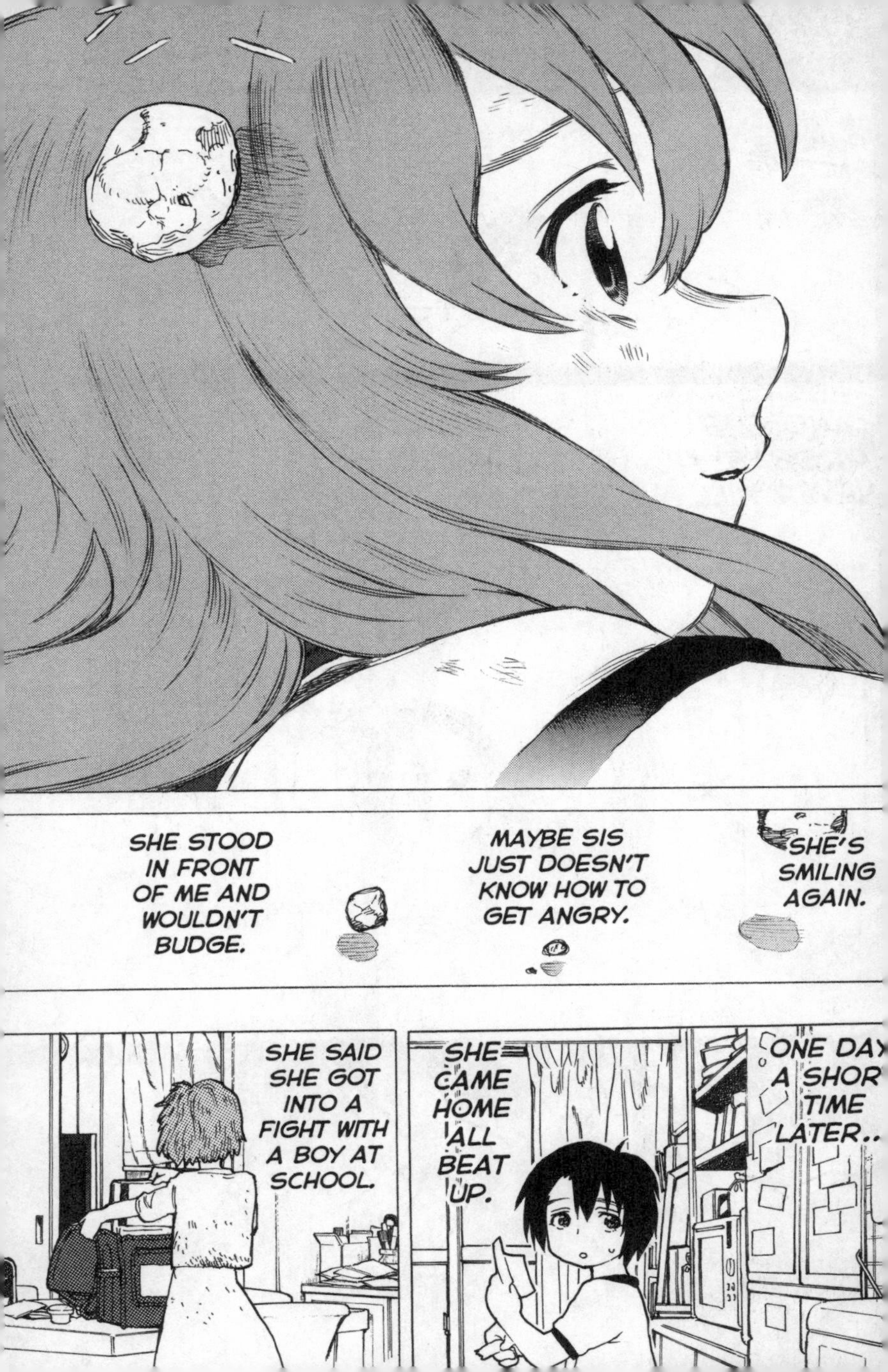
SHE'S SMILING AGAIN.
MAYBE SIS JUST DOESN'T KNOW HOW TO GET ANGRY.
SHE STOOD IN FRONT OF ME AND WOULDN'T BUDGE.
ONE DAY A SHOR TIME LATER..
SHE CAME HOME ALL BEAT UP.
SHE SAID SHE GOT INTO A FIGHT WITH A BOY AT SCHOOL.

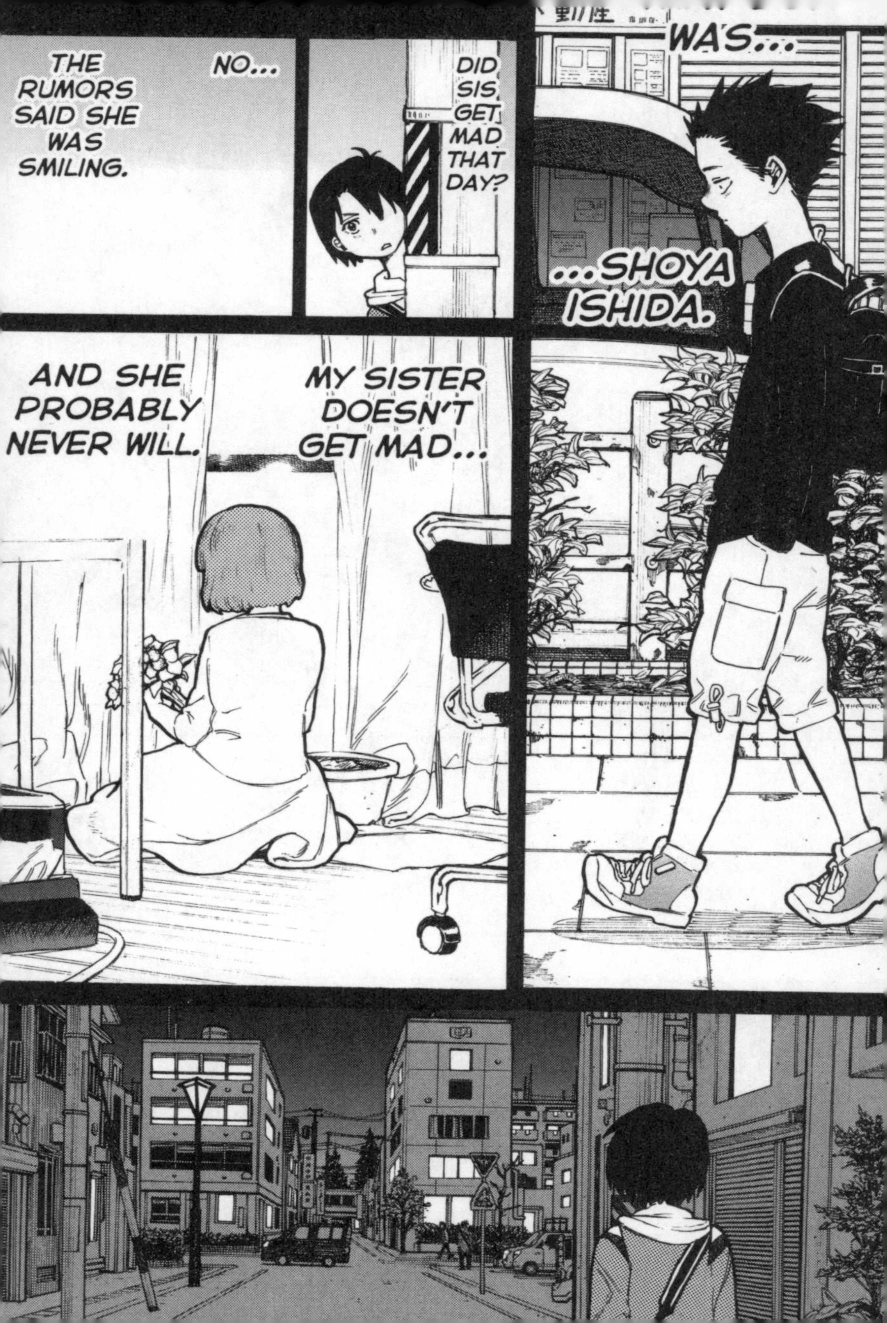
WAS...
...SHOYA ISHIDA.
DID SIS GET MAD THAT DAY?
NO...
THE RUMORS SAID SHE WAS SMILING.
MY SISTER DOESN'T GET MAD...
AND SHE PROBABLY NEVER WILL.

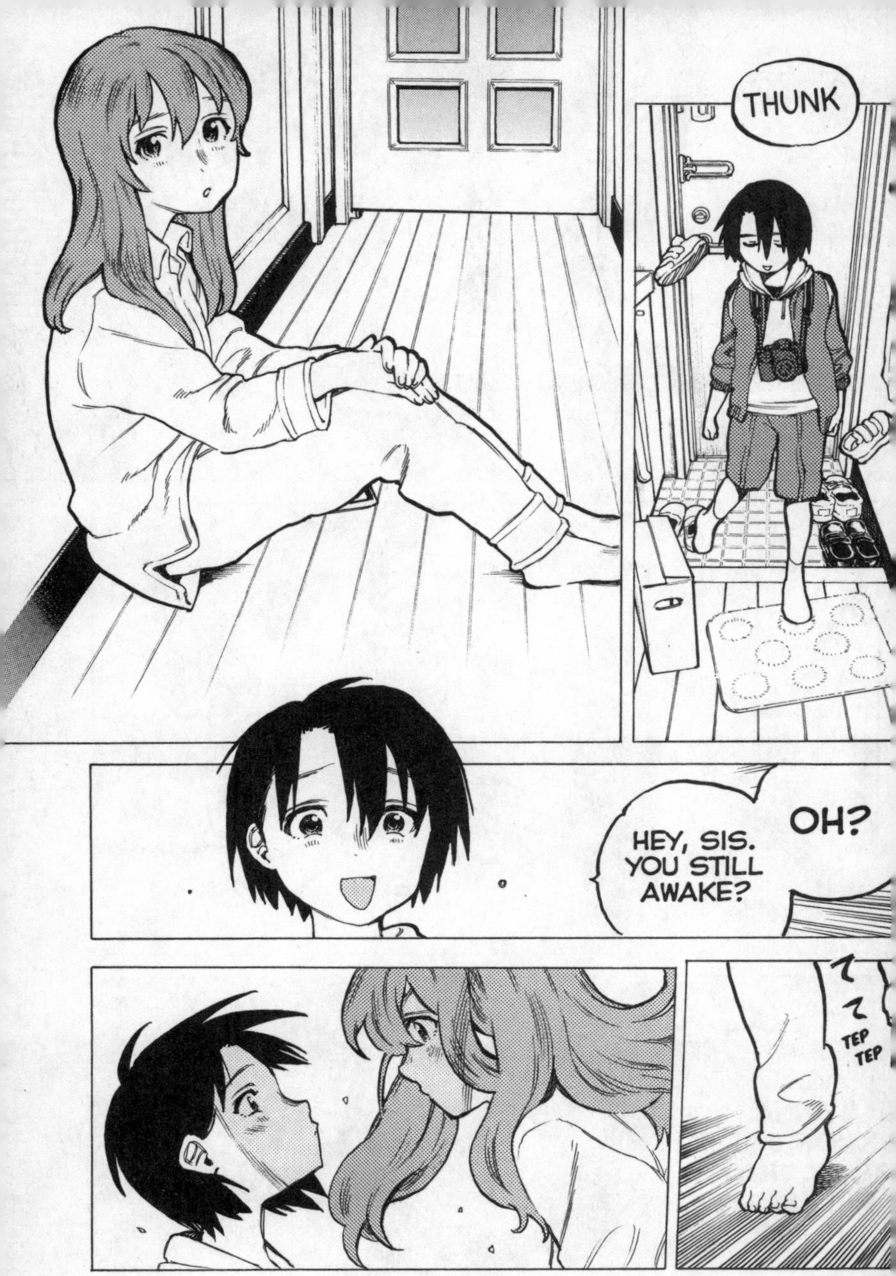
THUNK
OH?
HEY, SIS. YOU STILL AWAKE?
TEP TEP

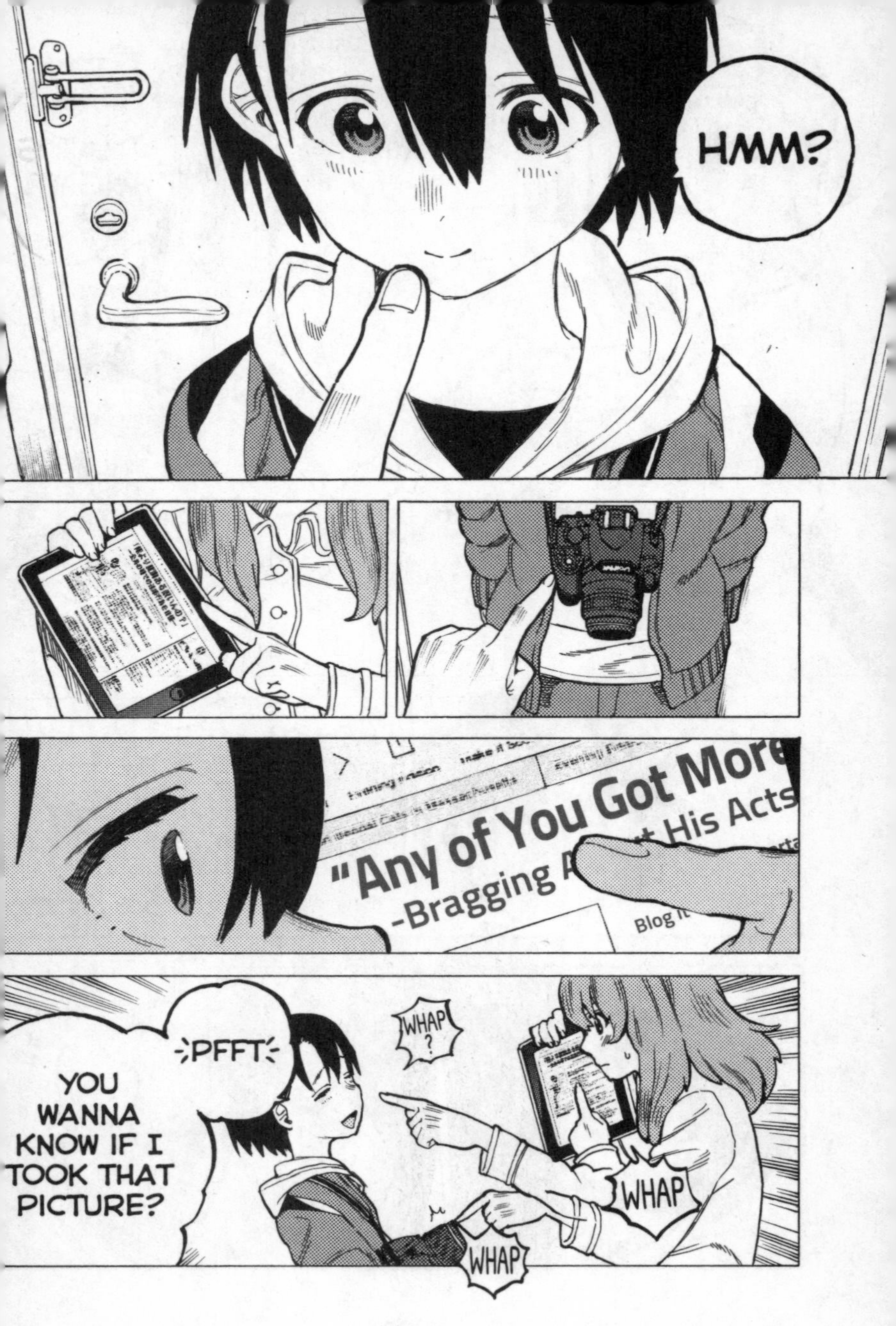
HMM?
"Any of You Got More
-Bragging
His Acts
Blog it
WHAP ?
WHAP
WHAP
PFFT
YOU WANNA KNOW IF I TOOK THAT PICTURE?

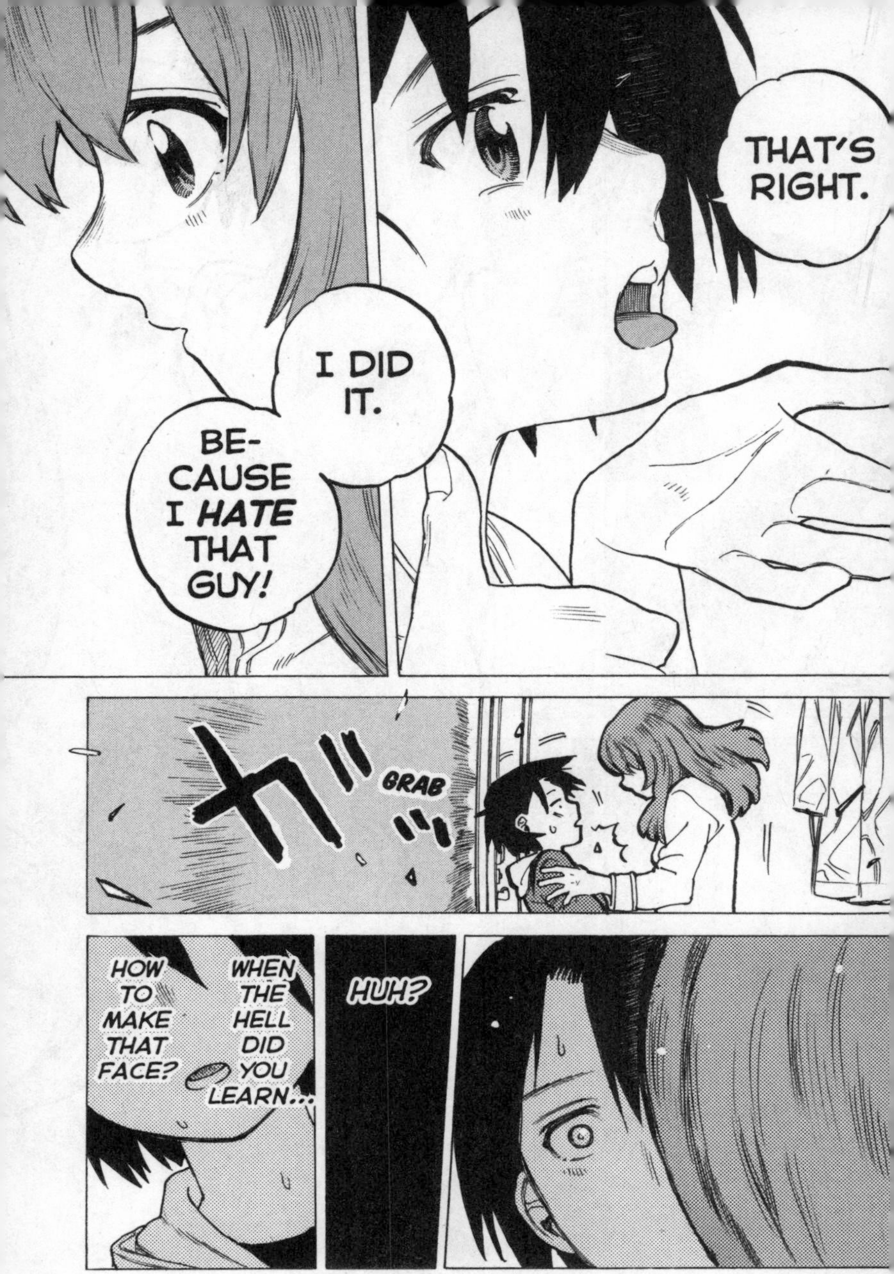
THAT'S RIGHT.
I DID IT.
BE-CAUSE I *HATE* THAT GUY!
ガッ
GRAB
HUH?
WHEN THE HELL DID YOU LEARN...
HOW TO MAKE THAT FACE?

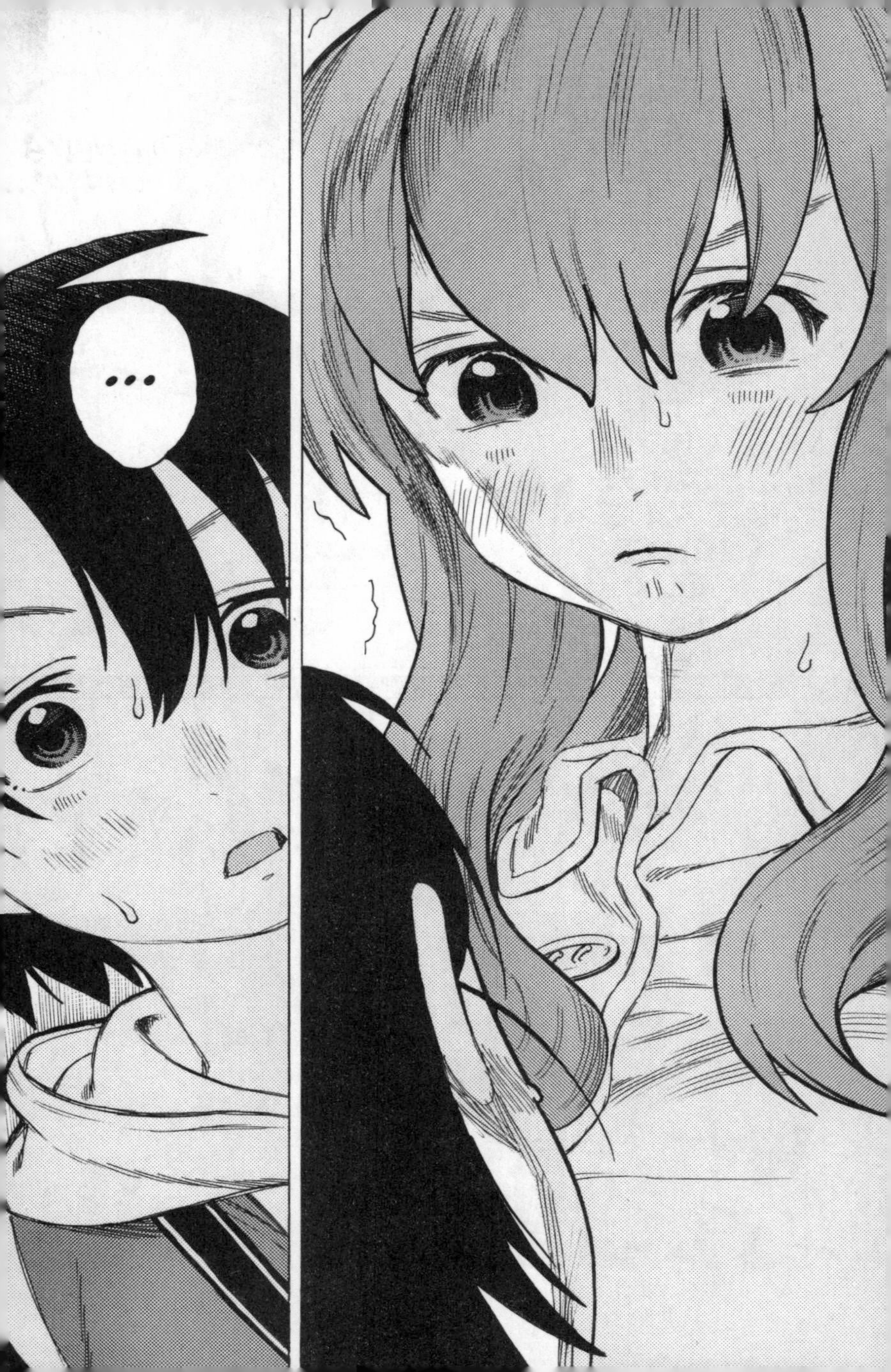
...

CHAPTER 12: SIS

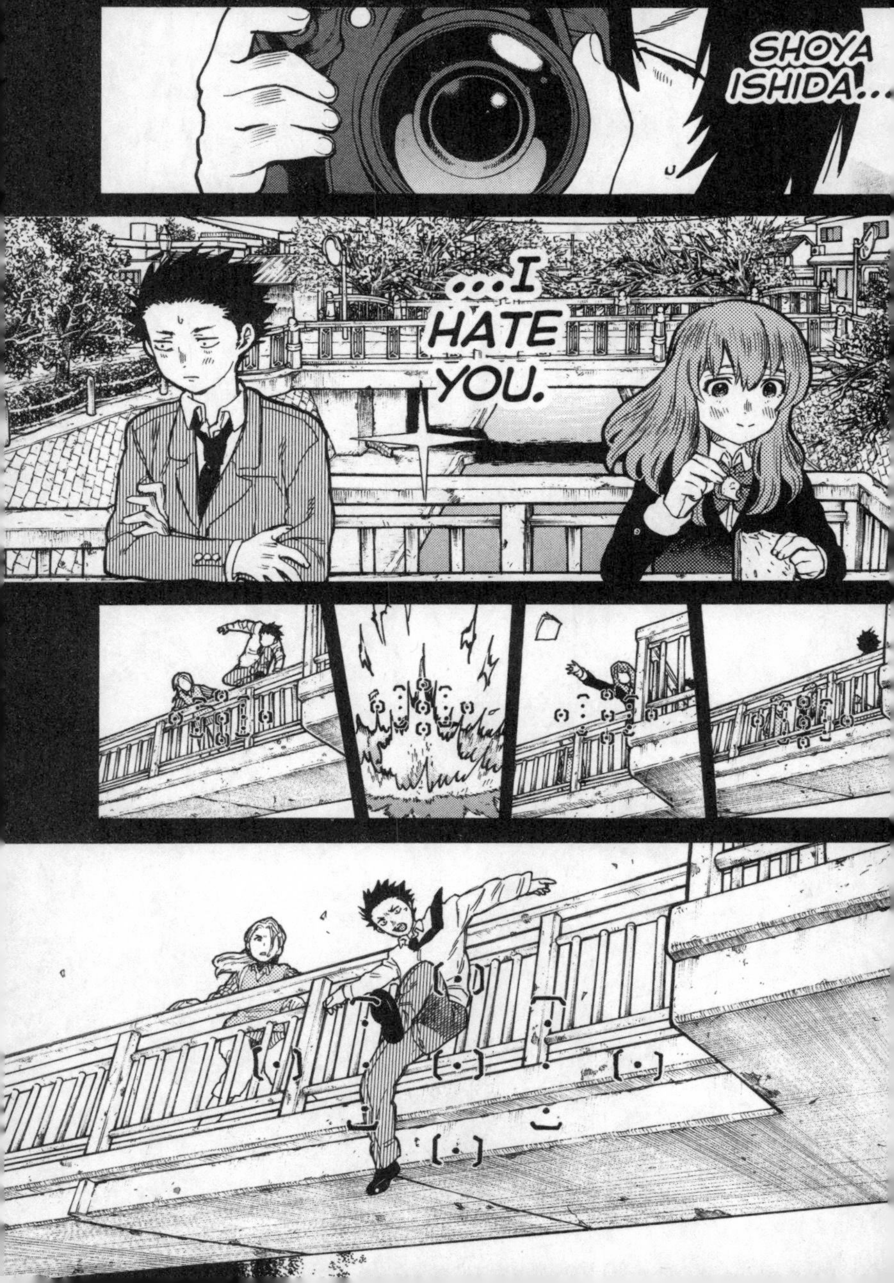
SHOYA ISHIDA...
...I HATE YOU.

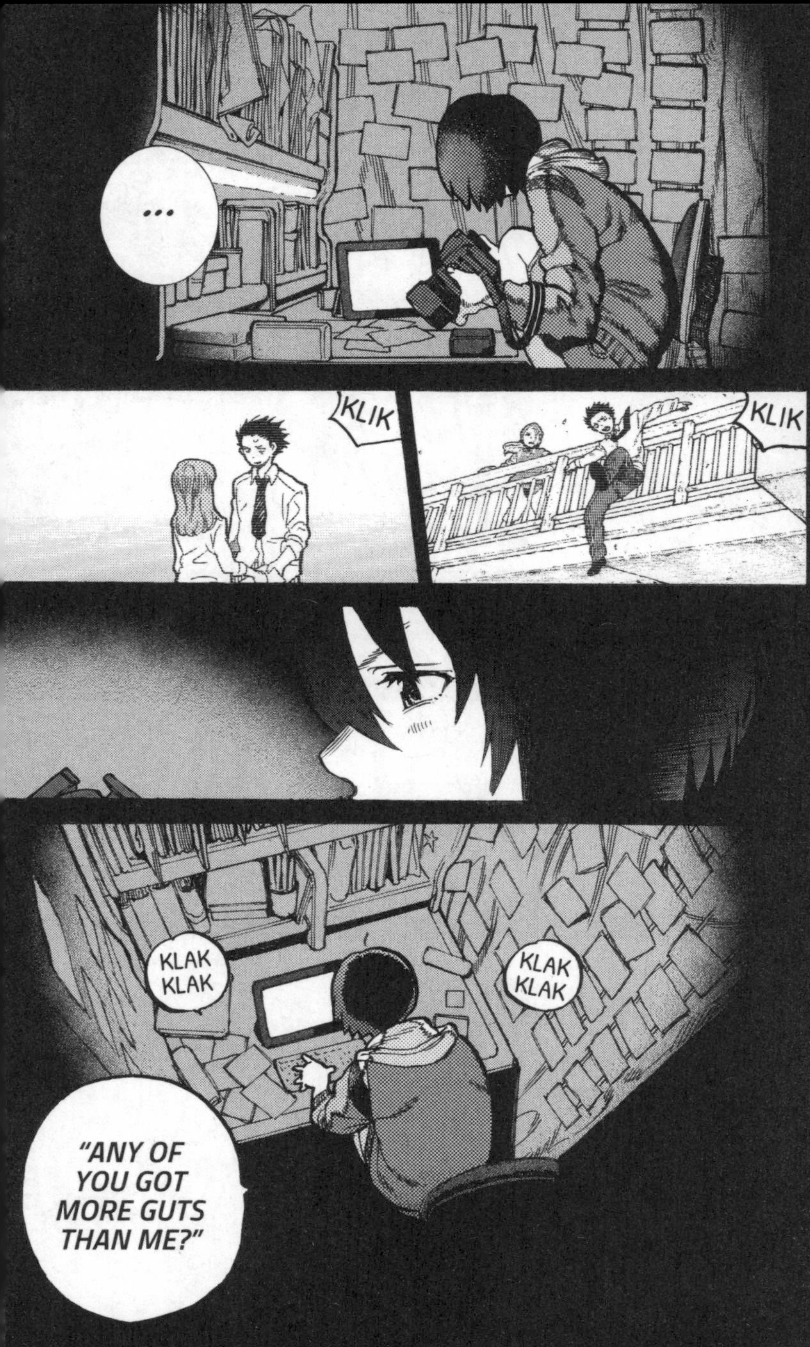
...
KLIK
KLIK
KLAK KLAK
KLAK KLAK
"ANY OF YOU GOT MORE GUTS THAN ME?"

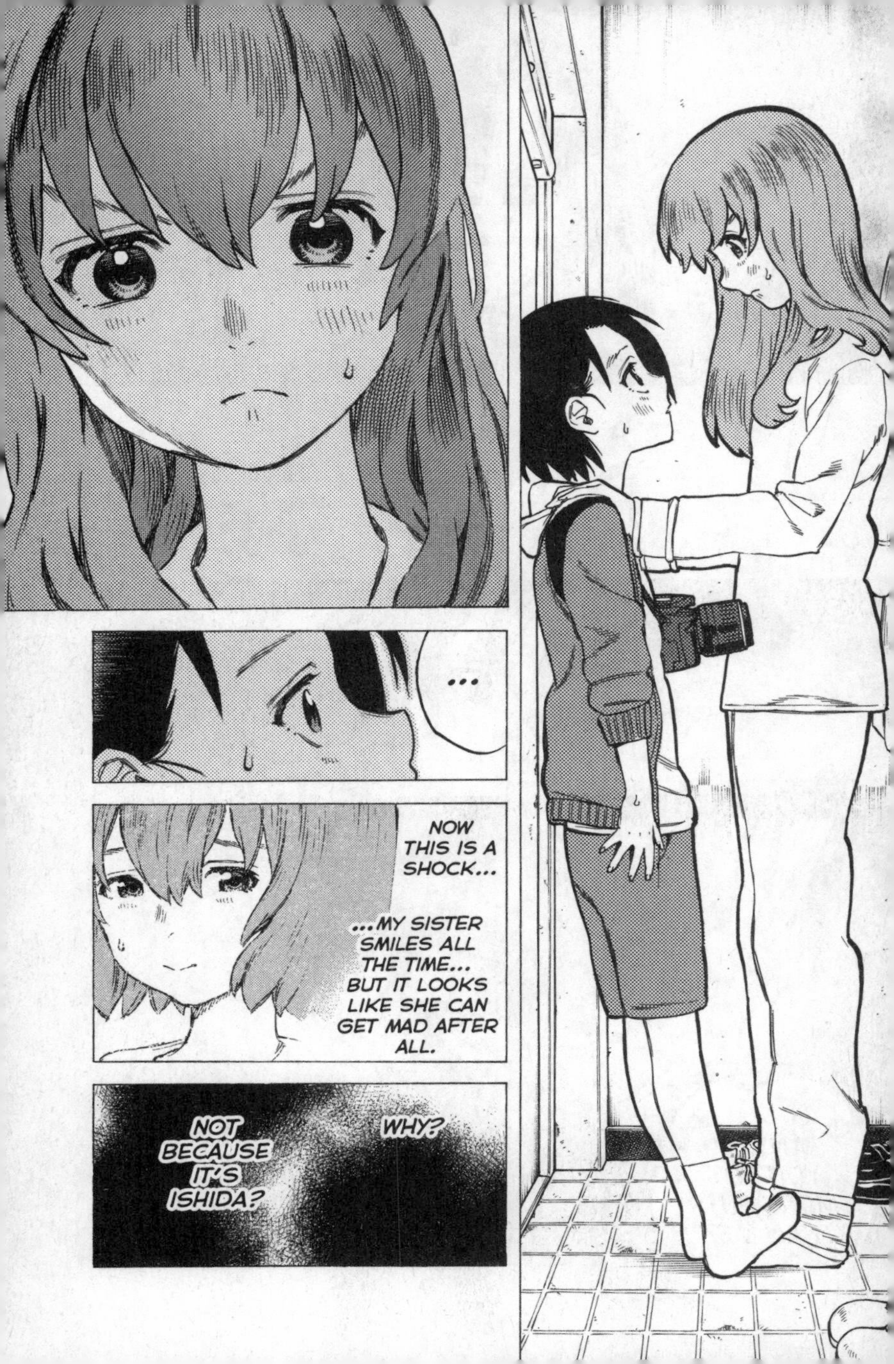
...
NOW THIS IS A SHOCK...
...MY SISTER SMILES ALL THE TIME... BUT IT LOOKS LIKE SHE CAN GET MAD AFTER ALL.
WHY?
NOT BECAUSE IT'S ISHIDA?

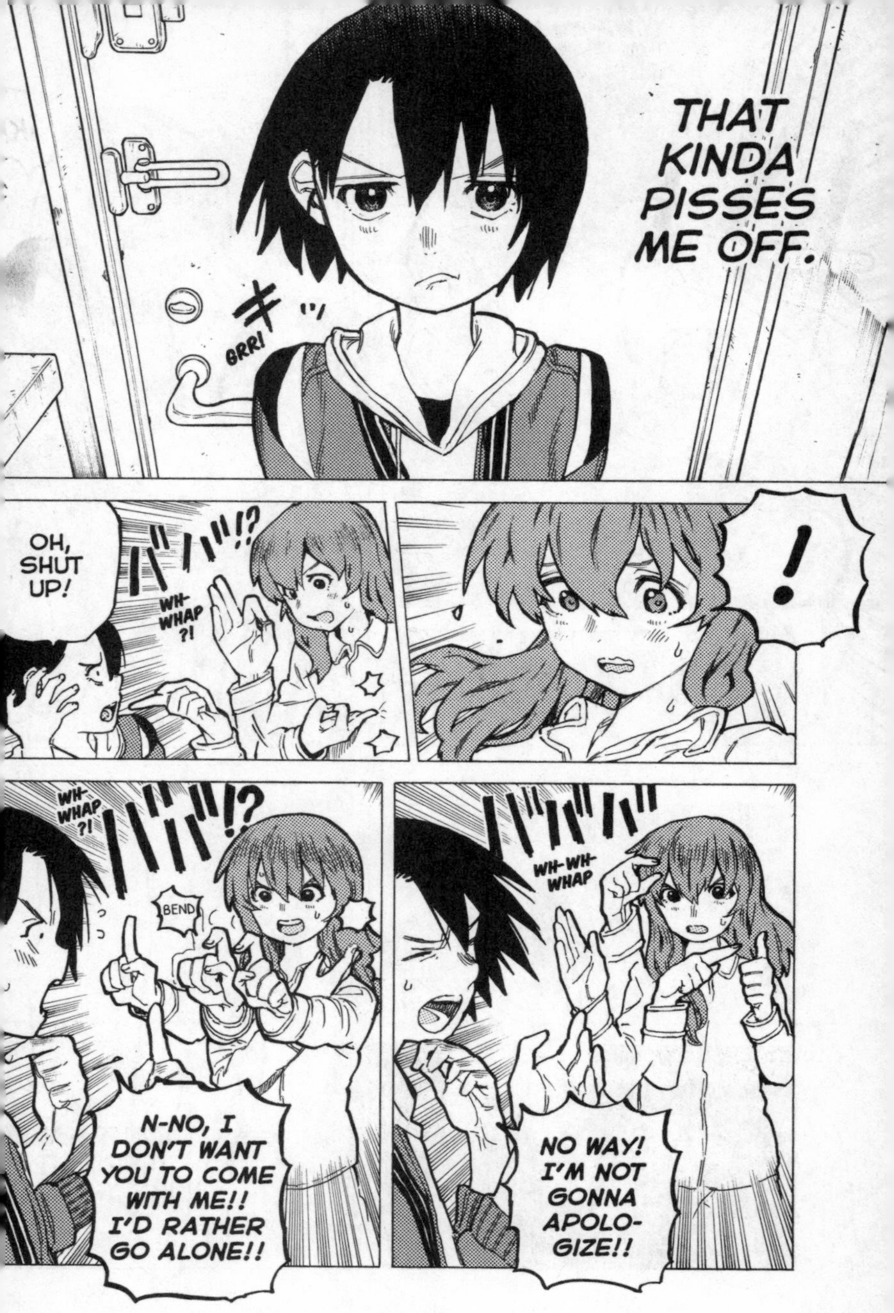
THAT KINDA PISSES ME OFF.
GRR!
!
OH, SHUT UP!
WH-WHAP ?!
WH-WH-WHAP
NO WAY! I'M NOT GONNA APOLO-GIZE!!
WH-WHAP ?!
BEND
N-NO, I DON'T WANT YOU TO COME WITH ME!! I'D RATHER GO ALONE!!

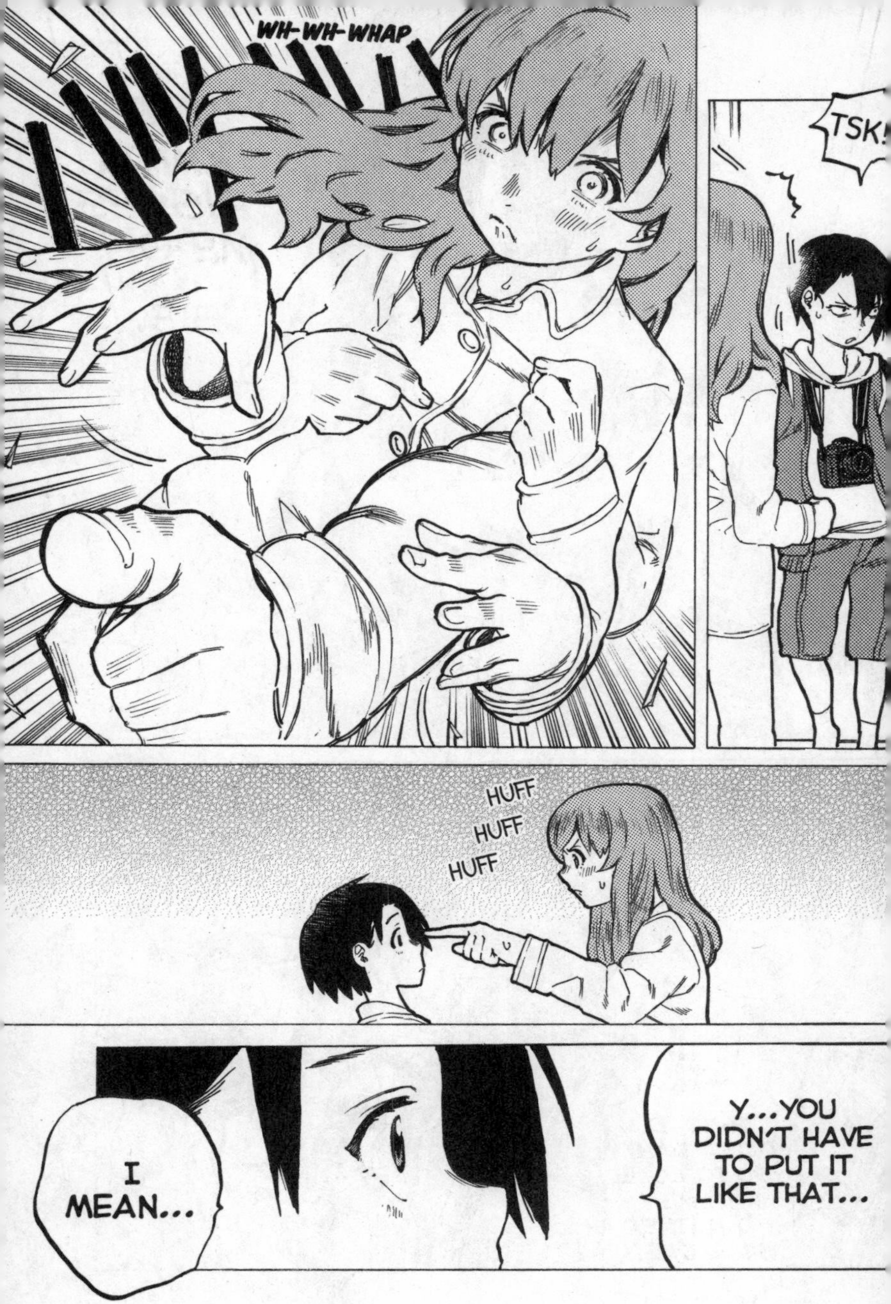
TSK!
WH-WH-WHAP
HUFF
HUFF
HUFF
Y...YOU DIDN'T HAVE TO PUT IT LIKE THAT...
I MEAN...

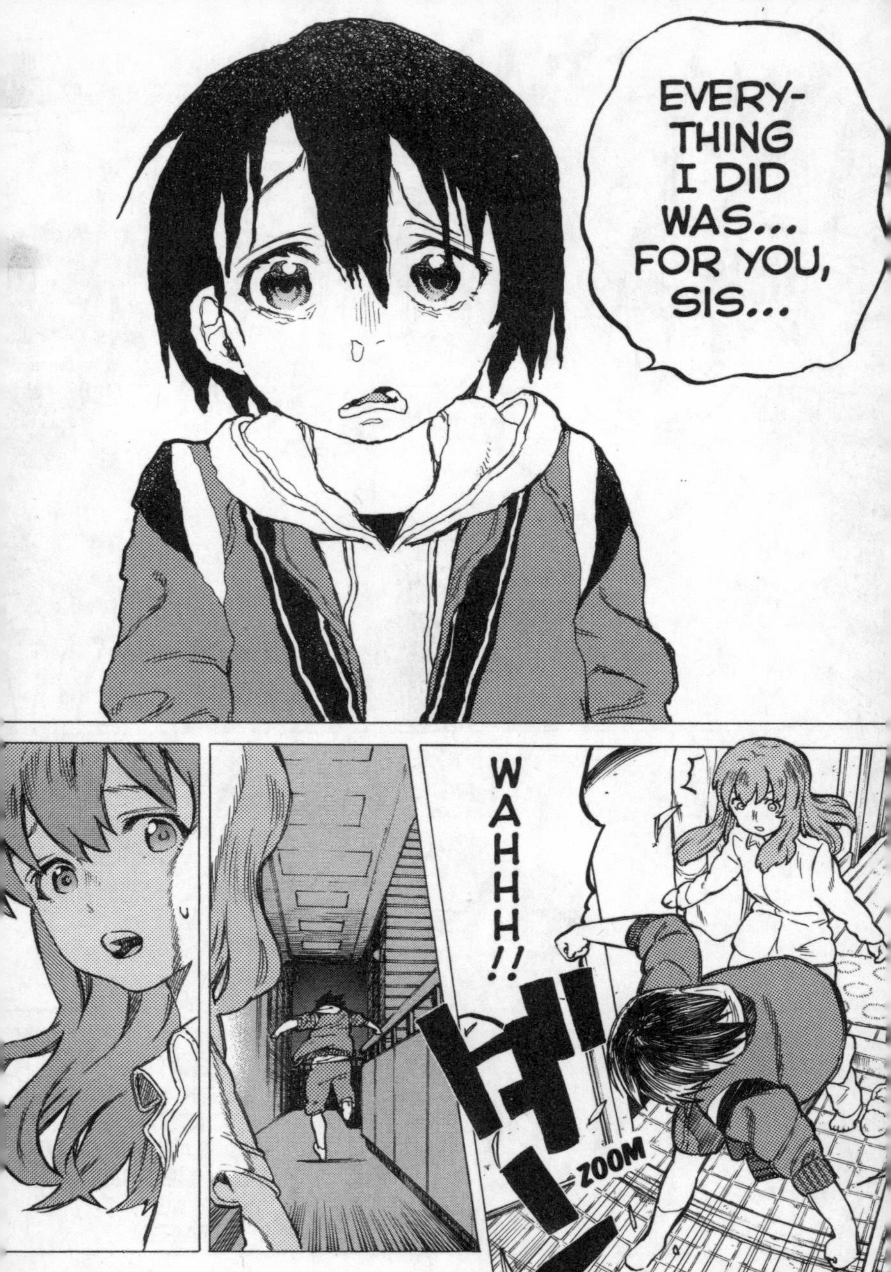
EVERY-THING I DID WAS... FOR YOU, SIS...
WAHHH!!
ZOOM

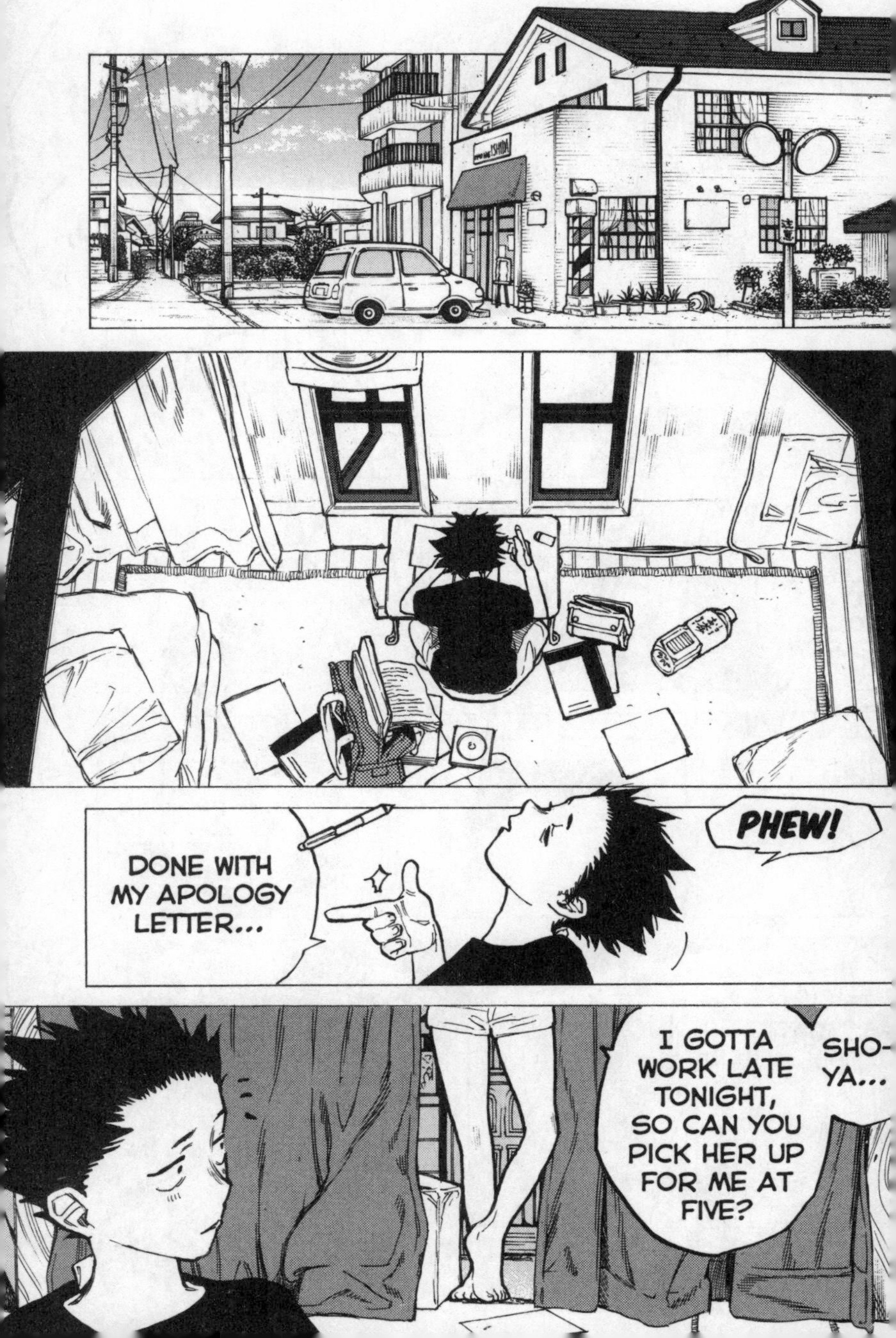
ISHIDA
PHEW!
DONE WITH MY APOLOGY LETTER...
SHO-YA...
I GOTTA WORK LATE TONIGHT, SO CAN YOU PICK HER UP FOR ME AT FIVE?

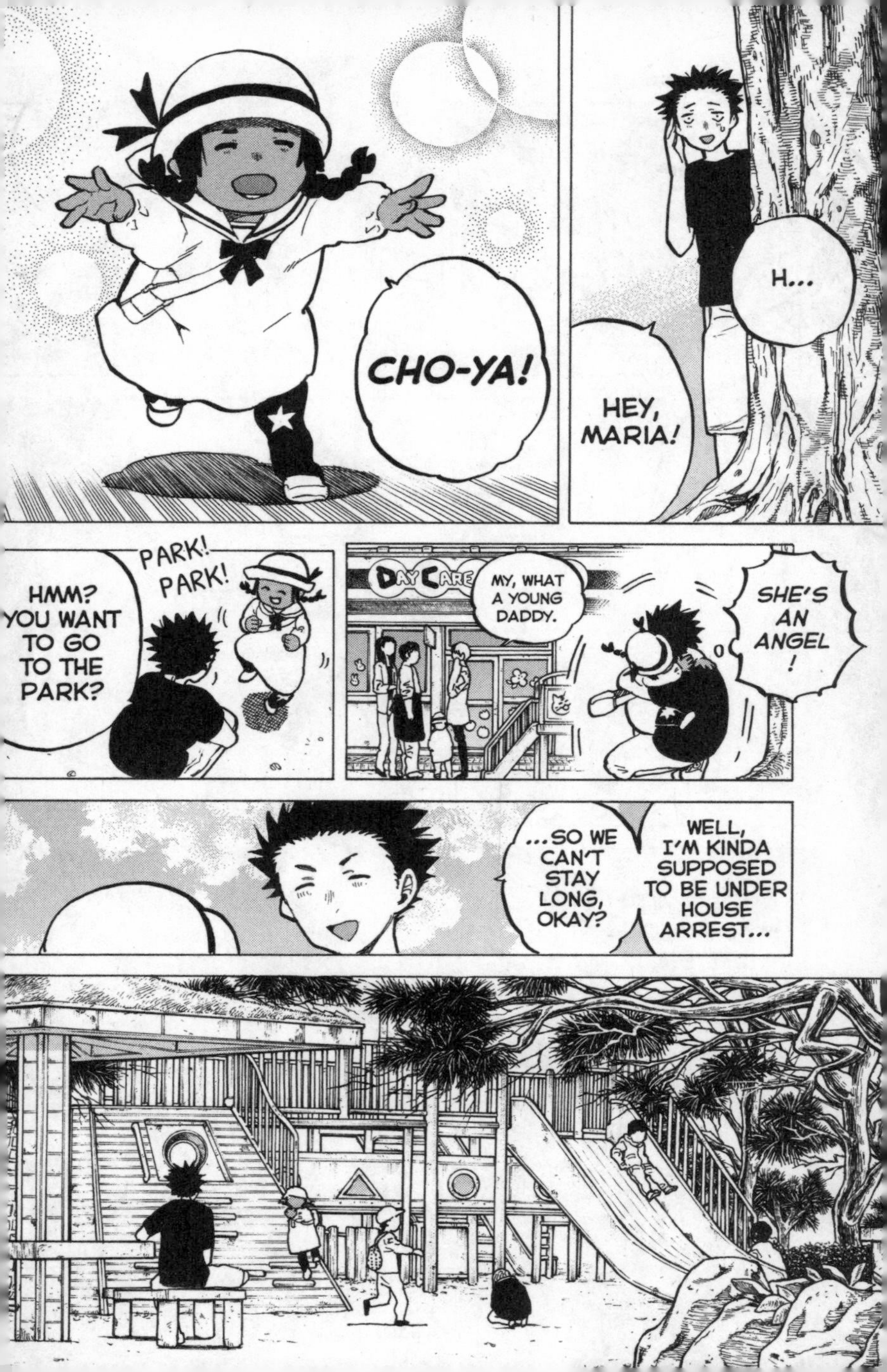
H...
HEY, MARIA!
CHO-YA!
SHE'S AN ANGEL!
MY, WHAT A YOUNG DADDY.
DAY CARE
PARK! PARK!
HMM? YOU WANT TO GO TO THE PARK?
WELL, I'M KINDA SUPPOSED TO BE UNDER HOUSE ARREST...
...SO WE CAN'T STAY LONG, OKAY?

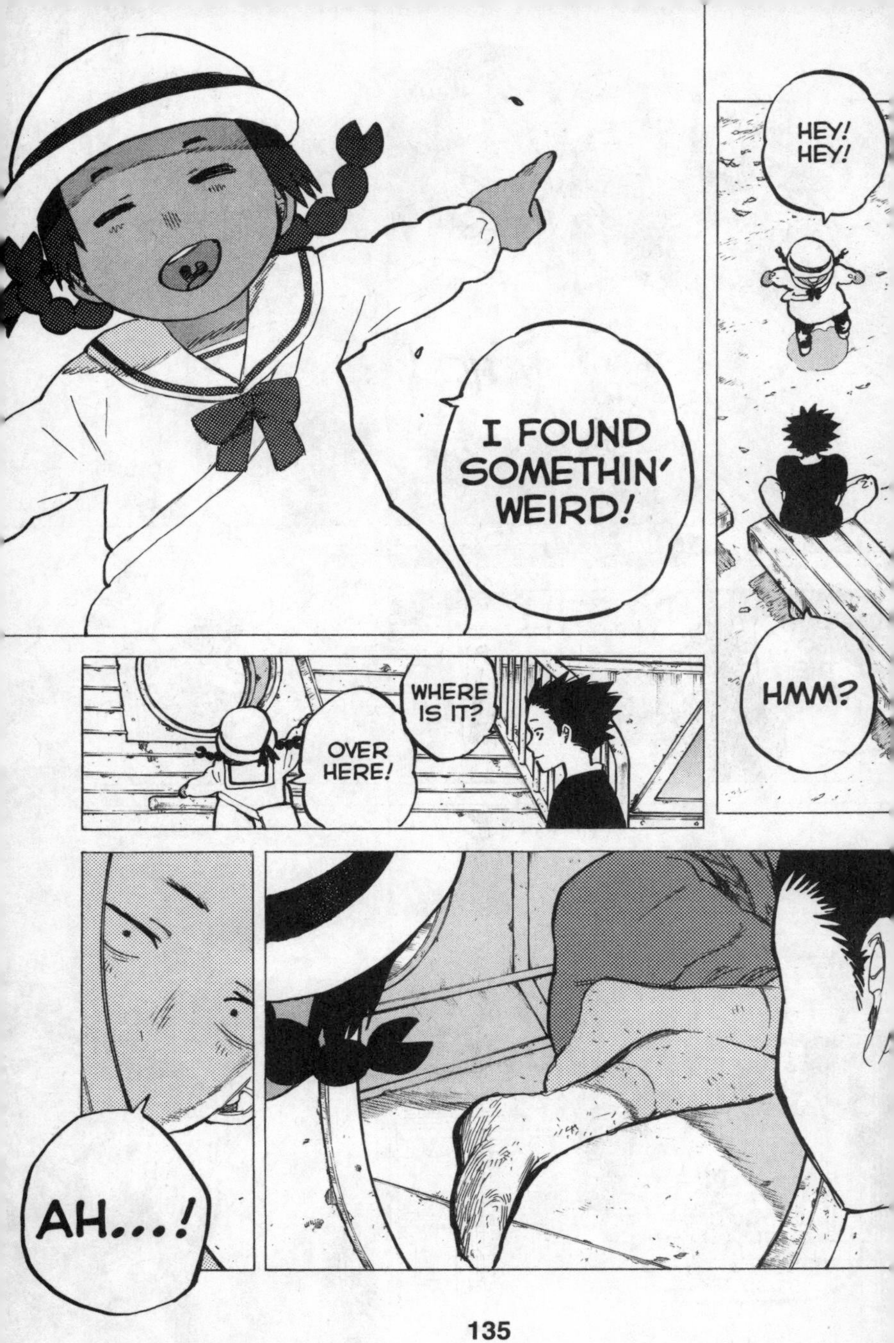
HEY! HEY!
HMM?
I FOUND SOMETHIN' WEIRD!
WHERE IS IT?
OVER HERE!
AH...!

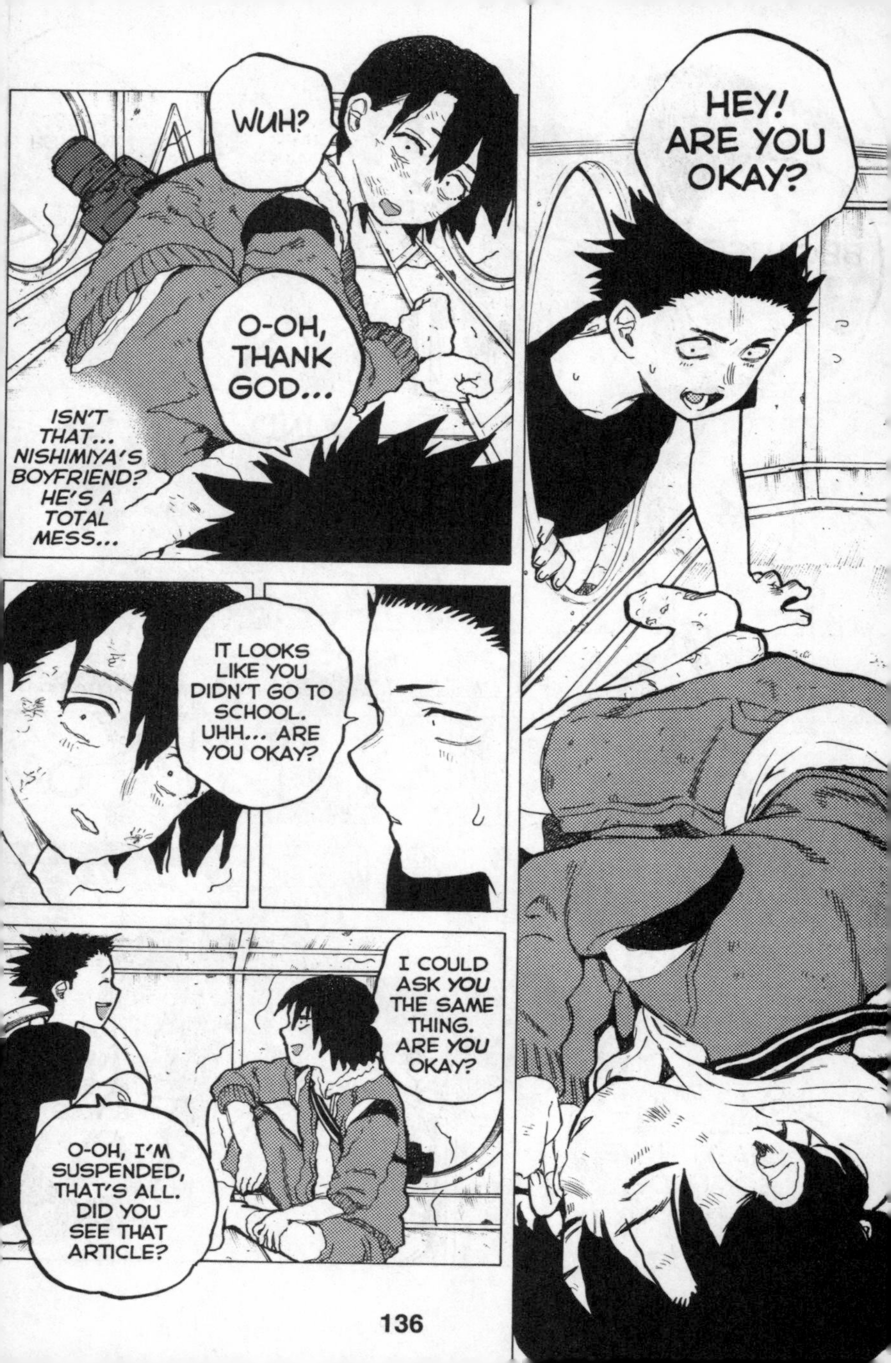
HEY! ARE YOU OKAY?
WUH?
O-OH, THANK GOD...
ISN'T THAT... NISHIMIYA'S BOYFRIEND? HE'S A TOTAL MESS...
IT LOOKS LIKE YOU DIDN'T GO TO SCHOOL. UHH... ARE YOU OKAY?
I COULD ASK *YOU* THE SAME THING. ARE *YOU* OKAY?
O-OH, I'M SUSPENDED, THAT'S ALL. DID YOU SEE THAT ARTICLE?

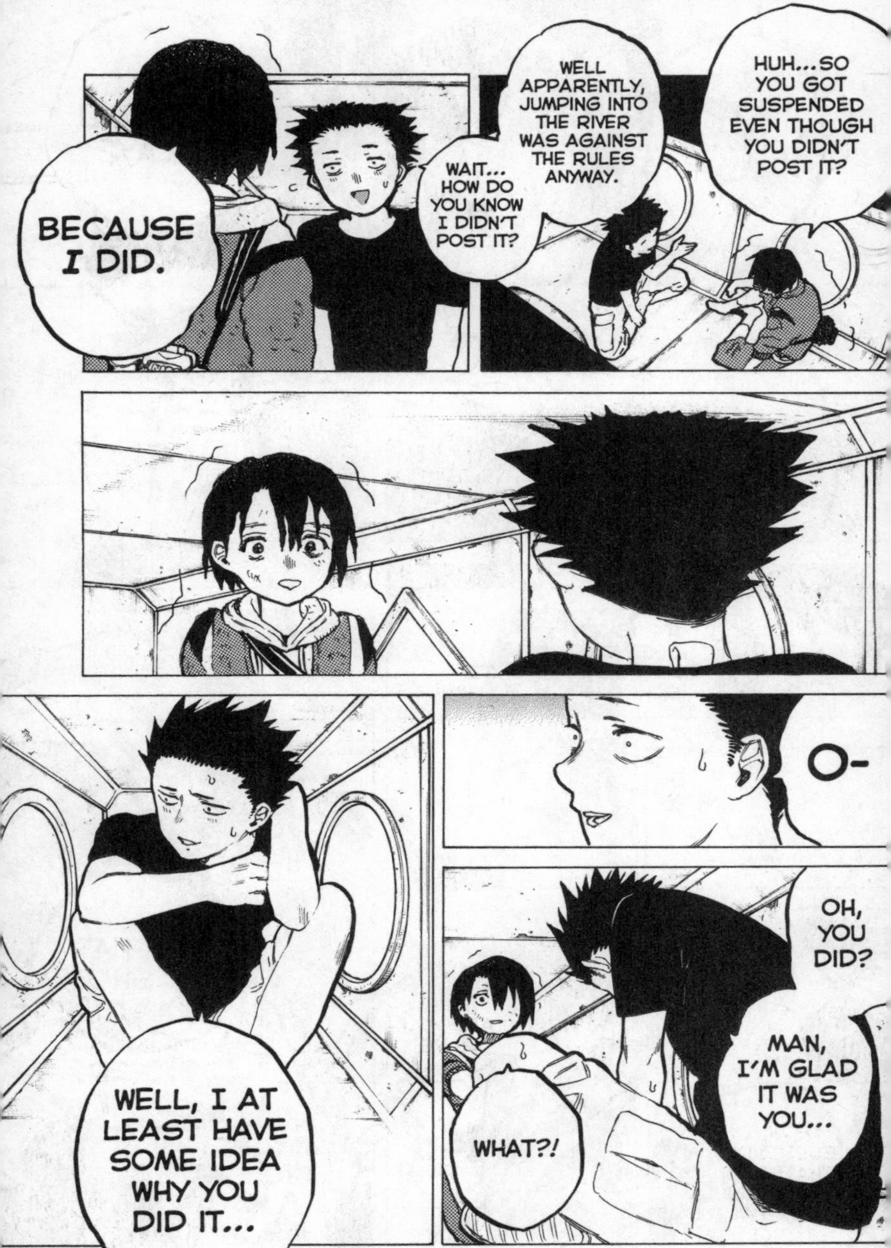
HUH...SO YOU GOT SUSPENDED EVEN THOUGH YOU DIDN'T POST IT?
WELL APPARENTLY, JUMPING INTO THE RIVER WAS AGAINST THE RULES ANYWAY.
WAIT... HOW DO YOU KNOW I DIDN'T POST IT?
BECAUSE *I* DID.
O-
OH, YOU DID?
MAN, I'M GLAD IT WAS YOU...
WHAT?!
WELL, I AT LEAST HAVE SOME IDEA WHY YOU DID IT...

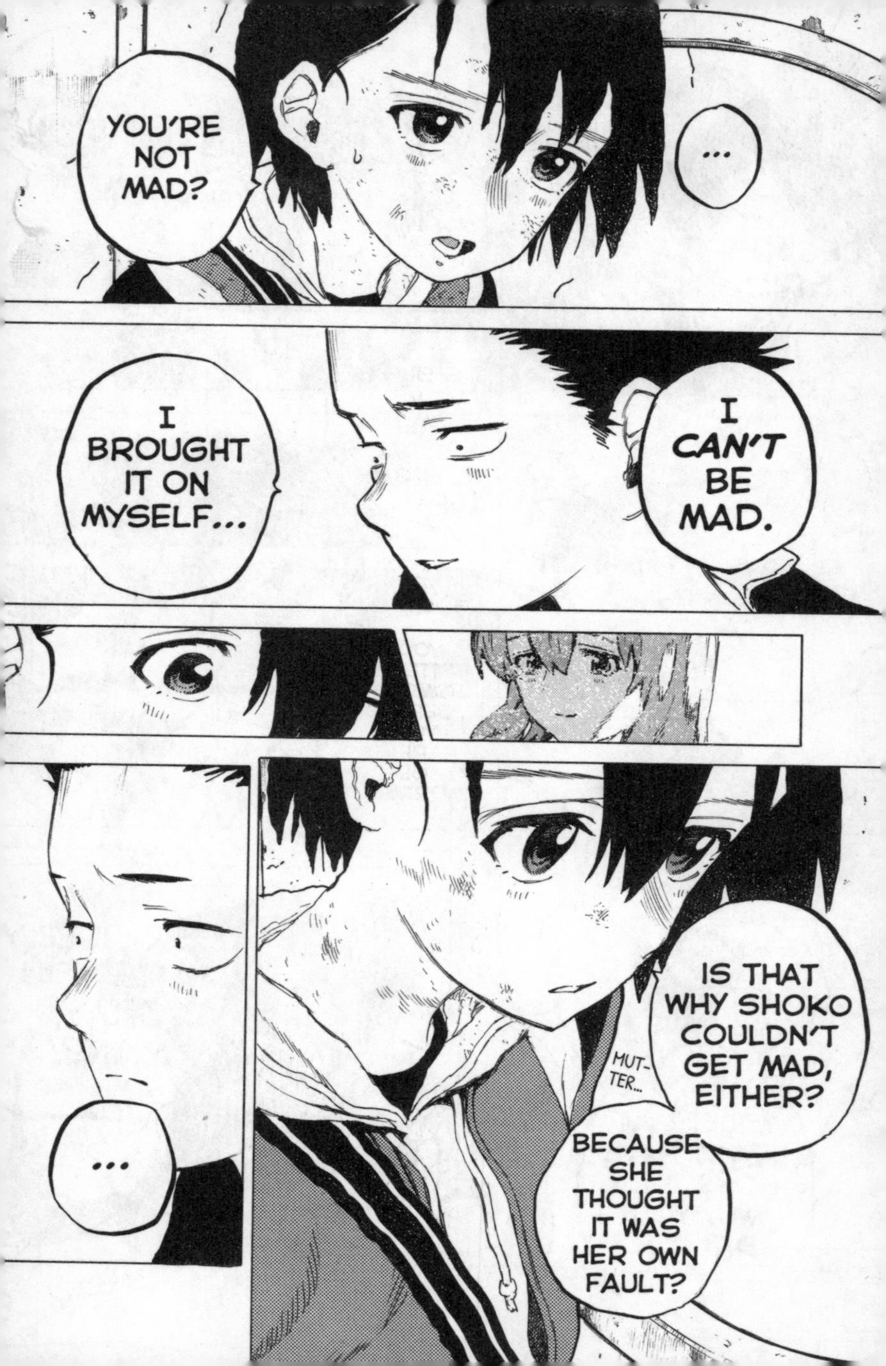
...
YOU'RE NOT MAD?
I CAN'T BE MAD.
I BROUGHT IT ON MYSELF...
IS THAT WHY SHOKO COULDN'T GET MAD, EITHER?
MUT-TER...
BECAUSE SHE THOUGHT IT WAS HER OWN FAULT?
...

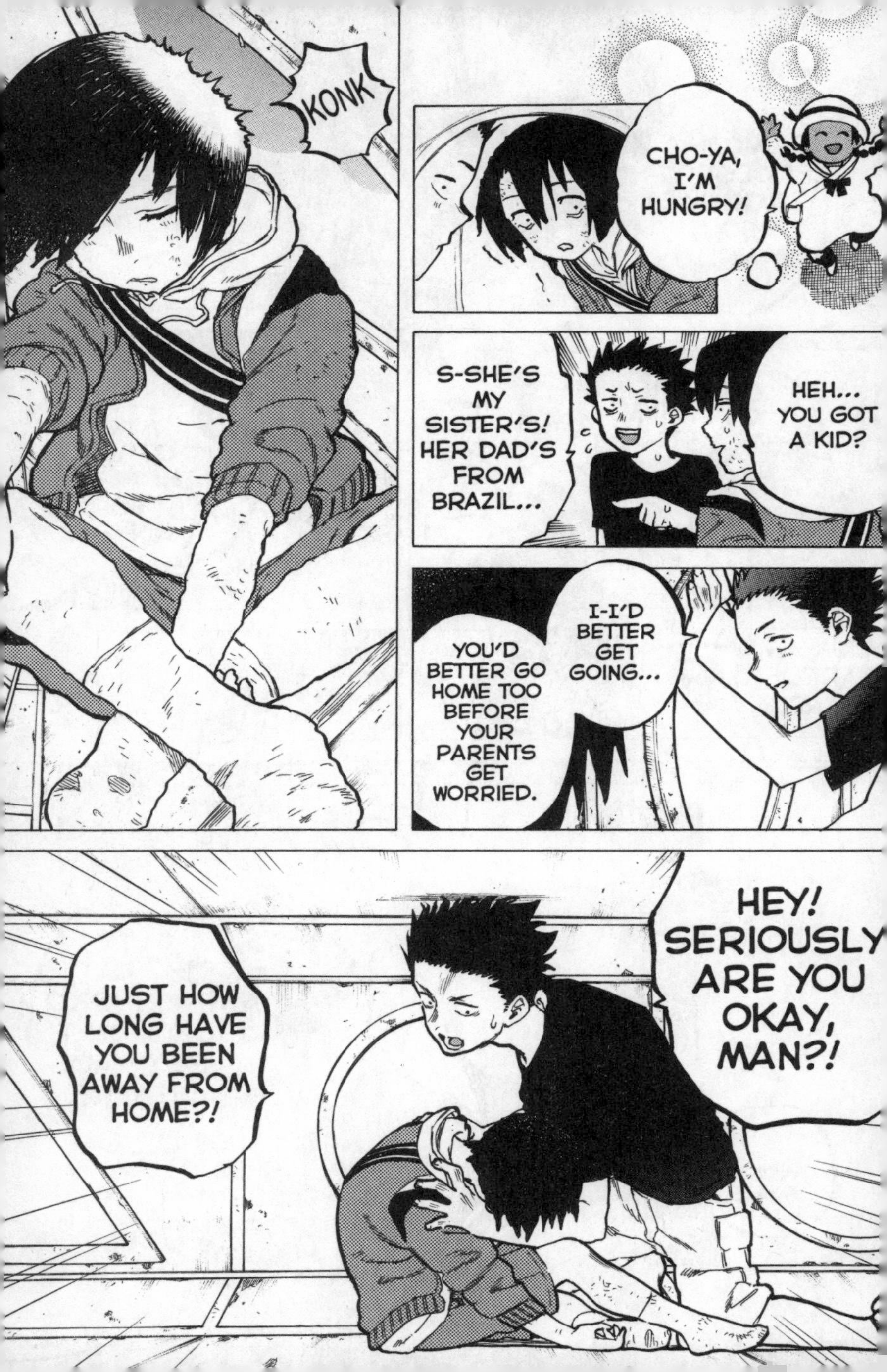
CHO-YA, I'M HUNGRY!
HEH... YOU GOT A KID?
S-SHE'S MY SISTER'S! HER DAD'S FROM BRAZIL...
I-I'D BETTER GET GOING...
YOU'D BETTER GO HOME TOO BEFORE YOUR PARENTS GET WORRIED.
KONK
HEY! SERIOUSLY ARE YOU OKAY, MAN?!
JUST HOW LONG HAVE YOU BEEN AWAY FROM HOME?!

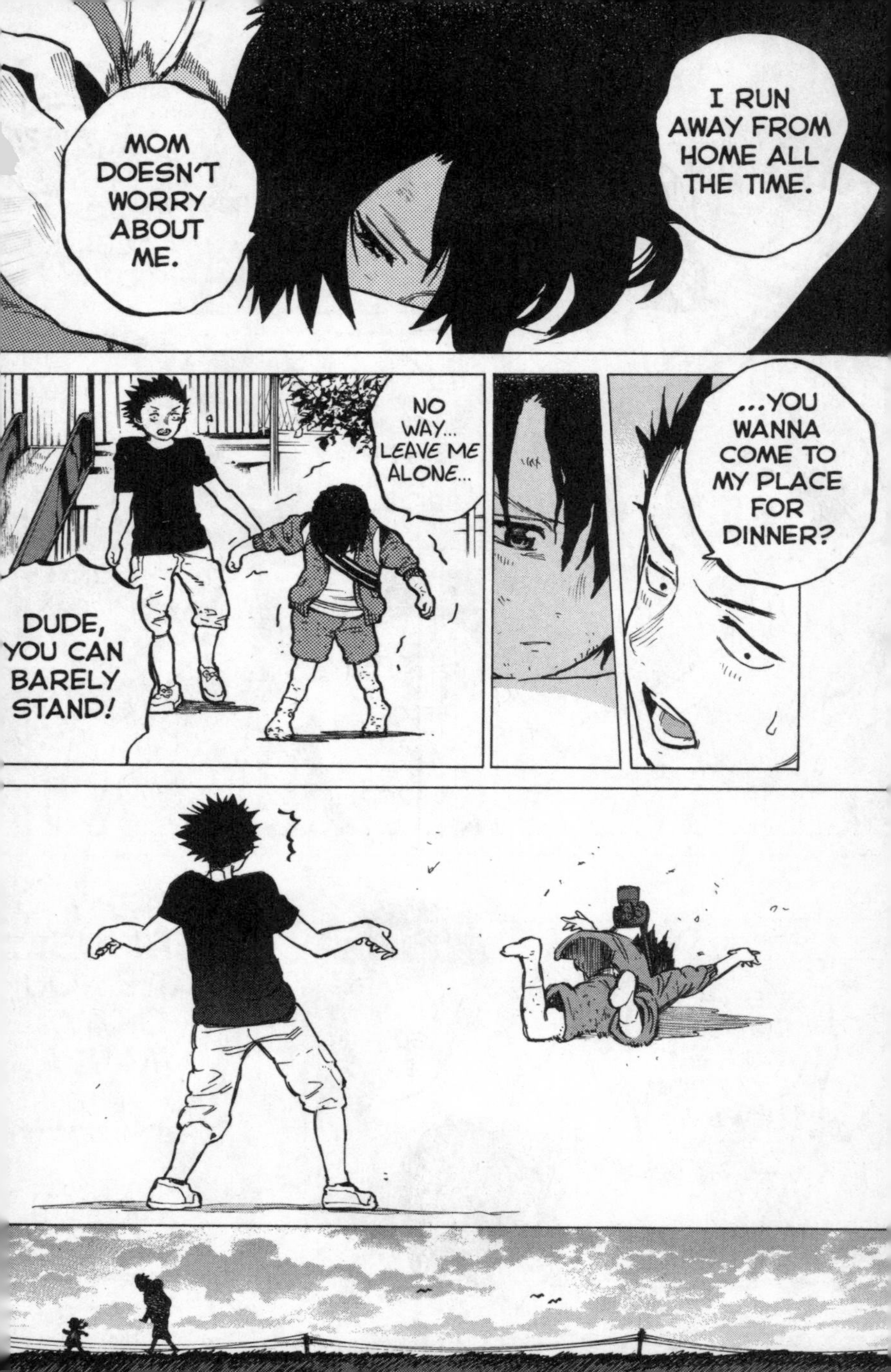
I RUN AWAY FROM HOME ALL THE TIME.
MOM DOESN'T WORRY ABOUT ME.
...YOU WANNA COME TO MY PLACE FOR DINNER?
NO WAY... LEAVE ME ALONE...
DUDE, YOU CAN BARELY STAND!

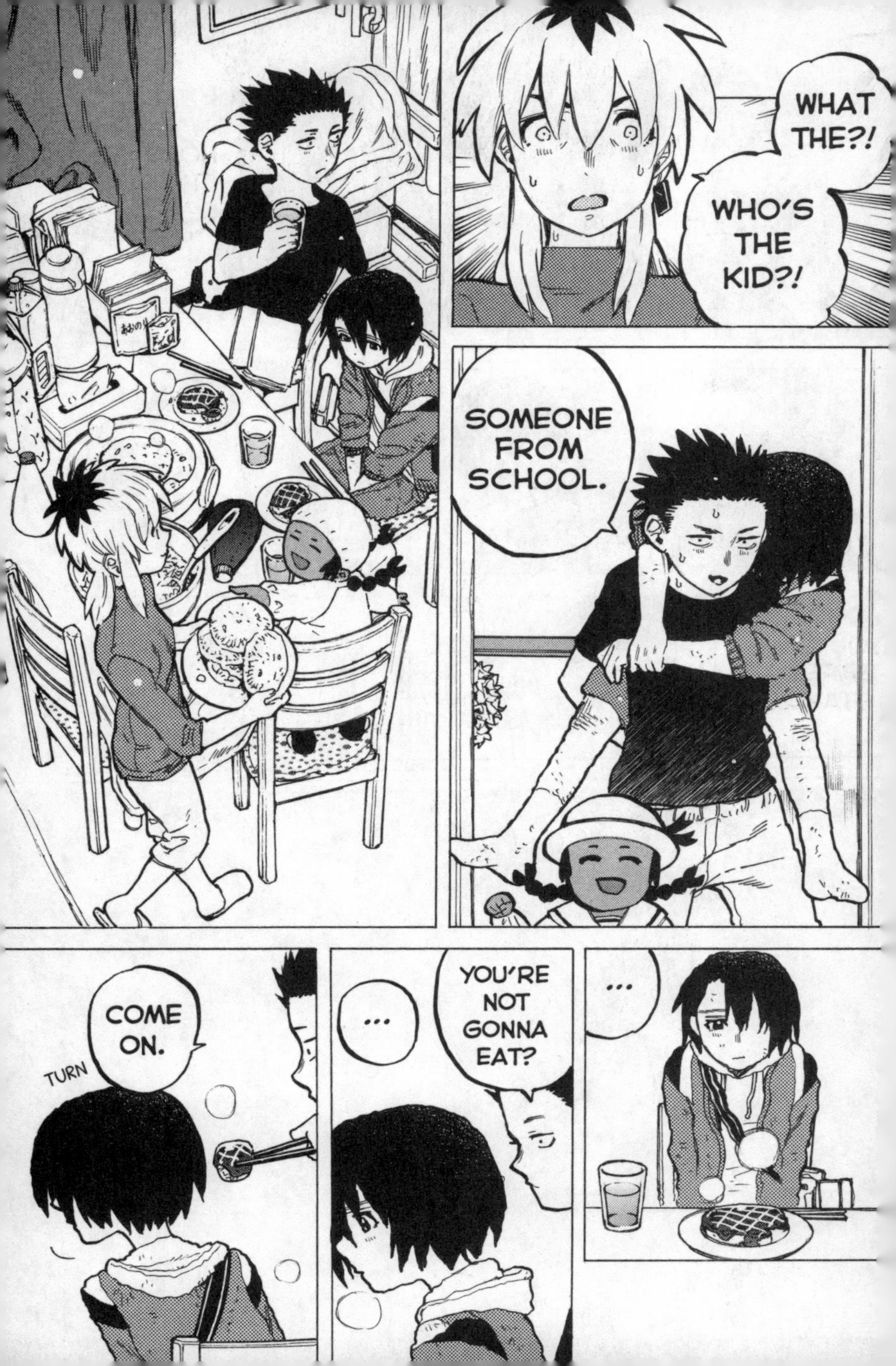

WHAT THE?!
WHO'S THE KID?!
SOMEONE FROM SCHOOL.
...
YOU'RE NOT GONNA EAT?
...
COME ON.
TURN

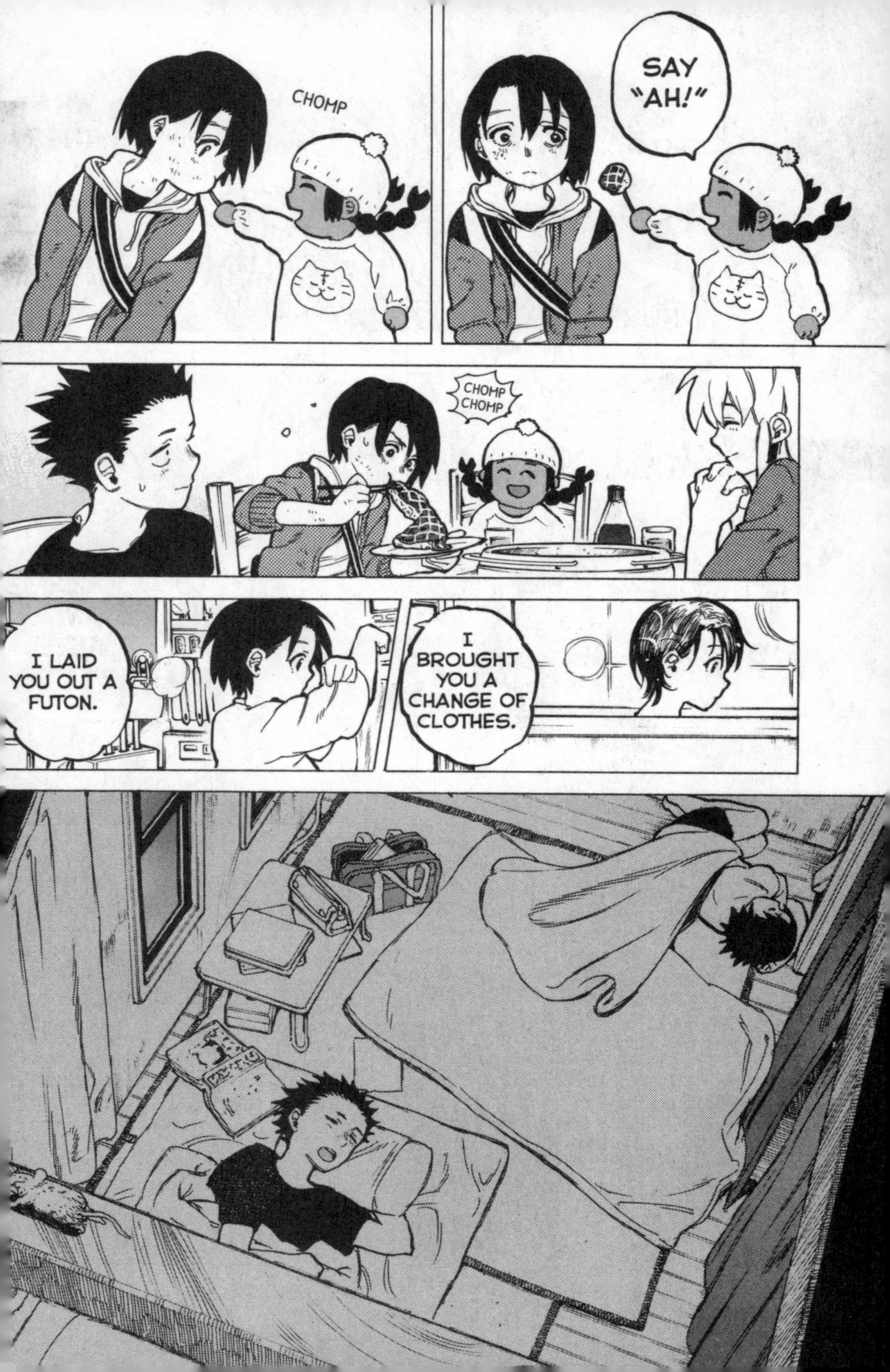
SAY "AH!"
CHOMP
CHOMP CHOMP
I BROUGHT YOU A CHANGE OF CLOTHES.
I LAID YOU OUT A FUTON.

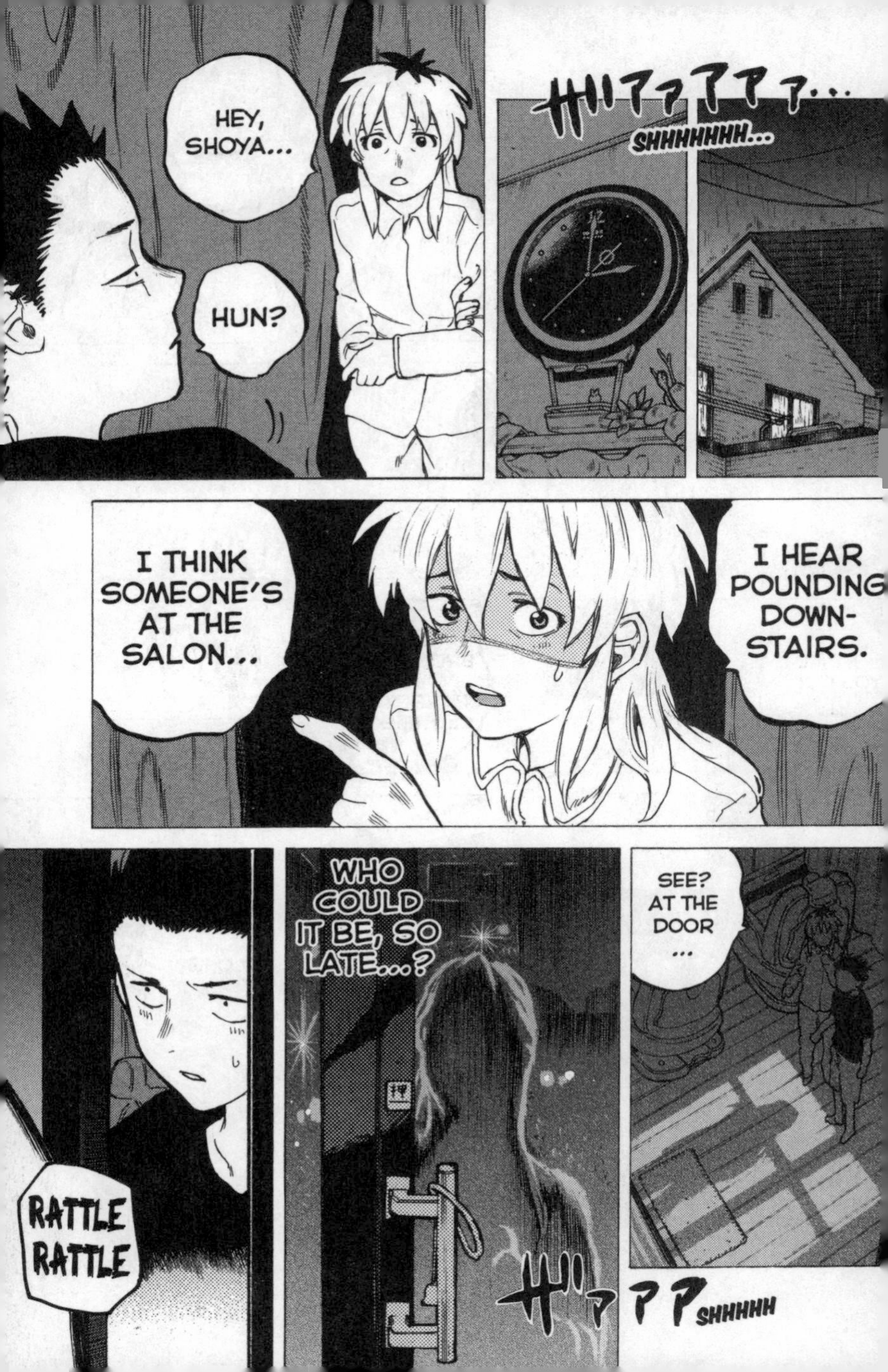

SHHHHHHH...
HEY, SHOYA...
HUN?
I HEAR POUNDING DOWN-STAIRS.
I THINK SOMEONE'S AT THE SALON...
SEE? AT THE DOOR ...
WHO COULD IT BE, SO LATE...?
SHHHHH
RATTLE RATTLE

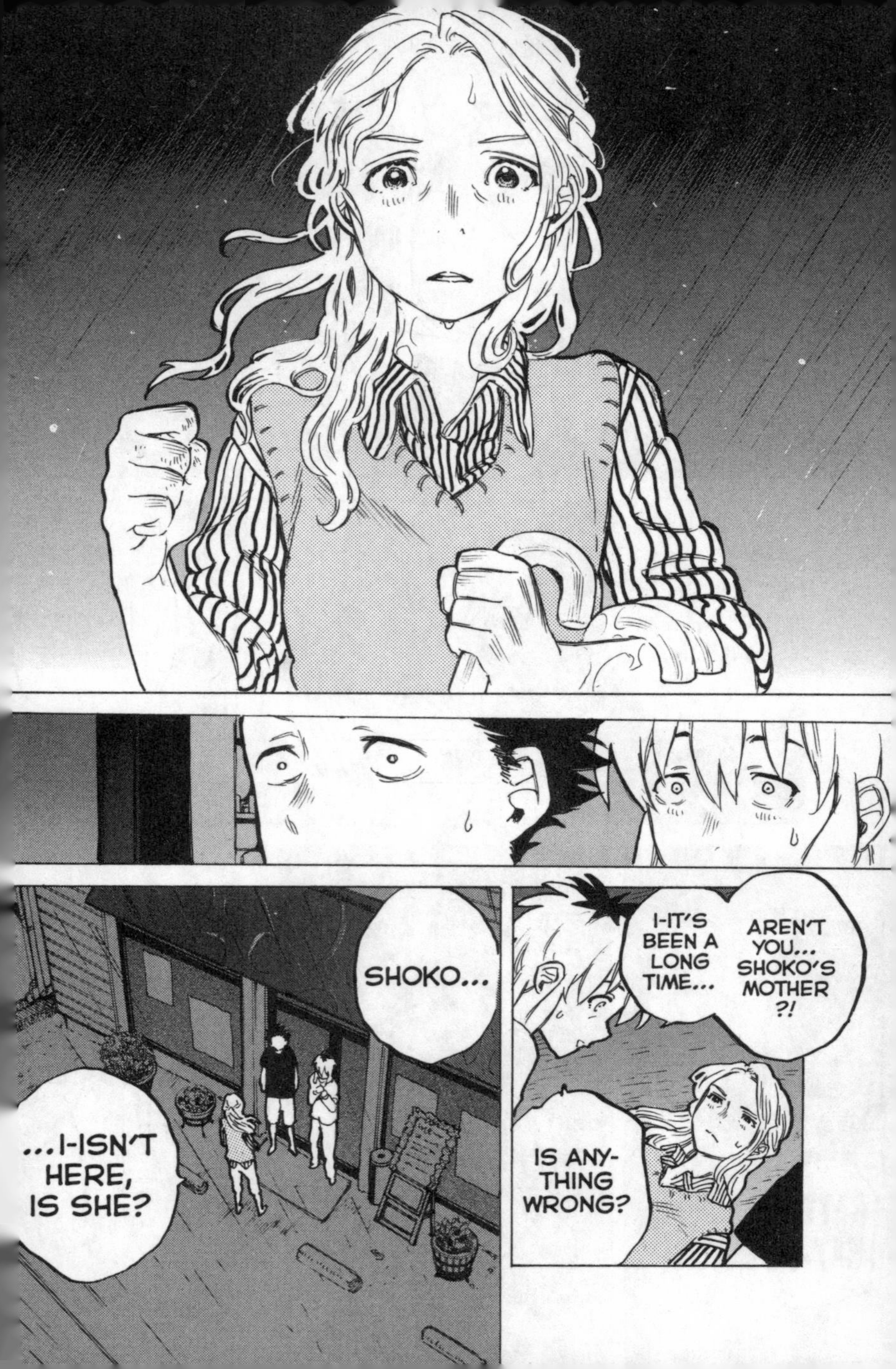
AREN'T YOU... SHOKO'S MOTHER ?!
I-IT'S BEEN A LONG TIME...
IS ANY-THING WRONG?
SHOKO...
...I-ISN'T HERE, IS SHE?

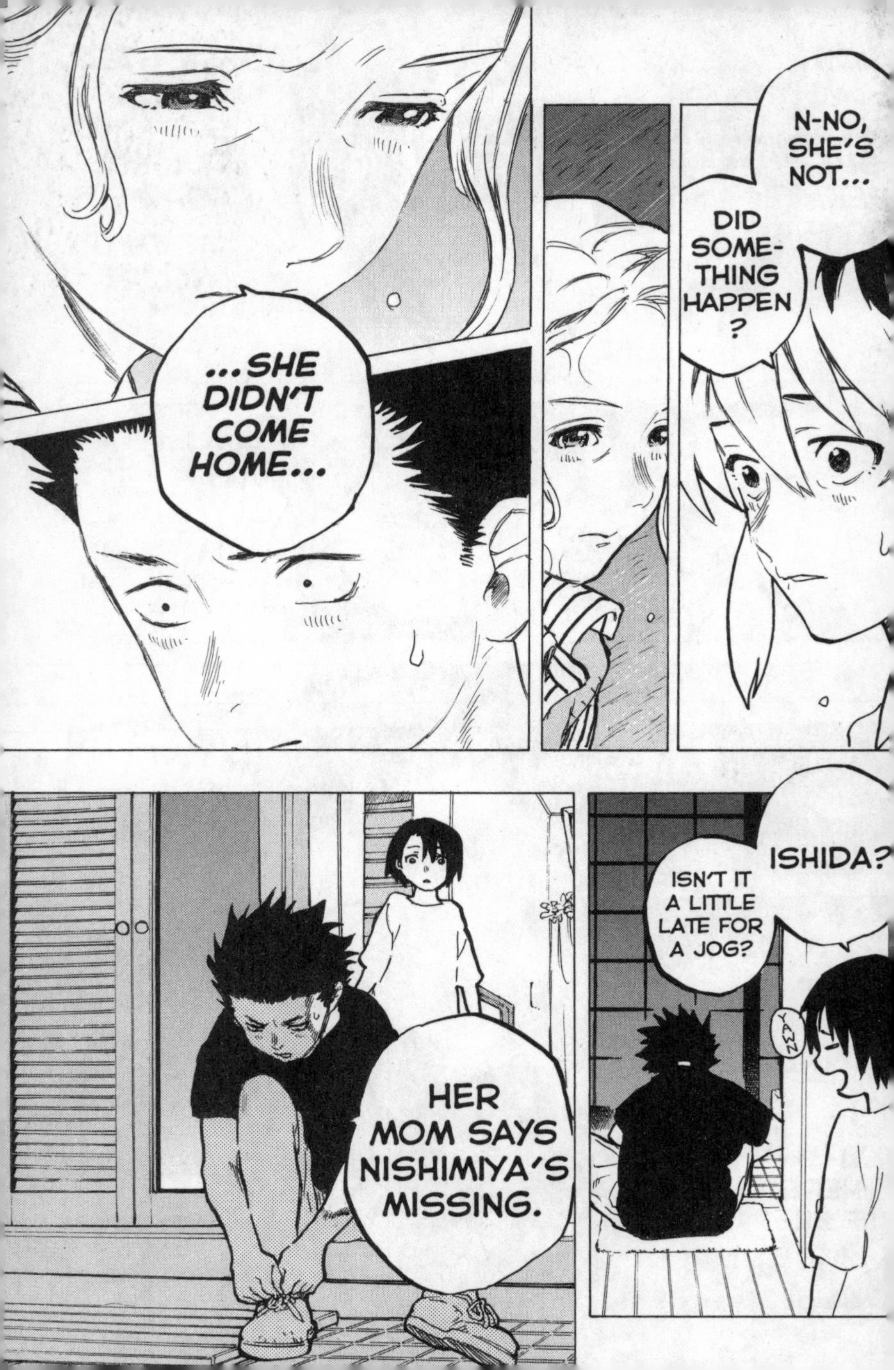
N-NO, SHE'S NOT...
DID SOMETHING HAPPEN?
...SHE DIDN'T COME HOME...
ISHIDA?
ISN'T IT A LITTLE LATE FOR A JOG?
YAWN
HER MOM SAYS NISHIMIYA'S MISSING.

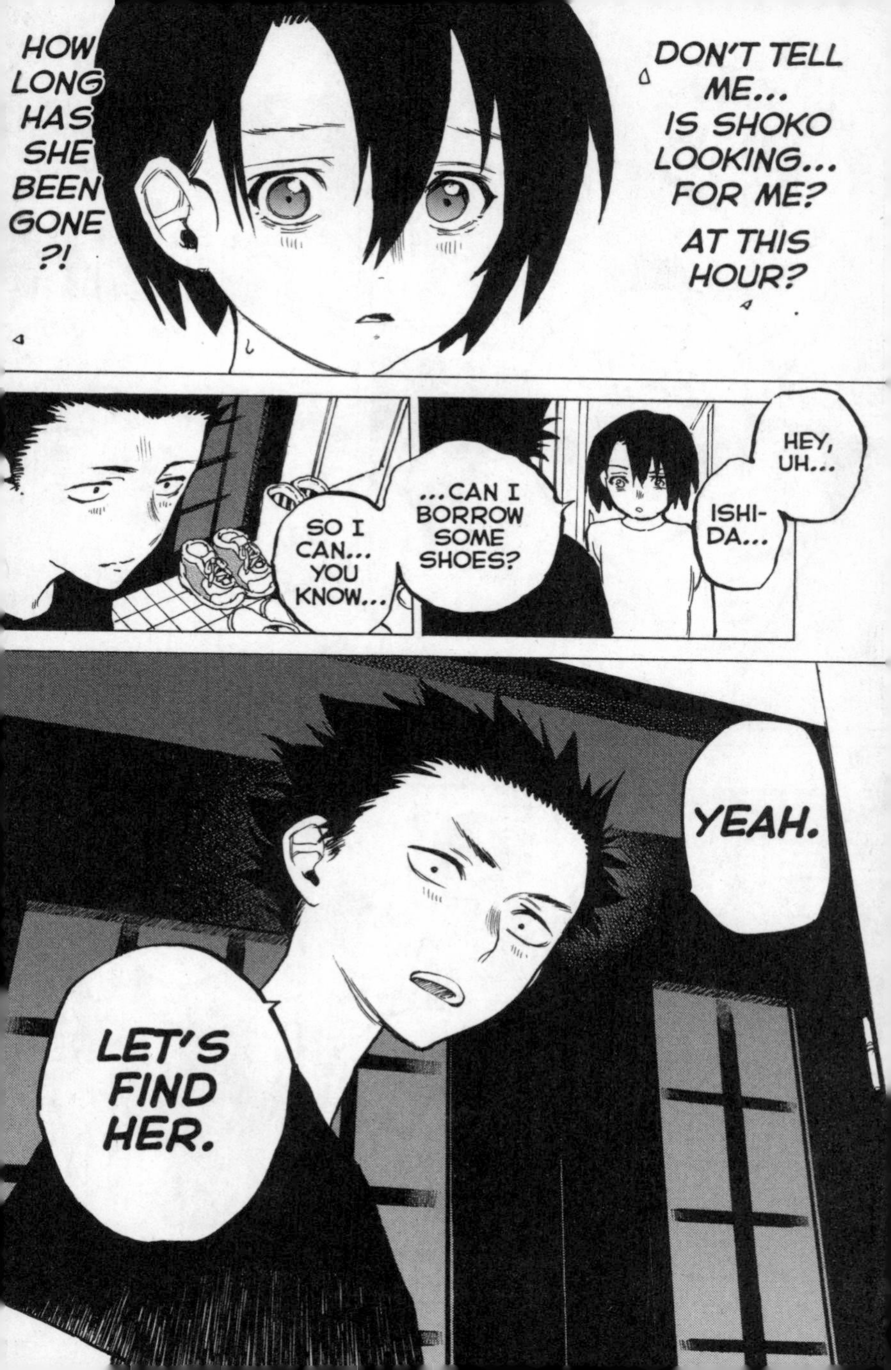
DON'T TELL ME... IS SHOKO LOOKING... FOR ME?
AT THIS HOUR?
HOW LONG HAS SHE BEEN GONE ?!
HEY, UH...
ISHI-DA...
...CAN I BORROW SOME SHOES?
SO I CAN... YOU KNOW...
YEAH.
LET'S FIND HER.

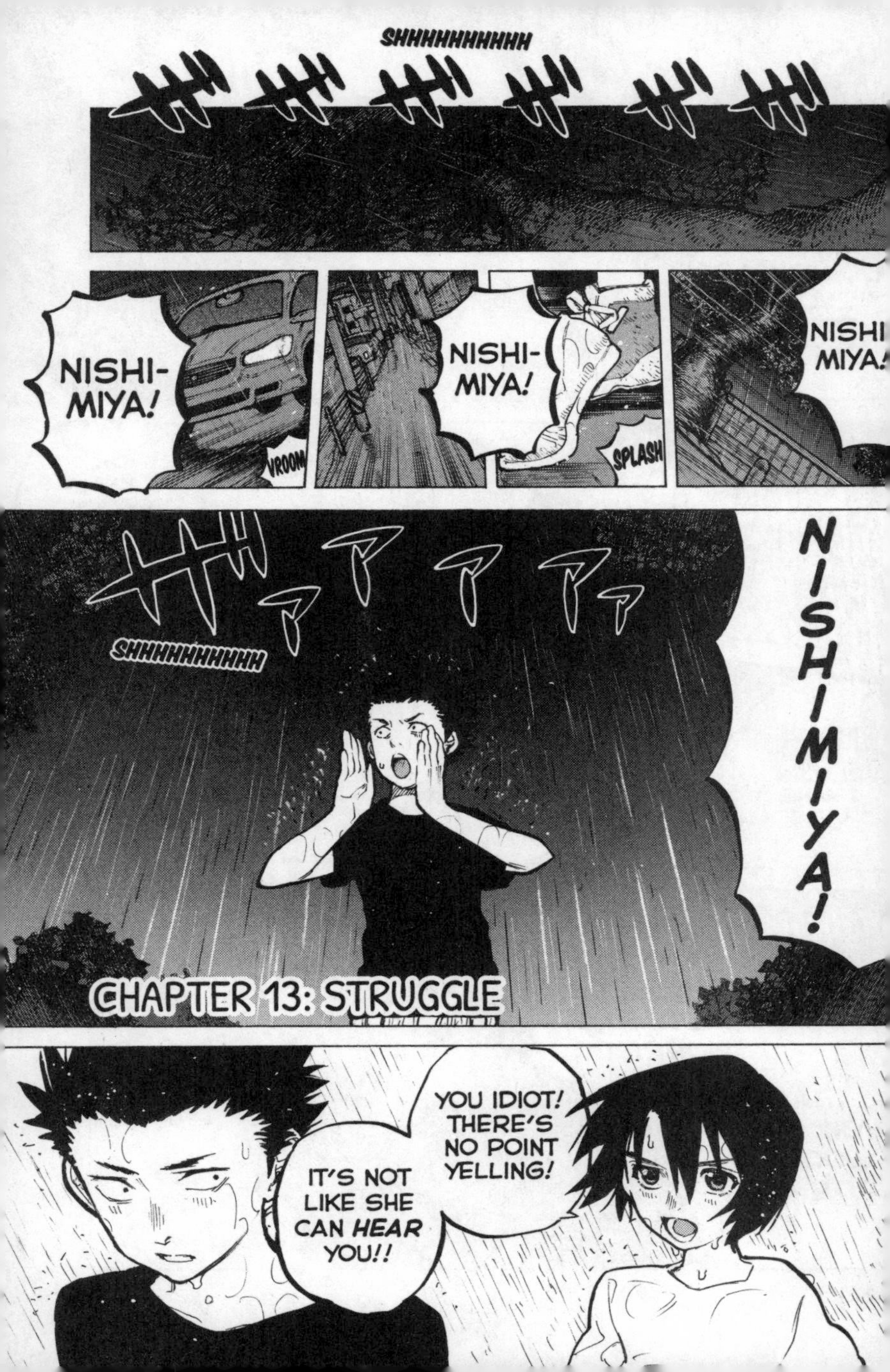
SHHHHHHHHHH
NISHI MIYA!
SPLASH
NISHI-MIYA!
VROOM
NISHI-MIYA!
NISHIMIYA!
SHHHHHHHHHH
CHAPTER 13: STRUGGLE
YOU IDIOT! THERE'S NO POINT YELLING!
IT'S NOT LIKE SHE CAN HEAR YOU!!

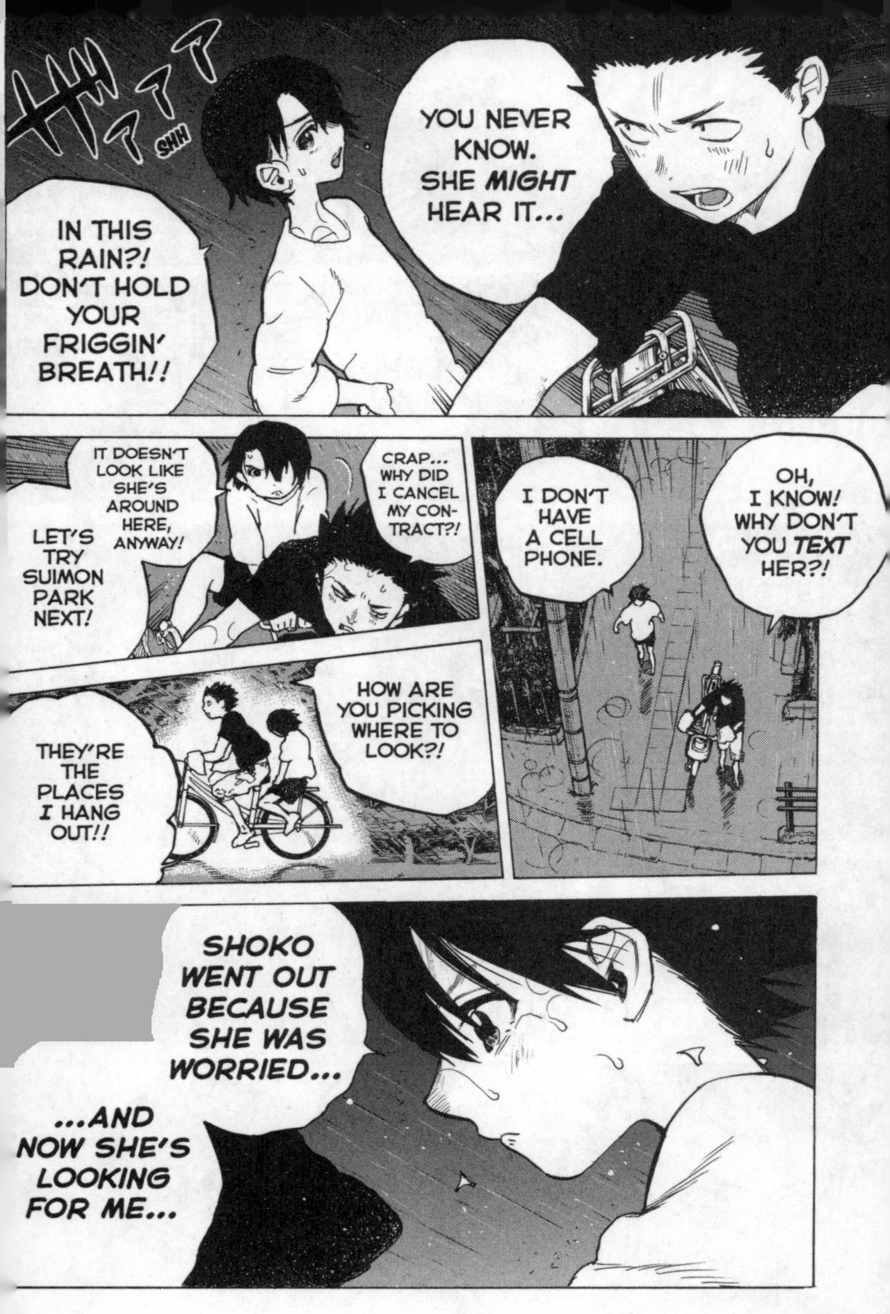
YOU NEVER KNOW. SHE *MIGHT* HEAR IT...
SHH
IN THIS RAIN?! DON'T HOLD YOUR FRIGGIN' BREATH!!
OH, I KNOW! WHY DON'T YOU *TEXT* HER?!
I DON'T HAVE A CELL PHONE.
CRAP... WHY DID I CANCEL MY CON-TRACT?!
IT DOESN'T LOOK LIKE SHE'S AROUND HERE, ANYWAY!
LET'S TRY SUIMON PARK NEXT!
HOW ARE YOU PICKING WHERE TO LOOK?!
THEY'RE THE PLACES *I* HANG OUT!!
SHOKO WENT OUT BECAUSE SHE WAS WORRIED...
...AND NOW SHE'S LOOKING FOR ME...

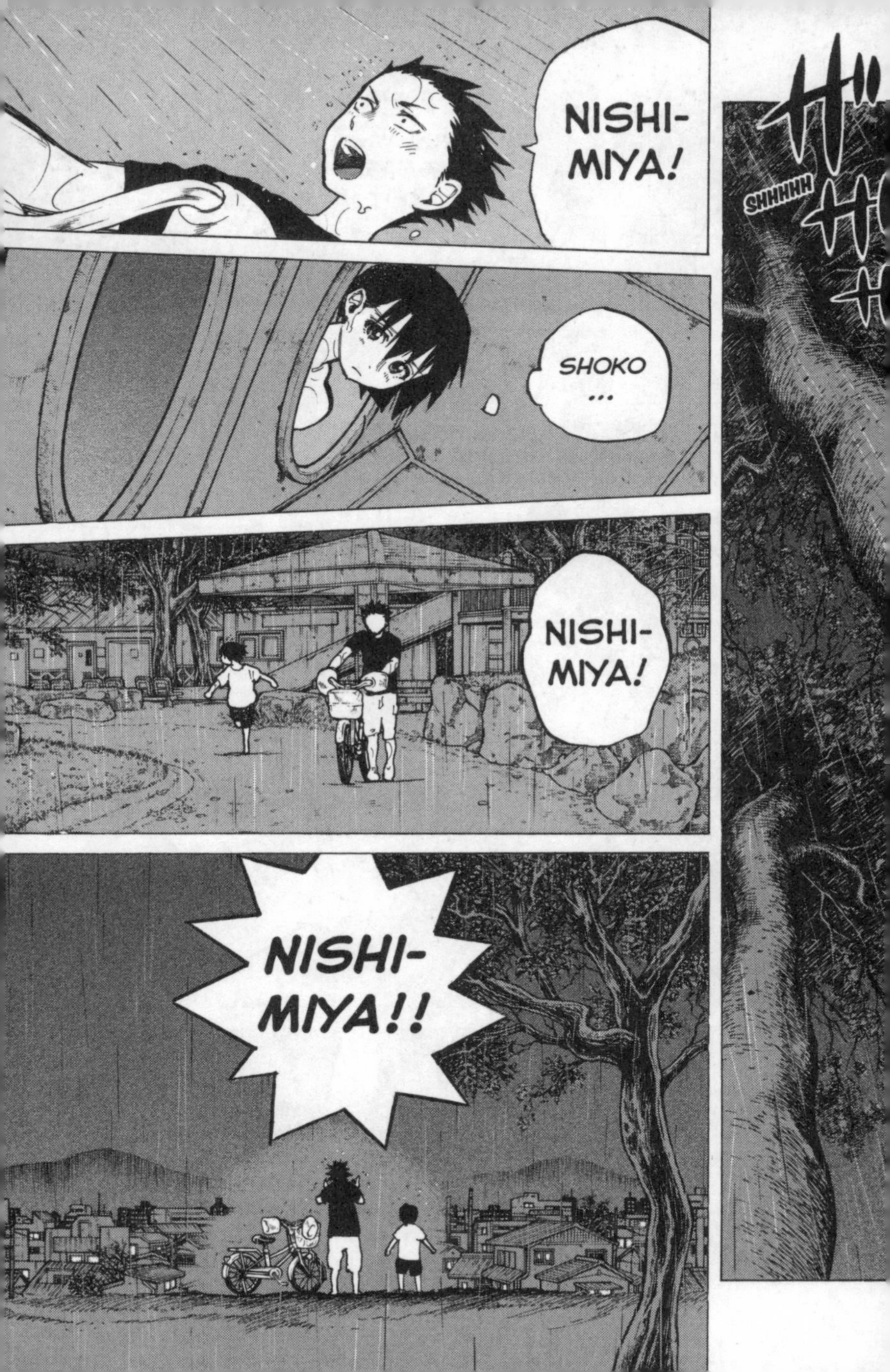
SHHHHH
NISHI-MIYA!
SHOKO ...
NISHI-MIYA!
NISHI-MIYA!!

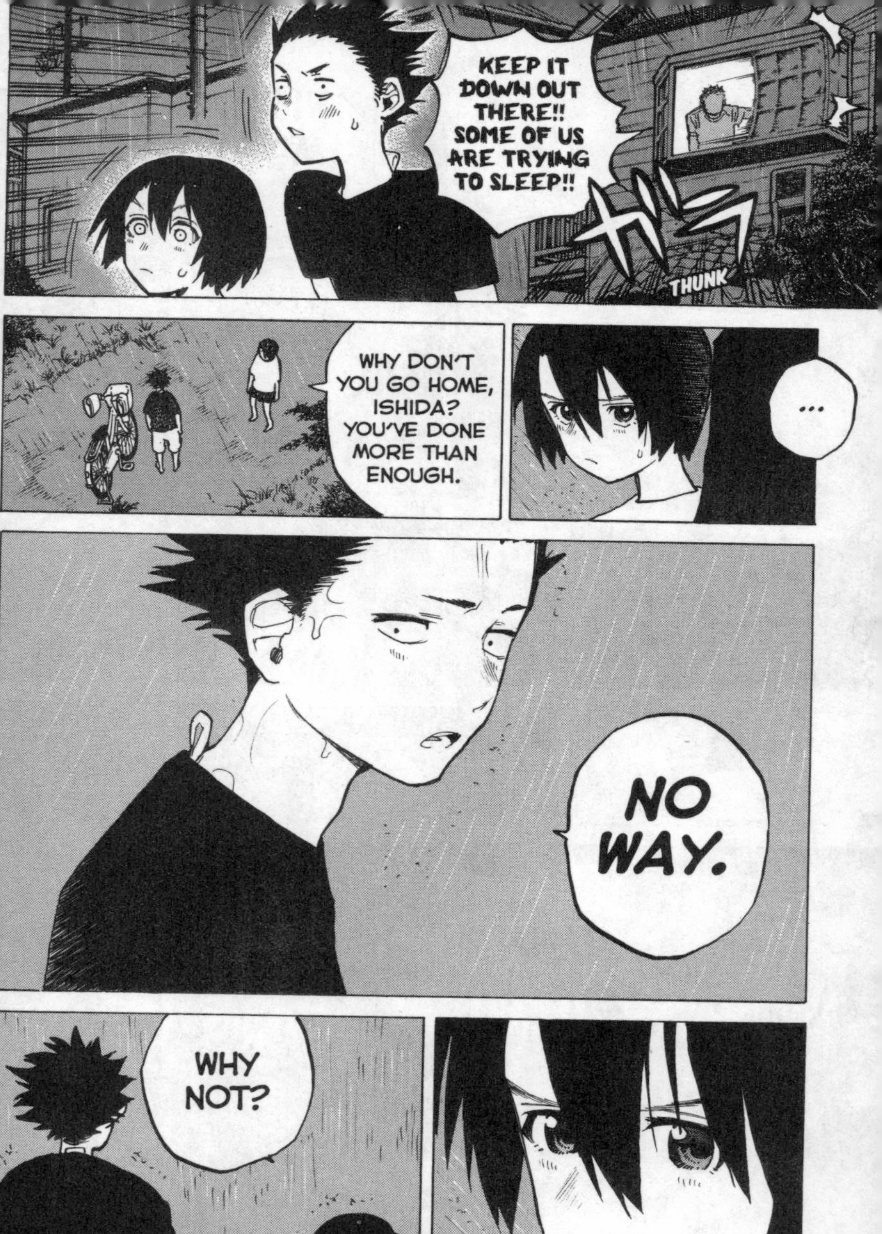
KEEP IT DOWN OUT THERE!! SOME OF US ARE TRYING TO SLEEP!!
THUNK
...
WHY DON'T YOU GO HOME, ISHIDA? YOU'VE DONE MORE THAN ENOUGH.
NO WAY.
WHY NOT?

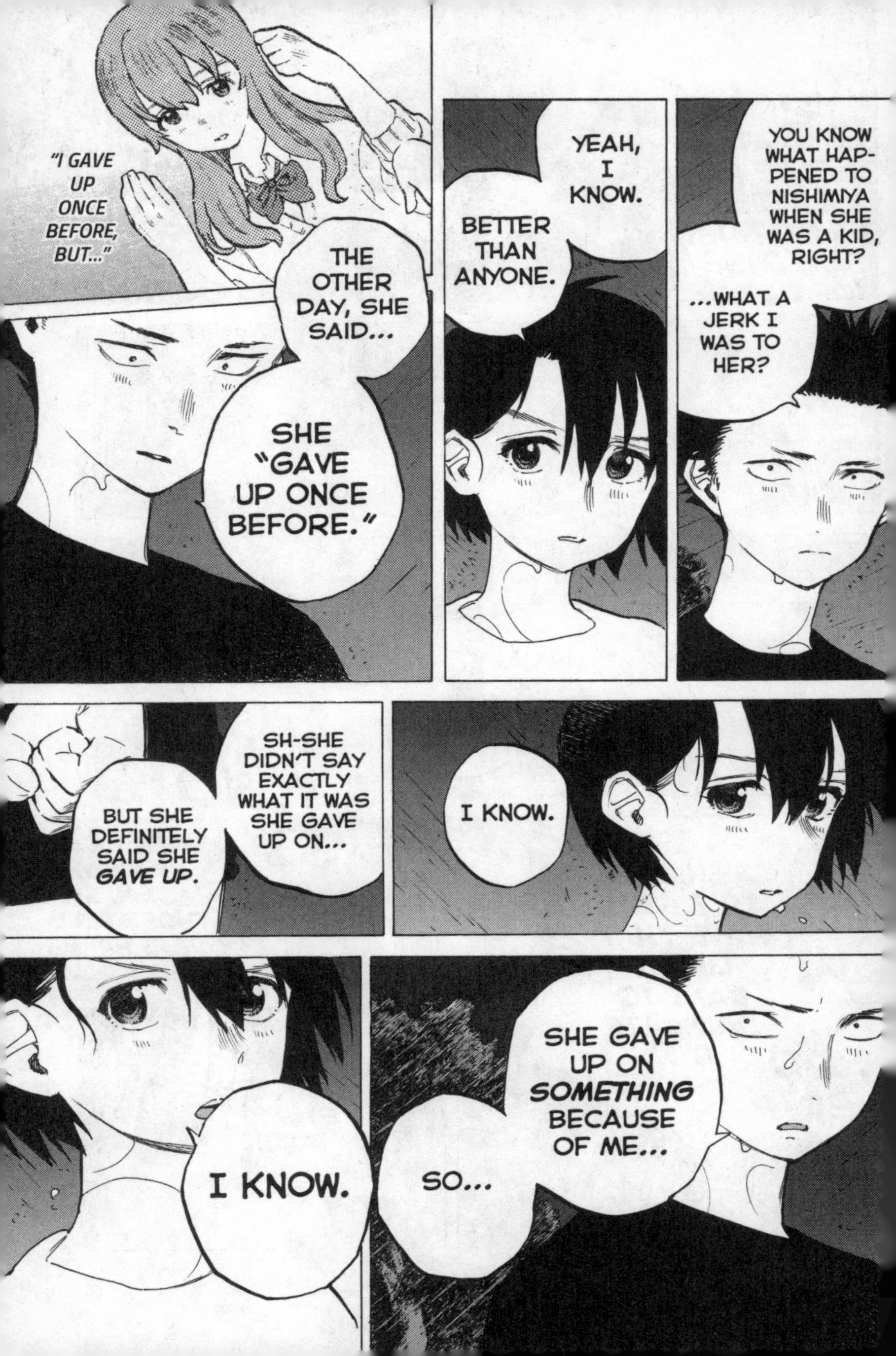
YOU KNOW WHAT HAPPENED TO NISHIMIYA WHEN SHE WAS A KID, RIGHT?
...WHAT A JERK I WAS TO HER?
YEAH, I KNOW.
BETTER THAN ANYONE.
"I GAVE UP ONCE BEFORE, BUT..."
THE OTHER DAY, SHE SAID...
SHE "GAVE UP ONCE BEFORE."
I KNOW.
SH-SHE DIDN'T SAY EXACTLY WHAT IT WAS SHE GAVE UP ON...
BUT SHE DEFINITELY SAID SHE *GAVE UP*.
SHE GAVE UP ON *SOMETHING* BECAUSE OF ME...
SO...
I KNOW.

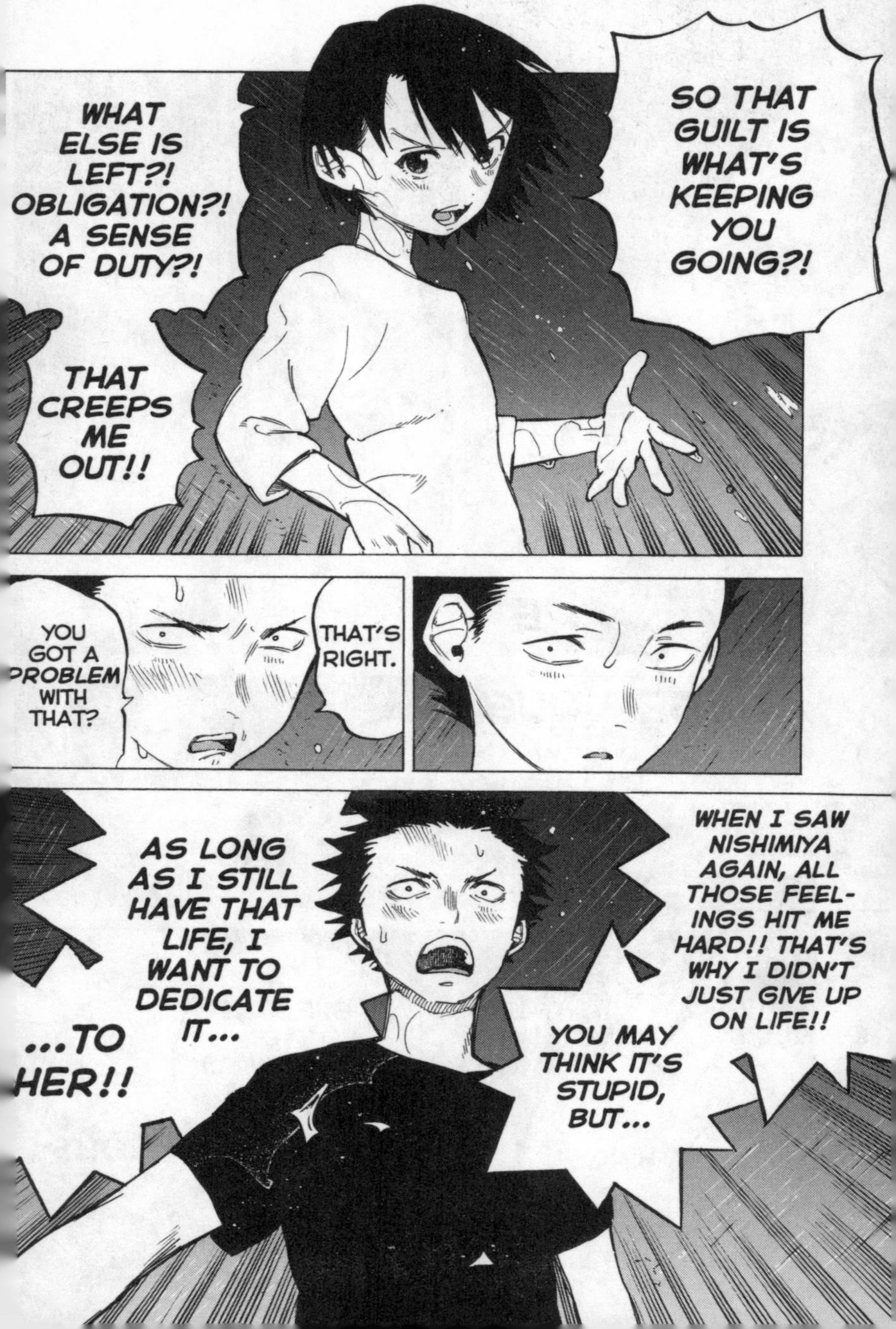
SO THAT GUILT IS WHAT'S KEEPING YOU GOING?!
WHAT ELSE IS LEFT?! OBLIGATION?! A SENSE OF DUTY?!
THAT CREEPS ME OUT!!
THAT'S RIGHT.
YOU GOT A PROBLEM WITH THAT?
WHEN I SAW NISHIMIYA AGAIN, ALL THOSE FEEL-INGS HIT ME HARD!! THAT'S WHY I DIDN'T JUST GIVE UP ON LIFE!!
YOU MAY THINK IT'S STUPID, BUT...
AS LONG AS I STILL HAVE THAT LIFE, I WANT TO DEDICATE IT...
...TO HER!!

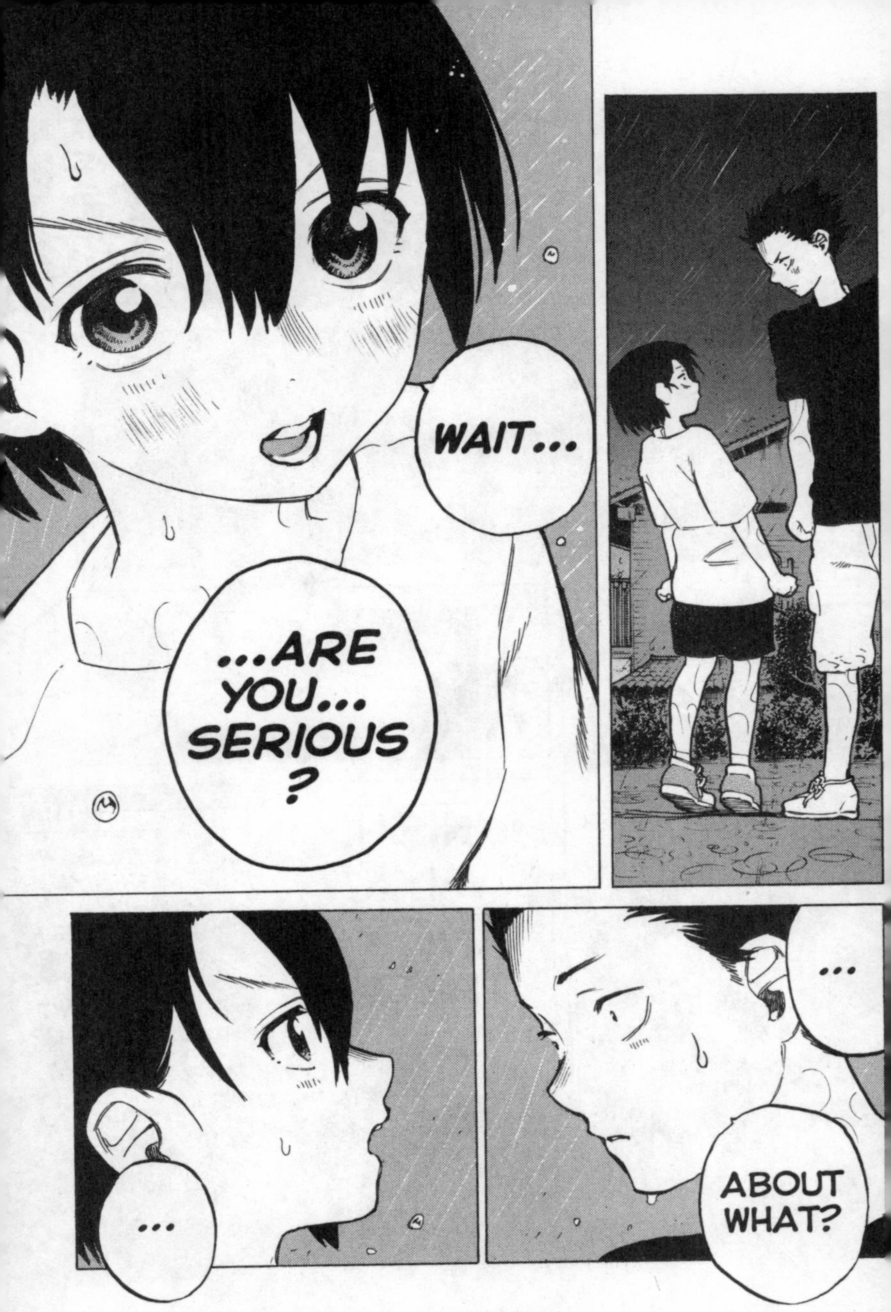
WAIT...
...ARE YOU... SERIOUS?
...
ABOUT WHAT?
...

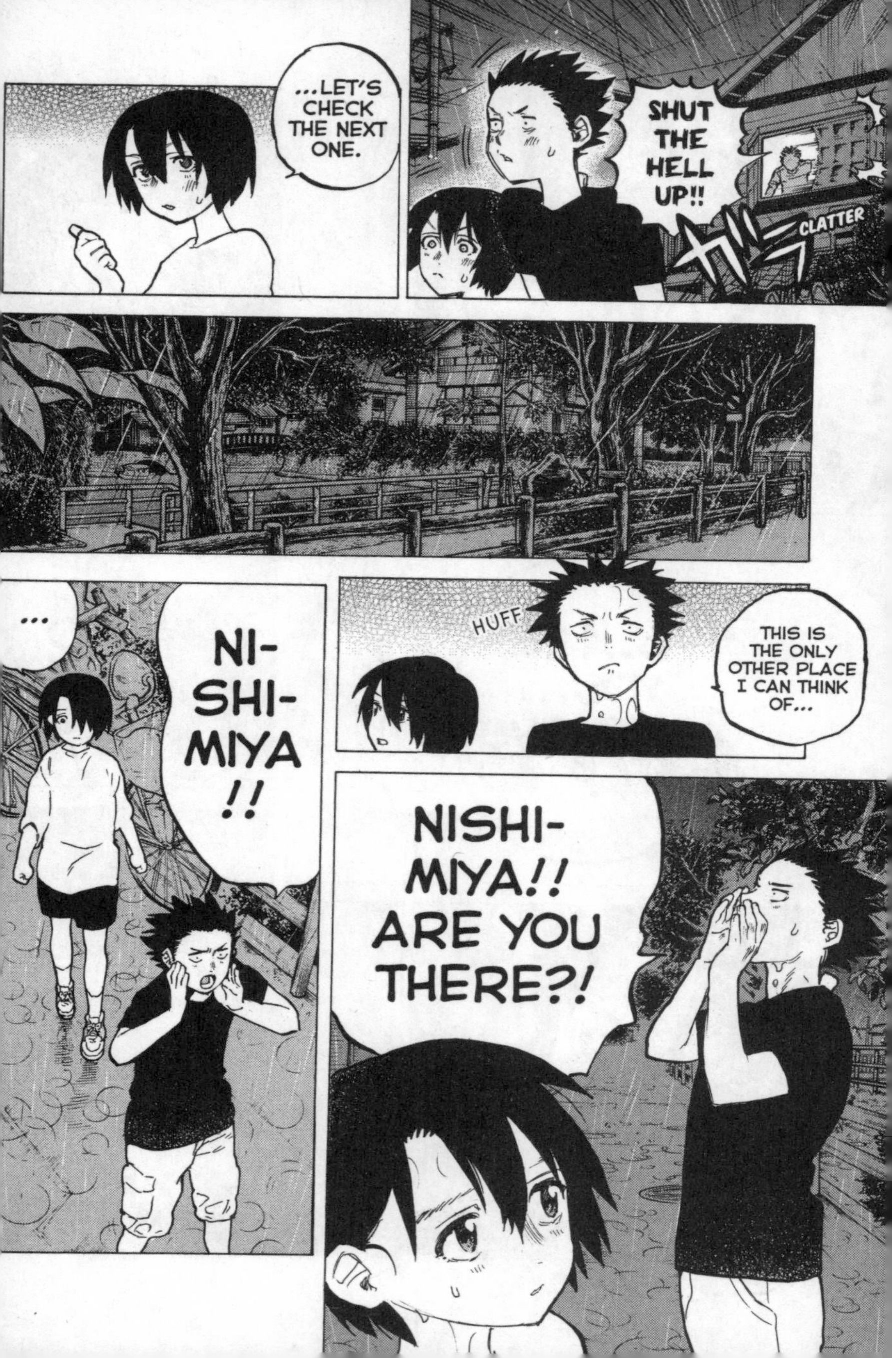
SHUT THE HELL UP!!
CLATTER
...LET'S CHECK THE NEXT ONE.
HUFF
THIS IS THE ONLY OTHER PLACE I CAN THINK OF...
NISHI-MIYA!! ARE YOU THERE?!
NI-SHI-MIYA!!
...

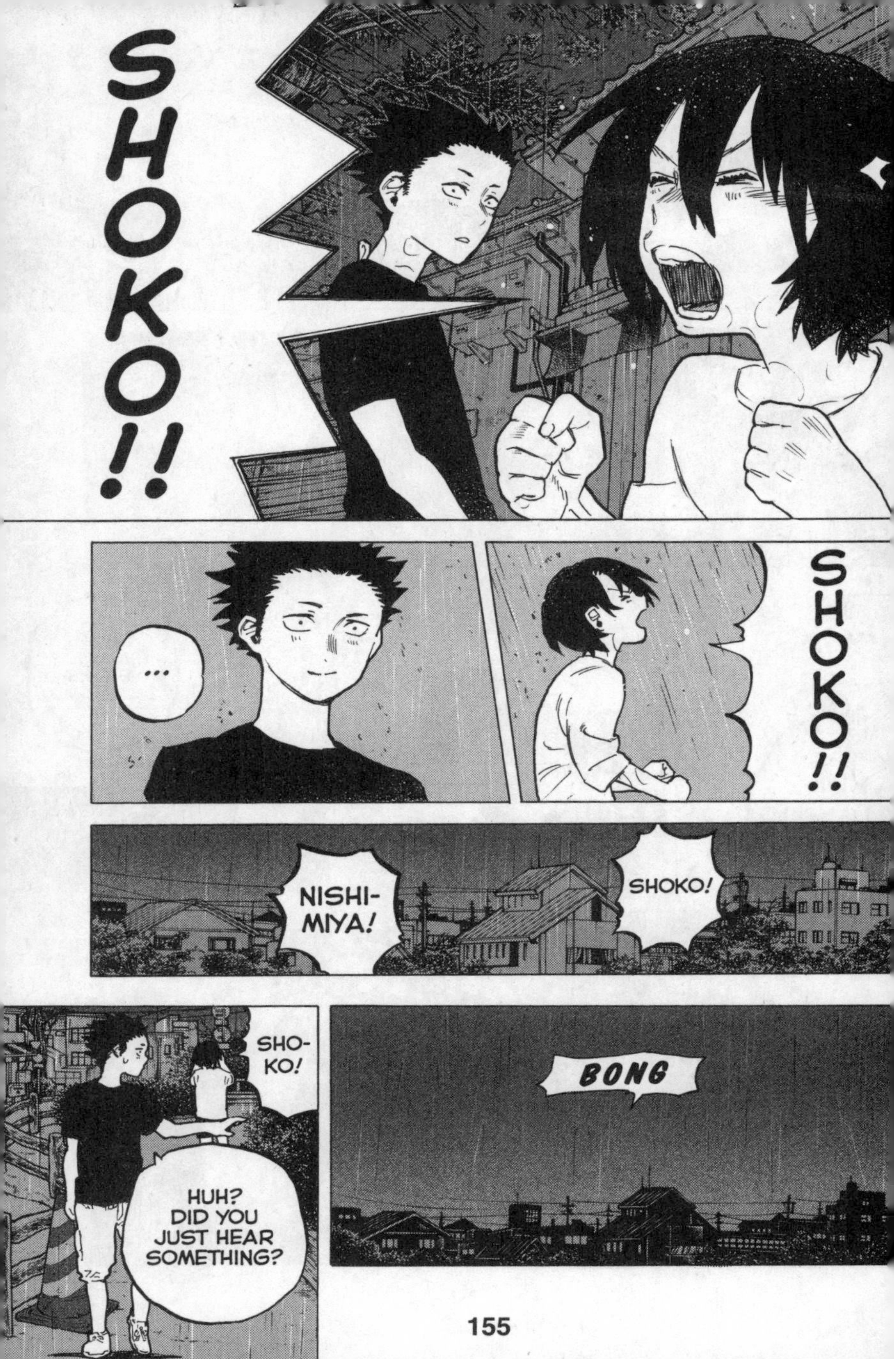
SHOKO!!
SHOKO!!
...
SHOKO!
NISHI-MIYA!
BONG
SHO-KO!
HUH? DID YOU JUST HEAR SOMETHING?

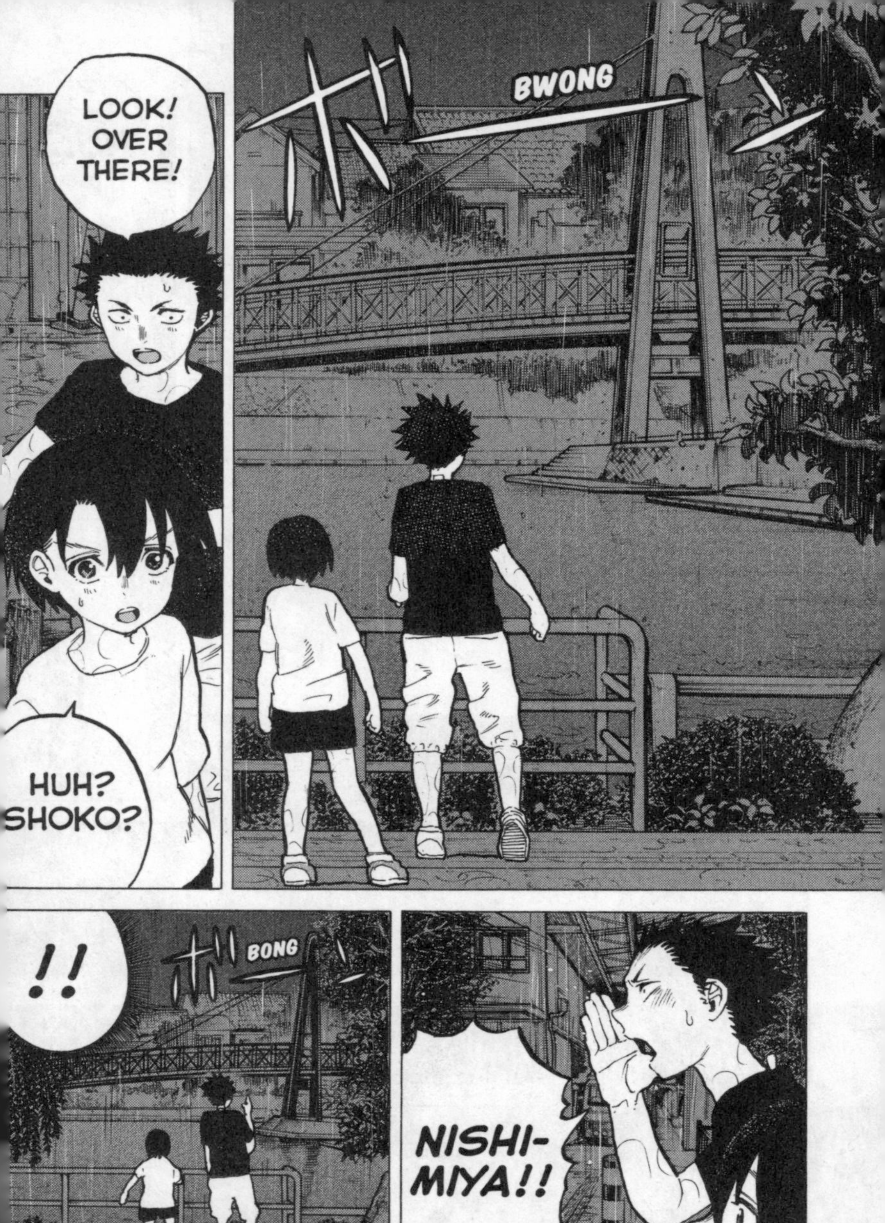
BWONG
LOOK! OVER THERE!
HUH? SHOKO?
NISHI-MIYA!!
BONG
!!

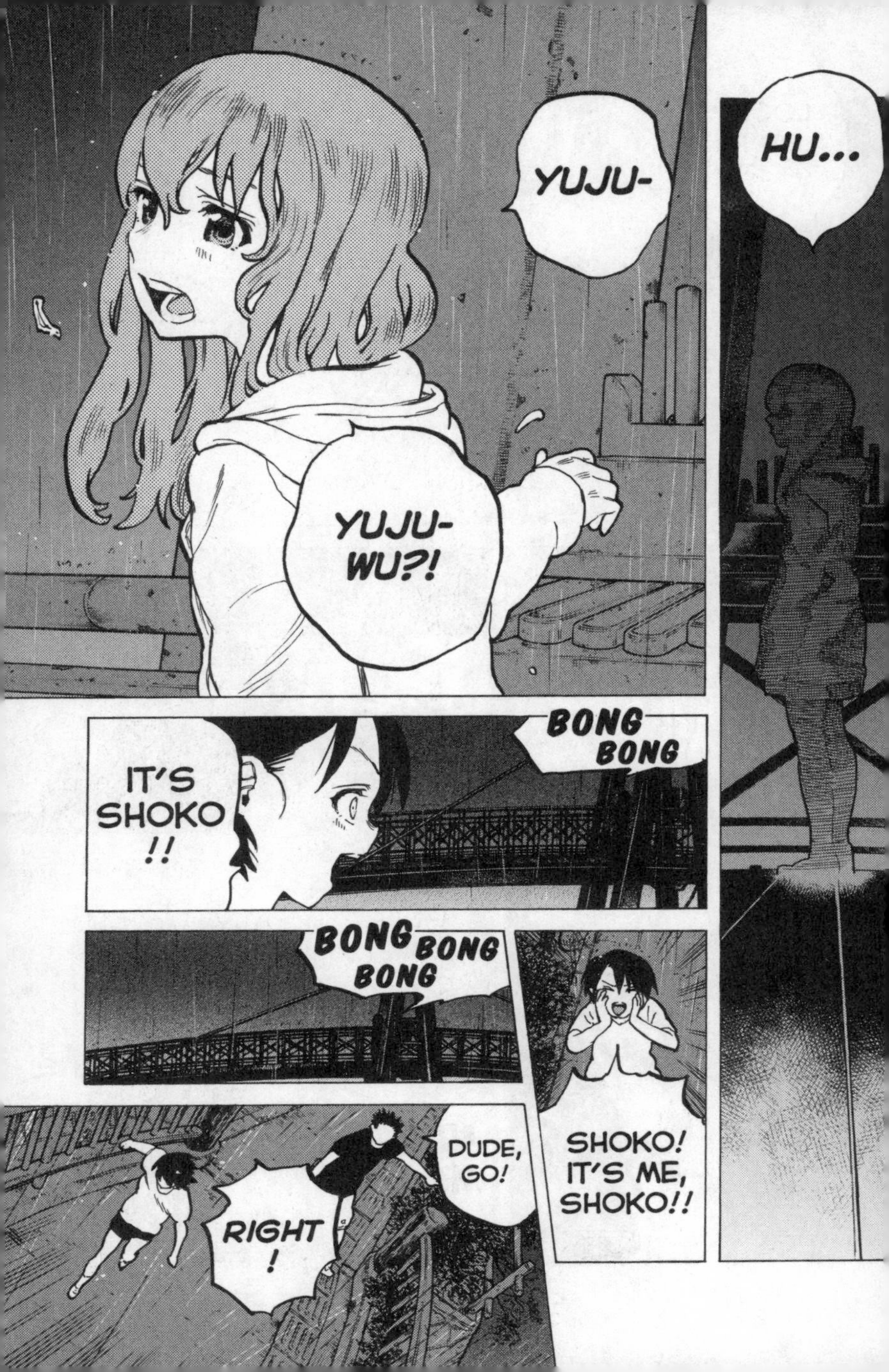
HU...
YUJU-
YUJU-WU?!
BONG BONG
IT'S SHOKO!!
SHOKO! IT'S ME, SHOKO!!
BONG BONG BONG
DUDE, GO!
RIGHT!

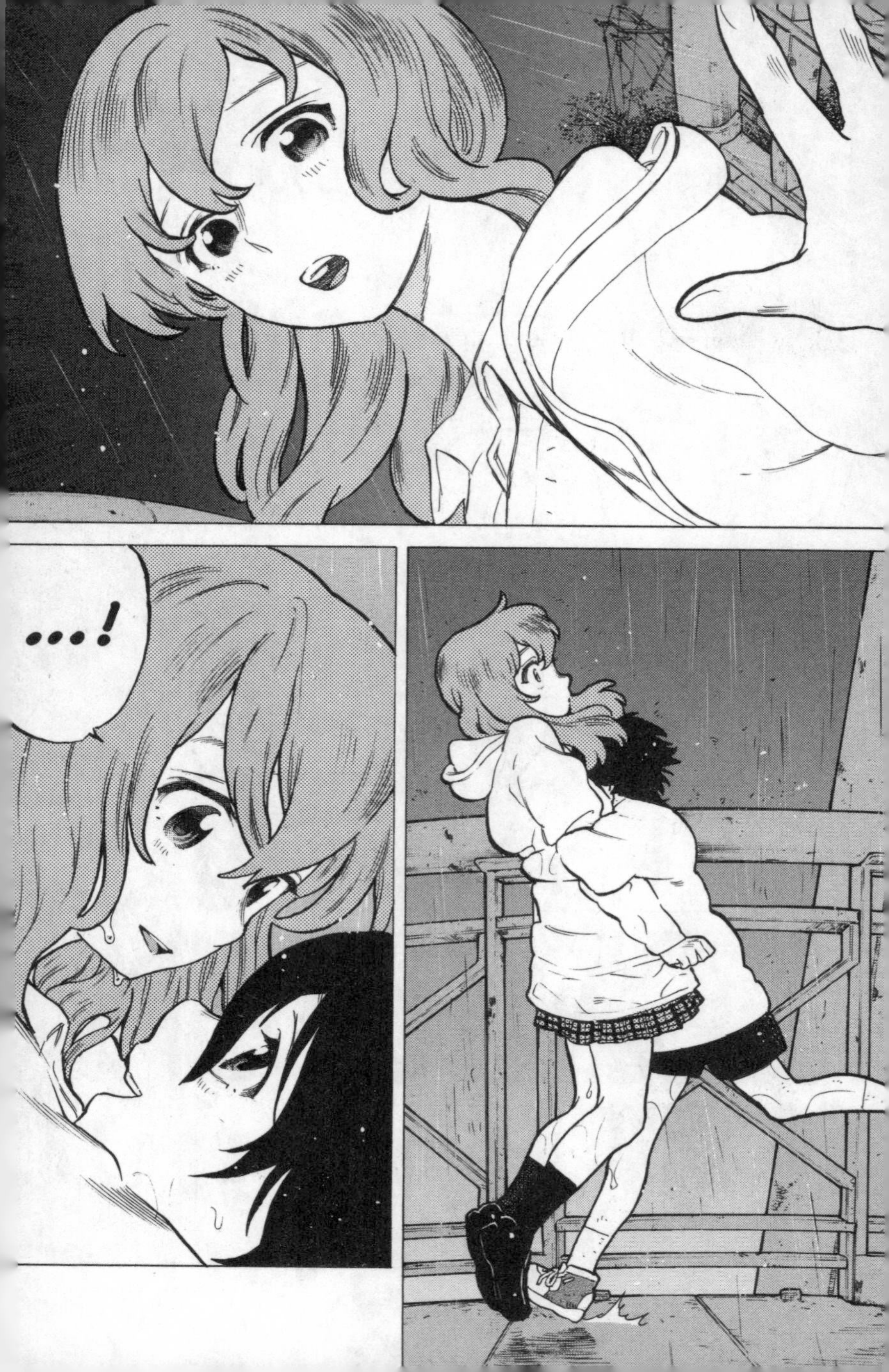
...!

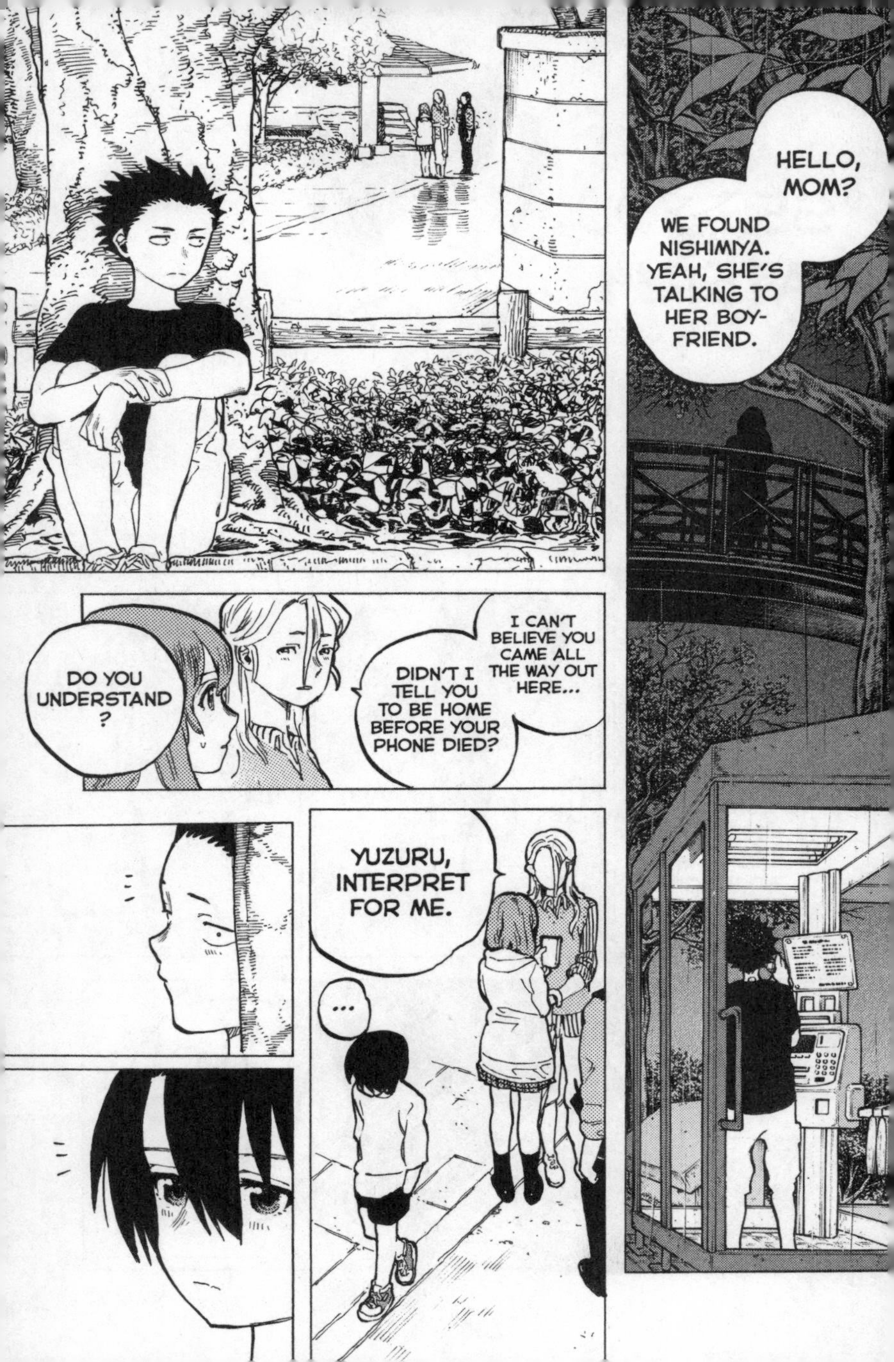
HELLO, MOM?
WE FOUND NISHIMIYA. YEAH, SHE'S TALKING TO HER BOY-FRIEND.
I CAN'T BELIEVE YOU CAME ALL THE WAY OUT HERE...
DIDN'T I TELL YOU TO BE HOME BEFORE YOUR PHONE DIED?
DO YOU UNDERSTAND ?
YUZURU, INTERPRET FOR ME.
...

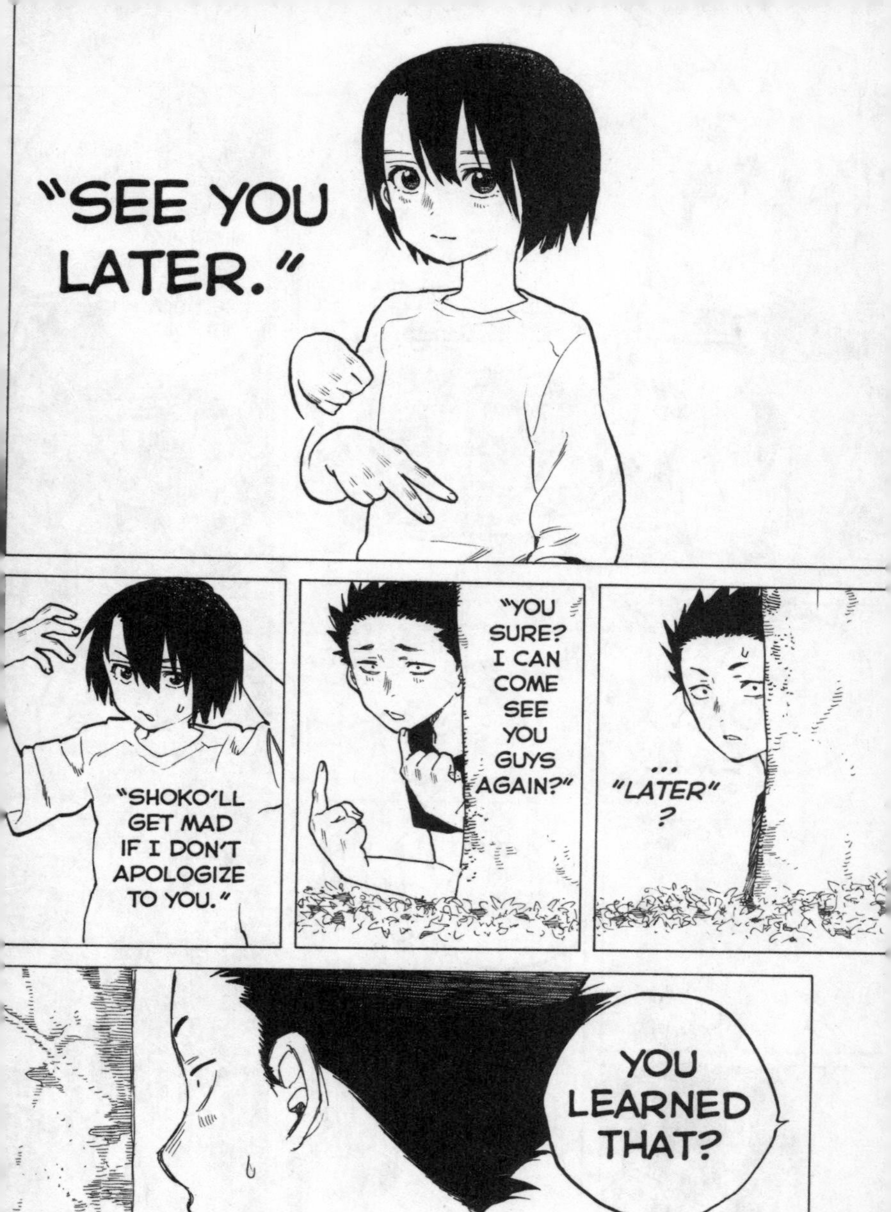
"SEE YOU LATER."
... "LATER" ?
"YOU SURE? I CAN COME SEE YOU GUYS AGAIN?"
"SHOKO'LL GET MAD IF I DON'T APOLOGIZE TO YOU."
YOU LEARNED THAT?

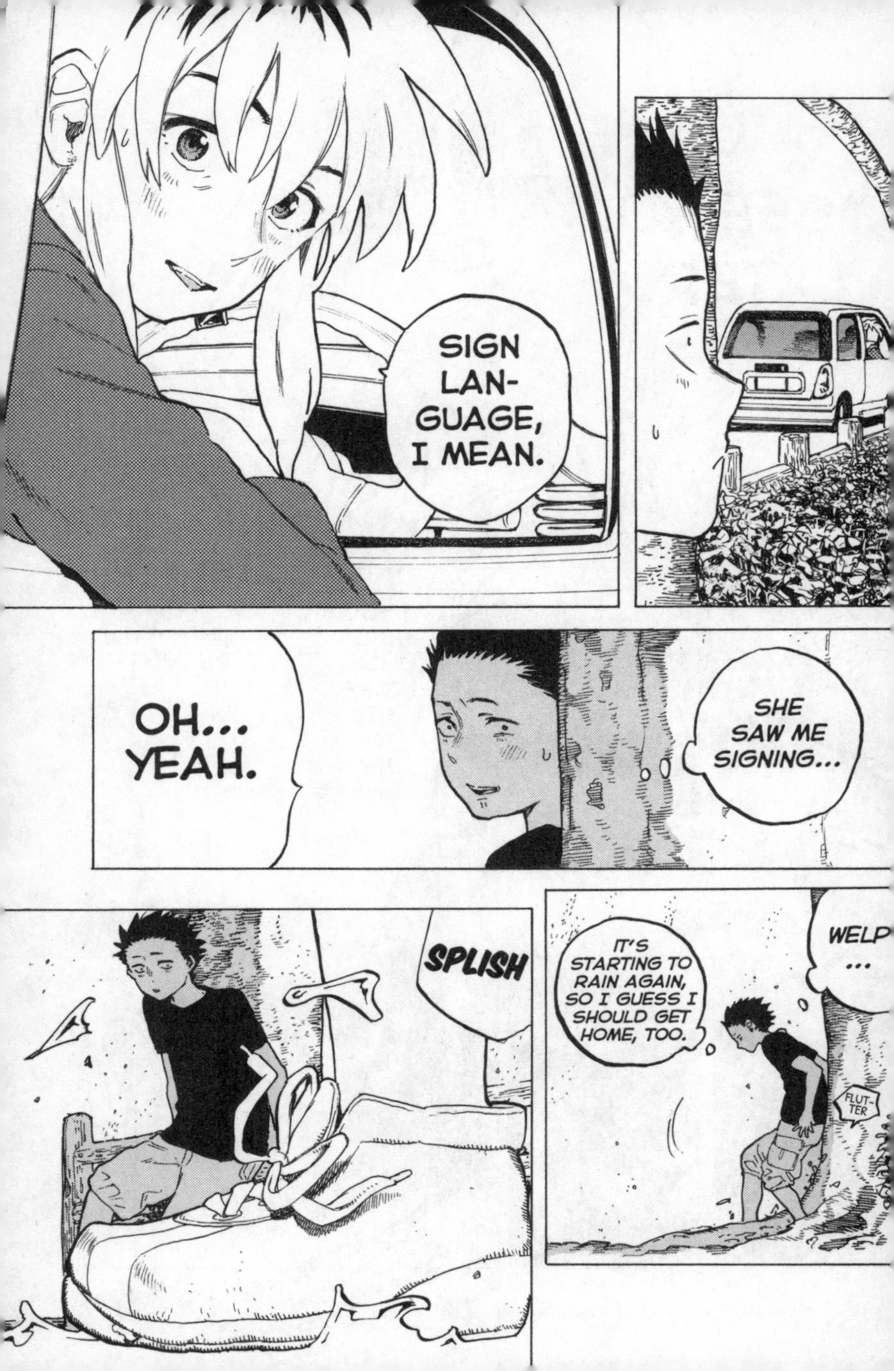
SIGN LAN-GUAGE, I MEAN.
SHE SAW ME SIGNING...
OH... YEAH.
WELP ...
IT'S STARTING TO RAIN AGAIN, SO I GUESS I SHOULD GET HOME, TOO.
FLUT-TER
SPLISH

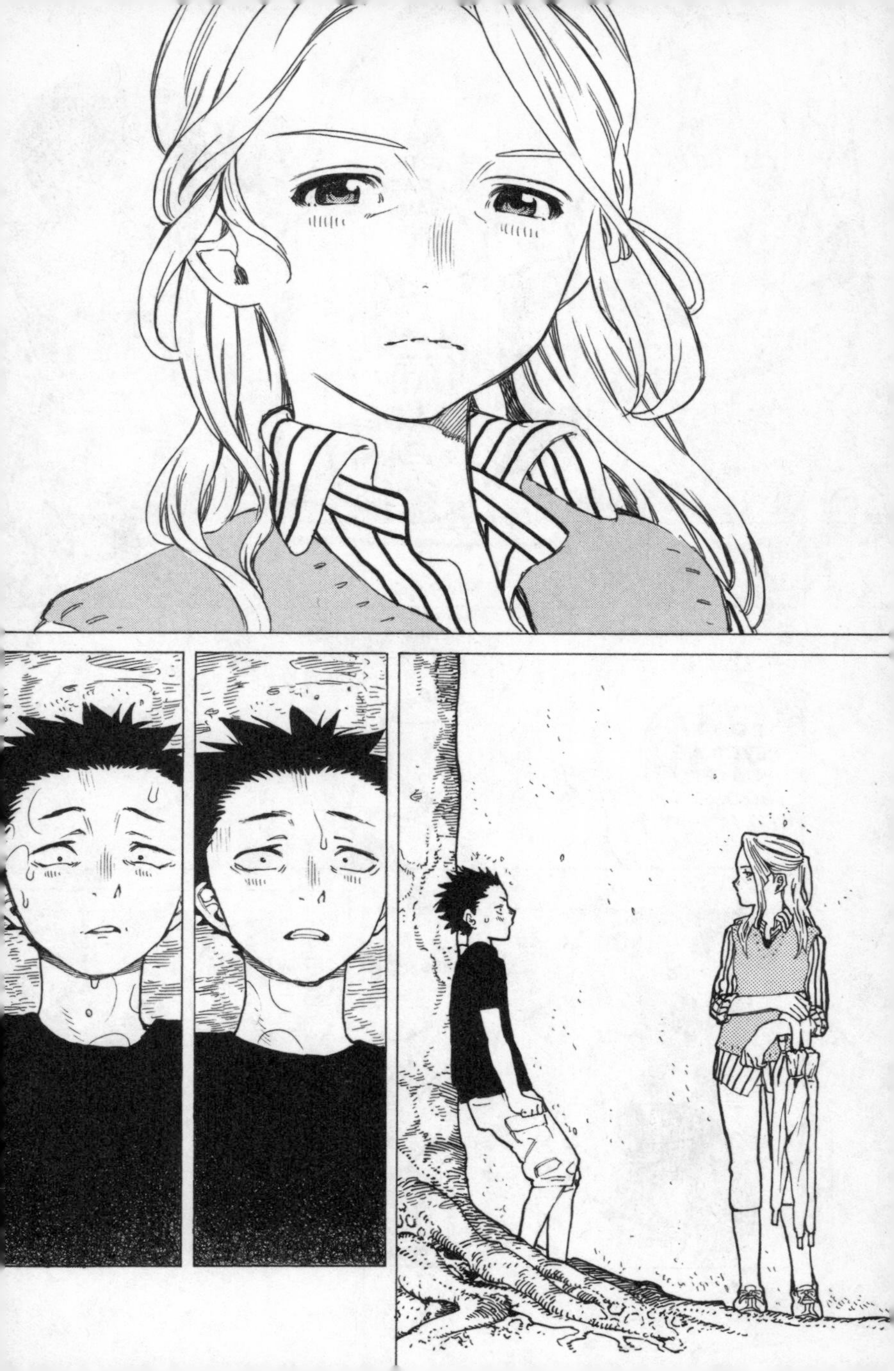

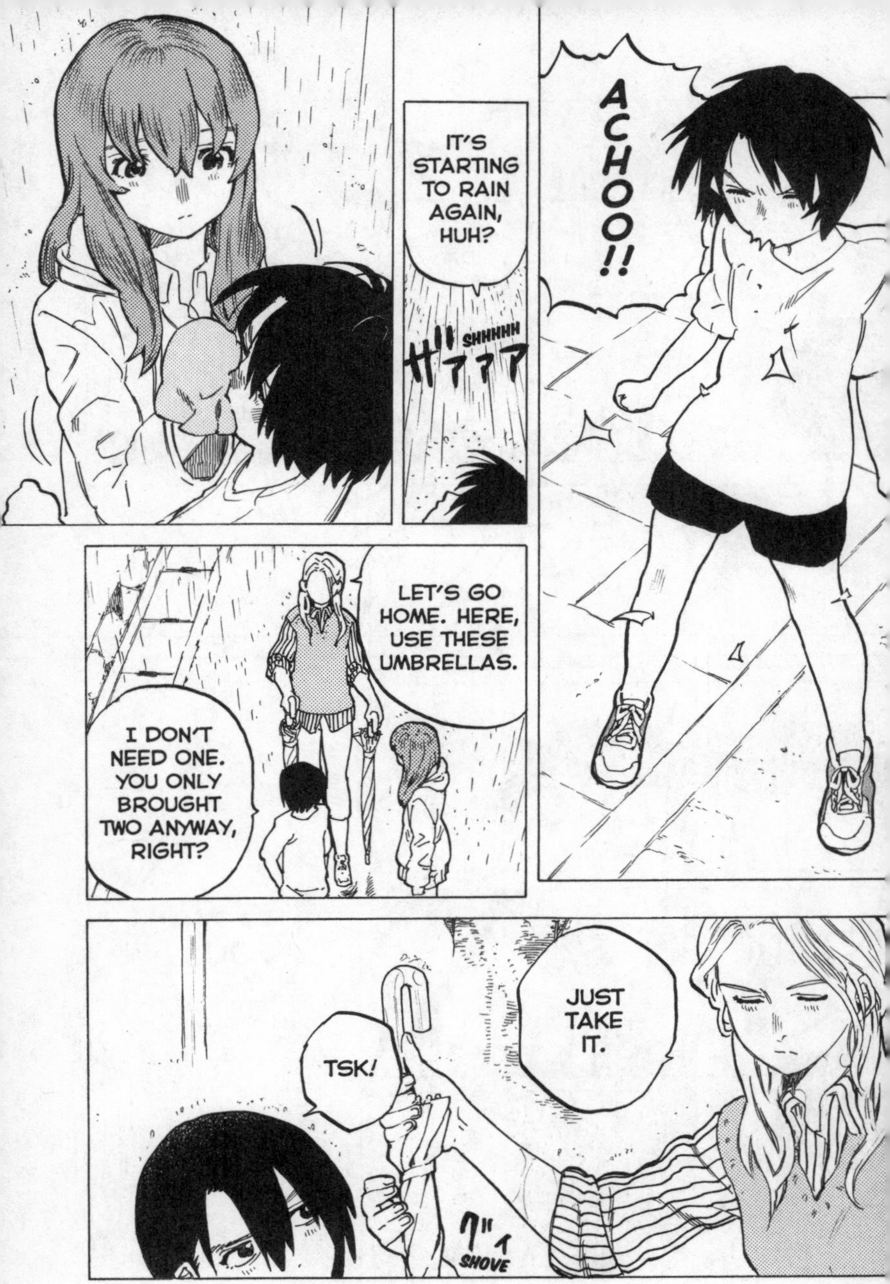
ACHOO!!
IT'S STARTING TO RAIN AGAIN, HUH?
SHHHHH
LET'S GO HOME. HERE, USE THESE UMBRELLAS.
I DON'T NEED ONE. YOU ONLY BROUGHT TWO ANYWAY, RIGHT?
JUST TAKE IT.
TSK!
SHOVE

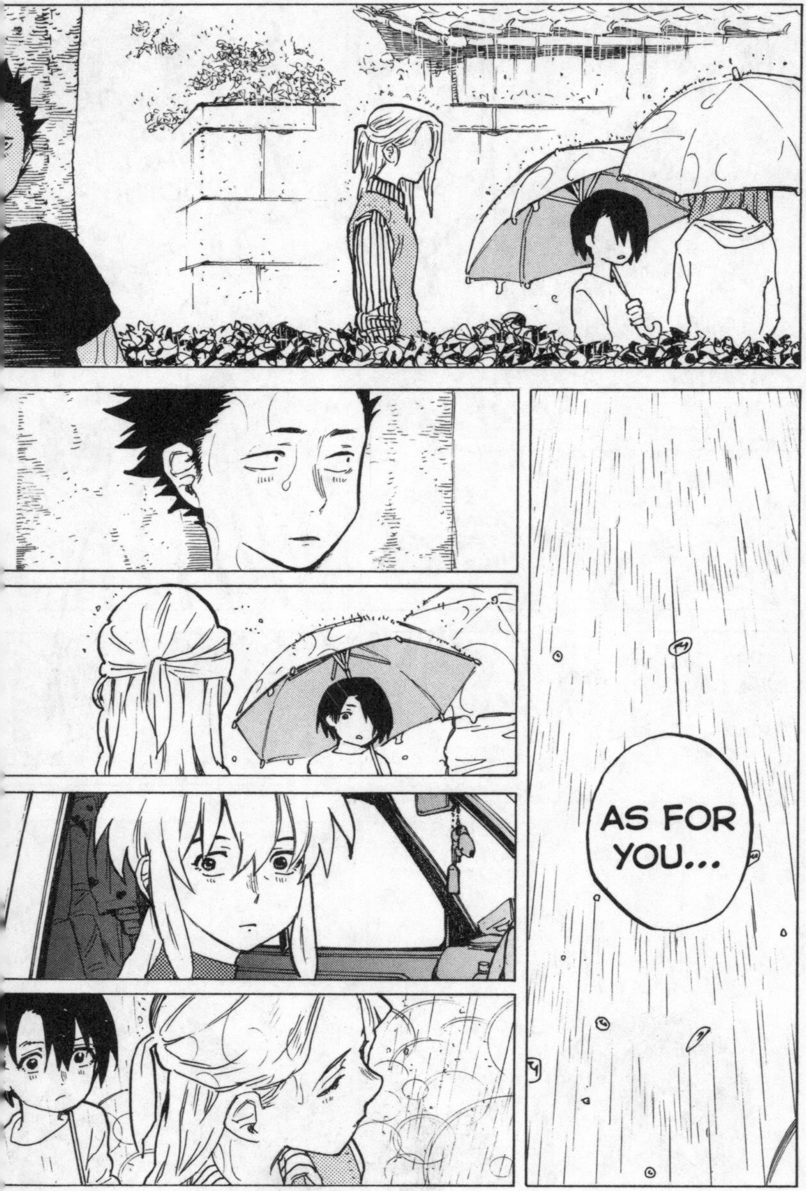
AS FOR YOU...

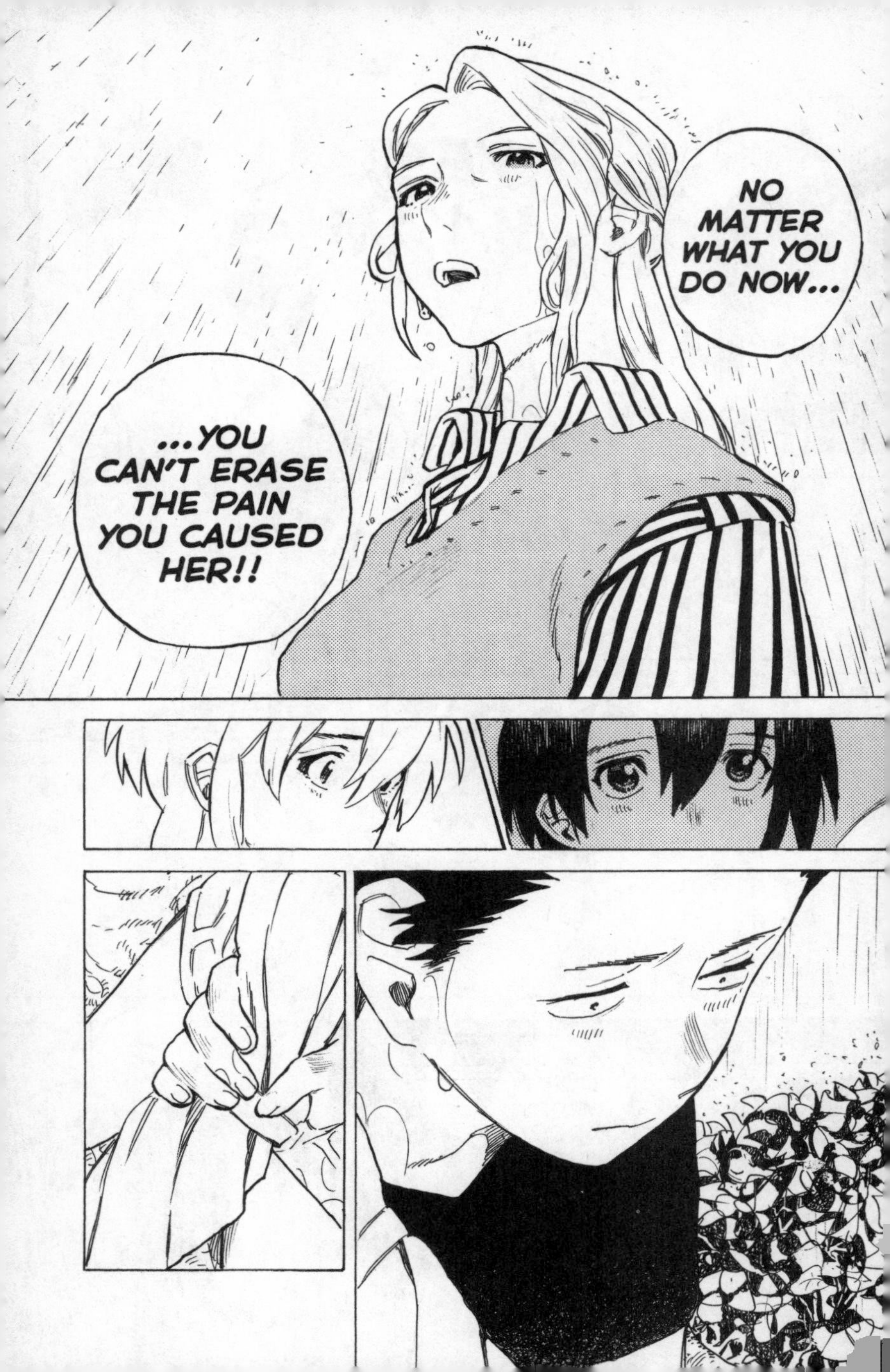
NO MATTER WHAT YOU DO NOW...
...YOU CAN'T ERASE THE PAIN YOU CAUSED HER!!

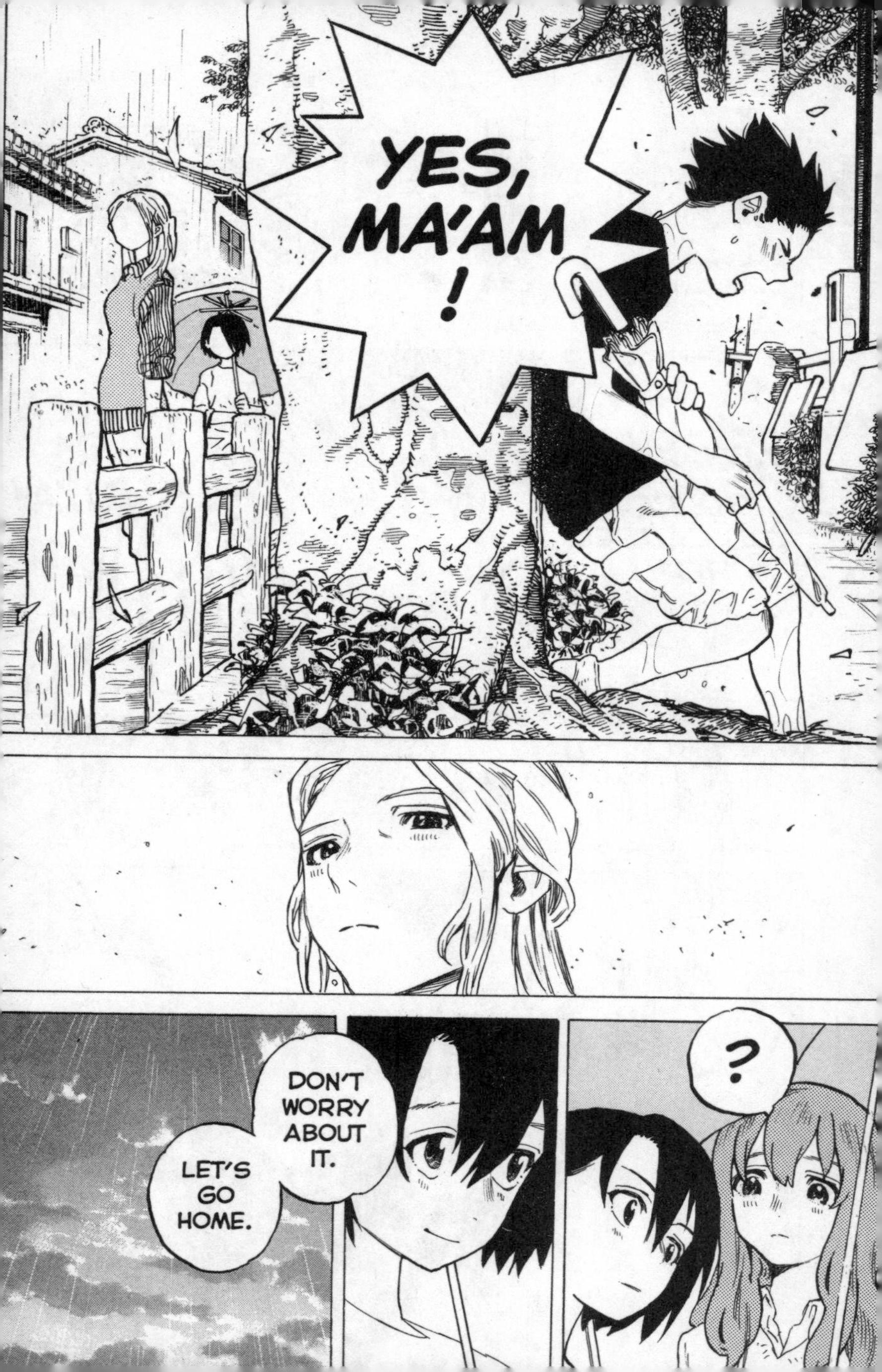
YES, MA'AM!
?
DON'T WORRY ABOUT IT.
LET'S GO HOME.

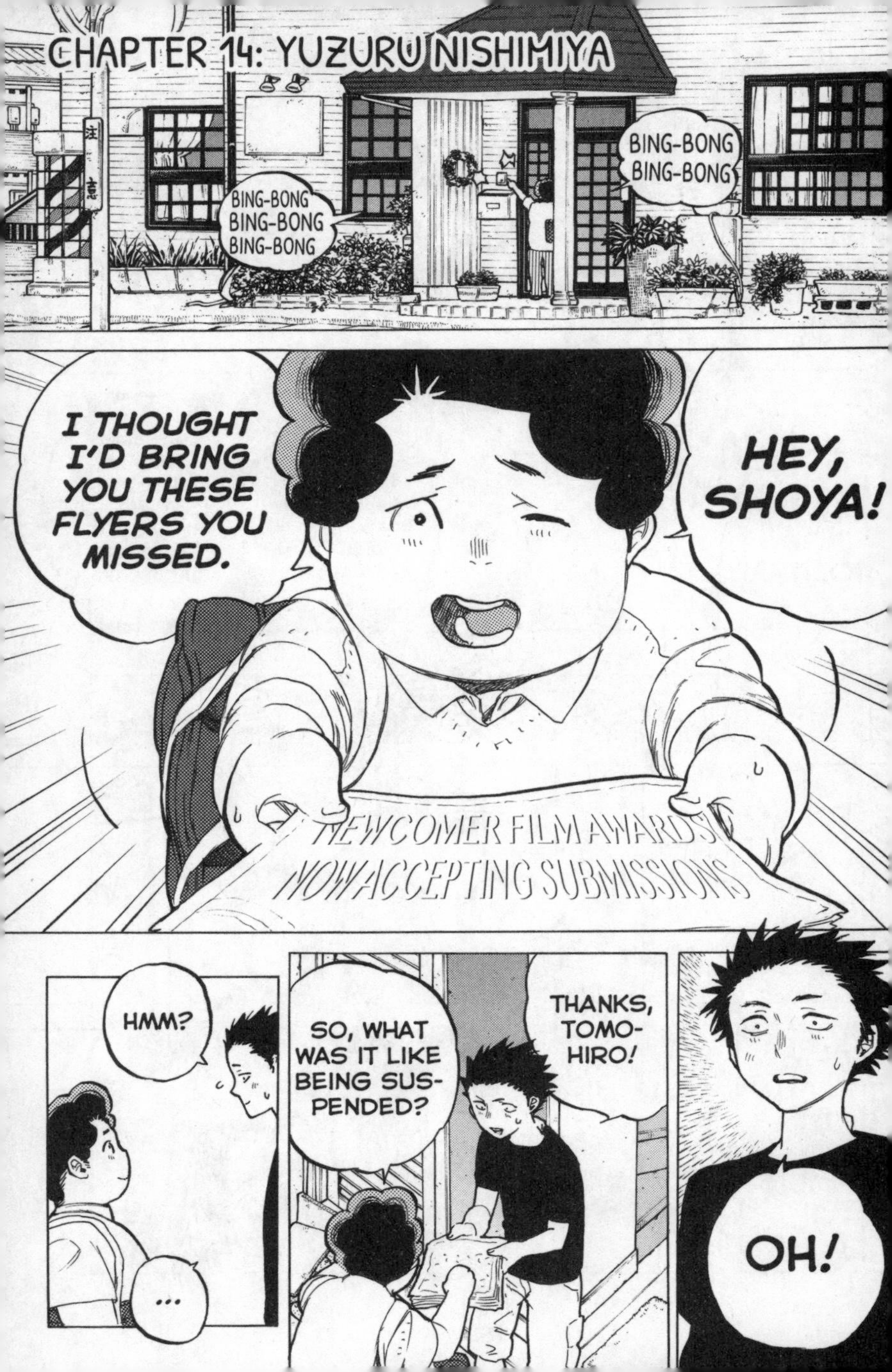
CHAPTER 14: YUZURU NISHIMIYA
注意
BING-BONG BING-BONG
BING-BONG BING-BONG BING-BONG
HEY, SHOYA!
I THOUGHT I'D BRING YOU THESE FLYERS YOU MISSED.
NEWCOMER FILM AWARDS NOW ACCEPTING SUBMISSIONS
OH!
THANKS, TOMO-HIRO!
SO, WHAT WAS IT LIKE BEING SUS-PENDED?
HMM?
...

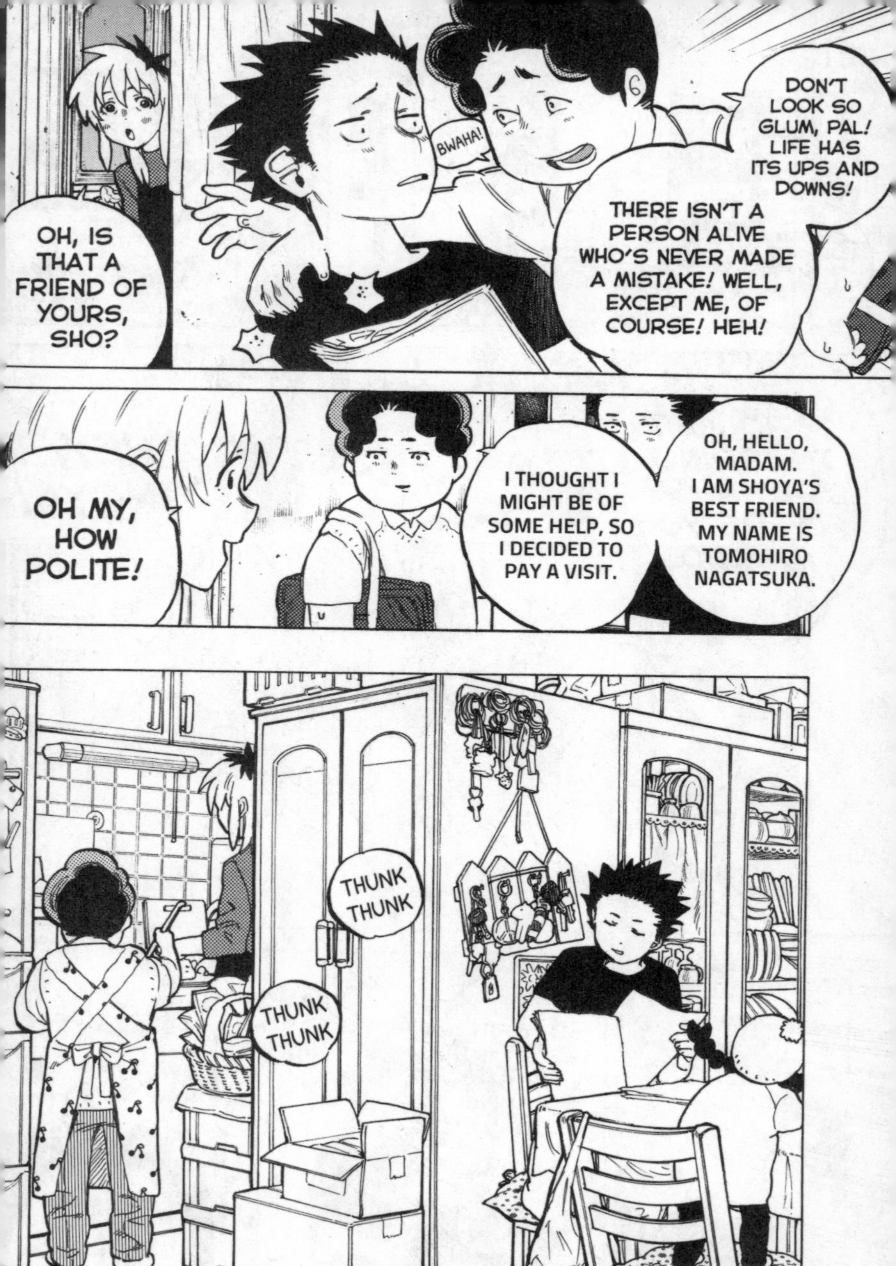
DON'T LOOK SO GLUM, PAL! LIFE HAS ITS UPS AND DOWNS!
THERE ISN'T A PERSON ALIVE WHO'S NEVER MADE A MISTAKE! WELL, EXCEPT ME, OF COURSE! HEH!
BWAHA!
OH, IS THAT A FRIEND OF YOURS, SHO?
OH, HELLO, MADAM. I AM SHOYA'S BEST FRIEND. MY NAME IS TOMOHIRO NAGATSUKA.
I THOUGHT I MIGHT BE OF SOME HELP, SO I DECIDED TO PAY A VISIT.
OH MY, HOW POLITE!
THUNK THUNK
THUNK THUNK

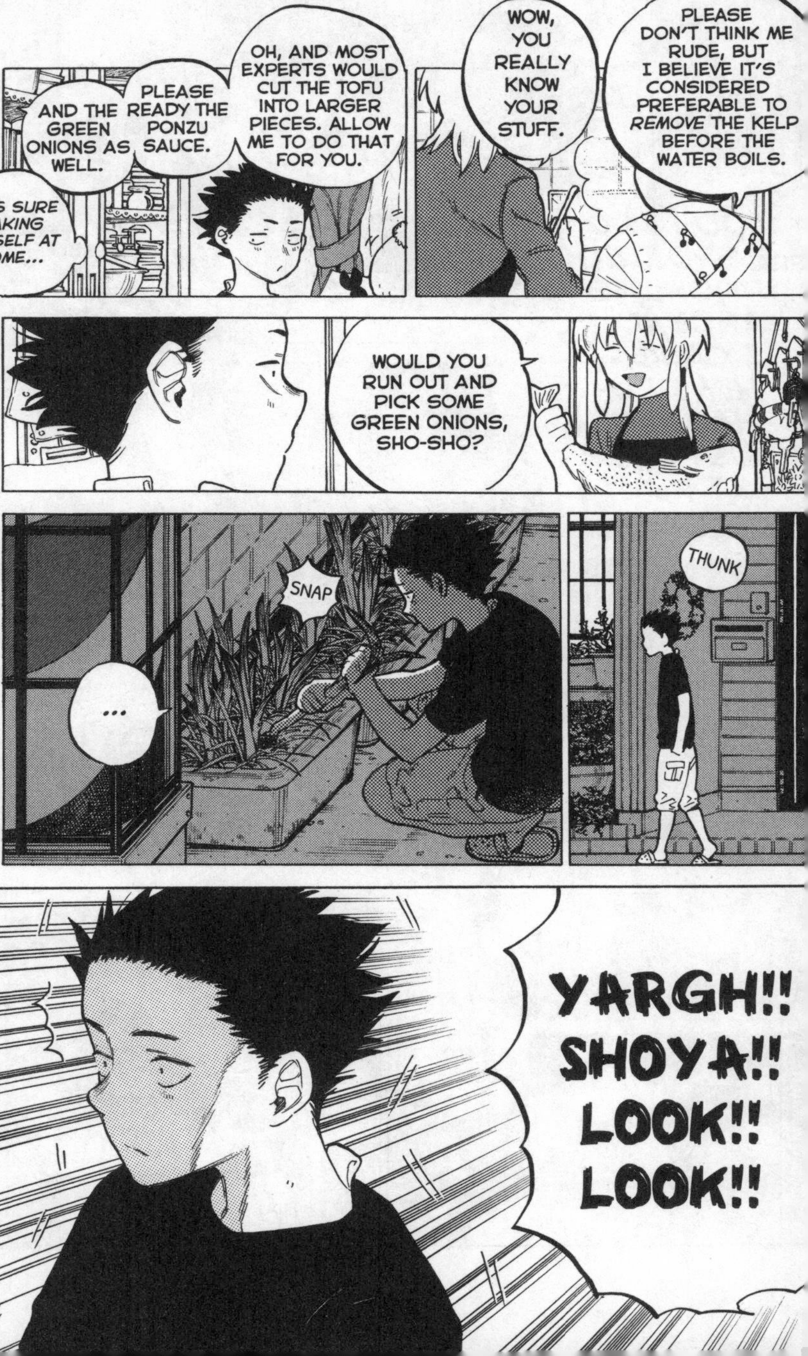
PLEASE DON'T THINK ME RUDE, BUT I BELIEVE IT'S CONSIDERED PREFERABLE TO *REMOVE* THE KELP BEFORE THE WATER BOILS.
WOW, YOU REALLY KNOW YOUR STUFF.
OH, AND MOST EXPERTS WOULD CUT THE TOFU INTO LARGER PIECES. ALLOW ME TO DO THAT FOR YOU.
PLEASE READY THE PONZU SAUCE.
AND THE GREEN ONIONS AS WELL.
HE'S SURE MAKING HIMSELF AT HOME...
WOULD YOU RUN OUT AND PICK SOME GREEN ONIONS, SHO-SHO?
THUNK
SNAP
...
YARGH!! SHOYA!! LOOK!! LOOK!!

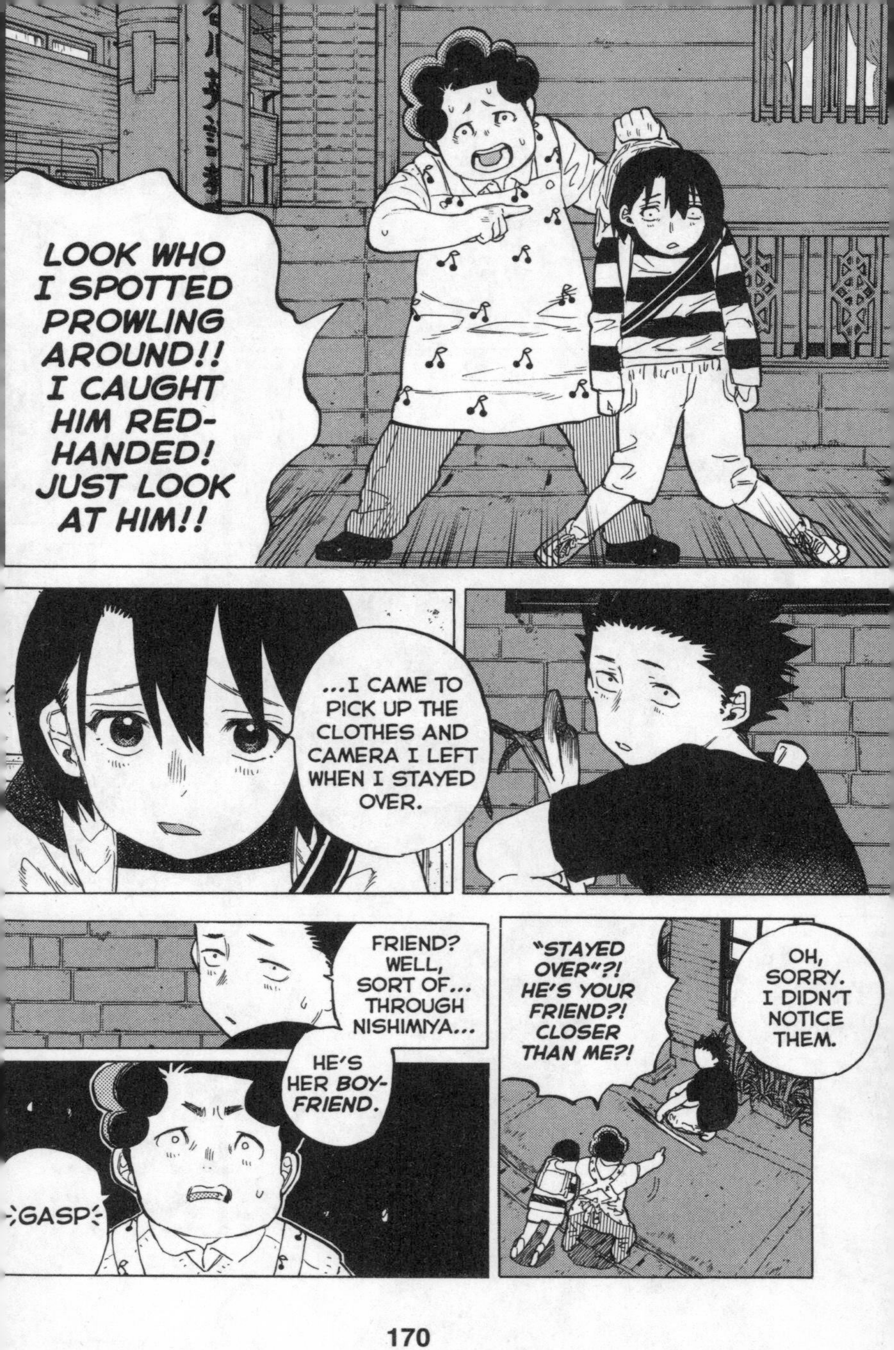
LOOK WHO I SPOTTED PROWLING AROUND!! I CAUGHT HIM RED-HANDED! JUST LOOK AT HIM!!
...I CAME TO PICK UP THE CLOTHES AND CAMERA I LEFT WHEN I STAYED OVER.
OH, SORRY. I DIDN'T NOTICE THEM.
"STAYED OVER"?! HE'S YOUR FRIEND?! CLOSER THAN ME?!
FRIEND? WELL, SORT OF... THROUGH NISHIMIYA...
HE'S HER *BOY-FRIEND*.
GASP

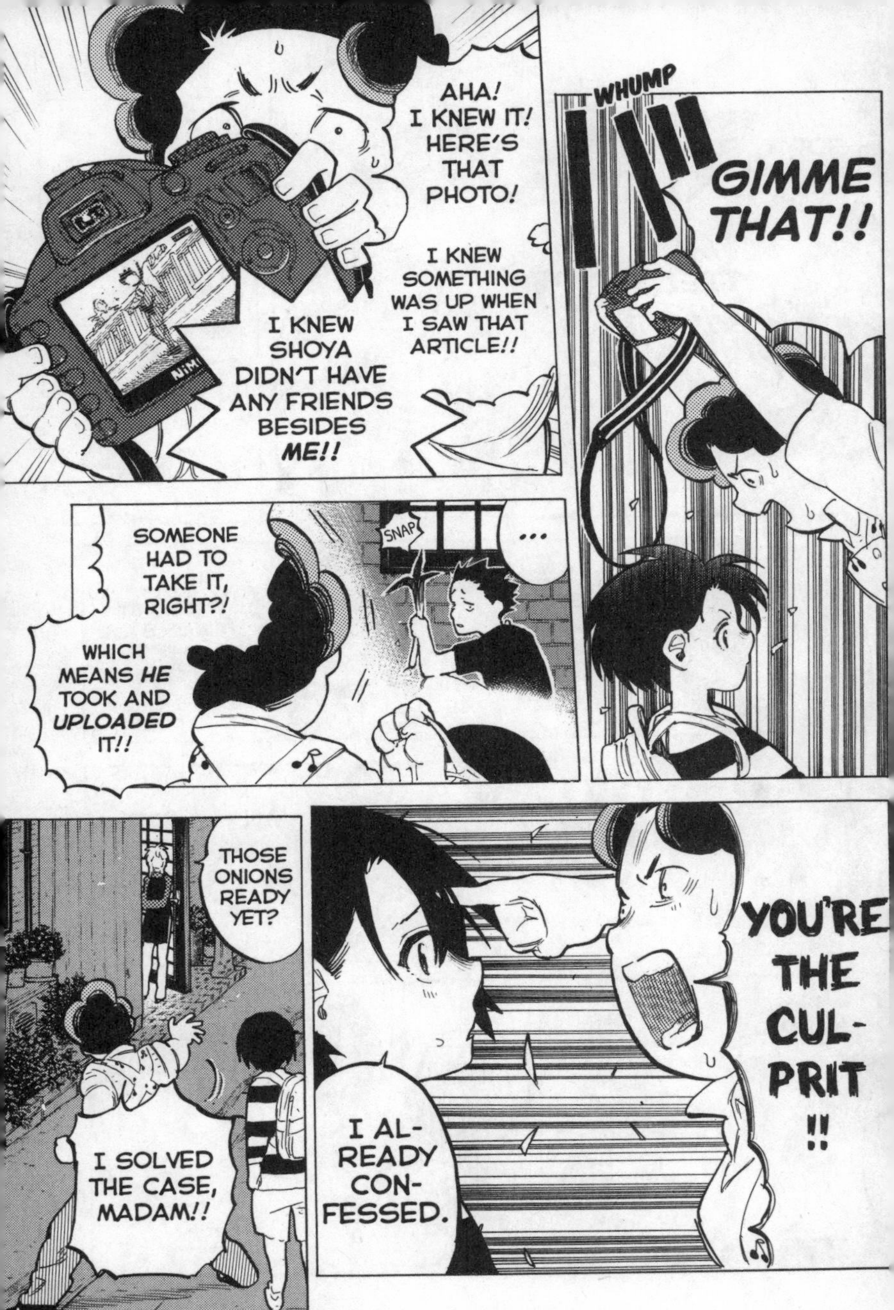
AHA! I KNEW IT! HERE'S THAT PHOTO!
I KNEW SOMETHING WAS UP WHEN I SAW THAT ARTICLE!!
I KNEW SHOYA DIDN'T HAVE ANY FRIENDS BESIDES *ME!!*
WHUMP
GIMME THAT!!
...
SNAP
SOMEONE HAD TO TAKE IT, RIGHT?!
WHICH MEANS *HE* TOOK AND *UPLOADED* IT!!
YOU'RE THE CUL-PRIT!!
I AL-READY CON-FESSED.
THOSE ONIONS READY YET?
I SOLVED THE CASE, MADAM!!

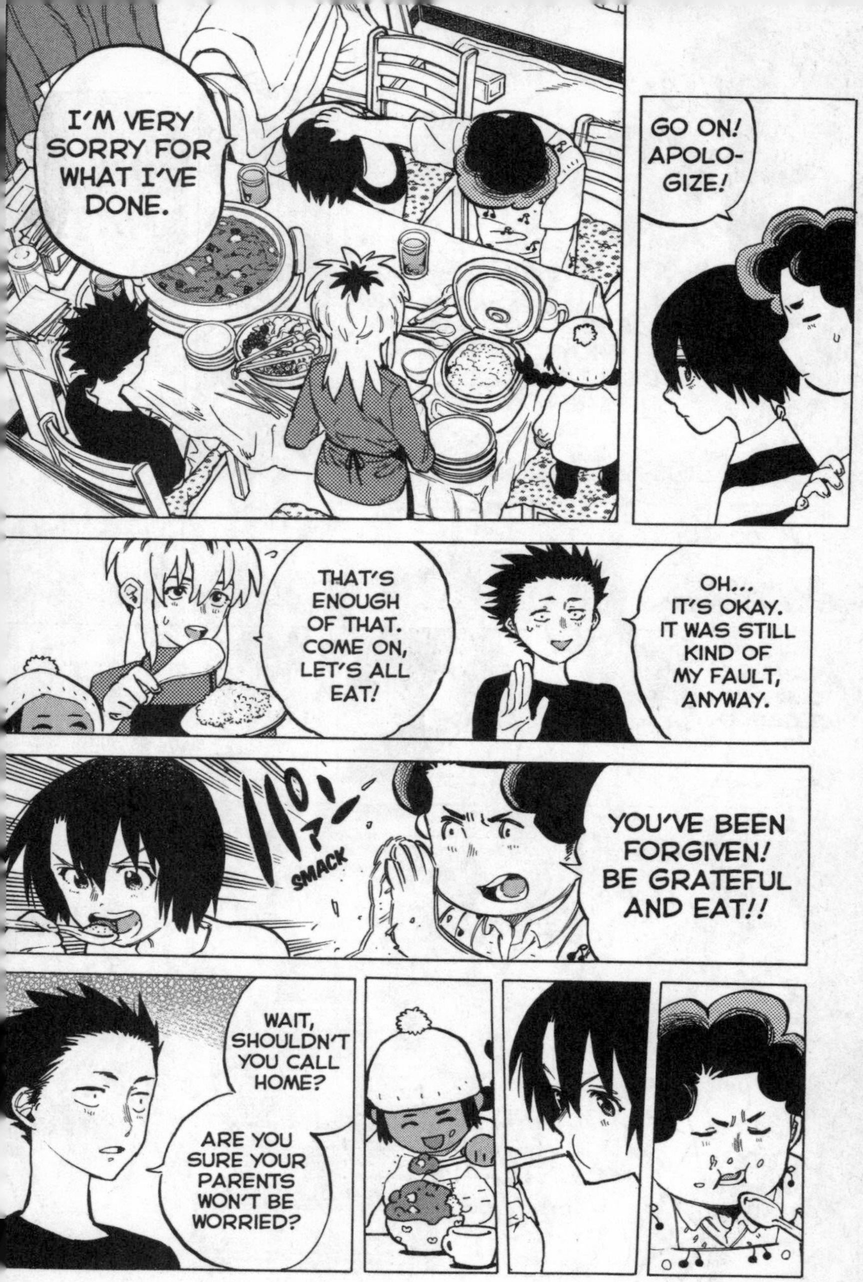
GO ON! APOLOGIZE!
I'M VERY SORRY FOR WHAT I'VE DONE.
OH... IT'S OKAY. IT WAS STILL KIND OF MY FAULT, ANYWAY.
THAT'S ENOUGH OF THAT. COME ON, LET'S ALL EAT!
YOU'VE BEEN FORGIVEN! BE GRATEFUL AND EAT!!
SMACK
WAIT, SHOULDN'T YOU CALL HOME?
ARE YOU SURE YOUR PARENTS WON'T BE WORRIED?

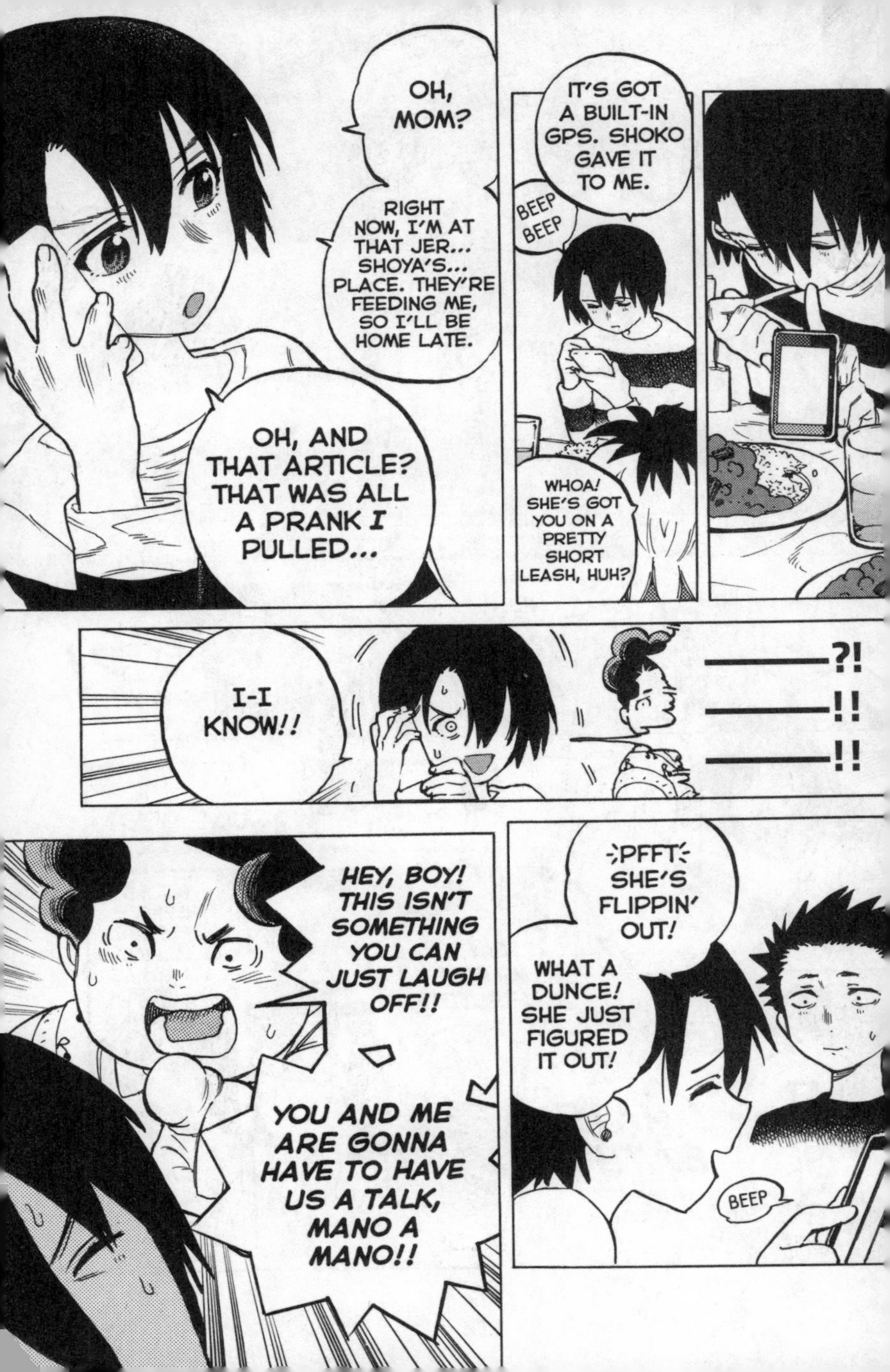
IT'S GOT A BUILT-IN GPS. SHOKO GAVE IT TO ME.
BEEP BEEP
WHOA! SHE'S GOT YOU ON A PRETTY SHORT LEASH, HUH?
OH, MOM?
RIGHT NOW, I'M AT THAT JER... SHOYA'S... PLACE. THEY'RE FEEDING ME, SO I'LL BE HOME LATE.
OH, AND THAT ARTICLE? THAT WAS ALL A PRANK *I* PULLED...
——?!
——!!
——!!
I-I KNOW!!
PFFT SHE'S FLIPPIN' OUT!
WHAT A DUNCE! SHE JUST FIGURED IT OUT!
BEEP
HEY, BOY! THIS ISN'T SOMETHING YOU CAN JUST LAUGH OFF!!
YOU AND ME ARE GONNA HAVE TO HAVE US A TALK, MANO A MANO!!

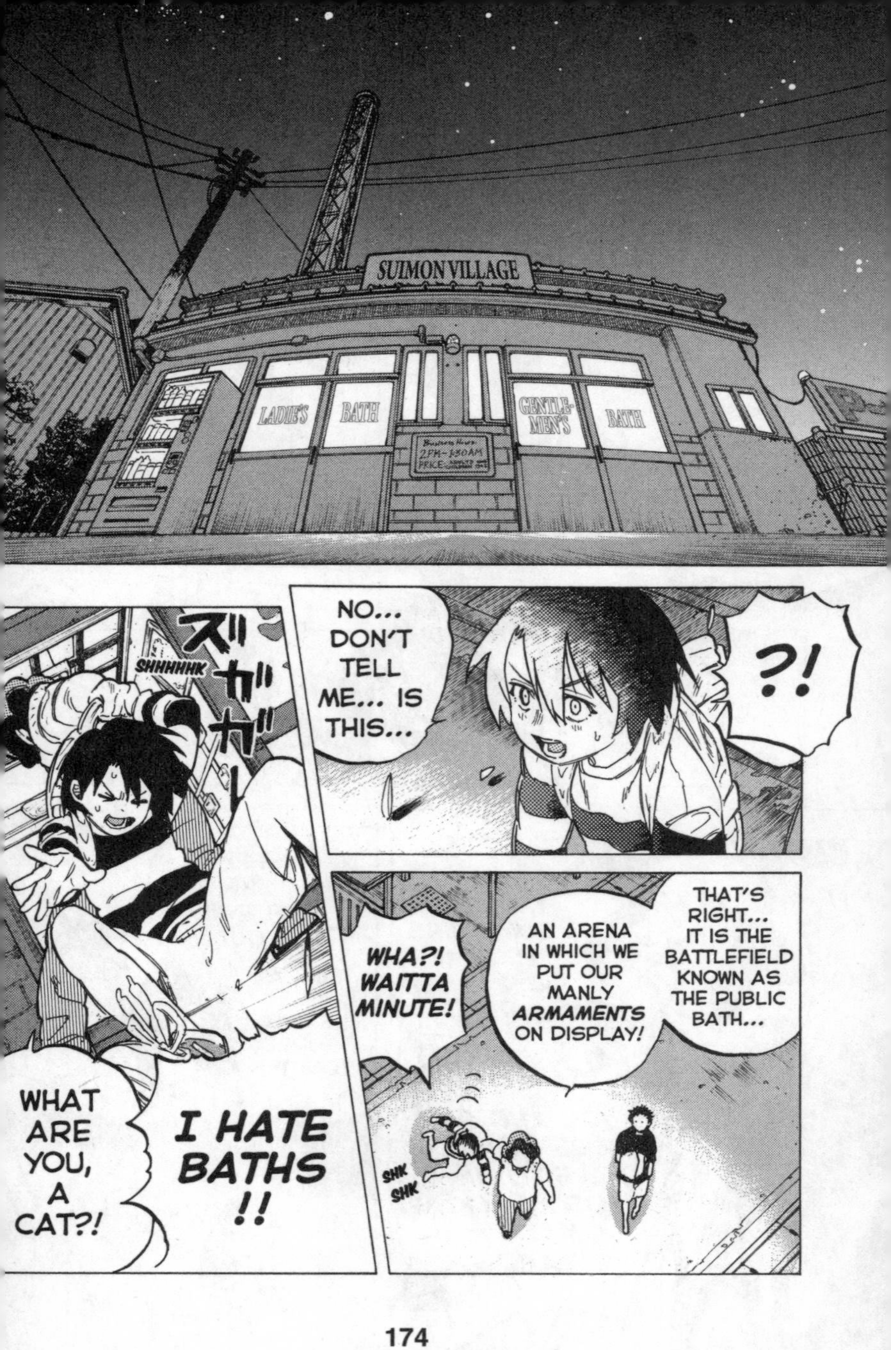
SUIMON VILLAGE
LADIE'S
BATH
GENTLE-MEN'S
BATH
Business Hours
2PM-1:30AM
PRICE
?!
NO... DON'T TELL ME... IS THIS...
THAT'S RIGHT... IT IS THE BATTLEFIELD KNOWN AS THE PUBLIC BATH...
AN ARENA IN WHICH WE PUT OUR MANLY ARMAMENTS ON DISPLAY!
WHA?! WAITTA MINUTE!
SHK SHK
ズガガー
SHHHHHK
I HATE BATHS!!
WHAT ARE YOU, A CAT?!

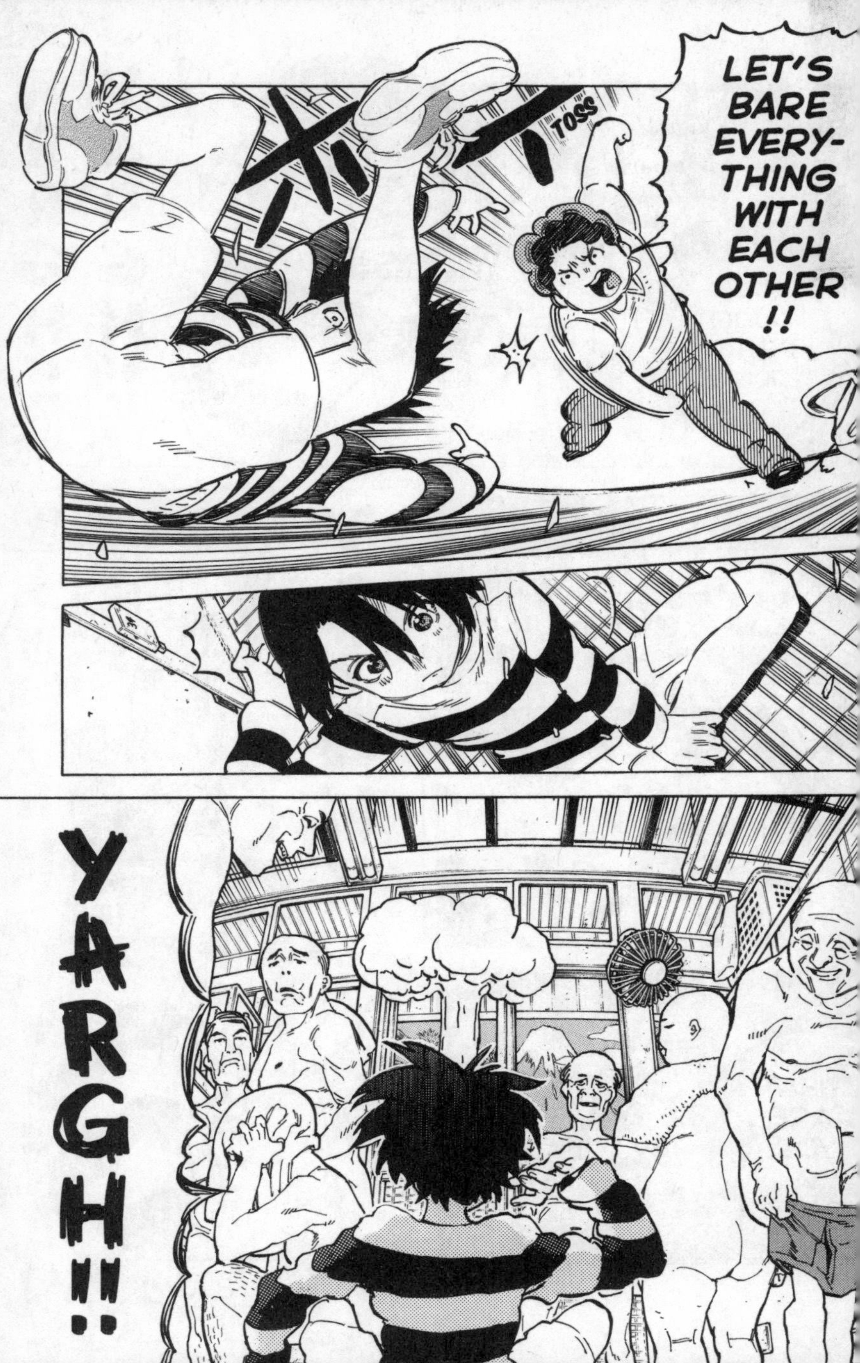
LET'S BARE EVERY-THING WITH EACH OTHER !!
TOSS
YARGH!!

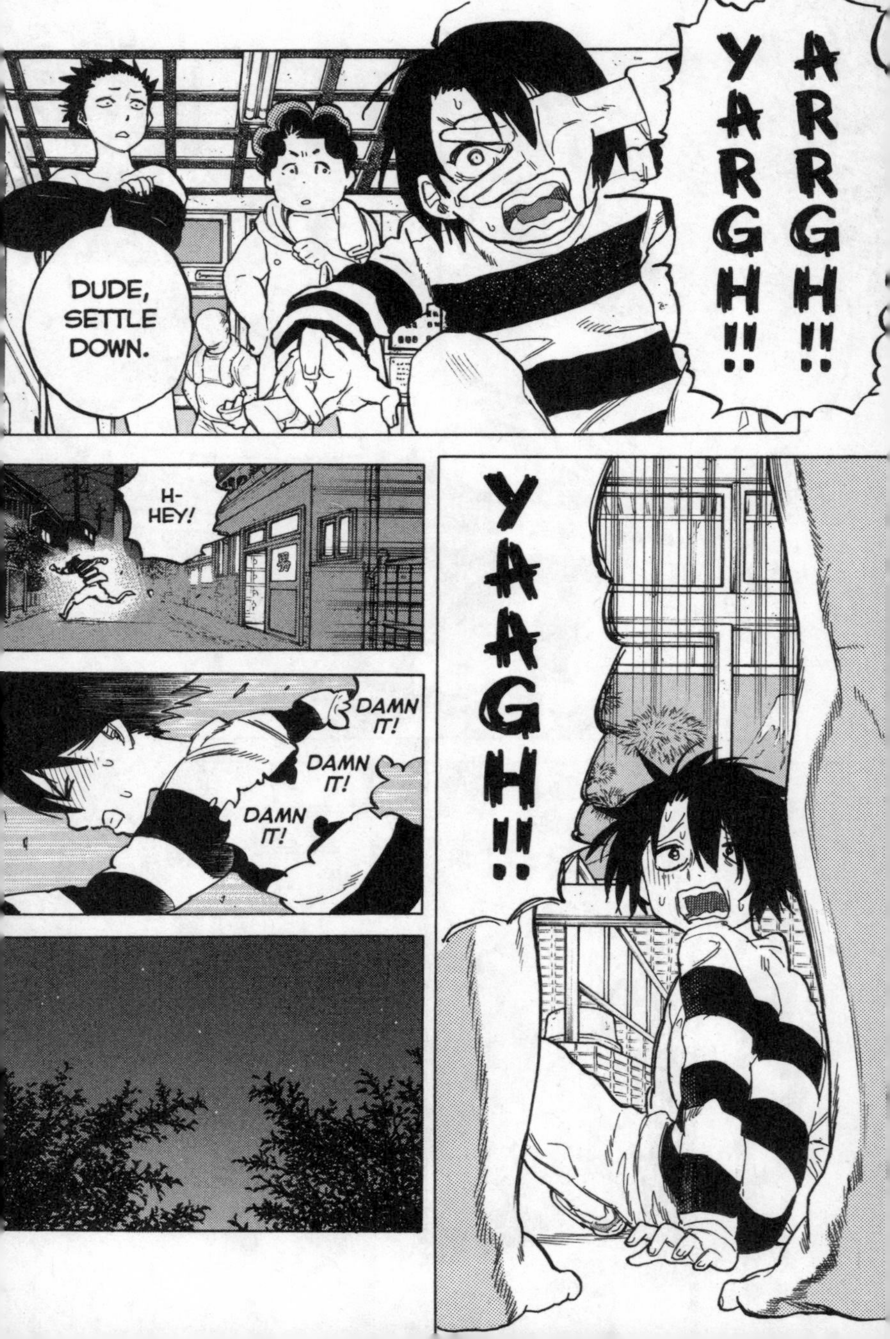
ARRGH!!
YARGH!!
DUDE, SETTLE DOWN.
YAAAGH!!
H-HEY!
DAMN IT!
DAMN IT!
DAMN IT!

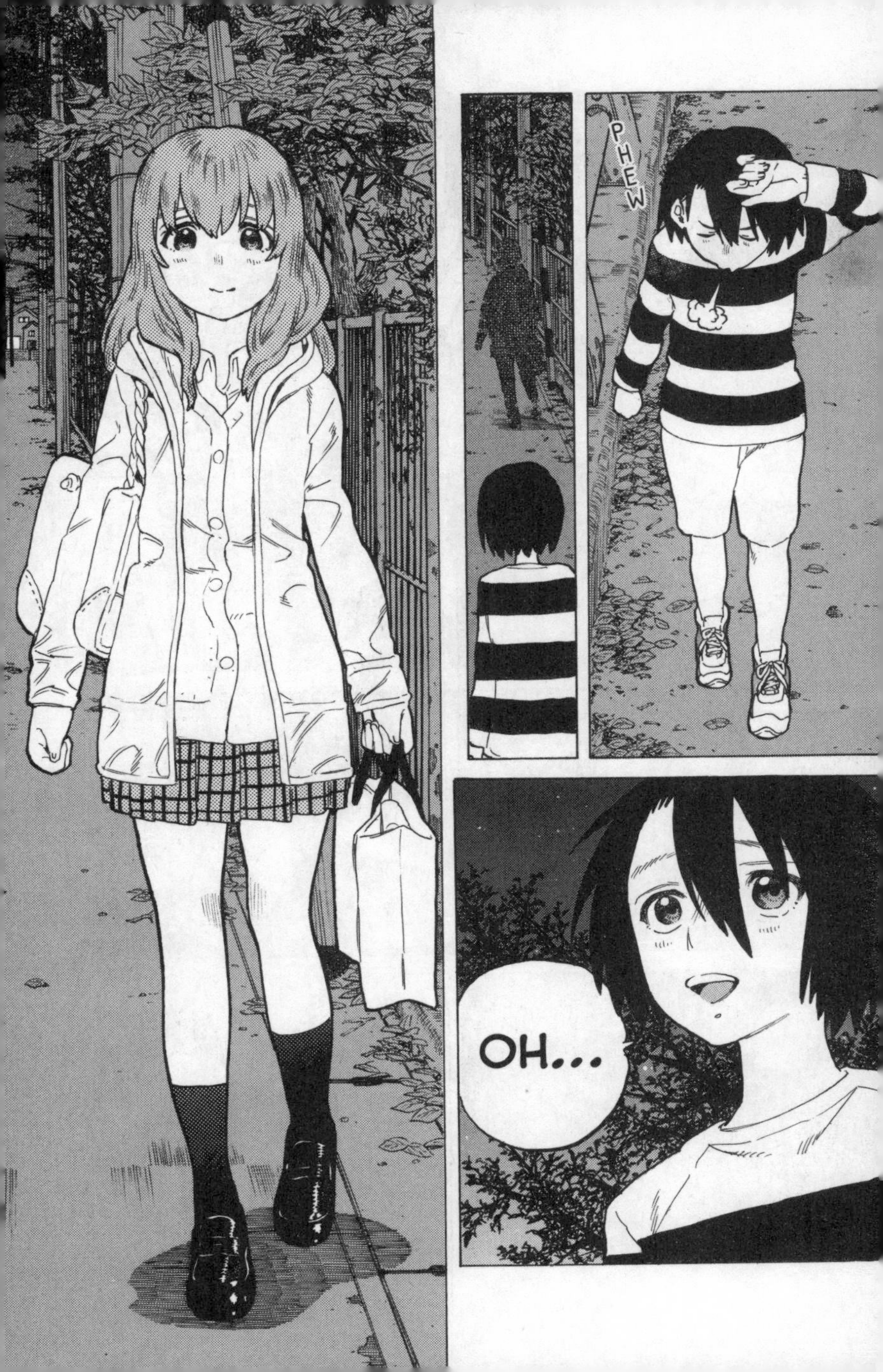
PHEW
OH...

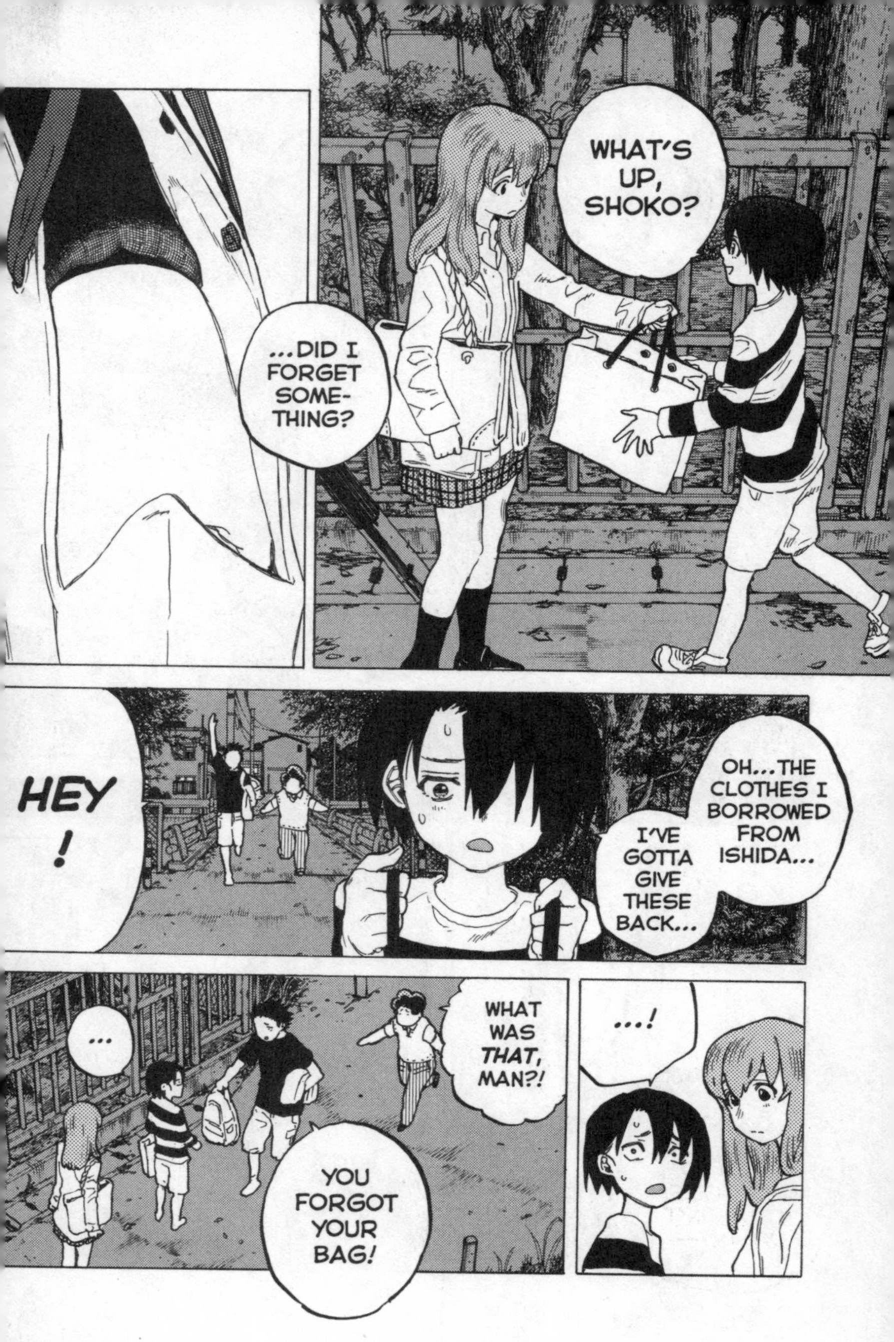
WHAT'S UP, SHOKO?
...DID I FORGET SOME-THING?
OH...THE CLOTHES I BORROWED FROM ISHIDA...
I'VE GOTTA GIVE THESE BACK...
HEY!
...!
WHAT WAS *THAT*, MAN?!
YOU FORGOT YOUR BAG!
...

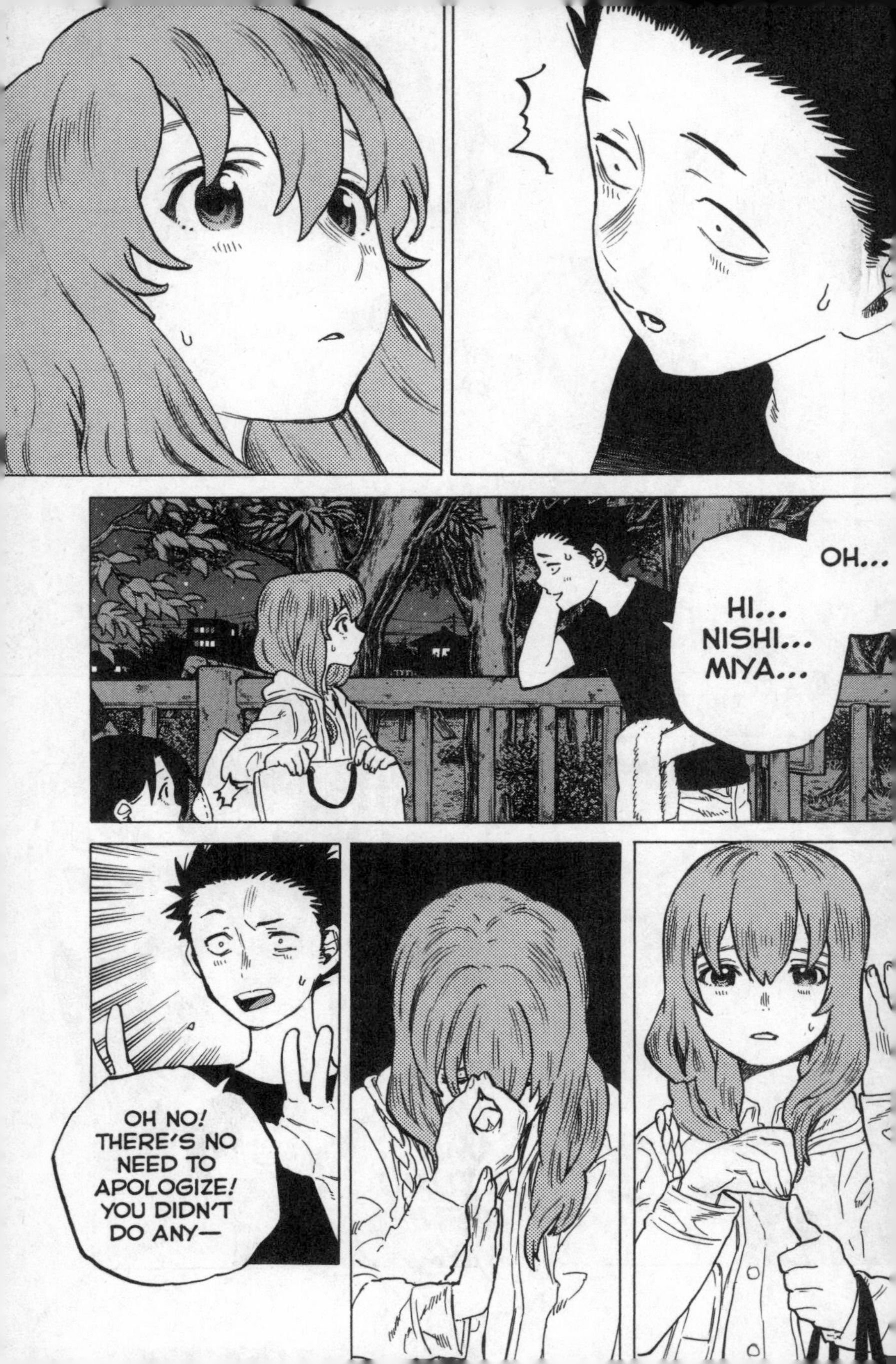
OH...
HI... NISHI... MIYA...
OH NO! THERE'S NO NEED TO APOLOGIZE! YOU DIDN'T DO ANY—

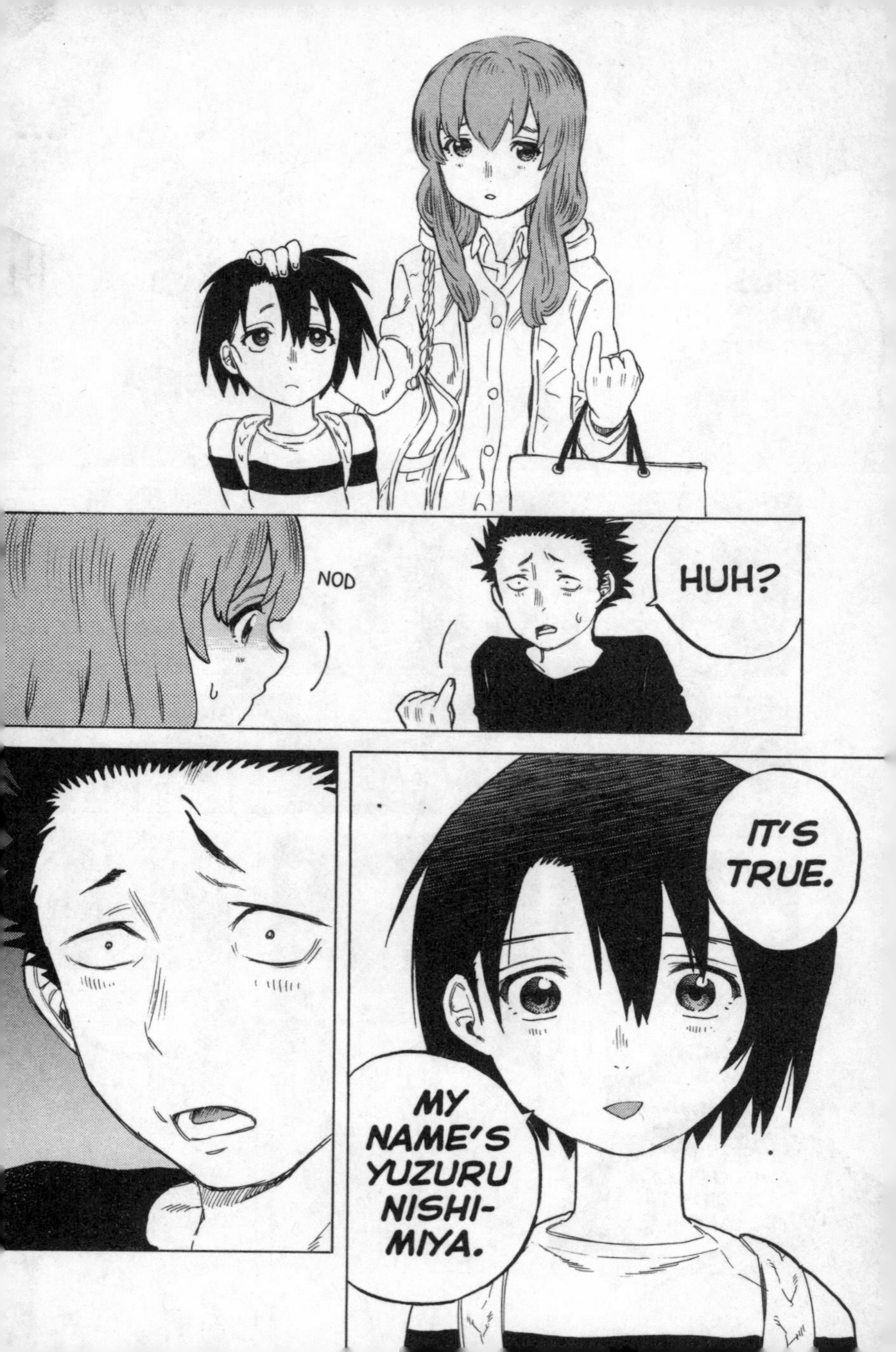
HUH?
NOD
IT'S TRUE.
MY NAME'S YUZURU NISHI-MIYA.

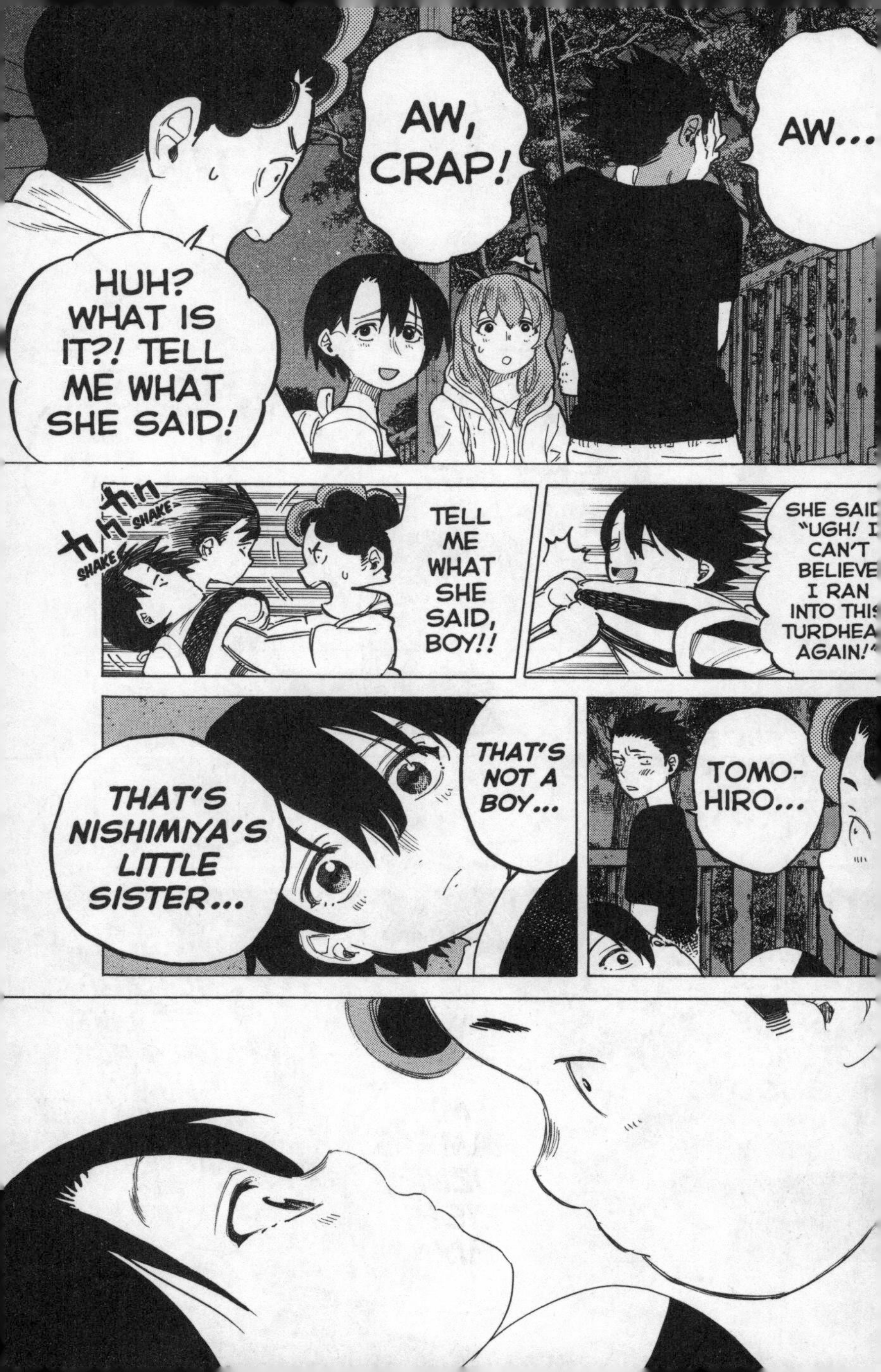
AW...
AW, CRAP!
HUH? WHAT IS IT?! TELL ME WHAT SHE SAID!
SHE SAID “UGH! I CAN'T BELIEVE I RAN INTO THIS TURDHEA AGAIN!”
TELL ME WHAT SHE SAID, BOY!!
SHAKE
SHAKE
TOMO-HIRO...
THAT'S NOT A BOY...
THAT'S NISHIMIYA'S LITTLE SISTER...

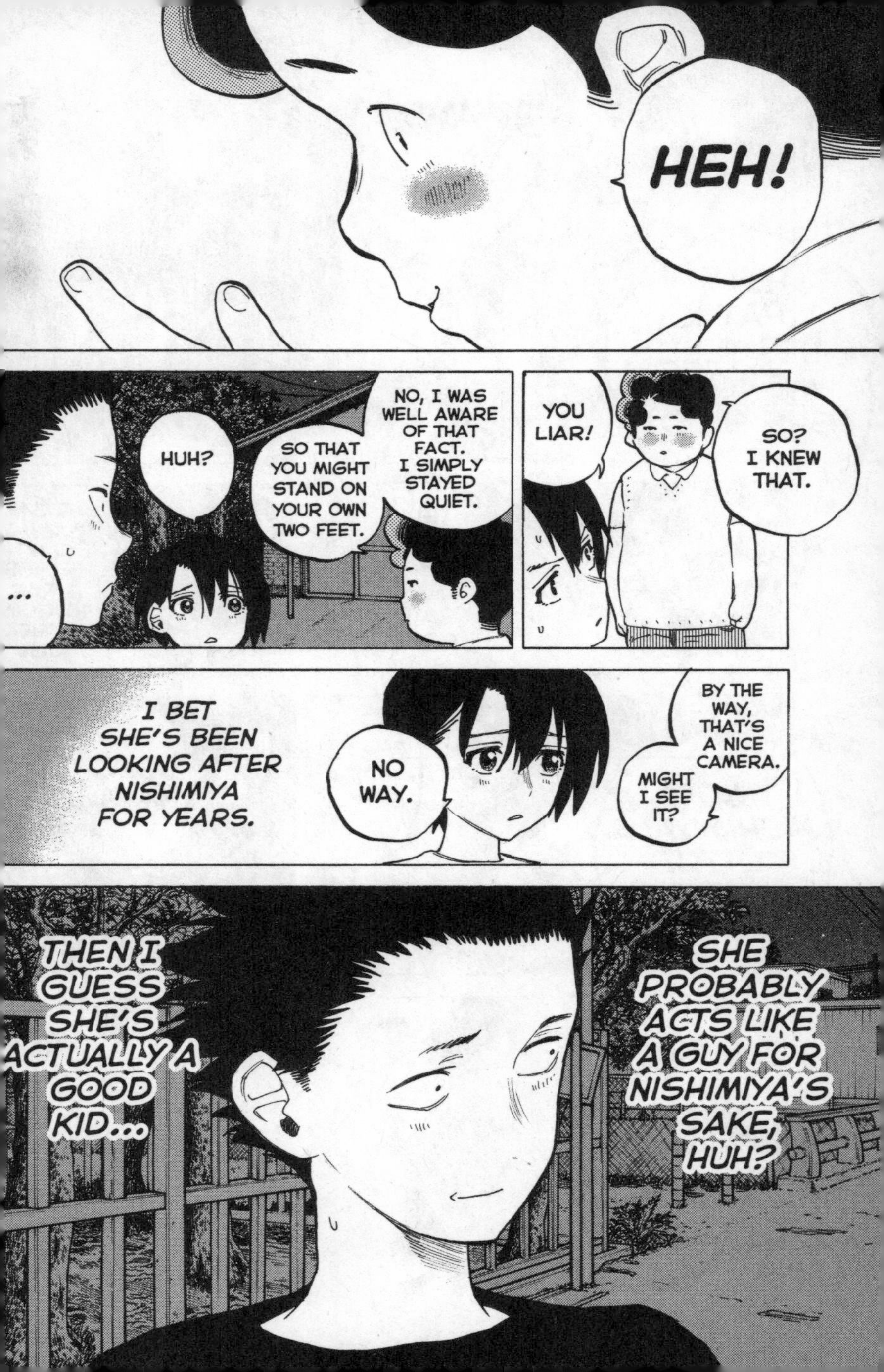
HEH!
SO? I KNEW THAT.
YOU LIAR!
NO, I WAS WELL AWARE OF THAT FACT. I SIMPLY STAYED QUIET.
SO THAT YOU MIGHT STAND ON YOUR OWN TWO FEET.
HUH?
...
BY THE WAY, THAT'S A NICE CAMERA.
MIGHT I SEE IT?
NO WAY.
I BET SHE'S BEEN LOOKING AFTER NISHIMIYA FOR YEARS.
SHE PROBABLY ACTS LIKE A GUY FOR NISHIMIYA'S SAKE, HUH?
THEN I GUESS SHE'S ACTUALLY A GOOD KID...

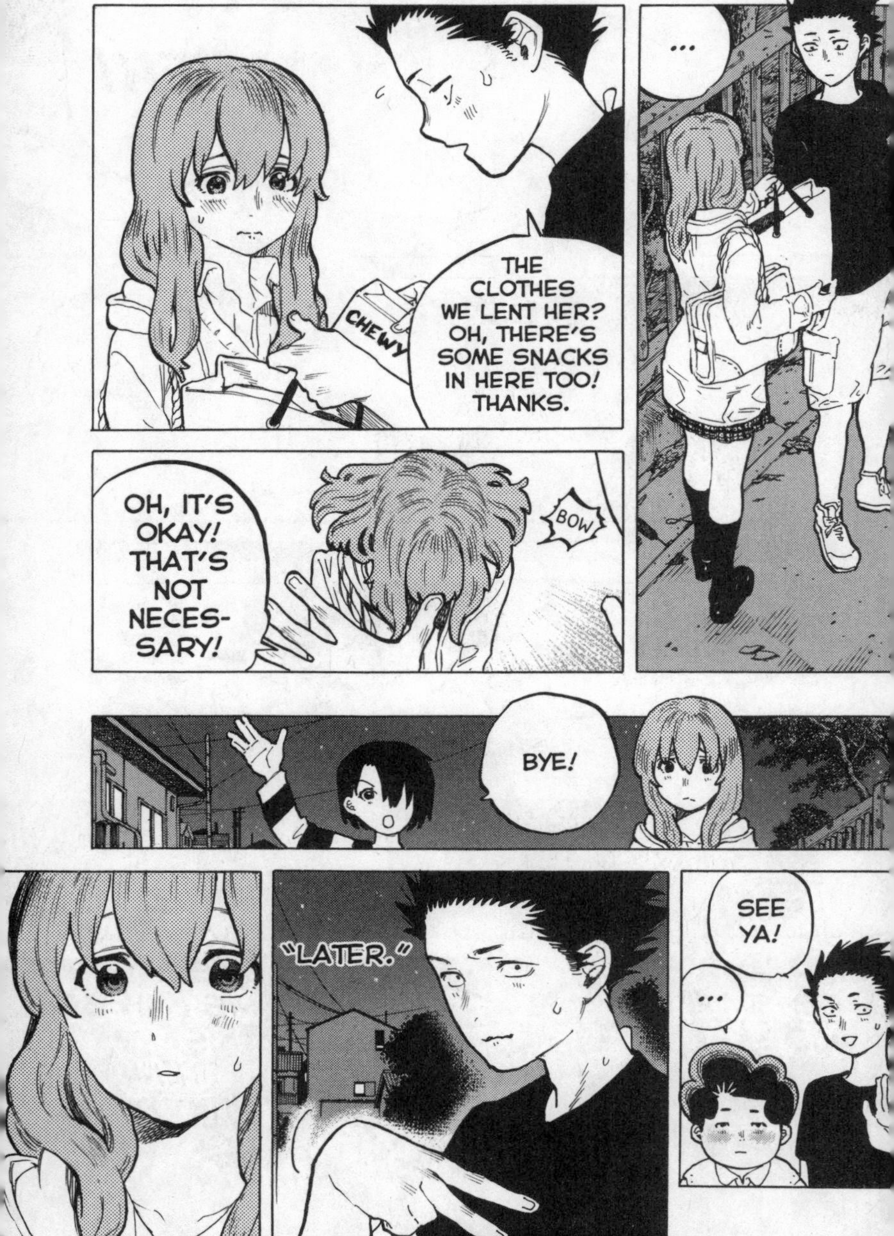
...
THE CLOTHES WE LENT HER? OH, THERE'S SOME SNACKS IN HERE TOO! THANKS.
CHEWY
BOW
OH, IT'S OKAY! THAT'S NOT NECES-SARY!
BYE!
SEE YA!
...
"LATER."

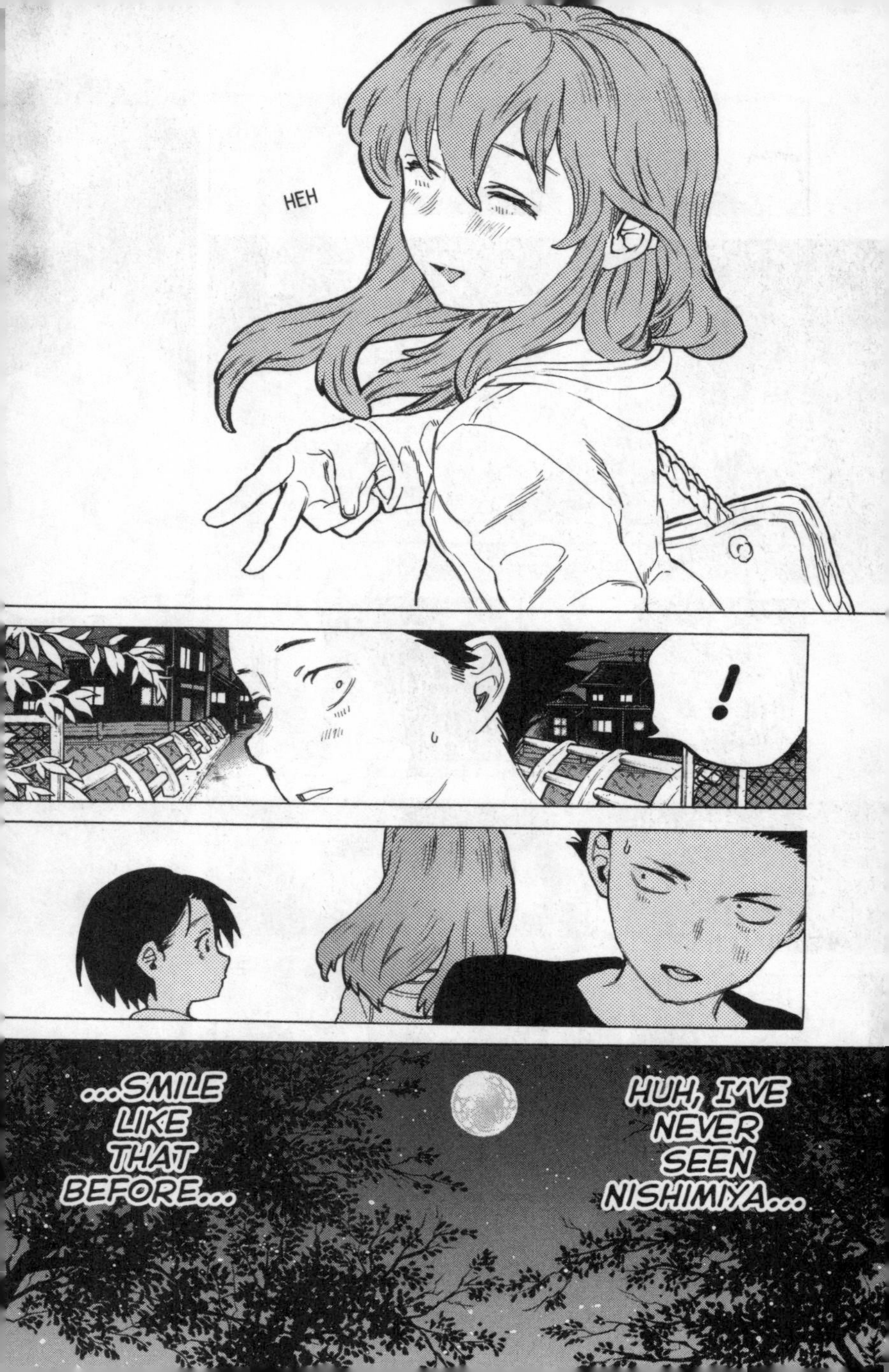
HEH
!
HUH, I'VE NEVER SEEN NISHIMIYA...
...SMILE LIKE THAT BEFORE...

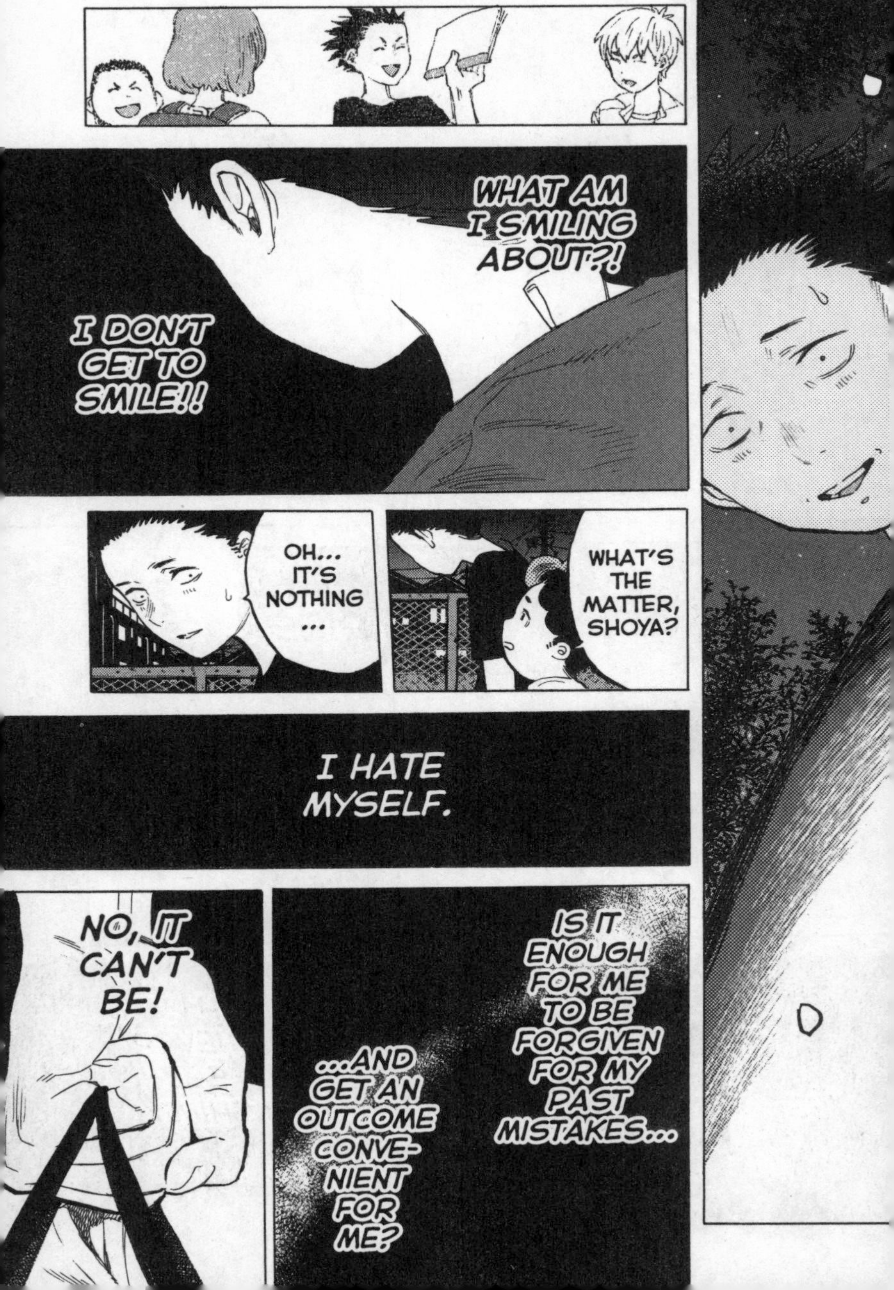
WHAT AM I SMILING ABOUT?!
I DON'T GET TO SMILE!!
WHAT'S THE MATTER, SHOYA?
OH... IT'S NOTHING ...
I HATE MYSELF.
IS IT ENOUGH FOR ME TO BE FORGIVEN FOR MY PAST MISTAKES...
...AND GET AN OUTCOME CONVE-NIENT FOR ME?
NO, IT CAN'T BE!

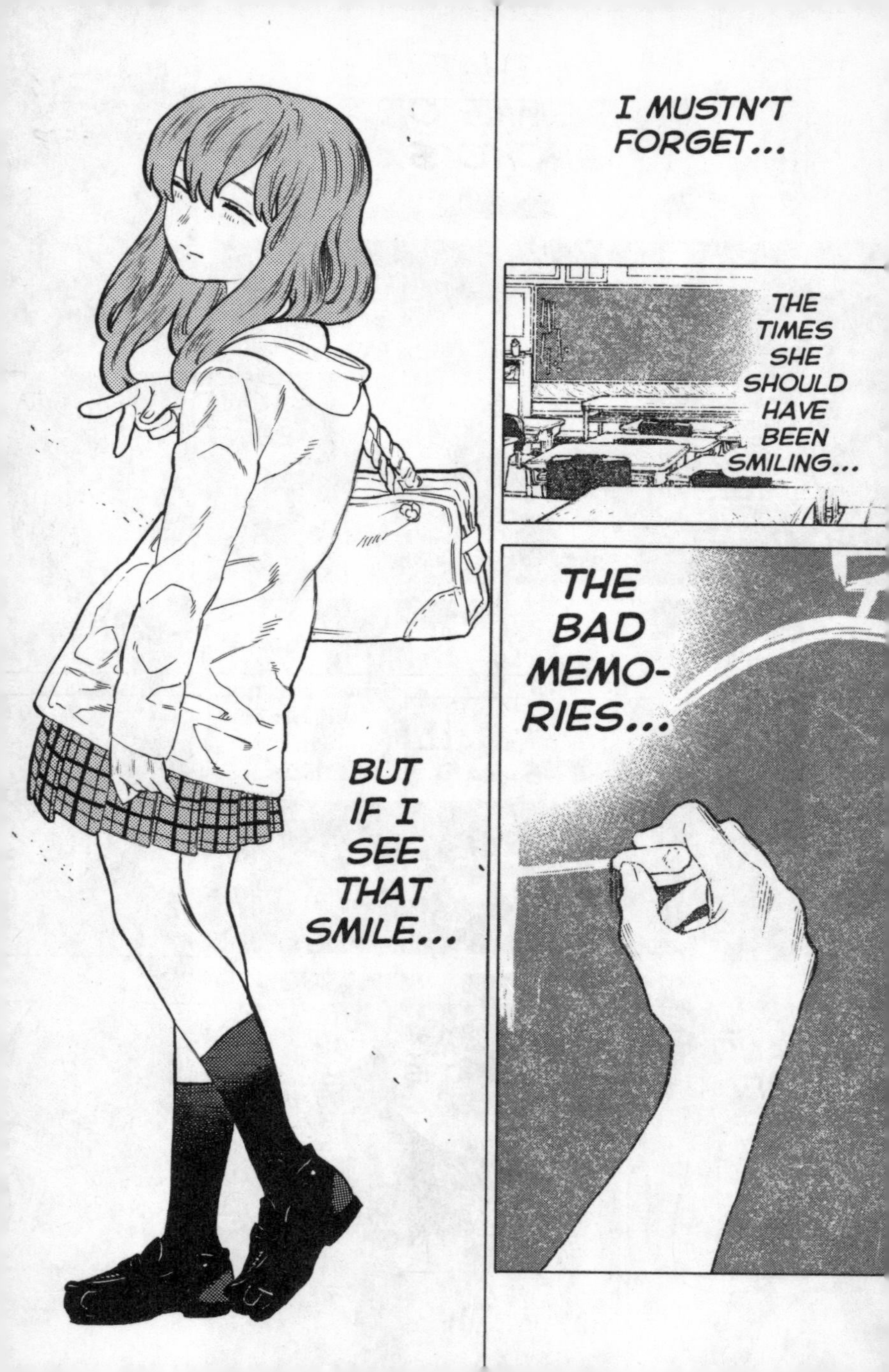
I MUSTN'T FORGET...
THE TIMES SHE SHOULD HAVE BEEN SMILING...
THE BAD MEMO-RIES...
BUT IF I SEE THAT SMILE...

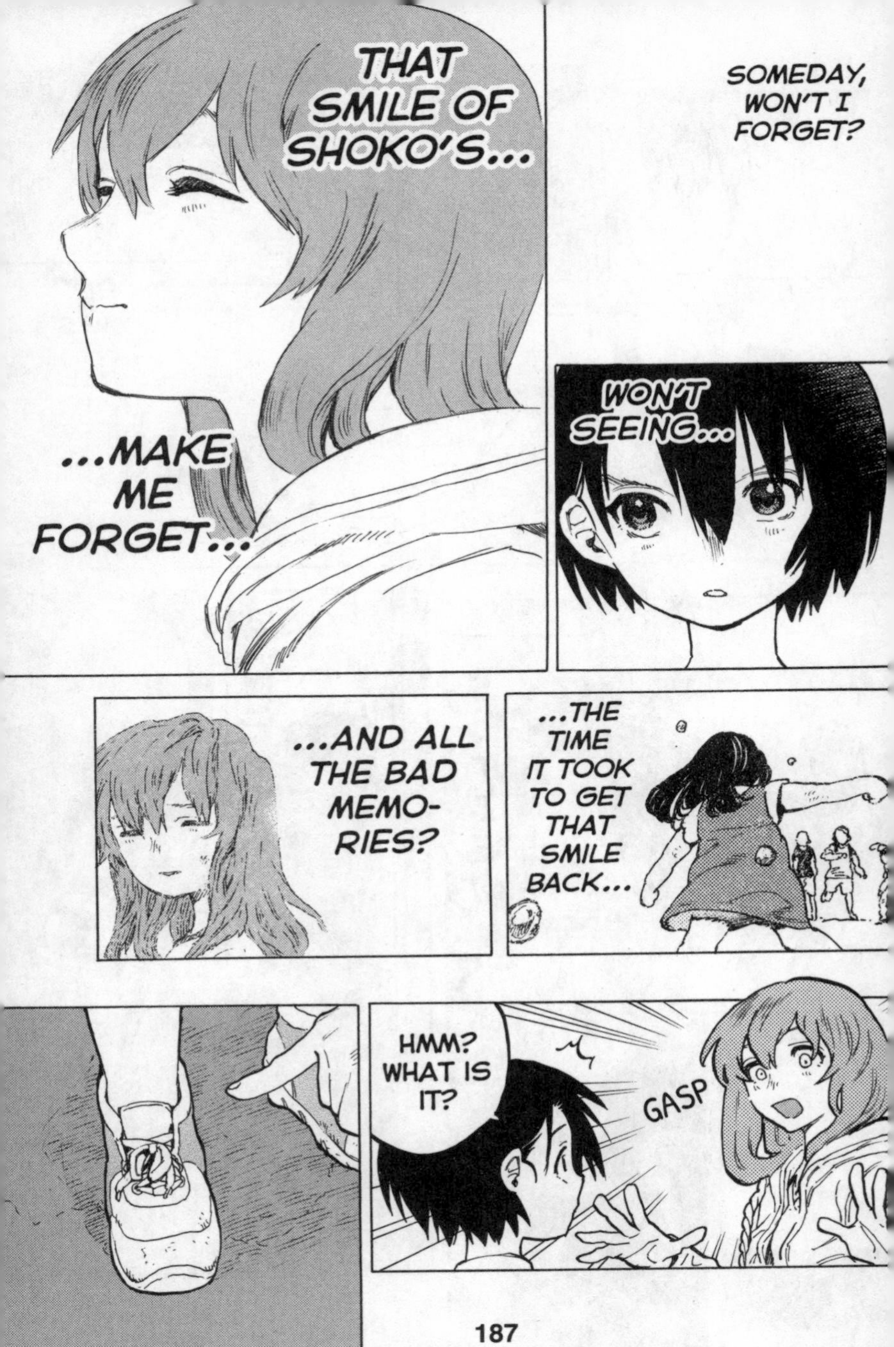
SOMEDAY, WON'T I FORGET?
WON'T SEEING...
THAT SMILE OF SHOKO'S...
...MAKE ME FORGET...
...THE TIME IT TOOK TO GET THAT SMILE BACK...
...AND ALL THE BAD MEMO-RIES?
GASP
HMM? WHAT IS IT?

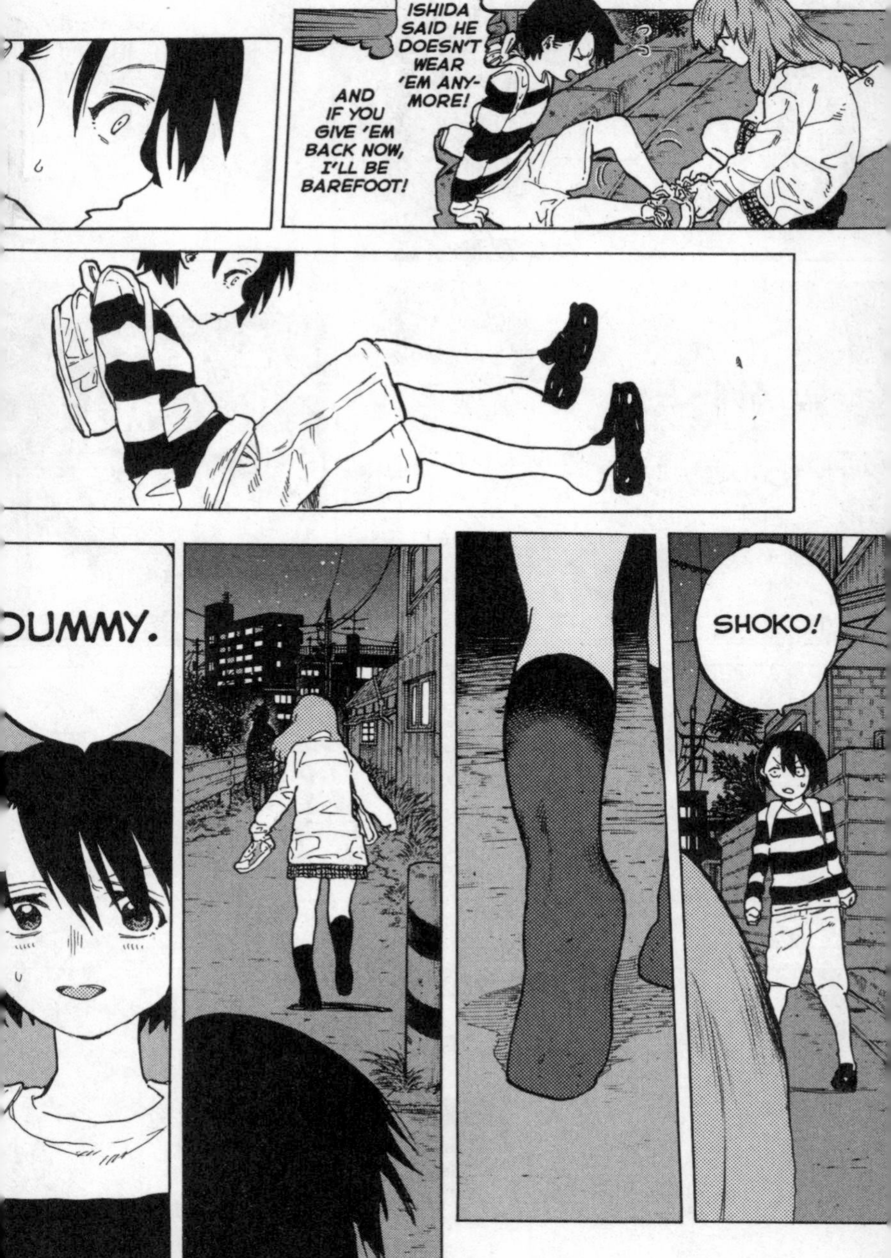
ISHIDA SAID HE DOESN'T WEAR 'EM ANYMORE!
AND IF YOU GIVE 'EM BACK NOW, I'LL BE BAREFOOT!
SHOKO!
DUMMY.

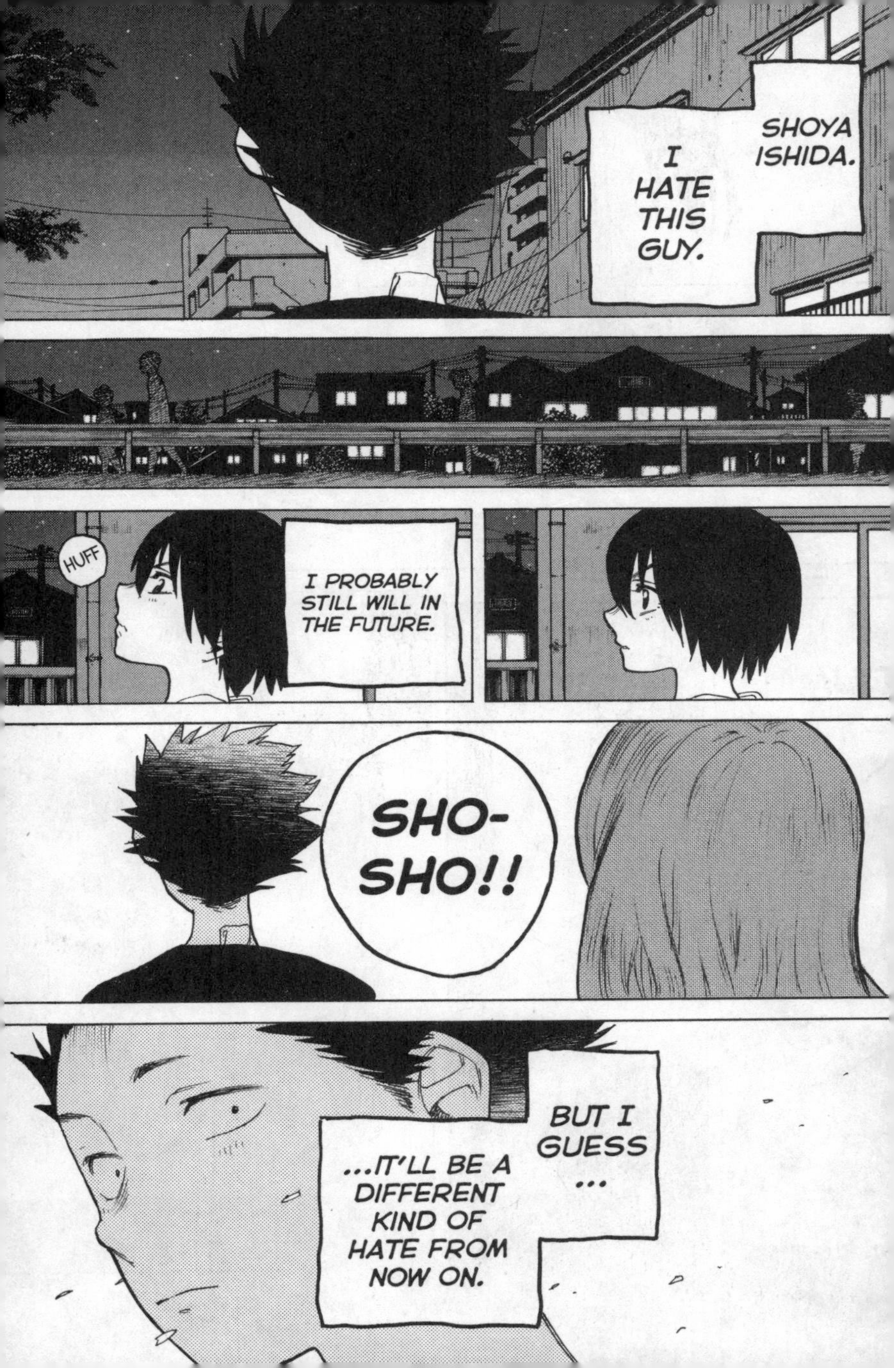
SHOYA ISHIDA.
I HATE THIS GUY.
I PROBABLY STILL WILL IN THE FUTURE.
HUFF
SHO-SHO!!
BUT I GUESS...
...IT'LL BE A DIFFERENT KIND OF HATE FROM NOW ON.

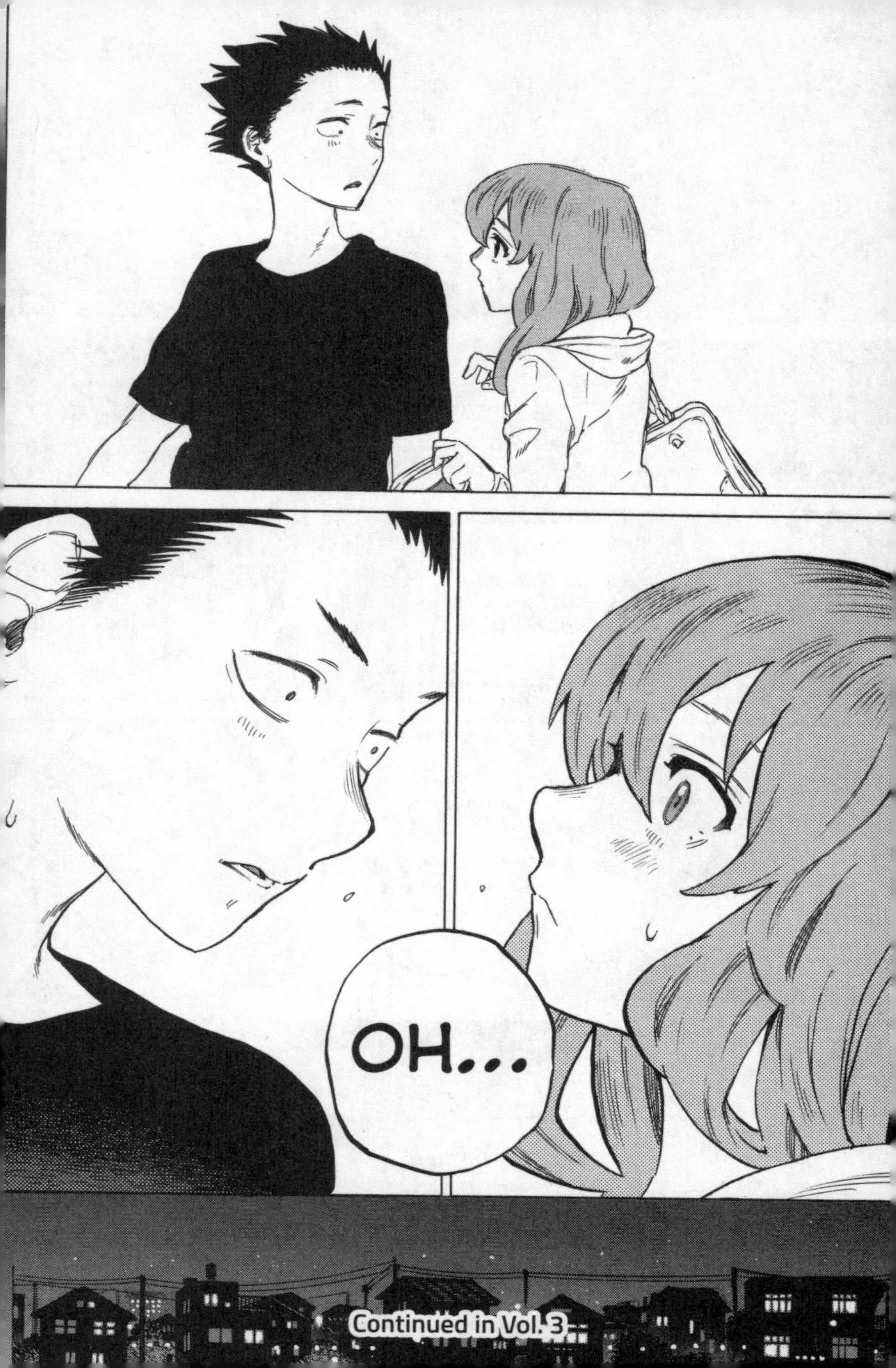
OH...
Continued in Vol. 3

a Silent Voice

SAY I LOVE YOU.

KC KODANSHA COMICS

Mei Tachibana has no friends — and says she doesn't need them!

But everything changes when she accidentally roundhouse kicks the most popular boy in school! However, Yamato Kurosawa isn't angry in the slightest— in fact, he thinks his ordinary life could use an unusual girl like Mei. But winning Mei's trust will be a tough task. How long will she refuse to say, "I love you"?

A Kodansha Comics Trade Paperback Original.

Silent Voice volume 2 copyright © 2014 Yoshitoki Oima
English translation copyright © 2015 Yoshitoki Oima

Published in the United States by Kodansha Comics, an imprint of Kodansha USA Publishing, LLC, New York.

Publication rights for this English edition arranged through Kodansha Ltd., Tokyo.

First published in Japan in 2014 by Kodansha Ltd., Tokyo, as *Koe no katachi* volume 2.

ISBN 978-1-63236-057-1

Printed in Canada.

www.kodanshacomics.com

9 18 17 16 15 14 13 12

Translation: Steven LeCroy
Lettering: Steven LeCroy
Editing: Ben Applegate
Kodansha Comics edition cover design by Phil Balsman